Dear Papa, Dear Hotch

N.L. Terteling Library

Swisher Memorial Collection

Dear Papa, Dear Hotch

The Correspondence of
Ernest Hemingway and A. E. Hotchner

Edited by Albert J. DeFazio III
Preface by A. E. Hotchner

University of Missouri Press   Columbia and London

Library of Congress Cataloging-in-Publication Data

Hemingway, Ernest, 1899-1961
    Dear Papa, dear Hotch : the correspondence of Ernest Hemingway and A.E. Hotchner /
edited by Albert J. DeFazio, III ; preface by A.E. Hotchner.
        p. cm.
    Summary: "The collected correspondence between Ernest Hemingway and A. E. Hotchner.
Includes more than 160 letters, cables, and cards the two friends exchanged from 1948 to
1961. With annotations and a textual commentary that enables readers to reconstruct the
features of the original manuscripts and envelopes"—Provided by publisher.
    Includes bibliographical references and index.
    ISBN-13: 978-0-8262-1605-2 (alk. paper)
    ISBN-10: 0-8262-1605-6 (alk. paper)
    1.   Hemingway, Ernest, 1899-1961—Correspondence. 2.   Hotchner, A. E.—Correspon-
dence. 3.   Authors, American—20th century—Correspondence. 4.   Journalists—United
States—Correspondence.   I. Hotchner, A. E.   II. DeFazio, Albert J.   III. Title.
    PS3515.E37Z484 2005
    813'.52—dc22   2005019673

$35

∞ This paper meets the requirements of the   OCLC
American National Standard for Permanence of Paper 60931389
for Printed Library Materials, Z39.48, 1984.

Designer: Kristie Lee
Typesetter: Crane Composition, Inc.
Printer and binder: Thomson-Shore, Inc.
Typefaces: Berkeley and Snell Roundhand

Frontispiece: Hotchner and Hemingway returning from a duck hunt in Ketchum,
Idaho, late 1960.

Photos on pp. 99, 100, 101 (bottom), 102 (bottom), 103, 105, 106, 110, 237, 242, 248, and
249 courtesy of Papers of Ernest Hemingway, Clifton Waller Barrett Library, Special Collections,
University of Virginia Library, Charlottesville; all other photos courtesy of A. E. Hotchner.

For Lynn

insular Tahiti, moveable feast

Contents

Preface

by A. E. Hotchner

These letters that Ernest Hemingway and I exchanged during the fourteen years of our friendship were conversation, not prose. In the beginning, my letters were awestruck and conciliatory, but later on a rapport developed between us that created an easy interaction: television, books, travel, writers and writing, friends, enemies, gambling, women, movies, health, bullfighting, baseball, boxing, wives, Venice, Africa, mothers, fathers, children, politics—in fact we touched upon anything and everything that involved our daily lives.

Hemingway's personality commanded his letters, which were as informal and as nonliterary as his conversation. In 1951 Ernest told Charles Scribner, Sr., "I like to talk with you even when it is only in letters and the conversation is lamentably stupid and one-sided." For him, writing a letter was an alleviation from the hard concentration of writing prose, and the way he wrote these letters to me was virtually indistinguishable from the way he spoke when we were together.

I first met Hemingway when I went to Havana in my role as a literary bounty hunter. It was 1948, I had just served four years in the Air Force, and the only job I could find was as a commissioned agent for *Cosmopolitan* magazine, a literary publication in those days before its conversion into a broadside for sex and the single girl. As a bounty hunter, my mission was to seek out distinguished authors and persuade them to write for the magazine. I was offered $300 and expenses for each author I bagged. Thanks to a combination of naïveté and persistence, I was able to obtain contributions from such literati as Dorothy Parker, Edna Ferber, John Steinbeck, and Ludwig Bemelmans, among others.

Ernest Hemingway was also on the list I was given but I procrastinated over going down to Cuba, where he then lived outside Havana in the little village of San Francisco de Paula, to ask him to write an article on the future of literature which was to be included in a series about the future of everything. But propelled by the necessity of paying my rent, I reluctantly went to Havana and sent him a note from the Hotel Nacional, where I was staying. Apologizing for my inane request, I asked simply that he send me a few words of refusal so I could prove to the *Cosmo* editor who sent me that I had actually contacted Hemingway, thus preserving the future of Hotchner.

To my surprise, Hemingway phoned me at the hotel and invited me for a drink at the bar of his favorite Havana haunt, the Floridita. Not only did we have drinks (too many for me), but in the three days I was in Havana he also invited me to go fishing on his boat, the *Pilar,* to accompany him to a jai alai game, and to visit him at his finca where I met his wife, Mary.

Ernest did not write an article on the future of literature but ultimately he did write a novel, *Across the River and into the Trees,* which was serialized in five installments in *Cosmopolitan.* It was this publication that was the main concern of the early letters we exchanged, but as our friendship became more intimate so did these letters, which cover the fourteen years from 1948 until Ernest's death in 1961. In the beginning, the letters are akin to a father writing to his son, and I suppose that was indeed my role back then, for at that time Ernest was not close to his own three sons and, it seems to me, I appeared at a time when he had a "papa" need not only to pass along his skills, his advice, and his affection, but also to have a young companion who eagerly shared his unique adventures.

I was young and struggling and vulnerable. During the years of our friendship, I saw this incredible generosity toward young people demonstrated time and again, both with money and with the commodity that Ernest regarded as infinitely more valuable than money—his time.

In retrospect, I think I arrived at a time when Ernest was lonely, when several of his close friends—Maxwell Perkins, his editor, and others—had recently died, and when his work was at a standstill; he had not published anything of importance since *For Whom the Bell Tolls* in 1940, and there was no stirring in him for a new book. I shared his interest in certain sports—baseball, football, prizefighting—as well as having an athletic bent of my own; I was a risk taker, a kid from the dead-wrong side of the tracks, an idolater of his writing, a person who exuded loyalty, which he prized. And I was someone who learned quickly, shared his love of adventure, and didn't complain or offer excuses. I state none of this as braggadocio, but as a retrospective assessment of that far-away young man, seeing him today as if he were someone I knew at the time.

I had gone to Havana anticipating that Hemingway, as widely publicized, was a hot-tempered, pugnacious soldier of fortune who roamed the world knocking over all objects, human and otherwise, that got in his way. What I discovered was that the world's impression of him as a battering ram of a man was virtually the opposite of the truth. His short stories and his two early novels, *The Sun Also Rises* and *A Farewell to Arms*, had brought to American literature a new style of writing, lyrically simple, direct, very realistic; writing the world over had been affected by it. But if Ernest had been the heavy-fisted giant of his reputation he could not have conceivably also been the sensitive artist whose work was eventually rewarded with both the Pulitzer and Nobel Prizes for literature.

Ernest was forty-nine when I met him. He had been married four times, been under fire in three wars, and had restlessly roamed the world—driving an ambulance in Italy in World War I, fishing for marlin in the Caribbean, hunting for big game in Africa, following the bullfights in Spain.

There were two deep currents that ran simultaneously through his life: one was to participate fully in and experience deeply the joys and sorrows of existence; the other was to assess those experiences and emotionally react to them on the printed page. Ernest was an original. No one else's word was good enough. He had to taste, smell, see, hear for himself.

Now, forty-plus years after his death, with ample time for reflection, I prize many of the tenets he lived by, as evidenced in many of these letters: true friendship requires forgiveness but no friendship can withstand the abuse of duplicity; anger and compassion are not too far apart and whenever possible spent anger should give way to compassion; pride is a desirable trait that rescues one from a fall and not vice versa—e.g., after the brutal critical assault that followed the publication of *Across the River and into the Trees*, it was Ernest's pride that defied the naysayers and goaded him into writing *The Old Man and the Sea*; deviousness is permissible if it is innocuous; good times should be orchestrated and not left to the uncertainties of chance; discipline is more desirable than inspiration; courage is a matter of one's conscience, not beholden to the evaluation of others; love is more durable than hate.

All of these facets of Ernest's convictions are on display in these letters. Many letters concern my dramatizations of Ernest's works for television, motion pictures, ballet, and the stage, all of which actually grew out of our friendship rather than any desire on my part to involve myself in those activities.

But, as the letters demonstrate, I came to enjoy and take pride in what was accomplished with many of the programs, particularly "For Whom the Bell Tolls," "The Fifth Column," "The World of Nick Adams," and "The Battler."

Ernest did not want to be involved with my scripts other than, at my request, to furnish background information about particular stories, information which is contained in several of these letters. But Ernest was completely involved in the business side of these productions, his letters reflecting the sharp eye he kept on the terms under which his stories were sold, for how much, for how long, and an especially sharp eye was focused on his lawyer, Alfred Rice, whom he constantly criticized but retained as a necessary evil.

"The reason I do not want to take an advance," he tells me, "is that I do not want anyone to have to look over my shoulder or see how it is going." In these letters, his confidence in his writing is manifest: "I can pitch double headers"; "Have been hotter, working, than the grill they roasted San Lorenzo on"; "Have been slugging it out with Mr. Shakespeare, the writer, today and I have him in bad shape."

He also vents his spleen on certain writers whom he skewers: John O'Hara, Kenneth Tynan, William Faulkner, Tom Lea, and especially James Jones. He even lowers the boom on me for my regrettable first novel, *The Dangerous American.*

He writes to me bitterly about his last three wives, saying of Pauline, "when women's have any feeling of guilt they tend to get rid of it by slapping it onto you"; and he is pugnacious about his brother Leicester's attempt to write a book about him and their family, "especially one as vulnerable as ours where my mother was a bitch + my father a suicide."

Since Ernest's death in 1961, scores of books have been written about him. His fourth wife, his first wife, his brother, sister, youngest son, assorted college professors who never met him, various cronies and phonies and even a self-proclaimed mistress have all written books about him, and, predictably, he emerges as a different man in each one of them. And despite explicit instructions in his will not to allow the publication of any of his letters, after his death Mary published vast numbers of those written to family, friends, editors, business associates, and others during his lifetime.

In 1949, when William Faulkner won the Nobel Prize for Literature, Ernest said, "No son of a bitch who ever won the Nobel Prize ever wrote anything worth reading afterwards." At the time, Ernest's observation was discounted as sour grapes, but, applied to his own life, it was certainly an apt prophecy. In his letter of December 7, 1954, he says of the Prize, "Had no chance to enjoy it, . . . just photographers, people mis-quoting you and yammer, yammer, yack, yack and my book, all I gave a shit about, and which I had been living in day and night being knocked out of my head like clubbing a fish." I think winning the prize was more contributory to Ernest's decline than the air crashes in Africa, what might have been the onset of impotence, the altercations with his wife, and having to leave Cuba and the finca, the *Pilar* and his good workplace. How often Ernest spoke with envy of Jean-Paul Sartre, who had had the prescience to refuse the Nobel Prize when it had been offered to him. "I guess Sartre knew," Ernest once said rather ruefully, "that the Prize is a whore who can seduce you and give you an incurable disease. I knew that once but now I've got her and she's got me, and you know who she is, this whore called 'Fame'? Death's little sister."

Ernest is preoccupied in many of his letters with his physical condition, especially after the two plane crashes in Africa. Blood pressure and weight readings predominate, but concussions, bowel movements, skin and eye afflictions, and X-rays (of the shell fragments in his leg, among others) are also included.

In addition to blood pressure and weight statistics, I also received daily word counts for whatever manuscript he was then writing; many of these notations were recorded on the walls of his bathroom, which probably explains why the finca was never painted.

After the airplane disasters in Africa, which produced a significant downturn in his life, Ernest became more confessional in his letters and his writing became cramped, less orderly, and, in his final letters, smaller to the point that certain words were unintelligible.

Approximately half these letters to me were handwritten, unhurried and flowing, as if Ernest was slowly paying out a trout line, the sentences slanting downwards from the horizontal.

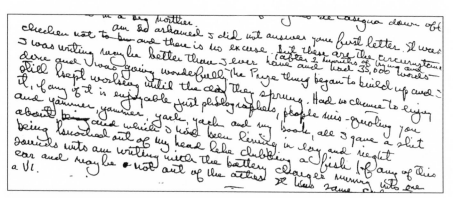

Letter 73 (Ernest Hemingway Collection, Library of Congress)

The typewritten letters were also composed slowly, manifested by the way that Ernest often spaced two or three times between words to slow himself down, like this:

FINCA VIGIA, SAN FRANCISCO DE PAULA, CUBA
15/II/50

Dear   Ed:
       Thanks   for   the   m ysterious   missive   from   Colliers   .
I   suppose   it   had   something   to   do   with   that   editorial   they
wrote   with   the   lovely   drawing   of   me   .   Or   maybe   they   had
a   surruptitious   opening   of   that   famous   corner   stone   and   found
my   message   .   Anyway   X   would   have   tried   to   write   something
very   good   about   Marle ne   for   them   .
       This   machine   ,   the   one   you   brought   ,   is   being   used   by
a   number   of   people   ,all   of   them   extremely   nice   ,   but   each   time
I   meet   it   again   something   new   has   been   lacking   .
There's   a   cat   too   ,   named   Sun   Valley   .   that   can   hit   five
keys   at   a   time   .

Letter 41 (private collection)

Ernest paid little attention to the niceties of spelling. "Charley Scribner can hire fifty dollars a week Princeton grads," he once said, "to correct the spelling—Princeton boys are good spellers." He claimed that he was a better speller than his friend Scott Fitzgerald, but actually they were equally bad. In these letters, it is customary for Ernest to retain the letter *e* when adding "ing" or "able" so that such spellings as *liveable, produceing, driveing, figureing, loveing, comeing* are commonplace. When I suggested the title "A Moveable Feast" for his posthumous book of Paris reminiscences, I retained the *e* out of deference.

Part of the mystique about Ernest stems from the manner in which he blurred the demarcation between fiction and fact. Fiction is a magnification of reality, he once observed, and when he told a story (and a splendid storyteller he was), it was hard to know whether it was fantasy laced with fact, fact seasoned with fiction, or pure fantasy. Did he really enter a circus cage with a bevy of tigers armed only with a rolled-up newspaper? Did he really lie down in the cage and induce two tigers to put their feet on his chest, getting "raked" in the process? When in Africa, as he writes in his letter of March 14, 1954, did he actually "take a Wakamba bride and inherit her sister, a widow of 17," who were "stacked better than M. Monroe" and sleep with them on "a bed about 14 feet wide"? This Wakamba troika figures prominently in the latest posthumous Hemingway "discovery," *True at First Light,* but Ernest's son Patrick, who was a white hunter and present during much of that safari, says he has no knowledge of any such matrimonial liaison. Ernest never mentioned writing this book to me, though he did confide to me, "September I will have an African son. Before I left I gave a herd of goats to my bride's family. Most over-goated family in Africa. Feels good to have African son. Never regretted anything I ever did." I can honestly say I believed him, although how he received word about the pregnancy and how in deepest Africa, without benefit of sonogram, they could foretell the sex of his offspring, went unexplained.

Ernest kept no diaries or notebooks but at any given moment he could conjure up vivid details of events that had transpired long ago, as quickly and surely as a computer screen reveals its stored data. One day as we drove across the Riviera, he pointed out the exact itinerary he had followed with F. Scott Fitzgerald when they had bicycled through there in the 1920s. When we walked the streets of Paris, his recall of places and people was prodigious: when we climbed the steep ascent to the Place du Tertre in Montmartre, he gave a running commentary on the houses, stores, cafés, and restaurants that we passed, recalling who lived in them in the twenties and with whom he had dined—even incredibly recalling special wines and foods that were on the menus. The knowledge he shared with me was far-ranging: the nuances of oysters from the lowly Portuguese to the imperial Belons, the poetry of waterbirds, the classic faenas of a great matador who literally dances with the bull, the difference between Titian and Tintoretto, Monet and Renoir, Gauguin and Seurat, Picasso and Braque and why he felt Cezanne could not be compared to anyone else. He described how to use one's built-in shit detector, how best to enjoy idle time, when to be aggressive and when to give ground, how to set your hook on a hit from a sailfish, how to swing your shotgun to transect the flight of a pheasant, how to evaluate a racehorse during the paddock parade, how to trim the fat from the sinews and bones of writing.

I am often asked, "What was he really like?" and as one of the few people still extant who knew him well, I suppose I should record a few of his characteristics that might enhance these letters: his enjoyment of stimulating conversation; his wide-open laughter and the way he would ball up his fist against his mouth to filter the laughter; the fury of his anger when someone he trusted didn't "measure up," an anger which could quickly rise to a boil and just as quickly subside; his courtly manner with women; his wonderfully informed observations when we attended prizefights, the World Series, jai alai matches, and particularly bullfights; his disdain for sycophants, phonies, tycoons, politicians, losers, braggarts, writers of undeserved acclaim, poseurs, neckties, wine connoisseurs, hustlers, bullies, self-servers, dandies, do-gooders, lawyers, agents, gourmands, gossips, automobile salesmen, the telephone, the camera, Texans, alcoholics, to name a few; the way his mobility was restrained by the leg wound he suffered in World War I, making him stiff-legged in manipulating stairs or entering an automobile, but nevertheless walking lightly on the balls of his high-arched feet; his intense involvement when friends were in serious trouble; his moments of comic relief when he hilariously mimicked someone in power; his remarkable patience and perseverance when hunting and fishing; his tendency, without warning, occasionally to break out in song with a voice that was buoyant but noticeably off-key; his compassion for street people, especially gypsies; his enjoyment of the company of beautiful, intelligent women, like Marlene Dietrich, Ingrid Bergman, and Ava Gardner.

I was surprised that Ernest had retained all my letters in a separate file that Mary Hemingway bequeathed to the John F. Kennedy Library. Of course I had kept all his letters, which in essence reflect the life he lived from his middle years until his death. Denied by Mary from publishing portions of his letters, I was compelled to disguise some of them in my memoir *Papa Hemingway,* published in 1966, feeling that they were vital to depicting Ernest's life between the times I was with him. But now the complete letters, interwoven with mine, in a sense constitute Ernest's autobiography, for he writes these letters with a freedom, with deep personal revelations, with an honesty about himself, his family, his fears, his pain, his melancholy (which he calls "black-ass") that has not surfaced in his other writing. There are passages that utter cries of anguish, of frustration, of a kind of combative helplessness.

Ernest has never been very far out of my life. How I have lived, the principles I live by, my attitude toward survival, toward love, toward friendship, toward trust, toward believing in myself and in the simple truths he impressed upon me—I owe that to him and more. As these letters reveal, he was my father, my brother, my ancestor who passed his secrets along to me. In his letter of March 14, 1954, written on board the S.S. *Africa* after his plane crashed, he writes: "I get lonesome and you know my problems and I can see all the freckles on your funny face and remember all our problems and the fun at Auteuil and on the trip and how you liked Venice and stayed better than any brother."

Looking back on the years since his death, those years that have passed without him, I'd say that the most resounding thing I learned from him was this:

Don't fear failure, and don't overestimate success. It was a tenet he lived by and a legacy I treasure.

When my book *Papa Hemingway* was about to appear, Mary Hemingway attempted to obtain an injunction against its publication, at the same time embarking on a vindictive campaign to impugn my account of my friendship with Ernest and to cast doubt on the validity of the book's contents. The New York courts dismissed her petition, and now, with the publication of these letters, I believe my long friendship with Ernest is effectively validated.

The real reason for Mary's actions was the fact that she claimed Ernest had not committed suicide but had accidentally shot himself in the head while cleaning his shotgun (why Ernest was cleaning a loaded hunting gun in July was never explained). After she filed her petition for an injunction, Mary came to me and said that she would withdraw it if I would eliminate those chapters that dealt with Ernest's suicide. Of course, I refused, and these letters demonstrate the chaotic state of his mind leading up to the suicide. When she wrote her own book, *How It Was* (1976), she rather reluctantly admitted that her account had been a subterfuge and that his death was indeed a suicide.

When I went to visit Ernest at the Mayo Clinic, finding him confused, suddenly very old and confined to a locked room with bars on the windows, I suffered a severe attack of despair. Yes, I knew from his letters, like the one on pages 299–300 about the bullfight pictures, that he had become irrational, but not until that visit to the hospital did I accept the fact that, having failed twice, he was hell-bent on suicide and that this time he would succeed.

When I left Ernest at the Mayo Clinic that cold June day and headed my rented car back to the airport, overwhelmed by the impact of my visit, I started to weep. I have rarely cried in my life and in any event tears do not come easy, but I wept at the tragedy of Ernest's decline, the fact that he had committed himself to suicide, this man who had been so vibrant, so in control of his destiny, now a victim of his delusions.

His was a deep, abiding friendship, like no other in my life. Rereading these letters, after all these years, fills me with sadness, exultation, and the realization that an extraordinary man infiltrated my life with wisdom, love, fortitude, and an indomitable spirit that I now gladly share with others.

Acknowledgments

In progress for nearly two decades, this edition owes much to many. For the essential permissions, I thank A. E. Hotchner, the Ernest Hemingway Foundation, Patrick Hemingway, and Michael Katakis. Mr. Hotchner made available his privately held letters and patiently answered my queries by letter, phone, in person, and through e-mail. I am grateful to several members of the Foundation who have overseen this project, particularly presidents Robert W. Lewis, Michael Reynolds, Linda Wagner-Martin, Scott Donaldson, and James Meredith and board members Susan F. Beegel, J. Gerald Kennedy, Gerry Brenner, Fred Svoboda, and especially Bickford Sylvester for his keen eye and good heart. For providing me with the education that led me to this edition, I am indebted to my parents.

For encouragement when this project was in its infancy, John H. N. Hemingway, William White, Anthony J. Colaianne of Virginia Polytechnic Institute and State University, and David L. Vander Meulen of the University of Virginia. For their support, colleagues Catherine Hailey, Roger Lathbury, and Mark Craver. For his humane guidance through the publication process, Clair Willcox of the University of Missouri Press; for his editorial scrutiny and acumen, Gary Kass.

For providing generous answers through the mail, Lillian Ross, Peter Viertel, and Matthew J. Bruccoli. The same and additional thanks to Rose Marie Burwell for her *Hemingway: The Postwar Years and the Posthumous Novels,* Miriam Mandel for material from her forthcoming *Hemingway's "The Dangerous Summer": The Complete Annotations,* and Robert W. Trogdon for his *Ernest Hemingway: A Literary Reference,* all of which were invaluable resources. For their generous contributions, Sandra Spanier and LaVerne M. Maginnis of the Hemingway Letters Project, Pennsylvania State University. For everything from

A to Z, including food and shelter in Charlottesville, Charles and Helen Oliver. For an afternoon's interview in University Park, Philip Young; for briefer explanations in Boston, Charles Scribner IV. For help transcribing and translating, Brian Dickson, José Fuentes, Dr. Monika Bilby, Schuyler Stephens, Manfred and Ben Zorn. For recollections of baseball from the forties and fifties, my father, Albert J. DeFazio Jr. For their willingness to share, participants in the Hemingway listserv, especially Paul Montgomery. For two years' toil, research assistant Patrick Gregg, who arrived on the scene when only the vexing questions remained and helped answer them with admirable perseverance. For forever tricking me into talking about Hemingway, my students.

I am indebted as well to the Special Collections and Interlibrary Loan Departments of George Mason University and the University of Virginia, where Ann L. S. Southwell provided timely and expert service; the Manuscripts Department of the University of North Carolina at Chapel Hill, and the John M. Olin Library at Washington University in St. Louis. Dr. Alice L. Birney and Jeff Flannery of the Library of Congress in Washington, DC, were prompt and professional. I am especially grateful to the staff of the John F. Kennedy Library in Boston, including Megan Floyd Desnoyers, Stephen Plotkin, Lisa Middents, Susan Wrynn, and Alyssa Pacy. A travel grant provided by the John F. Kennedy Library Foundation facilitated my research.

Jackson R. Bryer has been taskmaster and advocate. For his careful reading of the manuscript, his knowledge of the diamond and the track, and for his example, I am grateful.

Abbreviations

AEH   A. E. Hotchner

Choice   *Choice People: The Greats, Near Greats, and Ingrates I Have Known,* by A. E. Hotchner (New York: Morrow, 1984)

EH   Ernest Hemingway

Final   *Hemingway: The Final Years,* by Michael Reynolds (New York: Norton, 1999)

HIW   *How It Was,* by Mary Hemingway (New York: Knopf, 1976)

JFKL   Ernest Hemingway Collection, John F. Kennedy Library, Boston, MA

LOC   Ernest Hemingway Collection, Library of Congress, Washington, DC

PC   Private collection

PH   *Papa Hemingway: A Personal Memoir,* by A. E. Hotchner (New York: Random House, 1966)

Story   *Ernest Hemingway: A Life Story,* by Carlos Baker (New York: Scribner's, 1969)

ViU   Papers of Ernest Hemingway, Clifton Waller Barrett Library, Special Collections, University of Virginia Library, Charlottesville

Textual Policy

These letters are transcribed in a "clear text" intended to serve as a reliable substitute for the documents in the archives: while only the author's final intention is transcribed within the body of this edition, all emendations are noted in the textual commentary at the back of the book. The commentary will enable readers to reconstruct most of the features of the original manuscripts and envelopes. A complete list of these features and an explanation of the methodology for reporting them can be found at the beginning of the commentary.

The transcriptions reproduce the texts of the documents in their entirety except where authorial intention manifests itself in the form of cancellations, alterations, and proofreader's marks. In such instances, only the latest version is transcribed and the alternate readings are recorded in the commentary. Similarly, slips of the pen and typographical errors are corrected and so noted in the commentary. All of Hemingway and Hotchner's correspondence that is known to the editor is included in this edition (the sole exception is paragraph 4 of letter 54, which is restricted by the John F. Kennedy Library). Where the text refers to correspondence not yet located by the editor, this is indicated in an explanatory note accompanying the letter. Hotchner alludes to at least a dozen such letters written by Hemingway and Hemingway refers to eight written by Hotchner.

This, then, is a transcription of the authors' final drafts of their correspondence. It most often follows the form of the manuscripts in matters of spelling, punctuation, and capitalization; underlining in the documents is rendered as such. Exceptions to this general policy include unclear words in the manuscript, which are represented by the abbreviation *indeciph.* in brackets along with the number of characters involved when this is discernible. When people other than the correspondents and their wives are referred to by a nickname or a first name, the full name is provided in brackets at the initial mention in each letter. Idiosyncratic and nonstandard spellings that are consistently adopted by the correspondents have been preserved. Omitted periods and apostrophes have been inserted and so noted in the commentary. When used to represent the number *1, 1s* and *ls* have been silently altered to *1s*. Words hyphenated in the original documents are listed on page 367.

Brief annotations and cross-references also appear in brackets within letters; lengthier explanatory notes are appended to the letters. These notes are most often based on published scholarship or sources contemporary with the correspondence, such as the *New York Times*. Occasionally Hotchner is the only source for information and this is indicated in the notes. Hotchner is also the primary source of information in the photo captions.

Spacing has been standardized. Extra spaces between words are silently omitted; where a correspondent fails to include any spaces between words, one has been added and the emendation noted in the textual commentary. Irregular spacing within words has been eliminated and partial overstrikes rendered as if they appeared side by side; these changes are also noted in the commentary. Hemingway's subscripted, circled *x*'s are depicted as periods. Page numbers of multipage letters have been omitted. Various representations for the conjunction *and,* including *&* and *+,* have been retained. A listing of word divisions is included at the back of the book to identify compounds or possible compounds that are hyphenated at the end of a line in the original documents.

Certain attributes of the documents are noted in headings that precede each letter. All headings include an identifying number, the sender's and recipient's initials, the date, and the form of the letter: ALS (autograph letter signed), TLS (typed letter signed), Cable, and, in one instance, AcardS (autograph card signed). Headings also note the number of pages of the letter (each side counting as a page) and its current location: the Ernest Hemingway Collection at the John F. Kennedy Library, Boston, MA (JFKL); Papers of Ernest Hemingway, Clifton Waller Barrett Library, Special Collections, University of Virginia Library, Charlottesville (ViU); the Ernest Hemingway Collection at the Library of Congress, Washington, DC, donated by John Hemingway and A. E. Hotchner (LOC); or Private Collection (PC). Finally, headers contain transcriptions of letterheads, which are preprinted unless otherwise indicated; handwritten (*hw*) and typewritten (*tw*) letterheads are identified as such. All conjectures about dates and letterheads appear in brackets, and conjectures based on post-marks (*pmk*) are so noted. Markings made on a letter or envelope by its recipient are typically described in the textual commentary; if they bear upon the content of the letter, they are described in the annotations. Conjectural dates added to the manuscripts by archivists or others are disregarded. Closings are standardized, appearing centered beneath the letters. All letters are signed by their authors unless otherwise noted.

Dear Papa, Dear Hotch

Introduction

This collected correspondence between Ernest Hemingway and A. E. Hotchner includes 161 items (letters, cables, cards) that span the final quarter of Hemingway's life, 1948–1961. It illuminates the least familiar section of his biography—the post–World War II years—and echoes persistent themes from his final decade: death, love, and art. The narrative that unfolds also documents his important friendship with the young man who adapted many of his works, helped him edit serializations of *Across the River and into the Trees* and *The Dangerous Summer,* and wrote *Papa Hemingway: A Personal Memoir,* a best-seller in 1966 and Book-of-the-Month Club selection that, translated into twenty-eight languages, continues to introduce Hemingway to new generations of readers.[1]

For much of his life, Hemingway was anxious to explore new places and experience new things; typically, these adventures became the basis for fiction that he would write once he had removed himself in time and space from the original events. This cycle began following his high school graduation in 1917, when he went to Kansas City to become a cub reporter, then to Italy to drive an ambulance for the American Red Cross. Wounded in war and thwarted in love, he recovered at home for a year, returned to journalism in Chicago and, newly married, considered returning to Italy but was persuaded by Sherwood Anderson to try someplace new—Paris. His passion for newness took him to the Left Bank, to Gertrude Stein's salon and Sylvia Beach's

1. According to Hotchner's publicist, *Papa Hemingway* was "published in 34 countries in 28 different languages." Fass Speakers Bureau, http://www.fasspr.com/fsb/A.E.Hotchner.html (accessed June 23, 2005).

Shakespeare and Company bookstore; to Ezra Pound, James Joyce, and Ford Madox Ford. France midwifed Modernism while Spain preserved the strange and ancient bullfight. His dalliance with team sports in high school gave way to skiing in Schruns, Austria. Lake and river fishing was soon replaced by excursions on the Gulf Stream. Solitary hunting grew into African safaris. Reporting took him to Europe, China, the Spanish Civil War, and to World War II.

After World War II, his movement continued but his exploration of new places and recreations ceased. When this correspondence opens in the summer of 1948, Hemingway has already embarked on what would be a series of return voyages. He had taken his fourth wife, Mary, to the American West, as he had done with previous wives Pauline Pfeiffer and Martha Gellhorn, and he would later revisit Italy, Paris, Spain, and Africa. The places and activities that the young Hemingway had discovered and written about now became the subjects of the author's guided tours: repetitions rather than explorations. Places provided a continuity that people did not; many of his literary comrades from the 1920s had fallen: Ford, Joyce, Anderson, Gertrude Stein, Scott and Zelda Fitzgerald. His editor and his publisher since 1925, Maxwell Perkins and Charles Scribner, died in 1947 and 1952, respectively. In 1951, his mother, Grace, passed away, as did Pauline, mother of his two youngest boys and a perceptive critic of his work. Good friends were disappearing, too— Evan Shipman from his Paris years died in 1957 and Taylor Williams, his oldest friend in Ketchum, Idaho, died in 1959.

Death, divorce, and Hemingway's penchant for severing friendships left him, after World War II, on a literal and metaphorical island. His new wife and new friends, particularly the younger set—which included Hotchner, Peter and Virginia Viertel, Antonio and Carmen Ordóñez, Luis Miguel Dominguín and his lady friend Ava Gardner, siblings Adriana and Gianfranco Ivancich, George Plimpton, and Valerie Danby-Smith—were interested in visiting Hemingway and retracing his steps through old haunts. He had become the destination for a new generation of explorers. Not only were his friends interested in his past, but the general public also craved information that scores of interviewers sought to provide: Malcolm Cowley (*Life,* 1949), Lillian Ross (*New Yorker,* 1950), Sam Boal (*Park East,* 1950; *Gent,* 1957; *Escapade,* 1959), Robert Manning (*Time,* 1954), Jed Kiley (*Playboy,* 1956–1957), and Plimpton (*Paris Review,* 1958).

At the same time, Hemingway found himself the recipient of many awards, most notably the Pulitzer and Nobel Prizes (1953 and 1954, respectively), and these, as well as the premature obituaries that followed the first of two devastating air crashes in Africa in 1954, occasioned more recitations of past deeds, turning his gaze inward and backward. Scholars also contributed to this self-consciousness: Lee Samuels (1951) compiled a checklist; Carlos Baker (1952), Philip Young (1952), and Charles Fenton (1954) produced book-length critical studies; and John K. M. McCaffery (1950) edited the first critical anthology on Hemingway. The autobiographical element of his journalism from the 1920s expanded in his *Esquire* pieces of the 1930s and war reporting for *Collier's* in the 1940s. By the 1950s, biographers and interviewers were circling, and each time they persuaded Hemingway to talk about his life, he seemed to have less control over it. Once he began speaking on the record in widely circulated periodicals, his self-created incarnations begin to contradict one another. Yet, despite his violent tirades against "publicity," he was fatally attracted to self-promotion and powerless to reverse its effects. All his life he had been an incredibly successful one-man operation: chief executive and financial officer, sole agent and publicist, and also the creative artist whose genius sustained the entire enterprise. These tasks overwhelmed him in the 1950s.

In matters of the heart, he was seldom content for long, but after World War II his needs to have a devoted wife and an inspirational muse were in constant conflict. He was married almost continuously, beginning with Hadley Richardson (1921–1927), Pauline Pfeiffer (1927–1940), and Martha Gellhorn (1940–1945). In March 1946 he wed Mary Welsh and their rancorous marriage endured despite her frequent threats to divorce him. When they met, Ernest was still handsome, physically fit, and only a few years removed from the enormous success of *For Whom the Bell Tolls* (1940). Mary was petite and vivacious—Ernest's "pocket Rubens"—and the prospective mother of the daughter he had always wanted. But her ectopic pregnancy and miscarriage in August 1946 precluded her from bearing a child, and ill health, accidents, alcohol, and animosity jaded their relationship and began to accelerate the aging process of both Hemingways. In the end, it was not an abiding love that bound them but accident and circumstance—plane crashes, concussions, broken bones, the Cuban revolution, and Ernest's mental demise. There was never an opportune time for Mary to depart, and the longer she remained, the more determined she became to reign as the final Mrs. Hemingway.

Ernest complicated his last marriage by seeking creative inspiration from a series of asexual affairs with attractive muses. Mary managed to end Ernest's flirtation with Virginia Viertel quickly, but she hardly seems to have understood it. "Jigee," married to the screenwriter Peter Viertel, joined the Hemingways' entourage in November 1949 as they sailed to Paris, where they stayed at the Ritz and attended the races. When Ernest spent ninety minutes alone with Jigee in her private room, Mary became furious, but Ernest later explained that he was parrying the young woman's romantic advances, and Mary seems to have accepted his explanation.[2] This flirtation proved hardly more than an arguing point in the Hemingways' marriage, but Mary resented it (see letter 38).

Adriana Ivancich, the beautiful Italian teenager whom Ernest met in December 1948, more profoundly affected the Hemingways. She so obviously inspired Ernest's depiction of Renata in *Across the River and into the Trees* (1950) that the novel's gondola scenes brought scandal to her family when European papers identified her as the heroine.[3] Mary was especially offended by this relationship as well as by her husband's general maltreatment of her, writing to Charles Scribner in October 1950: "The reason I have to leave Ernest—not easy for me since I have no other home and no money—is that in his program of being a tough guy, he has destroyed what I used to think was an inexhaustible supply of devotion to him. He has been truculent, brutal, abusive, and extremely childish."[4] Later that month, Adriana and her mother visited the Hemingways in Cuba, staying through February 1951, and Ernest's literary productivity surged: having just finished revisions of *Across the River* for Scribners in June, he completed the "Bimini novel" (posthumously published in 1970 as *Islands in the Stream*) by December; in January he began *The Old Man and the Sea*, which grew out of "On the Blue Water: A Gulf Stream Letter" (*Esquire*, 1936), finishing his first draft just after the Ivanciches left Cuba. Ernest and Adriana corresponded from 1950 through at least 1955, with Ernest sometimes playing the role of heartsick lover and at other times mentor and partner. Adriana designed the jackets for *Across the River and into the Trees* and *The Old Man and the Sea* (1952) and illustrated "The Good Lion" and "The Faithful Bull" for *Holiday* in 1951. When the Hemingways left Europe in June 1954 following their plane crashes on safari, Adriana and her mother saw them off as they departed from Genoa.[5] This was the pair's final meeting.

When another young woman, Valerie Danby-Smith of the *Irish Times*, entered the Hemingways' volatile lives in Spain in July 1959, they were enduring a summer that was as dangerous for them as it was for the matadors whose skills they had come to witness. Ernest's purpose in returning to Spain was to update *Death in the Afternoon* (1932), a doubly reiterative endeavor in that it

---

2. Mary Hemingway, *How It Was* (New York: Knopf, 1976), 290.

3. See N. Ann Doyle and Neal B. Huston, "Letters to Adriana Ivancich," *Hemingway Review* 5:1 (1985): 14–29.

4. Mary Hemingway to Charles Scribner, October 12, 1950, quoted in Rose Marie Burwell, *Hemingway: The Postwar Years and the Posthumous Novels* (Cambridge: Cambridge University Press, 1996), 228.

5. Michael Reynolds, *Hemingway: The Final Years* (New York: Norton, 1999), 280.

returned him to a familiar place and a previous creative effort. His behavior toward Mary during this trip was atrocious and friends could not persuade him to mend his ways.[6] When Ernest gathered his Pamplona entourage at a picnic site along the Irati River that he remembered from his explorations in the 1920s, Mary slipped on a stone in the water and suffered a broken toe, but her greater misery was that she had grown expendable, perhaps even invisible, to her husband. He and the teenaged reporter who had come to interview him quickly became inseparable, and he soon persuaded Valerie to become his secretary.[7] Mary decided to return home in advance of Ernest in order to set up a separate residence in New York, a first step toward extricating herself from his life.[8]

Mary's ambition to leave Ernest was delayed: first, when she arrived home in advance of Ernest after being away from their Cuban home, the Finca Vigia (Lookout Farm), for a year, she had to repair the residence and prepare for guests—Ernest had invited Antonio and Carmen Ordóñez to join him in Cuba and then accompany him on hunting expeditions in Ketchum, where the Hemingways had purchased a new home that, again, Mary felt obliged to make ready. Having dutifully prepared both residences, she encountered a second problem when she slipped while hunting and shattered her elbow, which required surgery and physical therapy. When the Ordóñezes were suddenly called away on family business, the Hemingways returned to Cuba together and Mary's window for exit from Ernest's life temporarily closed.

Back in Cuba, with Mary unable to type, Ernest called upon Valerie for her secretarial skills. She joined the Hemingways in June 1960, residing in the "little house" and typing the revised chapters of the Paris sketches, later published as *A Moveable Feast,* as Ernest finished them.[9] When it became clear in July 1960 that the Cuban revolution would force the trio to leave the island, Valerie helped the Hemingways pack; Ernest was traveling again to Spain to update his bullfight article for *Life,* and Mary would enjoy New York until his return. Just after Ernest arrived in Spain, Mary and Val received news, relayed to them by Hotchner, that he had been stricken ill. The report proved false but Ernest had

6. Ibid., 328–34.

7. Valerie Hemingway, *Running with the Bulls: My Years with the Hemingways* (New York: Ballantine, 2004), 34–35. Valerie later married Hemingway's son Gregory. Her memoir includes almost no documentary evidence. She claims to have "removed every trace of communication between Ernest and me" (294) when she sorted his papers following his death but does not seem to have retained his letters.

8. Mary Hemingway, *How It Was,* 550.

9. Valerie Hemingway, *Running with the Bulls,* 98.

grown fretful and inconsolable, so Valerie joined him in Spain. Their parting in early October—he to go to New York, she to Ireland—was their last.

While Ernest's return to Spain and *Death in the Afternoon* was doubly reiterative, his final writing task was trebly so. Not only were the Paris sketches about the past, but portions of the manuscript may also have been written years earlier. And the muse for this manuscript about youth and love was not a teenager from the 1950s but his wife from the 1920s in Paris, Hadley Richardson, about whom he wrote: "When I saw my wife again standing by the tracks as the train came in by the piled logs at the station, I wished I had died before I ever loved anyone but her."[10] With no tangible muse at hand, Ernest's last pages were written in that terrible isolation he had identified in his Nobel Prize acceptance speech: "Writing, at its best, is a lonely life."

If his young women were muses and surrogate daughters, his male companions like Antonio Ordóñez (b. 1932) and Hotchner (b. 1920) were close in age to his own sons, John (b. 1923), Patrick (b. 1928), and Gregory (b. 1931). Following Pauline's death in 1951, Ernest became permanently estranged from Gregory, and Patrick, after graduating from Harvard in 1952, went to Kenya with his new wife. John, who had two young daughters in 1957 and who lived in Cuba, complained to Hadley that he felt unwelcome at Ernest and Mary's house: "They hate to see the kids out there. Makes them feel they may be out of their thirties."[11] In Hotchner, Hemingway found not only a friend but also a fellow writer, a jovial travel companion, and a surrogate son.

Their personal acquaintance began in the tropical warmth of Cuba and concluded in the cold chill of Rochester, Minnesota. Between these times and in an international array of places, they became friends and business partners. Initially Hemingway helped the fledgling freelance writer, but soon the older man would turn to the younger for small and then more substantial editorial services. In the 1950s Hotchner wrote and produced several adaptations of Hemingway's works for the new medium of television, and in 1966 his *Papa Hemingway* became a best-selling and influential memoir. It also alienated him from Mary Hemingway, her husband's literary executrix. Until her death two decades later, scholars and biographers would minimize Hotchner's role in Hemingway's life. This failure to acknowledge his contributions as a friend and associate has limited our appreciation of Hotchner as adaptor and editor of Hemingway's works.

10. Ernest Hemingway, *A Moveable Feast* (New York: Scribner's, 1964), 210.

11. John Hemingway quoted in Gioia Dilberto, *Hadley: A Life of Hadley Richardson Hemingway* (New York: Ticknor and Fields, 1992), 275.

The Hemingway/Hotchner correspondence testifies to an abiding friendship and a mutually beneficial business partnership. The two met when Hotchner, a young associate editor with *Cosmopolitan,* arrived in Cuba in June 1948, hoping to persuade Hemingway to write an article on "The Future of Literature." Not only did Hemingway surprise him by agreeing to write the piece, but he also asked Hotchner to negotiate the sale of two as-yet-unwritten short stories to *Cosmopolitan.* More startling was the author's request that Hotchner investigate the possibility of serializing his work-in-progress, the Bimini novel, which would be his first major publication since *For Whom the Bell Tolls.* The article was cancelled, and none of the short stories that Hemingway wrote seemed appropriate for *Cosmopolitan,* but one grew into a new novel. In August 1949 Ernest offered *Across the River and into the Trees* in lieu of the short stories or the Bimini novel, and he asked Hotchner to conduct the negotiations.

Hotchner not only secured very favorable terms—$85,000 for the serialization—but he also read the typescript for language and situations that might be objectionable in a magazine. The typescript bears more than three dozen of his corrections and revisions. The most substantial of these involve emending or omitting passages that could be construed as anti-Semitic. Arguing that readers would identify Hemingway with his protagonist and brand the author an anti-Semite, Hotchner persuaded him to cut some of Colonel Cantwell's internal monologues, eliminating the word *Jew* several times, to temper remarks about public figures, and to tame erotic passages and eliminate profane language. These changes are minor but noteworthy, particularly as Hemingway chose to retain them when he revised the novel for book publication with Scribner's.[12] Hemingway thanked Hotchner for his "fine efficient performance" (letter 30) and wrote: "I am truly grateful for you helping me when I was too angry or wrong. The damn Col. was angry often; but you helped me see where to take out the parts that would be misunderstood and make a bigger gang up" (letter 38). The novel appeared in the February–June 1950 issues of *Cosmopolitan,* followed in September by the Scribner's edition. The critical reception was generally poor.

In January 1950, a cognac-inspired conversation with Ernest in Italy about converting one art form into another prompted Hotchner's first foray into

12. For Hotchner's precise editorial contributions, see the collation of typescripts, serialization, and Scribner's edition in Albert J. DeFazio III, "The HemHotch Letters: The Correspondence and Relationship of Ernest Hemingway and A. E. Hotchner," Ph.D. diss., University of Virginia, 1992, 953–1245.

adaptation. Deeply suspicious of Hollywood, Ernest was likewise disinclined to collaborate on teleplays, but as a professional writer with a living to earn, he understood that these were necessary and potentially lucrative venues. Hotchner's first unlikely assignment was to adapt Hemingway's short story "The Capital of the World" for ballet. He made it work, and it was performed in 1953 at the Metropolitan Opera House in New York and televised nationally. The performance at the Met earned virtually no money for either man, but it proved that Hotchner was a trustworthy and capable partner.[13]

As a young and hungry freelancer based in New York, Hotchner was poised to act occasionally as Hemingway's agent and adapter for television and, eventually, for stage and film. Only once did Hemingway review a script, and this was for a dramatic reading of "The Snows of Kilimanjaro" that was never produced (letter 81). On another occasion, he provided background information for "The Gambler, the Nun, and the Radio" in a rambling letter dictated to Valerie Danby-Smith (letter 138). The only production that Hemingway appears to have seen was the second part of *For Whom the Bell Tolls* (see notes to letter 105).

The adaptations are often hard to track through the correspondence: their working titles occasionally change; sometimes they are dropped from consideration; at other times, years pass between inception and execution. Therefore, the following list is provided to identify the adaptations referenced in the letters, including those that were produced shortly after Hemingway's death. All adaptations are by Hotchner unless otherwise indicated.

December 7, 1953	*The Capital of the World* (teleplay), broadcast on *Omnibus,* CBS
December 27, 1953	*The Capital of the World* (ballet), Metropolitan Opera House, New York
Spring 1955	*The Snows of Kilimanjaro* (dramatic reading featuring Marlene Dietrich, not produced)
October 18, 1955	"The Battler" (teleplay), *Playwrights '56,* NBC
1956	*The Undefeated* (motion picture development, not produced)
November 10, 1957	"The World of Nick Adams" (teleplay), *The Seven Lively Arts,* CBS
April 1958	"Fifty Grand" (teleplay), *Kraft Television Theatre,* NBC

13. A. E. Hotchner, *Choice People* (New York: Morrow, 1984), 168–72.

Fall 1958	*Scouting on Two Continents,* by Frederick Russell Burnham (not produced)
March 12 and 19, 1959	"For Whom the Bell Tolls" (teleplay, two parts), *Playhouse 90,* CBS
November 19, 1959	"The Killers" (teleplay), *Buick Electra Playhouse,* CBS
January 29, 1960	"The Fifth Column" (teleplay), *Buick Electra Playhouse,* CBS
March 25, 1960	"The Snows of Kilimanjaro" (teleplay), *Buick Electra Playhouse,* CBS
May 19, 1960	"The Gambler, The Nun, and the Radio" (teleplay), *Buick Electra Playhouse,* CBS
March 1960	"After the Storm" (teleplay; not produced).
October 1961	*A Short Happy Life* (stage play)
August 1962	*Hemingway's Adventures of a Young Man* (motion picture), 20th Century Fox
1962	*The Battler* (motion picture), excerpted from *Hemingway's Adventures of a Young Man*
January 1967	*The Hemingway Hero* (stage play; working title was *Of Love and Death*)

The two men's most significant collaborative venture, cutting the typescript of *The Dangerous Summer* for *Life* magazine, is scarcely discussed in the correspondence, and even Hotchner's own account of it in *Papa Hemingway* hardly suggests the magnitude or lasting significance of his contribution. Hemingway's difficulties with *The Dangerous Summer* began when he complicated his initial ambition to write an appendix that would update *Death in the Afternoon.* He had envisioned a task that was essentially documentary and would require minimal attention to plot and structure: he would portray the greatest matadors to have appeared since the mid-1930s, explain the technical modifications and rule changes since then, and account for the current state of affairs in professional bullfighting. But when he agreed to write a 5,000-word feature article for *Life* about the upcoming mano a mano between matadors Antonio Ordóñez and Louis Miguel Dominguín, he needed plot, conflict, climax, structure, and, most of all, resolution. He seems to have hoped that an outside force—the bulls, perhaps—would provide his conclusion: "This story," he wrote to *Life's* Ed Thompson, "is difficult to write and to make of any permanent value. Would have been easy to write if either Luis Miguel or Antonio had been killed." Despite being gored, both men lived. And Hemingway's manuscript swelled to nearly 700 pages. He labored for three weeks, alone, trying to cut it but managed to remove only 278 words.[14] Everything seemed essential and Hemingway's failing health was making him indecisive, so he called his friend for assistance.

During nine days in 1960 in the stultifying heat of a late June and early July in Cuba, Hotchner cut the 688–page typescript of *The Dangerous Summer* for serialization in *Life*. In two neat columns, he listed twenty-seven cuts. Hemingway objected to practically every one of them (see appendix). Sometimes he sought to preserve certain literary features of the manuscript—mood, motif, counterpoint—claiming in one instance that "cutting this piece of country out that we went through so often and is such a big part of the summer—is like cutting the country part out of The Sun Also Rises." Other times he rejected cuts on journalistic grounds or out of a sense of reportorial fairness: his description of a car trip "makes us seem normal [A]merican people with whom reader can identify self" and eliminating certain descriptions of Dominguín "would be grossly unfair." Hotchner edited the typescript based on his understanding that *Life's* editors sought the story of the mano a mano. Hemingway, despite agreeing to write such an account, actually created a much more ambitious work of art. It was his sentimental journey, a picaresque romp through Spain, a headlong jaunt away from injury and illness, away from mental staleness and impending old age. The tale of the mano a mano, framed by personal narrative, enters the typescript on page 250 and exits on page 488, occupying only the middle third of the text. Hotchner understood that *The Dangerous Summer* was more than an article about bullfighting and felt that "Scribners should have published the full manuscript because that was what Hemingway intended."[15]

Despite his initial objections, Hemingway eventually consented to cut all but a few hundred of the words deemed nonessential by Hotchner. In the end, he excised about half of the text. *Life's* editors trimmed another 7,000 words adjacent to those that Hotchner had cut, leaving Hotchner primarily or indirectly responsible for excisions totaling 67,516 words. When Michael Pietsch edited the volume for Scribner's in 1985, he restored about 16,000 words but concurred with more than 70 percent of Hotchner's cuts. Pietsch's edition essentially reemphasizes the narrative's scope as Hotchner had defined it twenty-five years earlier.[16]

---

14. A. E. Hotchner, *Papa Hemingway: A Personal Memoir* (New York: Random House, 1966), 240.

15. Ronald Weber, *Hemingway's Art of Non-Fiction* (New York: St. Martin's, 1990), 117.

16. Hotchner's editorial contributions to *The Dangerous Summer* are detailed in my collation of the typescript that the men edited in June–July 1960, *Life's* serialization, and the Scribner's edition. See DeFazio, "HemHotch Letters," 1246–87.

When the cutting was done, Hotchner took the typescript to New York; Hemingway arrived a month later, en route to Spain to gather photographs and update his narrative. Before departing, he tried to pay Hotchner for his editorial work, but the younger man demurred, accepting only reimbursement for the travel expenses he had incurred. Hotchner wrote:

> I was really touched by your wanting me to share some of the loot—came as a surprise since had no thought this was anything but your project that I enjoyed helping on. I appreciated the dough [reimbursement for travel], of course, but please remember we are not on a dough basis although we do seem to mutually make quite a lot of it. But that is only incidental to main business of being friends + helping each other. (Letter 144)

The "main business of being friends + helping each other" was what drove their fourteen-year association. After Hemingway's death, Hotchner continued to adapt his works, suggested the title for *A Moveable Feast,* and collaborated with Mary on the Caedmon recording *Ernest Hemingway Reading.* But the widow objected to the memoir that he was preparing for serialization in the *Saturday Evening Post* and publication with Random House.[17] Mary had been claiming that Ernest's death was accidental, and she seemed prepared to maintain this fiction indefinitely; when she learned that Hotchner's memoir would describe the death as a suicide, she tried to halt its publication. Failing that, she confessed in an interview that her husband had killed himself.[18]

17. Mary alleged that the memoir was inaccurate and contained conversations that were her husband's literary property. The errors that she identified and that Hotchner corrected were innocuous. For a complete record of the changes made between the original proofs and the Random House edition, see DeFazio, "HemHotch Letters," appendix 1B, 913–52. In his preface to the centennial edition of *Papa Hemingway,* Hotchner explained that in order to preserve Hemingway's voice and emotions, he used excerpts from Hemingway's letters and melded them into his rendering of the conversations they had when they were together. A. E. Hotchner, *Papa Hemingway,* Hemingway Centennial Edition (New York: Carroll and Graf, 1999), xxiv. For a collation of *Papa Hemingway* and its source materials, see DeFazio, "HemHotch Letters," appendix 1A, 810–912.

18. In January 1966, the *New York Times* reported that "Mrs. Hemingway was said to have 'steadfastly' denied that her husband committed suicide." Robert E. Tomasson, "*Papa Hemingway* Brought to Court," *New York Times,* January 29, 1966, p. 22. Two months later, however, in an interview with Oriana Fallaci, Mary conceded that her husband had committed suicide and elaborated on his decrepit condition. "Mio marito Hemingway: Intervista con la vedora del grande scrittore americano," *Europeo,* March 17, 1966, pp. 30–37. This admission was the subject of a *Times* article (Harry Gilroy, "Widow Believes Hemingway Committed Suicide," *New York Times,* August 23, 1966, p. 36), and a translation of the interview appeared in *Look* magazine ("My Husband, Ernest Hemingway," *Look,* September 6, 1966, pp. 62–68).

But Hotchner had fallen out of favor with Mary, to whom he had initially dedicated his memoir, and what was for fourteen years a genuine and heartfelt friendship came to a close.[19] The long-suffering widow who had sacrificed her career to become Mrs. Hemingway settled into a twenty-six-year reign as her husband's autocratic literary executor. Not surprisingly, Hotchner is scarcely mentioned and usually ungenerously characterized in scholarship of that era. Jack Hemingway acknowledges the attempt to exclude Hotchner in describing the sons' role in publishing *The Dangerous Summer*: "Our influence was first felt in the decision finally to publish *The Dangerous Summer* with the insistence that the comic and very human sequences in which A. E. Hotchner played a role not be deleted as had first been proposed to us."[20] Those responsible for this proposal, he implies, were Mary Hemingway and her lawyer, Alfred Rice. In their absence, we are free to explore Hotchner's place in the Hemingway milieu. Ernest was fond of repeating *"Il faut d'abord durer"* ("first one must endure"); Hotchner and Hemingway have both done this in their fashion. And now the story of their friendship will endure as well.

19. Twenty-two letters, telegrams, and cards written by Mary to Hotchner between 1950 and 1961 survive and are held in the Alderman Library, University of Virginia, Charlottesville. Addressing her missives to "Honey Hotch," "Hotch darling," and other affectionate nicknames, Mary, who had suffered a near-fatal miscarriage in 1946 and was consequently unable to bear children, typed a sympathetic letter to the Hotchners regarding the loss of their infant son (March 30, 1954); congratulated Hotchner on his publications and adaptations (November 14, 1952, August 26, 1958); invited him for visits—reminding him about swimsuits, hunting gear, and directions (June 21, 1955, November 5, 1958); and complained about her husband (November 8, 1959). Her letter of July 4, 1950, in which she reneges on her offer to provide Hotchner with her notes describing their Paris-Cannes trip, indicates that she had long intended to write about her relationship with Hemingway: "You know I've been keeping travel diaries for several years. They started on the notion that they might be helpful to Ernest, as reminders for his own personal recollections. Then he decided I should eventually put them into a book. A pretty remote prospect, but none the less they are practically the only property I have." Alderman Library, University of Virginia, 6250f.

20. Jack Hemingway, *Misadventures of a Fly Fisherman* (Dallas: Taylor, 1986), 322.

The Correspondence of
Ernest Hemingway and A. E. Hotchner

1948–1961

1948

{1} AEH to EH
June 11, 1948 (TLS, 3 pp., JFKL)
Hearst's International Combined with Cosmopolitan/Hearst Magazine Building/
Fifty-Seventh Street at Eighth Avenue/New York 19, N.Y./Arthur Gordon/
Editor

Dear Ernest:

I've passed along your regards to Mark [Murphy] and Arthur [Gordon], and both were delighted to hear from you. Mark just returned from Indianapolis where he has been gathering material for a Saturday Evening Post article.

Arthur thinks the deal which I discussed with you is fine and has suggested $15,000 as the price for the article and two short stories. I checked the income tax situation with the resident tax lawyer and he suggested that we put the terms into contract form so that you will have proof to offer the internal revenue people if they query you.

Also, Arthur is in complete agreement about the situation regarding the novel. If your manuscript gets to us too late for complete serialization before publication, it will be possible to run installments after the book has been published. Of course, the sooner the completed manuscript is in our hands, the better.

I certainly enjoyed our visits; it was most kind of you to see me on such short notice. After being exposed to your finca the concrete and soot around here look especially awful. I hope you and Mary will be able to route yourselves through New York in the fall so that I can collect the people you want to see.

My best to both of you and many thanks.   ·

Sincerely,

Ed

A. E. Hotchner

Associate Editor

The contract dated June 11, 1948 and drawn between Ernest Hemingway and Cosmopolitan Magazine is hereby amended to include this further paragraph: "In the event that no acceptable manuscript has been received by Cosmopolitan Magazine (which shall be the sole party to determine acceptability) by January 1, 1950, it is understood that the said $15,000 shall be returned by Hemingway to Cosmopolitan Magazine upon demand by said Cosmopolitan Magazine at any time after January 1, 1950."

This is the fight story I mentioned. Similar in some respects to one Runyon did but I think you'll find it interesting. Arthur thought you might like to read the fantasy, THE NEXT VOICE YOU HEAR; he thinks more highly of it than I do. If you'd like to make any changes, mark this copy + I'll have it re-done.

Ed

Mark [Murphy]: Freelance writer, friend of AEH, and acquaintance of EH. AEH worked with Sergeant Murphy and Major Arthur Gordon on *Air Force Magazine,* which he had joined following a tour of duty as adjutant of the 13th Anti-Submarine Wing of the Air Force (*Choice,* 80).

Arthur [Gordon]: AEH's editor at *Cosmopolitan* who sent him to Cuba to solicit an article from EH on "The Future of Literature" (*Choice,* 15). AEH was warmly received by EH at La Finca Vigía ("Lookout Farm"), the 21-acre hilltop home EH purchased in 1940, located about eight miles from Havana. EH introduced AEH to La Floridita, his favorite seafood bar-restaurant, and the *Pilar,* his cabin cruiser (*PH,* 3–9). EH agreed to write the article, which was later cancelled, and to provide two short stories which were not yet written.

the novel: "[T]he first volume of his long novel, the Bimini story, which was complete in draft" (*Final,* 174)—a portion of what would become *Islands in the Stream* (New York: Scribner's, 1970).

Mary: Mary Welsh Monks Hemingway (1908–1986) married EH on March 14, 1946 (his fourth marriage, her third). When she met EH in 1944, she was the London correspondent for *Time* magazine; during their marriage she produced little journalism but kept extensive journals on which she based her autobiography, *How It Was.*

This is: The final paragraph, typed on a half sheet of paper and found separately, is included here because of EH's reference in letter 2 to "the enclosures and the two stories." George Sumner Albee's "The Next Voice You Hear" was published in *Cosmopolitan* in August 1948. The "fight story" remains unlocated.

Runyon: (Alfred) Damon Runyon (1884–1946), writer of short stories, many of which were adapted for stage and screen, and sports journalist who emphasized human interest over objective reporting.

{2} EH to AEH
June 27 1948 (TLS, 1 p., ViU)
FINCA VIGIA SAN FRANCISCO DE PAULA, CUBA

Dear Ed:

Thanks for the letter, the enclosures and the two stories. They came the morning we were shoveing off in boat for Cay Sal and Double Headed Shot Keys in Bahamas with the kids who were here on ten days' vacation. That was why didn't answer sooner.

Enclosed is the contract. So he TOOK the fifteen thousand dollars. My lawyer is haveing prostrate gland trouble in Philadelphia and his assistant lawyer doesn't know his prostrate from a hole in the ground so I haven't heard from them yet. But if law still same as it was pieces contracted to write by a bona-fide non-resident written while out of country are tax free if non-resident out of country over six consecutive months. Maybe now it is changed but if my prostrated lawyers find that is so I can give the monies back or just write the piece and the stories and take the loss same as always.

Will you now please send me tear sheets (tear as in tear paper not tear as in eyes) or mss. of what any of your other master minds have written on the Future of Everything so I get the pitch. You and Arthur [Gordon] both know that I do not know a shit about the future of anything but will write a good straight piece about what I think and will try to straighten up and think as good as I can. Also tell me minimum and maximum length.

It was swell knowing you, Ed. This isn't the old craperoo between the writer and the editor. You're very welcome any time you can ever come down. Please give best to girl.

Wish you had been on this trip. We caught around 1800 pounds of game fish, turned three big turtles, got lots of crawfish and had wonderful swimming. That water is almost virgin fishing and the kids had a wonderful time. I got down to 210 which is about as low as should go. We have enough turtle meat to feed the cats for ten days and enough white eggs to justify open-

ing a whorehouse here in San Francisco. Have the deep freeze full of everything. On four days, fishing five hours a day we averaged a fish every four minutes. The Malabar Farm of the Seas and we didn't even have to use manure.

Give my best to Arthur; also Mary's. Everybody tired from trip but feeling
wonderful. Would like to take you there sometime if you would go. No insects, lonely island (un-inhabited), good sanddunes, African vegetation, sandy
beaches, salt pond in the middle, make a lee with almost any wind, water so
clear you think you will hit a rock when you have thirty fathoms over it.
Awfully good life if that is what you like and that is what I like. Took two tons
of ice and the fish paid for the trip. Also no god-damn photographer.

Write me the gen.

Best always and hope see you soon again

Ernest.

Mary sends her best to Arthur and his wife. I said this before but she says it
again.

the kids: Patrick (1928–) and Gregory (1931–2001), EH's younger sons from his second marriage (1927–1940) to Pauline Pfeiffer (1895–1951).
My lawyer: Maurice J. Speiser (1880–1948), EH's attorney and agent from the 1920s
   until his death. Friend, collector, and correspondent to many modernists, he took a
   professional interest in the legal rights of artists.
assistant lawyer: Alfred Rice (1908–1985) served EH until 1961 as attorney and occasionally as agent, and then served Mary until his own death.
best to girl: reference to Geraldine Mavor (1915–1968), who soon became AEH's wife.
Malabar Farm: Experimental farm in Pleasant Valley, Ohio, owned by novelist and con-
   servationist Louis Bromfield (1896–1956).
photographer: George Leavens, who photographed EH for the Hemingway pieces "Paris
   160 Miles Away," *Holiday,* January 1948, p. 52, and "The Great Blue River," *Holiday,*
   July 1949, pp. 60–63, 95–97.
gen: British Royal Air Force slang for "intelligence, the hand out at the briefing." EH to
   Malcolm Cowley, October 17, 1945, in Carlos Baker, ed., *Ernest Hemingway: Selected
   Letters, 1917–1961* (New York: Scribner's, 1981), 603.
On verso of envelope, EH adds: "Will write you about stories as soon as read them EH."

{3} AEH to EH
July 7. [1948] (TLS, 2 pp., JFKL)
Cosmopolitan [New York City]

Dear Ernest:

A bad ten days, passed now, but still bad to think about. Arthur Gordon got called in and relieved of his command—temporarily the pitch is—with Herb Mayes, now editor of Good Housekeeping, taking over Cosmopolitan too. I like Arthur. He's a good friend. This is a tough strain on loyalty. Actually, all that is wrong is that circulation is down quite a bit, as it is on most other books. Well, when the team drops to second division you change managers.

Of course, Mayes is just as anxious for you to follow through on our little money deal as Arthur was. One thing, though—the America's Future series is out and Mayes wants to run your piece on writing as a straight article. This doesn't make any difference to you, I'm sure, since it all adds up to the same thing. There won't be any tear sheets to send, however (plenty of the eye kind, you can bet) so you're loose at the plate.

I get confused by the quickness with which talent is disparaged and dismissed. A guy has it on Monday, on Friday he couldn't be an office boy. It happens in writing, too, only there's tangible evidence to back it up, not profit sheets. The profit sheet is a shitty kind of measuring rod for talent, and that's just what is used in this weird business. Arthur has gone to Bermuda for a few days to try to assemble loose pieces, then end of August will go with Pam [Gordon] to England and spend two, maybe more months there. I think it should be more. Arthur can write, although now he must be pretty rusty, and writing away from this neurotic center will be good for him. I told him.

I took a little farm house on top of a green hill for the summer and I get there when I can, but that's not often enough.

Your fishing sounds fine, especially the island. I'm anxious to see what the Picasso of the camera [George Leavens] has done for Holiday. Scheduled yet? There's a fast stream down the road from my place that's busy with trout; I haven't given it a real test yet but it shows promise.

I hope the book [*Islands in the Stream*] goes well. I had drinks with Mark [Murphy] at Costello's last night and he sends along his fondest.

My best to Mary, and you.

<u>Ed</u>

Mayes wants to run your piece on writing as a straight article: When Herbert R. Mayes proposed that EH's piece on "The Future of Literature" be run as a stand-alone article rather than as part of the "America's Future" series, EH demurred, thinking that his prophesying about literature would appear presumptuous.

Costello's: Tim Costello's, a bar-restaurant in New York City on Third Avenue (*Story,* 387).

{4} AEH to EH
Jul 21 1948 (Cable, 1 p., JFKL)
New York

CAN UNDERSTAND YOUR FEELING ABOUT PRESUMPTUOUS ASPECT OF ARTICLE ["The Future of Literature"] STOP FOR TIME BEING LET ARTICLE RIDE AND WE WILL SEND FIFTEEN THOUSAND CHECK TO BE APPLIED AGAINST TWO SHORT STORIES AS AGREED STOP IF YOU THINK OF AN ARTICLE IDEA IN NEAR FUTURE OR WE DO COMMA FINE STOP IF NOT THEN WE WILL BE HAPPY TO APPLY ARRANGEMENT TO FICTION ONLY GLAD YOU ARE GETTING GOOD FISHING REALLY APPRECIATE WAY YOU HAVE COOPERATED REGARDS TO MARY HOPE YOU CAN ARRANGE A NEW YORK STOPOVER BEST

ED.

YOUR FEELING: The correspondence to which AEH was responding remains unlocated.

{5} AEH to EH
August 17, 1948 (TLS, 1 p., JFKL)
Hearst's International Combined with Cosmopolitan/Hearst Magazine Building/Fifty-Seventh Street at Eighth Avenue/New York 19, N.Y./Arthur Gordon/Editor

Dear Ernest:

The financial wheels have been a little slow in turning, but here's the sum, as agreed. It would make our accounting masters happy if you would sign the enclosed paper which I think is pretty much what we agreed upon when I last spoke with you.

Arthur and Pam Gordon leave Friday for London, where they will stay for a couple of months. I saw them yesterday, and they seem pretty excited about the trip. Arthur seems to be thriving on his enforced vacation and has managed to sell a novelette already.

I have just come from lunch with Mark Murphy and his charming wife Mickey, and naturally we devoted some of our time to talking about you. Mark has just finished a brace of articles on the Indianapolis speed derby and is presently doing research on the city of Cleveland which he will expose to the readers of The Saturday Evening Post. The drinks were good and the talk was fine.

I suppose you are back on the book [*Islands*], although the lure of the summer seas must be mighty hard to pass up. I am sorry to say that there is no worthwhile fiction to pass along to you at this time.

My best to Mary and yourself.

Sincerely,

Ed

A. E. Hotchner

Associate Editor

the sum: Likely a reference to the "check" in letter 6, ¶2, and "your 10G check" in letter 18, ¶11.

enclosed paper: No copy of the enclosure survived with this letter.

a brace of articles on the Indianapolis speed derby: Mark Murphy, "Oh, It's Wild," *New Yorker,* June 18, 1949, pp. 54–61. The other articles remain unlocated.

{6} EH to AEH

September 7 1948 (TLS, 1 p., ViU)

FINCA VIGIA, SAN FRANCISCO DE PAULA, CUBA

Dear Ed:

Thanks for letter and check. Enclosed is the codicil to the contract. Will try to write the best stories I can.

Excuse short letter as have put off writing due to general effup due to Speiser, my attorney and agent dying (go for a shit we called it in Raf).

My permanent address for next six months is Guaranty Trust Co. of N.y. 4 Place de la Concorde, Paris, France.

Write there.

Best always, kid. Boat sailing in ½ hour and have to make it (like always).

<u>Ernest</u>

(Mister Papa)

codicil to the contract: Presumably a copy of "the enclosed paper," letter 5, ¶2.

Speiser . . . dying: Maurice Speiser died on August 5, 1948. *New York Times,* August 6, 1948, p. 17. EH learned of his death on August 9 (*Final,* 174).

Raf: Royal Air Force. As front-line correspondent for *Collier's,* EH accompanied RAF pilots on practice and bombing missions in June 1944 (*Final,* 98–99). See Ernest Hemingway, "London Fights the Robots," *Collier's,* August 19, 1944, pp. 17, 80–81, which describes the RAF's efforts to intercept the pilotless aircraft V-1 German buzz bombs.

Boat sailing: The Hemingways boarded the *Jagiello* on the afternoon of September 7 and arrived in Italy on the 21st (*Final,* 175, 177).

1949

{7} AEH to EH
2/17 [1949] (TLS, 1 p., JFKL)
Hearst's International Combined with Cosmopolitan/Hearst Magazine Building/
Fifty-Seventh Street at Eighth Avenue/New York 19, N.Y./Arthur Gordon/
Editor

Dear Ernest:

Hope this gets passed along to you—I feel like I'm tossing a saucer that sails up and then curves back down to Italy—if that's where you still are. Sorry I've been so long in answering your last letter.

Strange how Italy, after the intense furore of the last elections, suddenly dropped from the news here. At one moment, this was the most strategic spot in the universe—we even sent the very best American publicity agents to do a job for the Cause—and the next moment, Italy could be a New Jersey suburb, for all we care. It would be interesting to know just what those elections did mean to the Italians; I suspect not much, one way or another.

It's too bad you weren't here for the last presidential election. You probably read all the events and know what happened from a blow-by-blow viewpoint, but, Ernest, there was a feeling in the air that I remember only once before—it was the morning after Roosevelt had defeated Landon. A strange, alcoholic atmosphere; little people felt big and the big ones looked like you always hoped they would. Somehow you felt like you'd just received an inheritance and Political Opinion was a thing no longer to be respected, either from Fulton Lewis, Jr., or Roper. A fine, fine day it was.

The article on you in Life, the one you told me about, was really second-rate. It sounded like Cowley had simply put transitions between all the prefaces for your books. I haven't seen the Holiday stuff—has it run yet? Perhaps I missed it.

And the project? Do you work hard on it or is Italy too distracting? I'm still hoping you route yourself through here on your return; good people for you to see.

All the best,

Ed

presidential election . . . defeated Landon: Refers to Harry Truman's defeat of Thomas Dewey in 1948 and Franklin Roosevelt's defeat of Alfred M. Landon in 1936.

Fulton Lewis, Jr.: Conservative journalist and broadcaster who supported the America First movement and Sen. Joe McCarthy.

Roper: Elmo Roper, a research consultant for the *New York Times,* was among the first to develop objective methods of political forecasting. *New York Times,* October 10, 1948, p. 13.

article on you: Malcolm Cowley, "A Portrait of Mister Papa," *Life,* January 10, 1949, pp. 86–101. This article included inaccuracies that were perpetuated for decades. Cowley (1898–1989) was an American literary critic, social historian, and editor of the *New Republic* from 1929 to 1944. He edited the *Viking Portable Hemingway* in 1944.

the Holiday stuff: Probably "The Great Blue River," which would run in *Holiday* in July; see notes to letter 2.

{8} EH to AEH
March 9 1949 (TLS, 1 p., ViU)
Villa Aprile/Cortina D'Ampezzo/Italy. [*tw*]

Dear Ed:

It was good to hear from you. You sound fine too.

Things quiet in Italy on acct. seven years between elections. Italians are a wonderful people. Probably have had the worst press in the world. Have learned a lot this trip I hope. Meeting people you fought against and seeing the places with more understanding, or anyway older, eyes been wonderful for me.

So you know about the stories: It's March now and the deadline is the end of December. I owe two stories or give back the dough. Wrote one but think it is too rough for Cosmopolitan and better just save it for book. I always just write them and the ones that are suited for Cosmopolitan I give them. They've published the best stories I've written as you and the owners know. But I don't write a lot of stories.

Plan to get back in Cuba in early May, take the kids on a trip to Cay Sal Banks and then write two good stories for you. I may have to let them lay a while after I write and then go over them but think, if have no bad luck, should surely have two before the deadline. (Story written is about 4500 words. Is much better than that Waugh shit. But I can beat it for you.)

The Holiday piece is scheduled for June Ted Patrick writes. He said he liked it very much and wanted me to do any others I wanted. But I owe you two stories first and can't do anything else until then.

The Life piece made me sort of sick. Sure is a lot of difference between Life and life. Not to mention liberty and the pursuit of happiness or a fire-fight say. I try to be a good character and keep all promises, good or bad, keep deadlines, not abort on missions, hit it on the hour you say you will, be where you say you will even if you have to move other people out of it, etc. But I don't think Cowley knows anything about whatever material people like me are made of. I felt all the time, reading it, as though I were being formed in his image. Well the hell with it. I had a nice private life before with a lot of undeclared and unpublished pride and now I feel like somebody had shit in it and wiped themselves on slick paper and left it there.

Think it was fine Truman won but that it has gone to what he thinks of as his head.

Mary sends her best. She broke a leg six weeks ago ski-ing when she was running beautifully. But hit some heavy wet snow she didn't understand. Ski-ing now, with the lifts and all, is about like roller skating. Nobody has any strength in their legs because they never climb anymore and the best concession (had three tries at spelling that) around a ski joint is the X-Ray and Plaster Cast booth.

So long and good luck. Keep me in touch with events.

Ernest

We are going direct to Cuba and skip N.Y. Have my brain about as full as she will hold. We'll come up sometime quiet and have fun. Would certainly like to meet R. Flaherty and the other good people you know. Do you think we can get hold of a 16 mm. print of Louisiana story? Wish I could buy all his 16 mm. Do you know if this is possible.

Wrote one: Possibly "A Short Story," dated "March 1949" by EH (JFKL 1.1), which grew into *Across the River and into the Trees* (New York: Scribner's, 1950).
the best stories I've written: Stories EH published in *Cosmopolitan* include "After the

Storm," "One Trip Across," "The Short Happy Life of Francis Macomber," "Nobody Ever Dies," and "Under the Ridge."

about 4500 words: EH compulsively counted his words (as well as his weight) and often reported the results in his letters.

that Waugh shit: Probably Evelyn Waugh's *Brideshead Revisited: The Sacred and Profane Memories of Captain Charles Ryder* (1946), which EH owned.

Ted Patrick: Editor of *Holiday*.

R. Flaherty: Robert Flaherty (1884–1951), documentary filmmaker whose *Louisiana Story* (1948) is considered his masterwork. His editor, Helen Van Dongen, worked with Joris Ivens and EH on *The Spanish Earth* (1937). AEH was dating Flaherty's daughter, Monica.

{9} EH to AEH
10 June 1949 (TLS, 1 p., JFKL)
FINCA VIGIA, SAN FRANCISCO DE PAULA, CUBA

Dear Ed:

I am very sorry not to have answered you sooner but your letter followed us here since we came back to Cuba on a slow boat via various South American ports.

In regard to the money advance, I would rather carry it against two short stories as it is and try to make them the best short stories possible rather than to carry it against the novel [*Islands in the Stream*]. However, I can tell you personally that I will not give the novel to anyone else. You can count on this the same as you could on a contract.

The reason I do not want to take an advance on the novel is that I do not want anyone to have to look over my shoulder or see how it is going. If I should be unavailable and the novel not be finished I would have the two short stories to cover the advance on them or would return the cash.

I think this handles business but if they want something more formal we can always draw it up. Everything is fine here. Mary is very well and completely recovered from the broken leg she picked up in Cortina. The infection I had on my face and was hospitalized with is OK now. Our kids are here for about 30 days and we are making a trip to the Bahamas. After that I will settle down and work here until things are finished.

Would love to receive any 16 mm. prints as we have that fine projector that Mark Hellinger gave me and it is wonderful to be able to watch a moving picture in your own home with a drink in your hand. If you have anything that we ought to get they can always be sent down here through the local agent who will call us up and deliver them.

Hope Mark Murphy's trouble [alcoholism] will be OK. That seems to be one of the occupational hazards of our time. With best regards to you from Mary and myself and looking forward to when we can be together, either here or in New York, and see Bob Flaherty.

Yours always,

Ernest

ERNEST HEMINGWAY

your letter followed us here: This letter remains unlocated. The Hemingways returned to the Finca Vigia from Italy on May 27, whereupon EH hired Juanita "Nita" Jensen as a part-time secretary; she appears to have typed this letter. Jensen, a secretary at the American embassy in Havana, had begun moonlighting for EH in May 1948 (*Story,* 472).

infection: erysipelas, a contagious skin disease that EH had contracted in March (*Story,* 481).

Mark Hellinger: Producer of *The Killers* (Universal, 1946), one of the few film adaptations of his work that EH admired. Hellinger provided a private screening for EH and others at the Sun Valley theater before the film's premiere (*Final,* 149; *Story,* 457).

{10} AEH to EH
July 6, 1949 (TLS, 1 p., JFKL)
Cosmopolitan [New York City]

Dear Ernest:

Good piece in Holiday; much comment heard at Tim [Costello]'s and Blakes; all highly favorable. I was somewhat disappointed in the photos but I suppose it's difficult to get unusual stuff working on a boat. Yet, I've seen what my friend Roger Coster, talented little frenchman who was on Air Force Magazine with me, has done in color under worse conditions so it is possible. I've never fished deep sea and I've never realized until now that I was really missing something.

Have you read Tom Lea's book [*The Brave Bulls*]? Curious that every review I read used Death in the Afternoon as a measuring stick. I started it expecting much, too much I guess, because I finished strongly disappointed.

Mark Murphy and his wife have just published an effective anthology composed of writings about Brooklyn [*A Treasury of Brooklyn*], of all places.

Although the idea would seem to be special, actually it is not and the selections hold up well. My contribution was a volume of Henry Miller smuggled back in 1946. I presume you saw Mark's reportage on the Indianapolis race in the New Yorker [see letter 5]. If not, I'd like to send it to you.

Don't know your interest in baseball; mine fluctuates. Right now I think the DiMaggio story really dramatic and the guy as close to a national hero as we've got. Amazing how the heel of one individual can furnish continuous copy for three months. Actually, DiMaggio cared so much about playing that he made the fans care about him. Baseball fever is really high now, especially over the National League race between the Dodgers and the Cards. As a native St. Louisan I can't forget the Gas House Gang of my childhood and so I follow the fortunes of this year's crew which was given no chance at all and now is only a game out. I regret that baseball is rarely played after boyhood—it's a good, vigorous game and a lot more rewarding than golf and other accepted pastimes that properly belong to the middle years. I think shooting pool is a more legitimate exercise than walking around a golf course.

I have contacted my movie friends and you should be getting films shortly if there are no complications. A few years back the major cos. agreed to distribute all 16 mm. prints only to certain organizations like hospitals, orphanages, church groups, and the like, but I've had you classified as a church group and you should be getting prints regularly. I think you'll get a list to choose from. Should have details in a few days. Bet you've never been a church group before.

As I told you on the phone, I'm going to squeeze in a week or 10 day vacation at Varadero Beach the beginning of Sept. and if you have time for a drink and a talk, fine, but certainly don't disrupt the book schedule or any other plans. By the way, Ernest, it occured to me that since the book is taking more time than you had anticipated, you might feel better with a few more bucks in the larder. I can easily get some more dough tagged on to the amount advanced for the short stories if you need it. Your stock is very high here and it would be no trouble, I'm sure. Let me know.

Glad you and Mary are recovered. Hope the fishing is good.

Best,

Ed

I hope you followed the Flaherty profile in the New Yorker. Taylor did a magnificent job.

piece in Holiday: "The Great Blue River"; see notes to letter 2. The piece featured eleven
photographs by George Leavens, including one of EH and Mary aboard the *Pilar*
leaving Havana Harbor with Morrow Castle in the background and one of EH fishing alongside Gregorio Fuentes. In his text, EH described why he lived in Cuba, the
origins of the *Pilar,* and his method of catching marlin in the Gulf Stream.

Blakes: The correct pronunciation of Bleeck's, also called the Artist & Writer's Club, at
213 W. 40th St., formerly a speakeasy and celebrated gathering place for the news-
men of the *New York Herald Tribune.*

Roger Coster: Coster's photograph "Water Gadgets" was featured on the July 15, 1946,
cover of *Life.* In the 1950s he and his Haitian wife ran the Hotel Olofson in Port-
au-Prince, which was known as the "Greenwich Village of the Tropics" and attracted
writers, actors, and artists.

Tom Lea's book: The novel *The Brave Bulls* (1949), about bullfighters in Mexico.

the heel of one individual: DiMaggio was treated for calcium deposits, missing sixty-five
games. *New York Times,* April 14, 1949, p. 33, and June 29, 1949, p. 35.

Gas House Gang: The 1930s St. Louis Cardinals, including Dizzy Dean, his brother Paul,
Pepper Martin, Leo "the Lip" Durocher, Frankie Frisch, and Joe Medwick.

Flaherty profile: Robert Lewis Taylor's three-part profile of the documentary filmmaker
appeared in the *New Yorker* on June 11, 18, and 25, 1949.

{11} EH to AEH
July 8 1949 (TLS, 2 pp., ViU)
FINCA VIGIA, SAN FRANCISCO DE PAULA, CUBA

Dear Ed:

Thanks very much for letter. Glad you liked the Holiday piece. Everybody,
or almost, seemed to write for Holiday as though they were playing an exhibition game in spring training. So I thought I would bear down as any writing you do as well as you can is good for you. Agree on pictures except that
the shot outside the Morro is very good. [George] Leavens claimed he could
only use colour between 1100 and 1400. Fish bite on the tides which are of
course the positions of the moon and also when the plankton comes up to the
surface (bringing everything else with it; the little ones that feed on it and the
big ones that feed on the little ones). This is best just at sun-down. I think
George is a good photographer but fragile and nervous. Would like to work
sometime with Roger Coster. We might do a Bahama piece. It is very exciting
over there (not Cat Cay and that gilded shit) but the wild cays. Only place left
there isn't any law and the ocean is as unspoiled as the West was in 1840.

About Tom Lea's book [*The Brave Bulls*]. I read it in Atlantic (with one eye) in the hospital at Padova and up at Cortina. That may have influenced me. But I didn't think it was very good. The best parts I wrote a long time ago myself. That sounds conceited but isn't really. Also there never was a bull in Mexico really worth a shit. Also am getting sick of the mystique of bravery etc. being piled on and manufactured situations and crap in general.

Thanks for telling me about Mark [Murphy]'s book. Have ordered it. Missed the New Yorker with his Indianapolis piece. Would appreciate it if you can get it without trouble. The change of address hasn't caught up yet.

Am awfully glad Di Maggio is playing again. There certainly were a lot of basehits pent up in him. My interest in it is like yours I guess. I played it and loved it more than any other game. Was a mediocre fielder, worthless second baseman, pretty good emory ball, knuckle ball and nothing ball pitcher. Learned to throw knuckle ball from Eddie Cicotte (probably mis-spelled). Could always hit. My old man was Charley Murphy's doctor when he owned the Cubs and when I used to have piles bad in football season (they'd stick them in and tell you to hold them up all night and you would be awake all night thinking you were holding them up and they would be out already) I would say Dear Lord I know this isn't as bad as what Frank Chance has to go through every day but please give me courage to bear it like he does. Frank Chance couldn't duck if they threw at his head. After he had his first concussion when I think it was Marquard hit him he would freeze and nobody ever threw anything to him that wasn't high and inside. Finally he got such awful headaches that it was tough for me, a punk kid, to see him.

Down here Hughey Casey, Billy Herman, Augie Galan, Curt Davis always used to come out to the house. [Kirby] Higbe and I used to go on the town together. Higbe is really crazy. Mickey Owen was another good pal. So I am a Dodger man although PeeWee Reese is the only guy left on the team I know. It was a wonderful bunch of guys when those I mentioned and Larry French used to hang out together. Have to write a baseball story sometime. But the best one I know (Durocher as Thief) somebody wrote already. As an old St. Louisan you must be pretty comfortable in N.Y. this summer. Was there ever anything like that heat? I like heat but it can really get too hot in St. Louis, Senegal, Bilbao and Madrid when it gets hot.

Thanks very much about the films. It really means a hell of a lot to us. I am proud to be a church group and enclose my card as a plain clothes jesuit (Joke.) and six leaflets you can distribute to your friends. After being married twice out of the church you would think the Jesuits might have given me up as hopeless. I remember explaining to our priest in Key West that I was going to fight on the Republican side in Spain and he saying, "Ernest I know that you must have your reasons. Remember that I am always praying for you."

Life is very complicated Ed. Especially in the higher and lower echelons. Please return my card and don't show it to anybody. I just sent it as a rough joke and I shouldn't even though I am now a religious group.

Maybe I told you this before but we had a chaplain who handled the field artillery of the 4th Inf. Division. He was a very nice guy, hard shell Baptist, but learning fast in war. One night in Bleiauf (mis-spelled) we were getting the shit shelled out of us with very heavy artillery and one railway gun (impressive). Chaplain quite nervous but behaveing well. So I said, "Chaplain do you still believe this shit about there not being any athiests in foxholes?"

And he said "No <u>Sir</u> Mr. Hemingway. Not since I've known you and Colonel Lanham."

When you come down I will knock off work for two-three days and bring the boat to Varadero and we can have some fun. Will work hard good balance of July and August so that will rate the vacation. So keep in good touch and give me your gen.

Am ok on dough. Thanks very much just the same. Our fighting chickens won 38 out of 42 fights. The joint is produceing what we need to eat. The deep freeze is full. I'm shooting hot on pigeons and should be able to pick up 3/4 G. The kids are all suited, Italian moneyed, and leave on Tuesday. My oldest boy Jack is back as a Capt. of Infantry in Berlin and self supporting (so far). If Gavilan Kid wins over Robinson am ok through Xmas. He'll probably lose, now, and am covering. Have a piece of a new fighter that can hit harder than Sandy Saddler and keep hitting for 3 minutes. But he doesn't know anything and we have to strengthen his hands. The way he goes now he would as soon hit a elbow as your jaw. These cultural pursuits keep me happy after I quit work and I work when the spirit moves me and it moves me every day. (Pinched that crack from Faulkner.)

So things look good. So for christ sake let us all duck. The last time had everything set Hellinger died on me. That's a wonderful story. Will save it to tell you. Also won't send my card. Will show. Sending is funny and rough but bad taste I think. Sort of funny though.

Best luck, kid. Hope magazine going good. Read only one Flaherty profile piece. Others not come. Made me seem like a little boy reading it. Think you picked a good hero. We all need one and I think you got the best one.

<u>Ernest</u>

the shot outside the Morro: Color photograph of the *Pilar* cruising past Morrow Castle in Havana Harbor.

I read it in Atlantic (with one eye): Tom Lea's *The Brave Bulls* was serialized in the *Atlantic,* February–May 1949. At the end of March, EH's eye had become infected and he was hospitalized for ten days in Padua (*Final,* 190).

Eddie Cicotte: Pitcher for the Chicago White Sox from 1912 to 1920, expelled from baseball as a consequence of the Black Sox scandal in the 1919 World Series.

my old man: EH's father, Clarence Edmonds Hemingway (1871–1928), was a general practitioner in Oak Park, IL, located nine miles west of downtown Chicago.

Charley Murphy: Owner of the Chicago Cubs from 1905 to 1916.

Frank Chance: Played with the Cubs from 1898 to 1912; first baseman in their famed Tinker-to-Evers-to-Chance double-play combination. Beaned numerous times in the head, his hearing suffered and he was forced to retire due to chronic headaches.

Marquard: Richard William (Rube) Marquard pitched for the Giants from 1908 to 1915.

Hughey Casey, Billy Herman, Augie Galan, Curt Davis . . . [Kirby] Higbe . . . Mickey Owen . . . PeeWee Reese . . . Larry French: All played for the 1941 Brooklyn Dodgers, who trained in Cuba.

Durocher as Thief: This story remains unlocated, but the anecdote is well known: Babe Ruth entrapped his thieving roommate, Durocher, by marking $100 bills.

Bleiauf (mis-spelled): Bleiaf

Colonel Lanham: Charles T. "Buck" Lanham (1902–1978) became EH's friend in July 1944 while commanding the Twenty-second Infantry Regiment, Fourth Infantry Division (*Story,* 402). They endured the Battle of Hurtgen Forest together.

If Gavilan Kid wins over Robinson: Gerardo Gonzalez "Kid" Gavilan lost to welterweight champion Sugar Ray Robinson on July 11, 1949, in Philadelphia.

Sandy Saddler: 1948 featherweight champ.

Hellinger died on me: Following Hellinger's successful production of *The Killers* in 1946, EH agreed to sell him four stories at $75,000 each plus a share of the profits. Hellinger died in December 1947 before the project began, and EH promptly returned the $50,000 advance to Hellinger's widow (Baker, *Selected Letters,* 767; *HIW,* 320; *Story,* 460).

{12} AEH to EH
August 17th [1949] (TLS, 2 pp., ViU)
Cosmopolitan [New York City]

Dear Ernest:

Much good travels New England way, returned to find your letter which was fine and enjoyable. Also, found a carbon [copy] sent to me of a letter sent you re the movie film; what the hell, unless you plan on charging admissions $20 is too much dough. Let me knock on a few more doors and see if there isn't better doing. All they have to do, really, is cut Tyrone Power a G next year and it all evens out.

This typewriter clatter is unwelcome this morning after a weird party last night at Croton, New York, where friends of mine are spending the summer in George Biddle's home. Most of the art hanging is Biddle's, some of it quite good, but there are walls of Picasso like originals and considerable sculpting by Mrs. Biddle and more accomplished hands. In the midst of this rustic museum the martini pitcher did its deadly work on the assembled fifteen or sixteen so that by midnight I found myself in a Fitzgerald setting, just about the most uninhibited desperate little band I've ever seen. Today all hands are surprised that they were on the stage rather than in the audience and I'm sure that the two young colored maids are both suffering premature menopauses. This to explain why the eyes do not see clearly and the lines run up and down.

Mark [Murphy] returned from his enforced excommunication and had lunch with him and his wife. He did a really fine piece for the New Yorker, a good one for the Post and a rather ordinary one for Collier's. Thoroughly frightened of AA (first time knew Mark to be frightened of anything) he has strapped himself onto the wagon and there he sits for nine weeks now, no signs of tottering. More of a physical challenge than anything else, he says, and I for one hope this is the way back to family and good writing habits. Wife Mickey is back at work on LIFE where she hates people and ideologies but likes idea of working and not being at home to run the house and tend the kids and be a housewife.

Two books recently read, one old, one new, have impressed me. The old: BRIGHTON ROCK by Graham Green[e]; the new: A RAGE TO LIVE, John O'Hara. Regretful that Green is so uneven because certain chapters, passages, phrases are great. Sex in the O'Hara book weakens it, oddly enough, but there is much to commend it. Good sweep and power and the dialogue is sensitive and real. Want my copy or do you get books easily?

News this morning is that Southworth of the Braves, as easy-going, likeable guy as I have ever met (meeting: 1944), has quit, victim of nerves. That it cracked this guy seems incredible but there were many things, principal of which the death of Billy Jr. in the war. Saw the Braves once this year and they were nine men each playing by himself. All season the papers carried news items of fistfights in hotel lobbies between various players on the Braves and although none of them involved Southworth his shadow was on them. The Braves are a surly and sour lot and there is no doubt that in the last series with the Brooks [Brooklyn Dodgers] they aimed for heads and midsections; maybe

Southworth's leaving will ease the tension of the next series for the Brooks are mad and the prospect of two pitchers throwing for a strike between the eyes instead of over the plate is grim indeed.

I have sat behind this desk long enough now and plan to take a leave in November and look up old friends in Paris and maybe see Italy. First, though, a short vacation at Kawama [Cuban resort] which is due and gladly taken. Plan to be there around 6 Sept. till 14 or so with my wife (you remember girl who came to visit with me last year? We were married last winter.) and we will use that as a base of operations with a couple of visits to watch cock fights (which I missed last year) and prowl. Will phone you when there, Ernest, but for Chrissake, if you are working good on the book just say hello and let it go at that—don't consider me someone who has to be seen or entertained. Goes without saying that it would be great to spend some time with you but I really mean what I say about work before us. Perhaps Mary would like to come visit for a couple of days if you are strapped to the typewriter. Anyway, leave it all unplanned and I'll phone and we'll see how things are. Because of a small yelp from the jaundice which I picked up in England in 1947 and is so loathe to leave, I have postponed drinking for a while but rules will be relaxed to embrace the daiquiries at the Floridita. If there is anything you would like brought from here please ask because we're coming by boat and weight is positively no problem.

We have purchased a novel over my loudest protestations—THE CARDINAL by Henry Morton Robinson; sop, I presume for the cloth along with Going My Way and Come to the Stable and Bells for St. Mary and other ipecac variants, but no way to excuse the turgidness of this one. Please skip.

By the way, I have a fine movie camera—a Bell & Howell 16 mm. and I use it quite well—and it occured to me that if we are going to see one another we might shoot some reels on cock fighting in color. Breeding, training, actual combat. Could turn out interesting. What think?

Don't forget—let me know if you want anything.

Best,

<u>Ed</u>

Tyrone Power: Top box-office star in the 1940s.

George Biddle (1885–1973): Muralist and social realist who helped create the Public Works of Art Project in the Depression Era.

Southworth: William Harrison "Billy" Southworth, manager of the Boston Braves from 1946 to 1951. He took a leave of absence on August 17, 1949. *New York Times,* August 17, 1949, p. 26.

THE CARDINAL: Novel that follows the career of a priest; serialized in *Cosmopolitan* in January 1950. The films *Going My Way* (1944), *The Bells of St. Mary's* (1945), and *Come to the Stable* (1949) featured priests and nuns.

{13} EH to AEH
August 22 1949 (TLS, 2 pp., ViU)
FINCA VIGIA SAN FRANCISCO DE PAULA CUBA

Dear Ed:

Was awfully glad to get your letter and know when you are comeing down. That is only two weeks away, kid. It is wonderful down here now and if we don't get hurricane then hurricane months are nearly the best of the year.

What we'll do is: when you and your wife get here call us up. If you are driveing to Varadero you have to go by the joint and so stop and have drink. If you are <u>not</u> on an expense account I can send my chauffer to drive you down here. If you <u>are</u> on an expense account can send him the same way. (When I used to work for Mr. Hearst the only item I ever had turned down was Hire of a Felluca: $700. Items such as Costs paid for damages through collission with an Arabian Dowh (two drowned): $237.50 were always passed unquestioned. (You had saved them money by your prompt settlement.) But I think they thought a Felluca had something to do with Felattio (also misspelled) and that I was either over-extending myself or setting up a personal harem since had recently been includeing items such as LUNCH WITH THE GRAN VIZIER (Pera Palace)—18.25. Complete Corruption of the Chief Eunuch: (WE ARE IN) 28.60. CORRUPTION OF THE HEADS OF BRITISH INTELLIGENCE: $49.75 (I have their gen before it leaves on the wire to Malta E.H.) and finally Karl Von Wiegand (that Prince) was so impressed by my extraordinary gen that he said, Ernie we have always been friends and in a way I helped to bring you up as a newspaper man and I am an old man now and my eyes are bad and you would never double cross me would you? You want to be a writer and not keep on as a newspaper man don't you, really?

So I told him I did and it was true. And have never given him the elbow although sometimes get pretty pissed off at those things he dreams up from those different places except they are so comic.

Brighton Rock is very good. Spooks you. Haven't read John [O'Hara]'s book yet. When I first met him, or read him, it looked like he could hit: Appointment In Samarra [1934]. Then he started beating out bunts. He was fast and he had a pretty ear but he had the terrible inferiority complex of the half-lace curtain Irish and he never learned that it doesn't matter a fuck where you come from, socially, it is where you go. So he keeps beating out bunts and drinking instead of trying to learn to hit and I lose interest. Am awfully glad if he has a good book. I'd written him off and am always happy to be wrong. The writing Irish cannot stand either success or failure so we can expect him to become fairly insufferable but we can always keep away from those joints and if he writes good that is all that matters.

Poor Billy Southworth and god-damn near poor bloody everybody. When they start throwing at heads is bad but it always happens in the summer. In our family my youngest boy, Gigi [Gregory], used to try and knock everybody's cap off on the first pitch. He did it to me too in a pick-up game and I walked out to him, haveing got up from the dirt, and said, "Don't you know any better than to throw at your own father?" He had almost as good control as Old Pete, or Mordecai Brown or the late Mathewson.

So all it occurs to him to say, looking at me as mean as a wart hog, is, "Don't you know there aren't any fathers on a ball field?"

He is a very polite and attentive boy when he is not competeing and very loveing. I hit the next pitch solid on a line and thank Christ it went to third instead of to him. I suppose he threw it to make me hit it that way too. Gig is a very tough boy. He is the only one of the three that I declare to win with. Now he is on a motor bike visiting his bro. (½ bro.) who is a captain of infantry in Berlin and then going down through Switzerland to Italy and to Venice where have given him the addresses and telephone numbers of all my good girls. He has had this miserable, lace-curtain catholic education at Canterbury School where he hated the masters and did not like the boys and it has inhibited the hell out of him in all sorts of ways. But maybe Venice will loosen him up. He wrote a fine letter from Germany. I have a Cheyenne great, great grandmother (Don't tell Cowley) and it helps quite a lot. This Gig is the only boy that turned out Indian; not Cherokee, Digger, Pyute, Navajo, or any of those unfortunate peoples but Northern Cheyenne and he has all the problems of them, as I always had, and all the lack of problems that haveing that blood gives you.

Please bring the Bell and Howell and we will get some good stuff. We have quit training chickens on acct. of the moulting season. It is to fighting birds like the curse to a woman. There may not be any rooster fighting nor anybody training while you are down here. But we always have a chance for wonderful shots on jumping fish which are quite moveing. Have been hotter, working, than the grill they roasted San Lorenzo on. Last week we stayed out on the week-end (just Mary and I fished and made love nights and got back on a Tuesday night) and on Wed. did 315, Thursday 560, and Friday 2100 which is more inches than I ought to pull. But been going awfully good.

So what we will do (since I have a safe lead now the way I'm going; we have them around 11–0 going into the sixth and I have my stuff and am feeling good) will bring the Pilar down and anchor her off the Kawama pier and we will go out and try to meet some interesting fish and take you and your wife down to Puerto Escondido or over to Cayo Blanco where we can shoot the negro goose flight and have fun for two three days and I will just write that much better when we get back.

If you tell me when you are comeing (What boat) might have a couple of things delivered to your office that you won't have any trouble bringing in.

Haveing you come down here is not like haveing to see Ray Long, or that frustrated fairy Harry Burton [former editors at *Cosmopolitan*], nor that short order Ghoul that worked for them and went to the Reader's Digest Factory. It is, Mary agrees, a pleasure. And come down if you are <u>fired</u> off Cosmopolitan and they are garnisheeing me for the advance I took on the stories, and in connection with which, believe have a pretty nice surprise for you.

See you soon, kid. Our love to your wife.

Ernest

PS.

Thanks for all the work on the 16mm. pictures. Situation still sort of confused. Don't work hard on it but $20^{00} to look at a film yourself is ridiculous. Understand how they must protect themselves, basically, but they can make exceptions unless they are saw-dust heads. EH.

Beneath "Monday August 22 1949/0600" EH writes "(as John Mason Brown would write it. Or maybe I made that crack before)." Brown (1900–1969) was a critic and author who served in the U.S. Naval Reserve.

Mr. Hearst: William Randolph Hearst (1863–1951), American newspaper tycoon. EH filed stories for Hearst's International News Service and Universal News Service in the early 1920s. Michael Reynolds, *Hemingway: The Paris Years* (Cambridge: Basil Blackwell, 1989), 72, 83, 119.

Felluca . . . Dowh: Probably "felucca" and "dhow," double-masted sailing vessels.

Karl Von Wiegand: Foreign correspondent with Hearst newspapers from 1917 to 1961.

Old Pete, or Mordecai Brown, or the late Mathewson: Three pitchers from the early days of baseball. Grover Cleveland (Pete) Alexander pitched for the Phillies (1911–1917) and later for the Cubs and Cardinals; Brown for the Cubs (1904–1912); and Christy Mathewson for the Giants (1900–1916).

Canterbury School: College preparatory boarding/day school in New Milford, CT.

San Lorenzo: Saint said to have been martyred on a gridiron.

things delivered: According to AEH, EH requested "a tin of béluga caviar from Maison Glass and a Smith-Corona portable [typewriter], pica type" (*PH*, 22).

a pretty nice surprise: EH proposed publishing *Across the River and into the Trees* in *Cosmopolitan*, which would presumably release him from his obligation to provide the magazine with two short stories.

{14} AEH to EH
Agosto 29.949 (Cable, 1 p., ViU)
New York

Sailing ss jamaica glad to tote whatever delivered my office plans sounds great best.

Hotchner.

AEH and his wife, Geraldine, who was four months pregnant with their first child, arrived in Cuba in early September for a nine-day vacation.

{15} AEH to EH
9/23 [1949 pmk] (TLS, 2 pp., JFKL)
405 East 54th Street/New York 22, N.Y.

Dear Ernest:

Really first opportunity I've had to get to a writing machine since return. I've been to St. Louis to aid and abet parental problems and my kid brother, Selly, who is here in New York supposedly making his way against the elements, had the S.O.S. aloft, so I've gone down the boy scout pledge for them and this should keep them reasonably well organized for about six months. Then the seams come apart and I take to the hills to hunt game.

Trip back was first rate. We came up on the Venezuelan plane which is the only one that goes non-stop—took us a little over five hours and if you are as hostile to air travel as I am, then this is a blessing when speed matters. We hit only one air pocket and that was at the immigration office at Idlewild. Most of the passengers were immigrants so the few Americans aboard were called first. We stepped forward when our names were called and I handed the immigration officer, a pasty-faced pontifical type, our landing card. "Proof of citizenship," he said, without looking up. I said that we had come from Havana where passports were not necessary. "Passports, no" he said, "but you gotta have proof of citizenship. Don't you have your birth certificates?" I got a little surly and said that I do not as a matter of custom, carry my birth certificate with me; he tells me to sit down until I can think of some way of proving I am a citizen—the same, naturally, goes for Jerry. Now I am the thin wallet type, believing that one or two crisp bills are all that a billfold should contain, but faced with the dismal prospect of proving I was a U.S. citizen at 10 o'clock at night in the far recesses of Idlewild, I went through the wallet, more out of obeisance to custom than anything else, and for the first time since I got out, found a practical use for my army discharge papers which, by law, I am required to carry. We have resumed as citizens but I wish I hadn't found the papers because I wonder if, by my intimate knowledge of baseball standings, catfishing on the Meramac, Greenwich Village restaurants unknown to Baedaker, Chicago's South Side, and my listing in the N.Y. telephone directory, I could have established my right to entry. Anyway, it might be a nice thing for you to try when you come up.

Of course, [Herbert] Mayes was delighted with the news which I delivered as we agreed and his attitude is that I know what I'm doing and therefore my suggestions are to be followed—literally. We will publish installment one in the Feb. issue and installment two in the March issue and the book will come out around March 15th. I had a long chat with Scribner (he was out of town when I got back and only returned) and he seems to be reasonably satisfied that Cosmopolitan will abide closely by the rules as they appear on the back of the score card. I suggested this to him, in view of the fact that he has already informed several members of his staff (nobody on Cosmo knows anything about the book except Mayes) and the possibility of a leak and considerable speculation seems imminent—that Cosmopolitan and Scribner's issue a joint announcement of the publication of the book next spring. And Ernest, it seems to me that we must establish with our very first announcement that this is a major work and not a by-product. I think this can be best achieved by telling the true facts about the writing of the book as you told them to me. Naturally, I'd like to know your reaction to this suggestion before doing anything about it and I'd like to know how much detail you would like revealed. I think the announcement should be brief but I think it should have the dramatic impact that the real story has. In view of the fact that several Scribner's people know about the book (Scribner told me that he received a letter from LIFE stating that they had heard you were completing a new book) I think the formal announcement should be made as soon as possible; but I'll await word from you. Scribner agreed with me on the above.

Scribner wanted to know what I thought of the portion of the book I had read. I told him and I watched the excitement grow in his face. He told me that he plans a really fine edition of the book and that special pains would be taken with the typography. On our part, I'll see to it that the art work will be handled by someone of unusual merit, far from Whitcomb alley. Subject to change, of course, I'm now operating on the theory that you will leave the manuscript before you depart, that it will be set in galleys which I shall bring to Venice or wherever for you to work on (and I shall have the magazine gen on four letter words).

Spent an afternoon with Mark Murphy who slid to the bottom of the pit. From what I can gather, it was the worst, blind orgy of his existence and he has joined AA. Knowing Mark and his talent, you want to know why, as does Mark, but there is no answer and AA seems silly and a fine place for Woolcott Gibbs but not Murph. I don't believe in this truce and I shake the head sadly over inevitability. He was glad to hear about you; I didn't mention your coming but if there's a little free time, he'd be a good guy to see.

Being with you and Mary this trip was great fun and I can't tell you how fond we are of your lady. We're sorry we were such a pain in the ass as fishermen—you were really a good guy about keeping Jerry from being tossed about too much, and although neither of us is very good at caution, it's a good thing for us to learn in this case. Jerry tells me you offered to sponsor our fullback and we think it would be fine to have him arrive under your aegis; isn't it too early to be talking like this?

I've just had a great time getting you a house present—some wonderful fight reels which I saw twice and will see again anytime you care to show them. My best to Roberto and Sinsky; tell Sinsky if he's ever in port and with free time I am in the phone book.

I hope you take it for granted that if there's anything needs doing before or during your stay, just send word.

Ed

If you need $, there's plenty here. I wrote Cannon about his book—no answer. Forgot to give you The Aspirin Age. Will give it to you for Ile de France. E.

Idlewild: Common name for New York National Airport, which was renamed John F. Kennedy International Airport in 1963.
Woolcott Gibbs: Writer and editor for the *New Yorker.*

a long chat with Scribner: Charles Scribner III was the head of Charles Scribner's Sons publishing from 1932 to 1952. AEH remembers him as "a soft-spoken, gracious, private, good-natured man who had a deep affection for Ernest and a father's pride in his work. We lunched occasionally and I enjoyed his company and his publishing stories. He came from an affluent riding-to-the-hounds social set in New Jersey but there was an appealing, unpretentious quality about him that overcame the New Jersey stuffiness." AEH to DeFazio, September 27, 2004.

Whitcomb alley: Jon Whitcomb was a popular illustrator of young couples in love and provided many cover illustrations for *Cosmopolitan.*

sponsor our fullback: According to AEH, EH offered to be a godparent for the Hotchners' child. AEH, fax to DeFazio, November 29, 2004.

Roberto: Roberto Herrera, EH's secretary and man Friday in Cuba.

Sinsky: Juan "Sinsky" Duñabeitía, sea captain and frequent house guest of the Hemingways, accompanied EH during his sub-hunting adventures aboard the *Pilar* (*Story*, 374).

Cannon: Sportswriter Jimmy Cannon, whose collection of columns, *Nobody Asked Me,* was published in 1951 by Dial Press.

The Aspirin Age: A collection of essays edited by Isabel Leighton that recount major events between 1919 and 1941 (New York: Simon and Schuster, 1949).

AEH enclosed with this letter a clipping headlined "Rocky K.O.d. Fusari and Persecution Complex—Cannon" (*New York Post Home News*, September 15, 1949: pp. 3, 38).

{16} AEH to EH
September 28 [1949 *pmk*] (TLS, 2 pp., JFKL)
Cosmopolitan [New York City]

Dear Ernest:

I had a talk with Dick Berlin yesterday and I gave him the general details about the book and filled him in a little about you and the modus vivandi in Cuba. He has one helleva admiration for you and he appreciated hearing from you so quickly. The question of money for the book [*Across the River and into the Trees*] came up and I said, playing it straight, that it had not been discussed. "Tell Ernest," he said, "that the relation he has with our organization is such that we'd feel better if he just named his own price. He's a good friend and he should be guided by what he needs and what he thinks the property is worth." So I tell Ernest. I have always found the driver's seat a fine place to be and I'm glad you're there. If you want me to do any scouting or advising or whatever, you know whose side I'm on, but I can tell you that Dick's sincere and whatever you name will be <u>it.</u> So alert Roberto's registrar! and line up the

Gregorio heirs! and Mary might like to book a few showings and indulge a few fancies she's had her heart set on.

If you'd like me to arrange good hotel quarters or set up use of an apartment for the few days, you know I'd be delighted to do.

The plans which we drew up at command level have worked out nicely here in the operational room. I will depart here with galleys in hand and general knowledge governing shits, fucks, pisses and aw, fudges, around November middle and courier them to you wherever. Only problem I have is Miss Geraldine and I'd like your advice. She, of course, would like to make trip but she will be in her sixth month and she has the annoying complications of a couple of tumors which are growing right along with the child. Doctor says he can't see any harm in a short trip abroad but I'm inclined to think that a lot of moving around in unfamiliar territory under the circumstances is not good thinking. I've never been cautious in my life and this is a strange kind of thinking for me but I've been actual eye-witness to this kind of disaster on two occasions, therefore I bring up the matter. Naturally, you can't make any decision about it and you're certainly just asked for your thinking about it because I think it would be helpful. My inclination right now, since this is probably the only kid Jerry can have, is to go this one alone although it would be much more fun with her.

The climatic change from Cuba to New York really startles. This is full fall weather now and last week-end in Connecticut we had that crystal crispness that really pins your affections on New England, at least until Notre Dame is unlimbered [until Geraldine gives birth]. Friends of ours who have a beauty of a sailboat—sleeps six—hauled us aboard and we flew up the shore and explored islands and sang forgotten songs under the incredible stars. Watching familiar territory change abruptly, grow young, grow beautiful, fade away, is much more compensatory than just happening on it and looking and going. I must always live where the seasons change, but not necessarily here. I got so weepy about nature last week that I almost got lassod into a band of bird-watchers. I guess it is time I got my ass to Italy.

Although I haven't mentioned it, I keep remembering the chapters I read and I'm really dying to read the before and after—just as a reader, mind you, not editor. I pity the poor bastards who will have to wait a whole month to get installment two. Of course, it gives them something to look forward to which I am told, is very important in the lives of many. Personally, I've never had any shortages in this respect and I'm sure you haven't either. We're lucky.

Tell Mary we expect to make her give us the recipes for the pumpkin-lamb dish and the cold vegetable soup. Hope the entourage is well and that the matinees are well attended.

<u>Ed</u>

Dick Berlin: President of Hearst Corporation, which published *Cosmopolitan.*
Gregorio: Gregorio Fuentes, first mate aboard the *Pilar* from 1938 until EH's death in 1961.

{17} AEH to EH
Sept. 29 [1949] (TLS, 2 pp., JFKL)
405 East 54<u>th</u> Street/New York 22, N.Y.

Dear Ernest:

Just a note re the announcement which I prepared with Chas Scribner this morning. Contained in the announcement are several facts which you told me, perhaps in confidence. You see the problem is to make this announcement establish the new novel as a major work—not a by-product of the big book nor an over-length short story—and really, Ernest, only the true story can achieve this. Scribner had drafted an announcement which had no life nor importance to it and I screwed around with it, trying to get the effect we want. As I say, maybe you'd like to keep the details covered but I just wanted you to know motivation. I think the statement is too dramatic, perhaps, but a sturdy red pencil can fix that.

Arthur [Gordon] is waiting for me at some Midtown bar where we are to pop a bottle over the fact that today he divested himself of his book. S & S seem to put considerable stock in it (whatever that means) and Arthur is set on pouncing upon number two without breath. I sincerely wish the poor bastard all the good that ever fell on a first shot—he's had more than his share of the reverse side of that coin.

In case you are getting alarmed that I am about to send you daily dispatches, full of chat and book club notes, I promise to amalgamate in the future. I simply wanted you to have word about the announcement which should hit you about the same time this will.

By the way, the Cards dropped number 2 to the Pirates today and Brooks took 2 from Braves which makes the Cards about the biggest fold in history. They may get three from Chicago, though, and I don't think the Bums [Dodgers] can overcome the Phillie hex two straight, especially when they don't have [Preacher] Roe or [Don] Newcomb rested. The Cards' fold, though, depresses me; I was reared on St. Loo teams which stormed up from 9 ½ off and took the lead with two games to go. This is a sad bunch.

All the best to all.

Ed

the announcement: "Hemingway Novel Slated for March," *New York Times,* October 13, 1949, p. 25.

his book: EH owned Gordon's novel *Reprisal* (New York: Simon and Schuster: 1950).

{18} EH to AEH
29 September 1949 (TLS, 2 pp., ViU)
FINCA VIGIA, SAN FRANCISCO DE PAULA, CUBA

Dear Ed:

Delighted to hear from you and to know that you and Jerry made the trip back OK and were able to establish your citizenship at the port of entry. Hotchner is a very suspicious name. Where you come from boy, chouteaux avenue? Did your grandfather fight mit Sigel. I will try to bring something to try to establish mine when we come in. Have gone completely legal here and have permits for all the guns and even a carnet extranjero [foreigner's permit] which have never had before. Don't like this government and don't want to take any favors from it so thought I'd better legalize my status.

That is wonderful news about the fight films and look forward very much to getting them. Mary is up in Chicago with her old, and lovely, and fragile parents. Just got a good letter from her today. Roberto and I went out on a trip so as to kill the loneliness of her being away and to anchor in some good cove and do some work and then get exercise afterwards. We ran into a mess of small and worthless cyclones, hurricanes rather, which were moving around on all sides. It felt like being einheit-ed [squeezed out] by the other characters. But they passed us by and today it looks as though the whole business is over for the month. Since you left I did 1,174 on 14 September; 901 on the 15th; 474 on the 16th; 664 on the 17th. On 18 September thy servant rested and on 19 September did 1,077 and in the evening or around midnight rather, 564—making 1,641 for the day. Couldn't cool out on the 20th and did 1,224. Laided (I guess Nita can't write layed) off two days getting Miss Mary away and putting my affairs in order and then on the boat on 23 September did 1,266;

785 on the 24th; 1,257 on the 25th; and 1,206 on the 28th. The latter writ-ten from 0400 to 0830. At those hours nobody sells you any crap. Laid (she <u>did</u> it) off yesterday and shot pigeons and slept in the afternoon and then saw pictures on the machine in the evening. This morning wrote 705 and am going to shoot pigeons now. It is blowing so hard with the anti-cyclones that they ought to fly very well. Got Blackie to retrieve yesterday and he retrieved 17 straight. Want to work him out again today. He is very happy and proud and tired.

Bad news about poor old Mark [Murphy]. Hope to see him when we are in town. Have spent half my life straightening out rummies and all of my life drinking. But since writing is my true love I never get the two things very far mixed up. Drinking is fun; not a release from something. When it's a release from something, except the straight mechanical pressure that we are all sub-jected to always, then I think you get to be a rummy. But I am not a first stone caster.

Will read Jimmy [Cannon] on the fight as soon as I get through with this. Want to get it off so we can go and shoot and stop thinking about the God-damned book. It's all better, so far, than what I showed you. Don't need any dough at the moment but we probably[—]later on and before I finish[—] should have a contract because ["]contracted for stuff["] comes under a spe-cial category as we talked about last year. But don't let's go into that now for the next two weeks when I am still in the stretch. Believe it should run in three instalments as it will be plenty long. That's better for you guys, too. But any-way, will let you know in plenty of time.

If Dick [Berlin] wants to pay more money that is OK. It is really the best book that I have written, I think, but I am prejudiced, of course. Have only two more innings to pitch and I plan to turn their caps around. Also will get to bat once and as you know, all pitchers think that they can hit. Most of us started as out-fielders anyway.

About the element of surprise, you should do that with Charlie Scribner. He is not dumb at all even though he stammers; he likes you, and there is no reason why you two can't handle all that stuff and in the way that it should be handled for the best interest of both parties without any stealing on either part.

Since we are shoving off in half an hour this will have to be a dictated and unread letter with the signature forged by Miss Nita. Want you to get it as soon as possible or else would hold it and write something with my own fist.

Don't worry about any responsibility of the damned proofs, galleys rather, as we will have various copies and ship one to me registered to the Guaranty Trust Company of New York in case your plane comes down and you should lose your galleys.

There isn't any doghouse trouble any more at all. A man should know how to get out of that doghouse or else he should turn in his suit. The other thing that makes things better is that I love Miss Mary, truly. She knows this and it helps her to forgive me when I am in the wrong.

Haven't cashed your 10G check yet but thank you very much for sending same. Have done all right shooting lately. Now we better get going. Wish the Hell you and Jerry were along. We have had 11 different hurricanes kicking around here but have not been hit by any one. This is more or less like the war. It gives you something to look at even if it is only the barometer.

Hope that you and Jerry are both well and not destroyed by the last heat wave. Here the weather is every way but it is cold at nights. Must get going now or Miss Mary will tell me that I am not taking life seriously. Some day I might take it seriously and a lot of characters would hang by their necks until dead.

Best always, Ed,

Ernest

ERNEST

(Please excuse messy letter but am rushing this as fast as I can. Dictated and unread by Mister Papa and signature forged by Miss Nita.) Have written you since this one that has secretarial lag.

chouteaux avenue: Street in Hotchner's hometown of St. Louis.

mit Sigel: Refers to the Civil War song "I Goes to Fight Mit [with] Sigel," which parodied the tensions that arose after Col. Franz Sigel, commander of the Third and Fifth Missouri Volunteers, was passed over for an expected promotion.

Mary is up in Chicago: Mary was in Chicago from "late September" through October 6 to visit her parents and purchase a mink coat (*Final,* 208–9; *HIW,* 281–82).

Blackie: Black Dog, a stray adopted by EH in Idaho in December 1947 (*Final,* 165).

the element of surprise: EH wanted AEH and Scribner to craft an announcement that served *Cosmopolitan*'s interest in publicizing the serialization without detracting from Scribner's plans for the novel, which would follow the serial.

Dictated and unread by Mister Papa: EH did read and annotate the first page of this letter (through paragraph 5), which is in elite type; the Textual Commentary identifies his seven inserts. The second page, in pica type, bears no marking by EH. His secretary, Juanita Jensen, addresses AEH as "Esquire" in the inside address, next to which EH writes: "(I don't know why Nita gives you that [title,] Edward. She also capitalizes Hell. Probably early training.)"

{19} EH to AEH
Oct. 3 1949 (TLS, 2 pp., ViU)
FINCA VIGIA, SAN FRANCISCO DE PAULA, CUBA

Dear Ed.:

Been jamming again and am tired so excuse if can't make this letter sparkle. Black Dog is tired too. He thinks he has to get up and stick with me whenever I work and he's a boy that loves his sleep. He keeps his eyes open, loyally, and he's got his finger on his number. But he doesn't like it. He'll be glad when book is over and so will I. But by Christ I'll miss it for a while. Just wrote a god-damn wonder chapter, the man says modestly. Got it all, to break your heart, into two pages.

Yesterday Roberto COUNTED. He hates to count but counts accurately, and through this morning it is 43,745. This is so you know what you have as effectives. Think should go 60 or just under. Can cut it into three if you want. Arrange with Charlie [Scribner].

Mary gets back Thursday. Today is Monday.

About Jerry and the trip: I think you shouldn't. You take a chance with <u>both</u> the woman and the kid. We have to take plenty of chances without takeing any on purpose. After seven [months of pregnancy] would be safer. But why take a chance on who you love and your own kid?

About the monies: please advise me. What is ok with Dick [Berlin] is ok with me. We ought to make a contract before it's finished and then spread it, probably, for double security.

Hope you liked Charlie. He liked you very much and he likes almost nobody. Hates authors.

Mary got the coat, natural wild mink (I guess the natural wild mink fucks more like a mink than the ranch mink or mutation mink). Anyway she comes in with it Thursday. I am staying away from town and being a good boy and let it go into book. Had our new whore out for Saturday just to be sure my head was clear. She promised to show yesterday Sunday. But think she was, maybe, fatigued. So made up a Spanish proverb, doesn't translate as well as it is in Spanish, "Try To Nourish yourself on the word of honor of a whore."

In Spanish it's better. Whore wonderful. Would make Earl Wilson drool. I sent her mother 20 bucks' worth of flowers for her birthday.

We have changes in the seasons here too, kid. They are subtle, not abrupt, like New England where our parents took off from because it was cropped out and the soil no damn good (and who eats autumn leaves?) But have them in good in the long book where we come home from the ocean always super-sensitized (if there is such a word). Know Connecticut is fine and beautiful and a substitute for life. But let me have Red Lodge, Montana where my hands mended, or even Cody, Wyoming or West Yellowstone, with Big Jim Savage dealing off the bottom of the deck so wonderful that only the boys can see it, or Billings on a Saturday night, or even, shit, Casper which is an oil town where Miss Mary lost our kid. Which is why I tell you not to take any chances with Jerry to whom I send my love.

Can't wait for the fight films. When do you think they will get here? Did you send by air-express?

We made patriots of them with Mr. Smith Goes to Washington plus Zale and Graziano. That's been our best program so far. Wish I could get Bob Flaherty's. Would be glad to buy. Corrected the defect in the machine that you called to my attention.

Must pay bills today now, bank was closed on Sat., the First. Feels good to have the work done and the money in the bank to pay with. Borrowed 10 G from Charlie S. [Scribner] for operation mink coat at the usual 2% he charges. Very reasonable charge.

They had a circus here with two good five year old cats; brothers. It was wonderful to hear them roar in the morning. Circus was pitched just to the right of the entrance to the Finca as you come up. Made friends with the trainer. He pays 38 bucks a week for meat for the cotsies and he nets 45 to 50 a month. Made 350 with Ringlings but can't get a work permit for the states. Doesn't use the chair.

The cotsies are awfully noble and they hate the whip the boys have to use to make theatre. I worked them good with a rolled up newspaper but you have to be careful not to turn your back. As soon as book is done am going to work them one night in public. The Circus has moved to Los Pinos. Would rather work cotsies than do almost anything; if you do not have to use the whip, or chair, or make theatre. Have a wonderful number worked out. The trainer is going to announce me as "An Illustrious domador del norte, now retired from the profession, but who, through his aficion, dedicates this rather special number to the Cuban public."

The climax is when I lie down and both cotsies put their front feet on your chest. Got raked a couple of times when was gentling them. But we have a doctor in the house, Roberto.

So it <u>isn't</u> as fucking dull here as all that. Promised Miss Mary I wouldn't work with Cotsies any more until book finished. She left when I started gentleing them and got raked. In a way am her security and it is wicked, I guess, to lay it on the line just for fun. But know no other place as good to lay it as on the line.

Give our love to Jerry and take care.

Ernest

Roberto sends his best. He has you all mixed up with the statue of Liberty etc. like in Jimmy Stewart film.

0800 3/10/49.

ED: Please don't think any chance of this being a secondary or not top-drawer book. Have been throwing in my armour worse than Georgie Patton ever did and there isn't a plane on the ground that can fly. Brooklyn Tolstois grab your laurels and get out of that slip stream. Even throw in the takeing of Paris for free. Will probably never live to finish the long book anyway. So what the fuck? EH. This is going to be a jolly fall, or autumn. One of my Venice girls, the best one, has written she is comeing to Paris. Another writes that she has fixed up the pied á terre. We are going to have to manaever boy. In there with the cotsies is nothing. We can always go into conference with the proof. Bring lots of proofs.

OK

EH

new whore: Xenophobia, a seventeen-year-old who lunched at the finca at least once during Mary's absence (*Final,* 209).

Earl Wilson: Broadway gossip columnist for the *New York Post.*

Red Lodge, Montana where my hands mended: In November 1930, EH overturned his car and was treated at a hospital in Billings, Montana, for injuries he later described as "right arm—muscular spiral paralysis—three fingers in right hand broken—sixteen stitches in left wrist and hand" (EH to Maxwell Perkins, January 5–6, 1932, in Baker, *Selected Letters,* 351).

Cody, Wyoming or West Yellowstone: Along with Red Lodge, Montana, places that EH visited in 1930. Michael Reynolds, *Hemingway: The 1930s* (New York: Norton, 1997), 42.

lost our kid: On August 19, 1946, in Casper, Wyoming, Mary's ectopic pregnancy ruptured, nearly killing her (*HIW,* 216–17).

Mr. Smith Goes to Washington: Producer/director Frank Capra's popular and critical 1939 success featured James Stewart as an idealistic junior senator.

Zale and Graziano: Refers to film of the first bout between Tony Zale and Rocky Graziano, which took place on September 27, 1946. Norberto Fuentes, *Hemingway in Cuba* (Secaucus, NJ: Lyle Stuart, 1984), 61.

never live to finish the long book: In March 1949, EH had set aside "the sea sections of his long novel"—*Islands in the Stream*—to write what became *Across the River and into the Trees* (*Story*, 472).

One of my Venice girls, the best one: Adriana Ivancich, whom EH met in December 1948 while duck hunting with his friend Nanyuki Franchetti in Cortina. An aristocratic Venetian socialite, she was the object of EH's current infatuation and contributed to the prototype of Renata in *Across the River and into the Trees.* Adriana provided cover art for that book and *The Old Man and the Sea* and illustrations for EH's two fables (*Story*, 469, 476).

Another writes that she has fixed up the pied à terre: Possibly Afdera Franchetti, "the pretty schoolgirl sister" of Nanyuki Franchetti (*Story*, 486).

{20} AEH to EH
Oct. 3 [1949] (TLS, 2 pp., JFKL)
405 East 54th Street/New York 22, N.Y.

Dear Ernest:

So I'm two cents off but after all I've kicked into the kitty you'd think they'd do me the favor; I've never come face to face with a postal clerk who wasn't a prick and this proves it. Must mean my other letters, not returned, are in some hold or dead or don't open until Christmas file so for all I know you haven't heard from me since I got back. Which also means (since I put the wrong postage on all of them) I'd better recapitulate. Let's see the most important thing from the book standpoint was Dick Berlin's reaction to the news—tell Ernest that his standing with us is such that he fixes his own price—he knows best how much he wants, and needs and the price he would command in the market. If you didn't get that letter then I can only repeat that my hat's in the air because the M.D. is closing in on Roberto and Gregorio's heirs are about to be anointed. Most of the stuff in the other letters was trivia that you can easily be spared.

I received a letter from [Charles] Scribner with a cc [carbon copy] to Hemingway at the bottom (what a load of ccs you must get; I haven't used cc since I was sports editor on my high school paper and one day I sat on a piece of cc when I had put on for the first time a pair of highly coveted tennis flannels) and the point in issue was whether our Feb. issue comes out on the 4th of July. Like I said, I don't save ccs but the jist of my reply was that Feb. issue comes out in Feb., March issue in March. Since there is so much concern over this point perhaps I'd better state it clearly: we will publish first installment in Feb. issue; we will publish second installment in March issue; Scribner's will publish book around March 15th; Copies of the book will go to reviewers no later than Feb. 20 well ahead of the March Cosmo and notices will be sent to reviewers Feb. 1 telling them when copies will arrive (this precludes impossible situation of reviewers reading magazine—a thing no reviewer has ever descended to, I'm sure.) I explained to Dick that this arrangement means that the book sales will start while the March Cosmo is still on sale—which is highly unusual for pre-publication in a magazine—but as I told you long ago this is perfectly okay with us. I'm sure I made all this clear when I talked it over with you in Havana and I know I'm boring you with this re-recital but since you received a cc I figure maybe I had better retotal the box score.

I told you in one letter that the plan for the European junket worked fine and I am deeply in your debt for that. I haven't been back since 1947, early, and the teared eye from Air France posters was giving me permanently blurred vision. I'll fly in with the galleys and stay in the vicinity just long enough to be of actual help. Would you like an apartment or a good hotel or anything here during the stopover? We'd be delighted to repay a little for your kindness—it was probably a pain in the ass trundling us back and forth on the boat but Jerry will never forget consideration given her—letting her in on as much as her bearings would bear—and neither will I.

I've sent you some fight reels for your library—a couple of the fights are really great and I wish I could see them with you to talk them over. Be sure to tell Roberto that one of the reels is <u>not</u> sound.

Scribner mentioned that you decided to send him the poetry and I think a follow-up project involving shorts and the poetry is a good idea. Would you like us to read the poetry or do you think it is definitely beyond magazine use? It occured to me that you might need immediate cash money for the trip and I shouldn't have to tell you that a request is all that is necessary. If for some reason you'd like to phone talk, I'm at Columbus 5-7300 during the day and Friday to Sunday at Westport 2-6067.

The movies have just returned from processing and there's some good footage. Too bad we were such a hex on the fish—would have liked to take you in battle.

Scribner says you are working good and the typewriter smokes. I wrote you that the chapters I read really made me itch for the before and after—I can't tell you what a strange feeling it is to know this little piece of the middle—but I can tell you this, with no bull shit involved—what I read had tremendous pull, because it stays right with me and I'm sitting in a cafe with that girl, wanting to take her up to my room.

How's Mary? We're sure fond of her.

The best,

<u>Ed</u>

two cents off: AEH's letter 16 was delayed due to insufficient postage.

the poetry: Probably "To Mary in London" and "Second Poem to Mary," later published in the *Atlantic,* August 1965, pp. 94–100.

The movies: Some of AEH's footage of EH and others aboard the *Pilar* is housed at the Alderman Library, University of Virginia, Charlottesville.

{21} AEH to EH
Oct. 4ᵗʰ [1949] (ALS, 1 p., JFKL)
Cosmopolitan [New York City]

Dear Ernest—

One item forgot to mention in yesterday's letter. Would facilitate art work greatly if you had one chapter from first installment which could be sent up for artist to illustrate. As I told you, I'm anxious to have art work best possible + more time alloted to artist the better.

> Best,
> Ed

{22} EH to AEH
11 October 1949 (TLS, 2 pp., ViU)
FINCA VIGIA, SAN FRANCISCO DE PAULA, CUBA

Dear Ed:

Thank you for the lovely films. They certainly photographed worse in those days but they had much better fighters. It was fun to see the Kingfish die in front of Mr. Joe Louis. Where is Reel No. 2? Numbers 1, 3 and 4 arrived OK and rapidly when we came back from the trip. Am at 47,474 today. If that's of any interest to you. It interests the shit out of me.

I believe that we should do something so that we will not lose the element of surprise on the book. Let's try and work it out. Will not cash your check until I hear about this, because if there is no element of surprise there is no deal. I think that I can go 60 [thousand words] easily and jamming all the time. It is a rather rough racket but as Arky Vaughn said to Miss Martha when she said to him, "But you look so rough, Mr. Vaughn, when you are on the ballfield," and Mr. Arky Vaughn responded, "Lady, I am rough."

Since I have my stuff, and I can guarantee you that I have it, Scribner's have to do more or less what I say. I do not want to crowd anybody but I think it would be best if we made a good clean deal. We both have lots to win and I have [lots] to lose.

Roberto, full of his enthusiasm for photographing, showed Miss Mary the pictures of the whore that we now call Xenophobia. Since this I have been in a doghouse whose dimensions pass description. But will fight my way out of it as out of any other God-damned place. Miss Mary is far from dumb and she noted in the pictures which Roberto showed her, proud of his photography, that the girl wore 3 different dresses. I thought of a pretty fast answer to that but I could not make it stick. Try sometime to make a lie stick with Miss Mary. I think that it is the quickest way to starve yourself to death that is still available.

Book goes wonderful and don't worry, kid, at all. I can call in the outfielders and pitch like Mr. Rube Waddell if you want. But am just mowing them down now. We got the runs. Will be awfully lonesome for book once it is finished. Never had a better friend or a more severest critic.

Write me the gen on the money. The true gen. I may go through that town very fast on account of having to work up to the last minute and not be able to see Dick [Berlin]. You tell me what I should do and I'll do it. It has been a long time since I have had any son-of-a-bitch that I could take orders from happily. If you want to see any of this last part I can send it but I hesitate to ask Nita to copy it when she is so busy. We haven't got as many secretaries as Phillips Lord or that man who has disappeared into the wilds of the Himalayas and I dislike to overwork good people. But if you want any further samples or anybody up there is choking up I can send them. Have been slugging it out with Mr. Shakespeare, the writer, today and I have him in bad shape. I guess maybe he is old. Anyway, he can't take it good in the body. But who or whom can? Have this wonderful advantage on him that he was never in those towns and that I spent my boyhood and considerably more in them. TWO GENTLE-MEN OF VERONA and he was never in Verona. THE MERCHANT OF VENICE and he was never in Venice.

ROMEO and whatever that puta was that he went with, "Now wherefor art thee, Romeo", and in a town he never saw like the seacoast of Bohemia. This is a country which I now believe to be controlled by Mr. Tito. He once was Chief of Staff of the 13th International Brigade and did very well. Not for himself, for everybody.

Am glad if you like Charlie Scribner. At least he is something to deal with knowing that it will come out the way he says it will according to his abilities. He is as dumb as a horse which is not awfully dumb. Guess this is about all as do not want to burden Miss Nita who has to type this. Did 884 today. Roberto has gone in to see his lovely whore named Xenophobia or something like that and am afraid that nothing that he can do in that town will get me out of this doghouse that I roam in. Will send you enlargements of all the good pictures. Some of the Pilar, Miss Pilar, are very good. Don't take any bad $10,000 checks and keep in close contact with your friend,

Mister Papa

(forged by Nita)

It was fun to see the Kingfish die in front of Mr. Joe Louis: Louis knocked out Harris Krakow, known as Kingfish Levinsky, in a 1935 Chicago bout.

Miss Martha: Martha Gellhorn (1908–1998), author and journalist who was EH's third wife; they were married from 1940 to 1945.

Arky Vaughn: Shortstop for the Brooklyn Dodgers who probably met the Hemingways when the team trained at Varadero Beach, Cuba, in 1941–1942.

3 different dresses: Roberto's photographs suggested that Xenophobia visited the finca on three occasions or that she changed clothes during a visit.

Rube Waddell: Pitcher for several teams between 1897 and 1910, he often instructed his outfielders to sit down during exhibition games and then retired the side.

Phillips Lord: Writer who created a popular country preacher character named Seth Parker, whom he played on radio and in the movies.

that man who has disappeared into the wilds of the Himalayas: News broadcaster and traveler Lowell Thomas had recently been injured in the Himalayan Mountains and had to be carried by litter for three weeks. "Lowell Thomas Thrown by Horse in Himalayas," *New York Times,* September 24, 1949, p. 5; "Lowell Thomas on Litter," *New York Times,* September 26, 1949, p. 27.

Mr. Tito: Josip Brozovich, premier of Yugoslavia.

{23} AEH to EH
October 17 [1949 *pmk*] (TLS, 2 pp., JFKL)
[New York City]

Dear Doghouser:

I know that lock-up pretty well myself, but I usually try to leave the door off one hinge and try never to board up all the windows like you have. But as the wound of Roberto's sharp focus heals and the all-conquering image of E.H. replaces it, (a transition which has probably already been achieved) the boards will loosen and poor papa will hoist himself up and through and back into the sunlight. No, Miss Mary doesn't impress me as a lady likely to catch the first fast answer tossed her way and I would hate to be standing up there with the lights at me and the measuring rod on the wall in back of me and Miss Mary standing in front asking questions. Doesn't the soft purr of the minks help? And the lure of the Ile de France and Paris and Venice?

Glad you enjoyed the fights; a couple of reels to come as soon as Willoughby gets them from whatever black source runs them their contraband. Yes the photography of that early stuff is thin and uneven but enough gets on the screen to make it exciting. Ezzard Charles who would have had to train hard to stay in Louis' sparring camp, now wants New York recognition as world champ. Ezzard yet—even the names are all wrong. Kid Chocolate, Manassa Mauler, Gentleman Jim, Sailor Jack, Brown Bomber, and all the rest—good fight names, the way baseball names fit the great guys who wore them. I don't think sports writers are less inventive, they're simply less inspired. Woodling, Mapes, Brown, Coleman, Lopat, Raschi, Snider, Furillo, Olmo, Hermanski, Jorgenson, Hodges, and almost everyone else on those two rosters [Yankees and Dodgers] are fair to good ballplayers but they'll never earn any of the lovely nicknames lavished on the princes.

Ernest, that you have your stuff working like [Lefty] Gomez 10 years back with six days rest has long ago been conceded in this press box. I told Scribner that this is a great book; I told Dick Berlin that this is a great book; both accepted this statement as fact. That I or anybody else here wants to see plugs from the last part is ridiculous. There's less choking up here then there is on the Yankees right now; there's just a feeling of pleasant anticipation. The only material we would like to get is a few pages from the early part of the book that the artist could read and start to illustrate. Or, if you'd rather not send up a chapter or part thereof, a brief description that he could use as a guide would be sufficient. However, you might prefer not to be bothered with this kind of detail since you are going so great (47,474 interests the shit out of me too—really a sensational pace) and although it would make for better art work to have a little more time, nevertheless we can get an artist to work a benzedrine shift and get out something presentable with no time at all if need be. I wish you'd give me a quick word on this, however, so I can get the best artist to stand by at the right time.

This is Oct. 17 which means that you are practically on the boat and we ought to put ourselves in writing and sign names and cash checks. First, money talk. This is talk with me playing second base to your short stop and

Mr. Hearst is in the batter's box. As I told you I talked with a couple of very bright literary agency boys who agreed that a fat, unprecedented kind of price for a two-installment novel by Hemingstein (it was agreed that this was a unique property in a market all by itself) would be $50,000.00. I asked prices on Sat. Eve. Post biggest buys and on Collier's, Life, and Journal buys and this holds up, on comparison, with their top buys, since no purchase seems to have exceeded $37,000. However, I can give you this advice. Berlin wants you to be 100% pleased in the money department and I think that if you asked 65 or even 75 it would be paid with no questions asked. Now, the other matter which you discussed—not losing the element of surprise. Hard for me to discuss this since I'm pretty fogged as to just what you want done to accomplish this surprise. I don't have to tell you that I'm not a magazine go-getter trying to swing the best deal going to Father Hearst. I am a guy who likes you and admires you as a person as well as the best writer who is putting the English language between covers. So it behooves me to say (as the boys on the floor of the Senate say) that the contract will read as you want it to, insuring surprise in whatever manner you think best. When I came back from Cuba I told Berlin that my understanding was that you wanted a March 15th book publication and you wanted us to publish installment one in our February issue which comes out February 1, and installment two in our March issue which comes out March 1. Now this is where I am foggy for I do not understand how you would like that changed. If you mean that you would like the book to come out before the final installment appears in Cosmo then how would it be if we published it in three parts with part three coming out April 1, two weeks after the book is published? This arrangement would allow for the book to come out before the magazine has revealed all of it and it would allow the magazine to publish two parts before book publication. Does this talk hit the issues or am I still foggy? Ernest, there isn't much time for drawing a contract and getting terms all set before you go off so I suggest that you cable me collect or phone me and let me know exact thinking. Let me emphasize that in the final analysis the deal will be as you think it in your best interests—there is no reason why you shouldn't be satisfied on terms, have this extra dough and get the six or eight million magazine readers who, according to the surveys (if you want to believe Mr. Roper), rarely buy books. Tomorrow I shall phone a little man I know at Air France and book my galley mission. Shall I buy one of those diplomatic brief cases with the handcuff, for transporting the galleys? I'd have to keep it chained to my wrist until I located you with the key. Maybe I'd better not—the prospect of stranding me on the Champs

Elysees with a brief case growing out of my wrist might tempt you to steal off quietly to some obscure haunt, leaving me to the ineptness of the French locksmiths.

Tell Mary to give you a big kiss and restore (?) tranquillity.

<u>Ed</u>

Nita calls me "Esquire." Nobody's called me Esquire since I was a lawyer. All lawyers call each other esquire; they think it covers some of the fake + compensates them for not having been bright enough to invent a word like "doctor" which they could use all the time.

Willoughby: According to AEH, Willoughby's was the camera shop where he purchased fight films.

Ezzard Charles: Upon Joe Louis's retirement, Charles beat Jersey Joe Walcott to win the heavyweight championship in 1949.

Kid Chocolate, Manassa Mauler, Gentleman Jim, Sailor Jack, Brown Bomber: Eligio Sardinias, Jack Dempsey, James Corbett, Jack Sharkey, and Joe Louis, respectively.

[Lefty] Gomez: Yankees pitcher from 1930 to 1942.

Hemingstein: One of EH's nicknames for himself dating back to his teenage years.

{24} EH to AEH
23 October 1949 (dictated 20 Oct) (TLS, 2 pp., ViU)
FINCA VIGIA, SAN FRANCISCO DE PAULA, CUBA

Dear Ed:

Just received yours of 20 October and am answering before going off to fish at Escondido with Miss Mary, Roberto and Gregorio. Here is the gen that you can operate on. I broke 54 yesterday. Quality is better than ever.

Tell Dick [Berlin] it ought to run three instalments. Will be around 60. Give it a little more or a little less.

Nita is coming out to live in the little house since her colonel is coming back—not <u>her</u> colonel but some colonel whose house she has occupied while he was away. She will start typing it and I will deliver to you between first of November enough stuff for your illustrator, etc., to go ahead with. It will not be completely corrected since I plan to correct from the proofs. This worked out good with FOR WHOM THE BELL TOLLS and I wish to follow the same system.

About dough, whatever is OK with Dick is OK with me. I think that if it runs three, and it should at the length that it shapes now, it should be around 75 or over if Dick agrees. I have never put it in the open market nor bid anybody against anybody else. Have had offers from LIFE and the other local creatures but I told you that it was your book as far as that went and we both bet on the nod. Will have to have some papers from Dick to show I contracted for it before I wrote it. Please tell him all this gen and do not let him have the idea that I do not write because I am snotty or getting above myself in any way. I do not write because I am so God-damned pooped after I write that it is difficult to write letters.

On transport; we have decided to sail on the ILE [*Ile de France*] on the 19th instead of the first. That gives me time where before I would be crowded. By Miss Nita copying here we will be way ahead and when I hit the town it will be in the bag or on your table. I can pull all the inches that there are on the thing but think it is better not to lose any motors. So book your transport accordingly. We leaving on the 19th and therefore arriving about the 22nd of November in Paris, France. We can correct proof there or in Venice. If you have read a thing a couple of hundred times you don't need to do much proof correction. You will have to use your good taste in cutting out what you have to cut out and anything you cut out (MR. HOTCHNER: There was an interruption in the wire with the following explanation by Mister Papa—"That crash was a cat who decided to eat my breakfast." Papa never finished the sentence, either.)

About calling you "Esquire", neither Miss Nita nor I did it to be wrong. We always call Charlie Scribner "Esquire" and he calls me the same and she saw that you were going to be well up in this game and promoted you to "Esquire" automatically. I did not know that you were a lawyer; but I am glad. We are building a good new ball team now which will tell you about when I see you.

Sinsky [Duñabeitía] got off all right just making his ship on time. Roberto is still here and is getting some wonderful stuff with the Rollei and an old Zeiss Icon that I found that a girl gave me one time when I was a nice looking guy. This was a long time ago but I was able to get it repaired and it has a wonderful lens and we got some beauty shots on the trip. All our verbal arrangements hold and we can confirm them in print any time you want. It was wonderful seeing you and Jerry and we enjoyed every minute of it. Was only sorry that the fish would not cooperate. But I am sure it was on account of these storms coming up. They are as sensitive to the barometer as a woman is to the moon.

Better knock this off and get the house work cleaned up. Certain amount of leakage due to the heavy winds and rains and have to find the different sources and fix. Love to you and Jerry from Mary and me.

Ernest

ERNEST HEMINGWAY

Love to Jerry. Tell her she's beautiful.

yours of 20 October: Presumably letter 23, which is dated October 17. Following the date atop the present letter, Juanita Jensen typed "(dictated 20 Oct)".

(*MR. HOTCHNER: There was an interruption in the wire . . .*): This parenthesis was written by Jensen. EH apparently dictated this letter into his wire recorder.

{25} AEH to EH
October 24th [1949] (TLS, 2 pp., JFKL)
Cosmopolitan [New York City]

Dear Ernest:

Item in yesterday's TIMES about the book gave me a big start and I phoned Scribner first thing this morning to find out how it got into the paper since he was only one I had mentioned the book to. He explained that you had requested special dispensation for the Times and that he had told you the nature of the material which he gave them. I think item bad stuff in phrasing and information and I say this not to make trouble in any way but I know you would want me to state what I think as always and for what it is worth to you I think in future less specific stuff said about the book the better. I think contents of the book should not even be hinted at—for the Times or anyone else—and certainly comparisons with former works are pointless. Anyway, I have not seen any one on the Times or any other newspaper and I dislike being referred to second hand. What's more it's inaccurate as all I ever told Scribner were the facts I possessed—that I had read a few chapters, that those few chapters were largely in dialogue, that the dialogue was powerful and the characterization, as it came through the dialogue, was effected with great skill; that the characters in this brief material were an army colonel and a beautiful Italian girl.

I have seen Scribner several times now and I like him a little more each time and I don't want you to think that I'm pitching a bean ball; I'm sure he means well and is acting in what he thinks is your best interests—I just happen to disagree on this publicity and thought it might be useful if I brought it to your attention.

Scribner passed along news that you delay sailing until the 19th so I have changed my flying to the 25th. I had a conference with the art department today and here is the gen in that direction: in order for us to publish installment one in February as planned they will have to go to work no later than Monday morning, October 31st. This gives them practically no time at all. Now they have devised a simple but highly effective layout that will <u>not</u> make use of an illustration, thereby eliminating the necessity of our receiving any advance material BUT they must have the final title by the 31st if we are to make deadline. Apparently that is the only thing that can kill us for February. I have an eerie feeling that I may get a cable from you on the morning of the 31st—"Get pencil and paper stop Here is title stop Fuck You! stop"—but this is the shit part of having this job and I have to do it because I accept the couple of bucks I wring out of old man Hearst every week. But I really hate like hell having to push you of all people because I know you are pushing enough with natural pressure of the book and that is the important thing to you and, incredible as it may seem, to me too. But it's obligatory to give you the details on Cosmo's needs and if you can just send final title in letter or wire so that we get it by 31st then we can handle written portion of book as late as November 8th or 9th.

Lillian Ross had good piece in last week's New Yorker but lacked brilliance of the Franklin job. Woolcott Gibbs has just written brilliant piece for us—I'll send you a copy. Hope all goes well. Please give my love to Mary.

Ed

Item in yesterday's TIMES: AEH enclosed a clipping of this item, which read in part: "The manuscript has not been seen by the publisher yet, but a roving agent, just back from visiting Hemingway in Cuba, reports that the book's locale is Italy and its general style reminiscent of 'A Farewell to Arms'—encompasses a brief time span, concerns a love affair between an American soldier and an Italian girl, and is told largely in dialogue. The novel runs about 85,000 words—Hemingway knows, because he hired a man to count them. He thinks it may be his best book yet, but isn't taking any chances: the work he put aside at the time of his illness [*Islands in the Stream*] will be resumed when this one is packed off." David Dempsey, "In and Out of Books," *New York Times Book Review,* October 23, 1949, p. 8.

Lillian Ross had good piece in last week's New Yorker: "Symbol of All We Possess," *New Yorker,* October 22, 1949, pp. 35–61; the piece was about the 1949 Miss America contest.

the Franklin job: "El Unico Matador," Ross's profile of American-born matador Sidney
Franklin, ran in the *New Yorker* on March 12 and 26, 1949.

{26} EH to AEH
1949 NOV 4 (Cable, 1 p., ViU)
Cuba

AIRMAILING TODAY FIRST SIXTYTWO PAGES ALSO CHAPTER WHICH INTRO-
DUCES THE GIRL STOP BEST TO YOU KID=: EH=

{27} EH to AEH
1949 NOV 15 (Cable, 1 p., ViU)
Cuba

TRIED TO CALL YOU ALL LAST EVENING SECRETARY CRACKED UP SO WILL NOT
ARRIVE UNTIL WEDNESDAY AFTERNOON BUT WILL BRING ALL CORRECTED
COPY EXCEPT LAST CHAPTER LOVE TO JERRY BRINGING COPY IS FASTER THAN
MAIL=ERNEST=

*On November 16, the Hemingways were greeted at Idlewild Airport in New York
by AEH and Lillian Ross, who spent the next two days gathering information for her
upcoming profile of the author for the* New Yorker. *The Hemingways entertained a
constant stream of friends at the Sherry-Netherland Hotel and EH met with Charles
Scribner, who presented him with a contract for* Across the River and into the
Trees. *Before embarking on the* Ile de France *on the 19th, EH arranged for AEH to
pick up the final chapters of the manuscript in Paris (Story, 478–79). Accompanying the Hemingways abroad were Sam Boal, a wartime colleague of Mary's, and
Virginia "Jigee" Viertel, whose husband, Peter, would later write the screenplays for*
The Sun Also Rises *and* The Old Man and the Sea.

{28} EH to AEH
1949 NOV 23 (Cable, 2 pp., ViU)
Ile de France

URGENT TO HOTCHNER PLEASE CALL OTTO BRUCE HOME APPLIANCE COMPANY
605 SIMONTON STREET KEY WEST FLORIDA AND ASK IF HE CAN GO CUBA BRING

CAR STOP EXPLAIN CIRCUMSTANCES AND MY EFFORTS GET IN TOUCH STOP
THIS IMPORTANT STOP IF BRUCE CAN GO AIRMAIL HIM ALL CAR PAPERS REGIS-
TERED STOP IF NO BRUCE PHONE ANITA JENSEN AMERICAN EMBASSY HAVANA
AND ASK GET PACO GARAY TO OBTAIN EXTENSION ON CUSTOM PERMIT FOR
BUICK STOP THEN SQUARE AAA IN NEW YORK WITH PAPERS WHICH YOU HOLD
SHOWING WHEN CAR LEFT EUROPE TO AVOID LOSS OF BOND STOP ALSO IN
BOOK WHERE LIVING GENERALS CALLED JERKS YOU MAY CHANGE TO CHARAC-
TERS STOP ALSO WHERE GENERAL IS EXPLAINING HOW IS TO BE GENERAL TEXT
READS GIS WHEN SHOULD BE GS MEANING HIS STAFF G1 COMA G2 COMA AND
SO FORTH STOP HAVE ALL COPY CORRECTED LOVE TO JERRY PAPA PACO GARAY
GIS GS G1 COMMA G2

OTTO BRUCE: "Toby" Bruce, from Piggott, Arkansas, where he met EH though Pauline
    Pfeiffer, was EH and Pauline's friend and handyman during their Key West years;
    thereafter, the Bruces remained friends with EH and Mary (*HIW,* 238).
TO AVOID LOSS OF BOND: EH had to post a bond to take the car out of Cuba and
    needed an extension or permit to avoid losing the bond. AEH, phone conversation
    with DeFazio, June 14, 2005.
PACO GARAY: "[D]id something in the Immigration and customs and knew many
    Cuban government officials" (*HIW,* 238).
GS MEANING HIS STAFF: General Staff, division level.
G1 . . . G2: G1, administrative and operational level; G2, security level.

{29} AEH to EH
Sunday [December 4, 1949] (TLS, 1 p., JFKL)
[New York City]

Dear Ernest,

    Today we are having our first snow and unlike most first snows which are
meager and do not stick, this one has flakes the size of half dollars and there
is three inches on the ground although the fall is only two hours old. We have
just moved into a fine house on 21st Street between Ninth and Tenth Ave.,
across from St. Francis' Seminary where the carillons play sweetly every
evening at six o'clock and when the night is clear it is Christmas Eve. The
street itself is small and quiet and lined with young maples and we have two
floors with a back yard exclusively our own. I do not like living in New York
but this existence makes it less unpleasant. I am sitting in a little room we have

fixed up as a study and it faces our neighborhood backyards filled with many trees, now white.

The automobile has already been brought to Key West and Nita reports by letter that there is no Col. Richard Cantwell on the Army lists. She also writes that there was a rumor at San Fran. de Paula that you had come down with some mystic New York disease and that she and other of your friends have been concerned; I have just written her and put all fears to rest, assuring her that Dr. Cordon Rouge, '27 was in attendance and recovery was phenomenal.

Old man [Herbert] Mayes jitters, I tell him it's much too soon, he says go anyway, who am I to argue over such fine circumstance, so I fly next Friday Paris bound. Since we are good friends, I can tell you frankly, as I intimated to Mary, that I know you have many friends in Paris and wherever else you may be, whom you will be seeing and I think it's best, however much I like being with you and Mary, that I live completely apart and I'll only come around when there are things you would like us to do together. This is perhaps an unnecessary statement but I make it to resolve any possible awkwardness . . . after all, you're the Godfather of this fine, sponsored journey I am about to enjoy. If there is anything forgotten or just realized that you would like me to bring, you have only to cable. Charley [Scribner] tells me that he will not have the galleys ready, for you do not want him to set until he gets a corrected copy.

It's been almost three years since I've been in Paris and you know the eagerness with which I await next Saturday; the best things of my life happened in Paris and the best friends I ever had I met there; I was truly happy.

Gerry sends love to you and Mary—she feels thoroughly cheated over being left but I've been tenderly tough with her and she's reconciled pretty good.

See you in Paris.

Ed

Col. Richard Cantwell: **Protagonist of** *Across the River and into the Trees.* **AEH had asked Juanita Jensen to determine whether there was an actual Col. Robert Cantwell; she replied on November 22 that the "1949 edition of the 'Army Register'" listed no officer with that name (JFKL).**

On December 9, AEH flew to Paris, where he stayed at a small, inexpensive hotel, the Opal, while the Hemingways stayed at the Ritz. By December 10, EH had completed Across the River and into the Trees, *and the two men celebrated by at-*

tending the races at Auteuil, a steeplechase course in the Bois de Boulogne. AEH remembers, "We weren't doing too well until early one morning Ernest got a tip from the jockey room on a horse named Bataclan II posted at 27–1. It won by virtue of a rather questionable finish and our killings provided us with a very festive Christmas" (AEH to DeFazio, September 27, 2004). They edited Across the River and into the Trees and their revisions were transcribed onto a carbon by Jigee Viertel. On December 24 the Hemingways, AEH, and the Viertels drove to Nice. On December 28, AEH and the Viertels returned to Paris by train and the Hemingways went on to Venice. AEH retrieved the final chapters from the typist and delivered them to Venice around January 9 (Final, 214).

1950

{30} EH to AEH
2/1/50 [February 1, 1950 *pmk*] (TLS, 2 pp., ViU)
[Italy *pmk*]

Dear Ed:

Thanks for two fine letters. Latest received today with the gen and the contract.

There seems to be nothing especially pressing on business so let's skip it. Personal letter: Personal for Mister Hotchner Only.

We certainly miss you kid. If you liked us and our mob and the people we train with you can be very sure that you were liked as well or more.

When I told Philip, Anne-Marie's brother, that you were gone he took it about as cheerfully as the news that there weren't going to <u>be</u> any replacements. Every one in Venice really liked you. Maybe you should fight out of here instead of St. Louis.

Adriana asked me to write you to thank you for your note. She said she couldn't write because she would have to address you as darling.

Mary is fine and being damned good. If I were her—skip that one. She is pretty damned wonderful you know. She just called from other room to send you her love, for you to roll with the punches, and that at the fair in the Piazza San Margherita the merry go round has gondolas instead of horses. I don't know whether this is code or not. Is transmitted as received.

One time on the boat we had a new and terrific code to cover all possible situations which might arise includeing the most amphibious. I read the goddamn thing which had been devised by a mad man (USMC) and he asked me if I had any phrases or situations to add. So just wrote AM SHELLING FRIENDLY CRUISER.

Later on we worked out some better ones.

We go to Cortina tomorrow. Then back here and Nanyuk Franchetti and I are going to shoot Monte Carlo. Wish the old syndicate was here. The Grand Prix is going to be 2 million francs this year and the entry is only 20,000. If I'm not in form, and Christ knows I should not be, then we have two entries from here and Homer Clark who is the best pigeon shot we have in US. I don't know whether to shoot or bet. Neither of the guns I have here fit me; that Browning is much too long. Have been working on a new one and maybe o.k. But it is a very rough game; faster than baseball and one strike is out. You have to hit the first pitch and 90 percent of them are bad. Also they are so fast they look about the size of Walter Johnson's fast one and they cut the tails so you never get a straight bird. I shouldn't shoot it I guess but only two Americans have ever won it; one in 1876 and one in 1933. When I should have been shooting it was when [I] was in Spain. Eyes probably too slow now. Maybe Nanyuk or Homer can win it. They are about the same age.

What the hell else to write from here? My god-damned heart, that target of opportunity, sliced straight in half like the judgement of Herod. Only they sliced mine as clean as with a butcher's cleaver and Herod held up the attack.

So never worry, boy, if things are bad. They can be worse.

We are getting to be a bunch of morbids, it sounds like, but only on paper. There are no problems in real life I'm sure and How do you like it now, Gentlemen?

Thanks for good letters and for fine efficient performance all the time always.

Agree on [Alfred] Rice. Seems really good guy.

Any time I ever get gloomy I think about how you almost went into the FBI. Best luck and love from us both.

Papa.

Will send contract by registered letter. EH.

two fine letters: presumably letters written since AEH returned to New York at the end of December; these remain unlocated.

Anne-Marie's brother: In Venice, EH and Anne-Marie Lacloche discussed adapting "The Capital of the World" as a ballet and AEH agreed to pursue the venture when he returned to New York (*Choice,* 168). Anne-Marie Lacloche was married to Francesco

Aldobrandini—son of Don Clemente, Prince Aldobrandini—and was well-connected to the Italian aristocracy.

Adriana asked me to . . . thank you: EH introduced AEH to Adriana Ivancich in Venice.

Mary is . . . being damned good: Mary was aware of EH's infatuation with Adriana but "decided to avoid discussing the imbroglio with anyone including its protagonists. . . . I was sure that no cautionary phrases of mine could arrest the process. I held my tongue" (*HIW*, 292).

One time on the boat: During World War II, EH hunted for submarines aboard the *Pilar.*

Nanyuk Franchetti: Baron and shooting companion of EH who owned a lodge north of Venice.

Homer Clark: Son of Homer Clark Sr., both champion trapshooters.

Walter Johnson's fast one: Johnson, pitcher for the Washington Senators from 1907 to 1927, was known for his fastball.

My god-damned heart, that target of opportunity, sliced straight in half: Refers to EH's infatuation with Adriana Ivancich. Mary reports EH's saying: "But my heart is not subject to discipline. . . . It's a target of opportunity" (*HIW*, 296). See also *Final*, 217.

How do you like it now, Gentlemen? Pet phrase of EH. Lillian Ross used it as the title of her *New Yorker* profile.

how you almost went into the FBI: AEH recalls: "In 1941, before being drafted, I had an interview with the FBI, but the questions were so dumb and reactionary that, despite their encouragement, I decided I'd be better off as a buck-ass G.I." AEH to DeFazio, September 27, 2004.

Will send contract: Presumably for serialization of *Across the River and into the Trees* in *Cosmopolitan*. The first of five monthly installments appeared in February.

{31} EH to AEH
19/2/50 (TLS, 2 pp., ViU)
Gritti Palace, Venice [hw]

Dear Ed:

It was pretty bad timeing wasn't it, kid? No sense to cry over spilt shit. Let's do something practical.

Have you any money for comeing events and while you are makeing plans? Let me know anything I can do.

Wouldn't you think they might have realized that I would not have given them the novel except for you; that I turned down all other magazines cold; turned down the syndication deal that would have brought in many times the dough. Simply said had promised novel to Cosmo and refuse to let anybody bid on it.

Oh well.

We came down from Cortina last night and I was figureing on getting the second half here and doing the go-over while Mary went back up to ski. Good and warm to work here now. But have the first part anyway and wrote Charley Scribner in N.Y. last night with Copy to Savoy Hotel London to cable me when he arrived or sailed and whether he had MSS and I would cable him where to send it.

Scratched Monte Carlo because Nanyuk Franchetti had so many ducks and geese comeing in and the other boy I wanted for team couldn't go. Would have liked to shoot it myself but was out of training and without a gun I could shoot without thinking about gun. Thanks for what you said about shooting. The eyes are gone for certain lights but still have the other stuff. You have everything for a shooter includeing the necessary pair of balls and when things get worked out we will shoot plenty together.

We heard from Jidge [Viertel] finally but I've scratched all that too. Too complicated.

Here Adriana and Giovanna went with us up to Cortina and they had a fine time ski-ing. Giovanna I don't think you met. Awfully fine girl too. Then they had to go to Milan for Adriana to see her Aunt and I hit the Penicillina again in Cortina for an infection I had picked up shooting a week ago at Nanyuki's. Started like the same damn thing I had before but believe we aborted it with Aureomycin and this new Crstalymina. Anyway face a lot better today. Keep this one out of the funny papers. Will skip all publicity on this one.

Taking so much Penicillina etc. don't do you no good in social life. But I haven't got the old rale; true. Dr. thinks my face infects from the burnt particles of powder and wad that come down when shooting those straight up and down over-head ducks.

Mary is ski-ing well. She is fine and sends her love to you and Jerry. She will look after your commissions.

Gritti [Palace] kept our apt. for us with everything in it and did not charge us while we were at Cortina. The town's name is Venice.

Ingrid's been takeing her lumps and it did not occur to Rosellini to do anything more chic and gallant than to read my private letters to her to the press. So we all have a few troublies of one sort or another.

Must write Alfred Rice and send check for passage home. I still trust him. Am I right? I hope so. Trust you, Rice, Charlie's intentions, and Al Horwits. Also Gregorio. Trust Marlene [Dietrich] in the clutch and let's cut to the clutch. Trust lots of people you meet here but hate casualties.

Jige wrote and asked if we took Venice or if we bogged down. I wanted to write that re-took it and lost you early in the assault. That nobody came up on our left and the people never got up on our right. And that now we were counting our deads.

But instead I skipped it.

So let's skip everything includeing the Scandinavian [Bergman].

Love from us both,

Papa

Tell Jerry not to worry about Cesaerean. Is as simple now as appendicitis.

bad timeing: Friction with Mayes led to AEH's dismissal from *Cosmopolitan* following the first installment of *Across the River and into the Trees* (*Choice,* 83; Herbert R. Mayes, *The Magazine Maze: A Prejudiced Perspective* [Garden City, NY: Doubleday, 1980], 60–61). This information was probably communicated to EH in a letter that remains unlocated.

Jidge . . . scratched all that: According to Mary, Jigee had designs on EH (*HIW,* 286, 290).

hit the Penicillina again: Presumably to treat a recurrence of erysipelas, a contagious skin disease, for which EH had been hospitalized in March (*Story,* 471).

Ingrid's been takeing her lumps: In a much publicized affair, actress Ingrid Bergman had left her husband and daughter for film director Roberto Rossellini.

Al Horwits: Publicist for Universal Pictures who had discussed a film version of *Across the River and into the Trees* with EH (*Final,* 208).

Marlene [Dietrich] (1901–1992): Film star whose friendship with EH began aboard the *Ile de France* in 1934.

{32} EH to AEH
8/3/50 [**March 8, 1950**] (TLS, 2 pp., JFKL)
Gritti [*tw*], Venice [*hw*]

Dear Ed:

We get off tomorrow and just got your letter of March 3rd today. Congratulations to you and Jerry on the Baby. Am so happy everything is ok. Sounds like fine baby. What do you call her? Hotchnera?

Mary's leg was a two part break with tendon pull-out. But she is comfortable with it now and can travel o.k. If I see it isn't comfortable will put her on wagon-lit at Nice. She's had eleven days since the break.

Tomorrow we run here—Padova, Vicenza, Verona, by-pass Milan and down to Nervi. Next day Nervi—Nice or Aix.

Have my get-away money, we are packed and set to roll. Had last supper night before last with Adriana's mother and kid bro. Jackie [Giacomo], Adriana and Giovanna, Mary, me here at Gritti in the appt. Everyone spoke and asked about you. Wish would have known about baby so could have drunk to baby, Jerry and you.

Am running as a straight sad with built-in head wind but suppose I rate that. May win yet. Always have. Gave my christmas knife to Federico Kechler, Christmas boots to Jackie, money clip to some infant. Starting new same as 1950.

Look, when you see [*Holiday* editor] Ted Patrick you might tell him for me that you more or less control where my stuff goes and that I would not sell nothing to noplace where you were not working at unless you accepted service under the Woman's Home Upfuck or The Ladies' Home Compassion.

You can show him this. I believe he would understand what I mean. Don't show him the rest of the letter nor to anybody else. I have some new wonder stories. Wrote three here for friends when I couldn't cool out from writing. Been going good.

I'll tell you a couple of things when I see you.

Here's the gen. We sail, even with everybody in their floatable iron lungs, on March 21st on Ile. No publicity. Not on passenger list. If you want to come down would love to see you. Then Sherry-Neth unregistered until business done. Want to skip publicity in N.Y. for several varieties of reasons. Then direct to Cuba on train and pick up car either K.W. [Key West] or Miami. Will check with [Otto] Bruce.

Think Holiday really best bet for you. Probably me too but wish to preserve my re-entry at other place.

Was a big mistake this time to serialize as we did, but shit we both made it and does a man cry over spilt shit or a spilt horse or whores?

Answer is no. Will not enumerate recent chicken mss. difficulties as went in for surmounting. But when tackled that last Mme. LeGros section I felt like the Sea-Bees.

No communication with Pete and Jige lately. There was something pretty odious by a former Mrs. Schulberg here peddling something to Charlie Scribner that was to be written "under my direct super-vision" and I wrote Charlie covering Pete, sent Pete a copy of letter, wrote him and Jige good letter and decided I was in the wrong pasture and better haul my shit out of there quick. It's out.

Poor peoples. Anyway Venice Italy is a better town than Venice Cal., Venice Fla., or even The Coast himself and include N.Y. Poor all of us.

No word from Lillian. She has plenty family worries. Cables from Marlene.

I have done the re-write on the whole thing. Wish you had been around to help me with your good, clean, smart, just head and your heart as bad as mine.

Take care of yourself and let me know anything I can ever do.

Mary sends her love to you and Jerry.

Best

<u>Papa</u>

your letter of March 3rd: Remains unlocated.

Mary's leg: Mary broke her left ankle while skiing on February 25, 1950.

Adriana's . . . kid bro. Jackie: Giacomo, younger brother of Adriana and Gianfranco Ivancich (*HIW,* 295).

Federico Kechler: Count and sportsman who invited the Hemingways to fish with him in Austria in the fall of 1948 (*Story,* 468).

Wrote three here: Probably "The Good Lion," "The Faithful Bull," and "The Great Black Horse."

Mme. LeGros: Parisian typist of *Across the River and into the Trees.*

Sea-Bees: U.S. Navy construction battalions (CBs) that built shore facilities in combat zones.

a former Mrs. Schulberg: Jigee Viertel was the ex-wife of writer Budd Schulberg, but according to AEH this is a reference to Schulberg's mother. AEH, phone call with DeFazio, December 9, 2004.

She has plenty family worries: Lillian Ross's father was ill.

the re-write on the whole thing: EH had finished revising *Across the River and into the Trees* for book publication.

On March 21, the Hemingways left Paris aboard the Ile de France, arriving in New York on the 27th. Their visitors in the Sherry-Netherland included Patrick Hemingway, who ventured down from Harvard with Henrietta Broyles, seeking EH's approval to marry her, and Wallace Meyer of Scribner's, who came to discuss the book publication of Across the River and into the Trees (HIW, 229–300). The Hemingways left New York on April 6 and arrived in Cuba on the 8th (Final, 221).

EH left with AEH the following document, dated "April 6, 1950 New York City": "Be it known that Ed Hotchner of 415 West 21, New York City, is empowered to act as my sole representative, in whatever capacity necessary, in the adapting of the short story, THE CAPITOL OF THE WORLD, into a ballet; he is empowered to adapt the story, to negotiate terms for its ballet presentation and all matters germane to this transaction are to be handled by him. [signed] Ernest Hemingway" (ViU, 6250f).

{33} AEH to EH
April 13, 1950 (TLS, 2 pp., JFKL)
[New York City]

Dear Papa, when you leave town it is as if all the friends I ever had took off. There are so many good things to do that there is no time for; and so many others that do not take place at this particular time. But this was a good visit with good people around. I sent the photos to Marlene [Dietrich] with the information and I phoned George [Brown] who said to tell you that Paul de Kruif tried to reach you the day you left. He is a splendid guy, George, and I plan to drop up and talk once in a while. Evan Shipman's article seemed accurate and Lillian [Ross] says she has finally finished hers. I presume both of them have provided you with copies—I have not seen Lillian's.

Rice forwarded to me a letter from Ann-Marie [Lacloche], excitedly asking about the ballet. She appeared convinced, with young girl enthusiasm, that the debut was momentary and that it was being performed exactly as she had written it. I hated to disallusion her, even a little, but from the sound of her letter she had one foot on the boat. I told her, as nicely as I could, that the ballet was shaping fine but that things in the ballet world, as opposed to the real or actual world, move very slowly and not always in the direction planned. As a matter of fact it is taking more of my time than I'd like to give it, what with four meetings already and endless ones to come, but I appreciate their many problems. Dali is fairly certain to do the sets and Menotti may do the music. I submitted Ann-Marie's manuscript but, unfortunately, they do not think the story should be interpreted in that manner, & I have done an adaptation that better suits their purpose. I only tell you all these details so that you know I am respecting Ann-Marie's position and will do all I can to make her feel that she is part of the Project.

I had a real joy yesterday trying guns at Abercrombie and finding a Winchester that I really like. I can hardly wait to get to the country (we go up first time this week-end) and try my shooting eye. I will try to go against the crows that harass us but I understand they are very hard to hit. Week-end of May 5 I am going to spend with people at Quogue [NY] who are great gun fanciers and we will shoot at the local gun club and I may enter a stationery target shoot if I am going good with the .22. In other competitions, I usually improve under tough going but I have no experience with gun competition.

I have been to Philadelphia to see [Ted] Patrick and we got along fine. He is a normal and straight and virile guy as far as I could tell, all of which qualities are in vast contradistinction to the editor of my recent acquaintance, I told him that you had left two stories with me that were not yet ready for placement but that if he would like to read them he could. He phoned me next day, very excited about them, and suggested that if there were a third, it would be wonderful to run all three of them in one issue, since they are so brief. I showed the stories to [Wade] Nichols of Red Book also, telling him as I did Patrick, and he was equally enthusiastic. Papa, I think you should have Adriana do a sample illustration for each story so that when the time comes for definitely placing them, I can also arrange for her to do the illustration. I believe with you that she has fresh talent for this kind of illustration and she should get her samples to me as soon as possible. The problem of Holiday or Red Book is not an easy one to solve (I am thinking ahead—neither has offered anything definite yet, although it looks like they will). Red Book has a much larger circulation—it is ahead of Cosmopolitan, as a matter of fact. I would be able to get a better job, better in the sense that it would be a bigger job with more salary. Holiday, however, has more class and quality to it and runs material that is, from my point of view, more attractive. Guess the best thing to do is, as always, ride the horses that come by and let it go at that.

I hope you and Mary had a pleasant trip back to Havana and that your lovely house was not too disordered from Gig's revels. I grow to like Mary all the time more, as Mike Gonzales might put it, and it's too goddam bad New Yorkers and San Francisco de Paulans can't visit week-ends. Maybe with the jet-propelled cruisers. I threw baseballs yesterday and scared the shit out of myself with the way I could still snap a curve.

Your friend, as always,

<u>Ed</u>

George [Brown]: Friend of EH who ran a gymnasium in midtown Manhattan (*Final,* 358; George Plimpton, *Shadow Box* [New York: Putnam's, 1977], 20).

Paul de Kruif (1890–1971): Author of best-selling popular accounts of medical science; EH owned five of his books.

Evan Shipman's article: Remains unlocated. Shipman, a racing columnist for the *Morning Telegraph,* was a friend of EH from the early days in Paris.

Dali . . . and Menotti: Surrealist painter Salvador Dali (1904–1989) and composer Gian-Carlo Menotti (1911–).

Abercrombie: Abercrombie & Fitch department store.

editor of my recent acquaintance: Herbert Mayes of *Cosmopolitan.*

you had left two stories with me: "The Good Lion" and "The Faithful Bull." AEH was probably aware of the third story in this group, "The Great Black Horse."

Gig's revels: EH's son Gregory was known as "Gig" or "Gigi." In November 1949, EH had

invited Gregory "to come down to the Finca for his next vacation" (*Portrait,* 80). The "revels" probably involved Gianfranco Ivancich, who had moved into the finca in the Hemingways' absence and was fond of entertaining women there (*Final,* 217).
as Mike Gonzales might put it: The Cuban-born player and manager for the St. Louis Cardinals was known for his pithy phrases such as "Good field, no hit."

{34} AEH to EH
May 10 [1950] (TLS, 2 pp., JFKL)
[New York City]

Dear Papa:

I spent most of lunch with Lillian [Ross] yesterday trying to figure an angle to get her to Europe, since she has finally developed a head of steam in that direction. The New Yorker is willing to send her if she can think of some project not in conflict with Flanner or Wechsburg. We thought of a couple of subjects, interesting and requiring much travel, and I sincerely hope she can lobby one through because she needs the trip. I wetted the whistle thoroughly, as you might imagine, and for good measure I threw in several large adjectives in behalf of Venezia, land of the impossible. I suppose of all things I think about in the never-never, Venezia stays most consistently on the inside rail three lengths out.

Speaking of which, leads me to think of poor Evan S. [Shipman] who must have gone strongly with his Hill Prince who met a better animal in the stretch. From the newspaper accounts of the running, I would guess that the Prince was not well-ridden, E. Arcaro to the contrary, or at least, not well-handled at the crucial moments. Young female friend of mine threw everything including her cardigan on Mr. Trouble to come across and I, not having heeded, simply watched the counting of the green.

Last week-end with friends at the Westhampton went fishing Saturday, tennised Sunday, all greatly enjoyed, including a fine eating and drinking gathering at Ted Patrick's house Saturday night. He has a fine structure right on the sand beach of the Atlantic Ocean, that noble body, and we ate grosses of clams freshly trundled up out of the deep of the canal, drank innumerable glasses of various alcohol, and finished all off with a suckling pig, apple in mouth, that was real delight. I like Patrick fine and we discussed on Sunday the stories and there is no doubt they would go best in Holiday so I have told Patrick that he will get them and that you have asked an artist friend in Italy to submit a sample illustration. Meyers [Wallace Meyer] at Scribner's sent me the surplus jackets but I honestly think one cannot tell from them what Adriana's true ability is and it would be much better if she would do a thing for one of the stories. Don't you agree? I want to show her off to best advantage on her first run and these jackets would not; if she goes well this initial time out I could follow up with other assignments for her and for that reason the sample is important. And, Papa, don't you think the horse story could go, maybe with a few proper names changed? I think it a fine story and maybe not too sophisticated for *Holiday*. At any rate, I'd like to show it to Patrick because the plan is to run three together in one issue and make a big thing out of it. I don't have a copy of the horse story, so please send me it if you think it can go. I should also have some idea of what amount of coin of the realm you would like the *Holiday* money lords to pass into your coffers—or do you want to leave that up to me? Please let me know on these items because Patrick and his lads are excited about the stories and anxious to start planning.

I wrestle with many insignificants, which is wrong, but necessary, since the bank total reacts favorably even to the insignificants. I am trying to write six articles at the same time, wrongly imagining that the force of sheer numbers will distract me, but some of the recent accounts which I have heard regarding my distinguished alma mater [*Cosmopolitan*] make me glad that I am wrestling insignificants rather than neurotics. The magazine world generally moves slowly in relation to personnel, but it may be that in due time brother Patrick and I will link arms. I do not count on this, as I do not count on most pleasant eventualities.

I am re-reading "Death in the Afternoon" to give me true background for the writing of the "Capitol of the World" ballet, and I am currently filled with admiration for the writing and envy for the experiences, both of which I hope I have succeeded in keeping out of this letter.

Do you fish and shoot and relax some and does the badly torn heart begin mending? Scar tissue is not so bad but running sores are awful.

Please tell Mary that I love her as always and that I look forward to getting the notes on the trip when she has a little time.

Bloody Hotchsmear

Flanner or Wechsburg: Ross's colleagues Janet Flanner and Joseph Wechsberg covered Europe for the *New Yorker.*

Hill Prince: Horse ridden by Eddie Arcaro that placed second to Middleground in the Kentucky Derby on May 6. Mr. Trouble finished third.

the surplus jackets: Adriana Ivancich illustrated the dust jacket of *Across the River and into the Trees.*

the horse story: "The Great Black Horse."

badly torn heart: Another reference to EH's infatuation with Adriana Ivancich.

I look forward to getting the notes on the trip: AEH had requested the notes Mary kept during their excursion from Paris to Nice in December 1949. Mary consented but changed her mind and provided only the travel itinerary. Mary Hemingway to AEH, July 4 [1950], ViU, 6250f.

{35} AEH to EH
May 17th [1950] (TLS, 1 p., JFKL)
[New York City]

Dear Papa:

Marlene [Dietrich] phoned the morning the profile came out disturbed over what was said about her and disturbed that she had not been aware that Lillian [Ross] was present for the New Yorker. I said that I did not think the references to her were derogatory or disrespectful and she said perhaps not but that the stuff about taking towels from the Plaza made her look like a jerk. Later I checked with Lillian who said that not only did she inform Marlene that night that she was present for the New Yorker but that she even discussed with her the possibility of doing a profile of her. I have passed this information along to Marlene and since both sides have subsided I guess the flurry is over. Marlene asked whether you had seen the article before publication and I said I thought you had seen very late galleys but did not know whether you were entitled to make changes, which is the truth.

I think Lillian is a fine reporter and things are as she states them but I couldn't help musing, after I had finished reading the profile, how each observor sees differently. I was not on the Met or Abercrombie missions, but I was present with the Kraut [Dietrich] and I would have given the nod to matters other than the Plaza towel. However, I do not mean to belittle the profile, which apart from the defect of being terribly telescoped, was carefully and well written and, as I said before, honest. Conversations are reported accurately and for the most part the spirit is authentic. If Miss Lillian will travel and experience and grow she will one day sit on top of the heap—don't you think?

I know you are busy with rewrite and I can't help wondering if you have decided to include the long poem. If you ever have a free moment and an old carbon available, I would dearly love to read the rest of the poem—I think what you read to Evan [Shipman] and me was about half, wasn't it?

Love to Mary,

Ed Hotchner

---

the profile: Lillian Ross, "How Do You Like It Now, Gentlemen?" *New Yorker,* May 13, 1950, pp. 36–62.

taking towels: Dietrich used towels borrowed from the Plaza to clean her daughter's apartment (*Portrait*, 55).

very late galleys: Ross sent galleys of the profile to EH on April 26, requiring them back by May 1 or 2. Lillian Ross to EH, April 26, 1950, JFKL. Both EH and Mary marked minor corrections on the galleys. Ross remembers: "In a letter to me dated 1/5/50 (his style), Hemingway wrote: 'It is a good, funny, well-intentioned, well-inventioned piece and I made only the necessary deletion on my mother and corrected her age.' Mrs. Hemingway added on the same letter: 'Compliments on a fine piece—Mary.'" Lillian Ross to DeFazio, September 18, 1989.

Met or Abercrombie missions: Ross accompanied the Hemingways to Abercrombie's, where EH purchased a coat, slippers, and belt, and to the Metropolitan Museum, where they were joined by Patrick Hemingway (*Portrait*, 71–89).

the long poem: Possibly "First Poem to Mary," composed in London in 1944 (*Story,* 483).

{36} AEH to EH
May 31, 1950 (TLS, 2 pp., JFKL)
A. E. Hotchner/415 West 21st Street/New York 11, N. Y.

Dear Papa:

Have received the enclosed letter from Anne Marie [Lacloche] and have sent the enclosed reply; I imagine the thing you would least like to do at this time is delve into the intricacies of the ballet world. I don't know what I was doing there myself. Would you please return Anne Marie's letter after you've read it, for me to place among life's souvenirs.

The sea rolls rough, Captain, and the men are throwing up the dramamine. Every time you choose a street two guys sneak out from an alley and rabbit punch you to death. I used to have a strong neck but now it swivels like my desk chair, if I had a desk chair. But I figure you hang on and mark down the names and remember the faces, never figuring to give it back because you've learned that that wastes the energy in the wrong direction, but figuring to know the shit from the shinola when the sun comes out. But with the sun in, believe me, it all looks like shit.

The FBI now comes to query about some poor devil not seen since law school, 1940, about to have hot stiletto rammed far up. So they put the big glass on the guy—did he ever say anything about conscription; did he go to a lot of vague meetings; did he wipe his ass with Scott's Hammer & Sickle tissue, red tint?—and send in the report. The report. That's all we go by now, isn't it? At Cosmo, when you wanted a guy to write an article or wanted to buy a short story, first thing you phone down to Dr. Matthews and he looks him up in his little report book and gives you the nod or not on him. The report. They should bury <u>that</u> in the Collier's cornerstone. Anyway, all I know of this guy is that he was the best goddam wrestler I ever saw—pinned the Oklahoma A. & M. heavy AAU [Amateur Athletic Union] champ in 2:45; later was Great Lakes and All Navy weight class champ and only meetings I knew about were on the mat. He used to wrestle me one arm and me with my six could just as well have been blowing bubbles. But the report will get him though the Oklahoma man couldn't.

I guess this is the time for the big fish and you are on the Pilar more than off. I am sorry that I forgot to show you the Pilar pictures when you were here. How do the Cuban regulars like the photos of Our Town? I have made other prints and sometimes, when I am sad and I look at them, my eyes water.

My love to both of you,

<u>Ed.</u>

June 1—[Ted] Patrick just phoned again. Would like to give him horse story + word on others. Please let me know.

---

enclosed letter . . . enclosed reply: Lacloche was dismayed that her script had been rejected and that she no longer seemed to have a role in the ballet project. Anne-Marie Lacloche to AEH, May 8, 1950, ViU, 6250f. In his reply, AEH recounted his struggles in placing her script and his rationale for writing his own adaptation. AEH to Anne-Marie Lacloche, May 30, 1950, ViU, 6250f.

Dr. Matthews: J. B. Matthews, "a reformed Communist" who established "an espionage network, digging into the private lives of decent men. . . . In his files were collections of faked facts. He was a natural born mudslinger and had his minions everywhere" (Mayes, *Magazine Maze,* 271).

the Collier's cornerstone: After World War II, Collier's magazine erected a building on Fifth Avenue and EH contributed a note for the time capsule in its cornerstone.

{37} EH to AEH
July 4 1950 (TLS, 2 pp., ViU)
The Finca [*tw*] [Cuba]

Dear Ed:

Am very sorry to be so sloppy about writing but have been busier than a one-armed South Korean. I wrote Lillian [Ross] and told her to give you the Gen. Got the final page proofs done, and several thousand other things and then took a beauty spill up on the flying bridge (very heavy weather and I was just relieveing Gregorio at the wheel when he put her in the trough). Got a good sound concussion complete with fire-works; not stars, the ascending type and when get up it is arterial that is spouting. One of The clamps that hold the big gaffs went in all the way into the skull bone. We contained the hemmorage and made the Finca ok etc.

This is the thing that I always thought helped a writer the least.

Anyway that was Saturday and today is Tuesday. A brilliant sentence in itsself. But I am not at the peak of my best. Anyway I held onto the rail when I hit, broke the fall as well as I could with my shoulders (spine hit the big gaffs) but Pilar is fifteen tons, the ocean more, me 210 and I hit hard. But was up at the count of one and when I saw that bright red spurting I told Gregorio I had to go below and for him to anchor and let Roberto come up astern. (He was in the Tin Kid.)

Then I told Mary to get a roll of toilet paper and put big folded packs on and I would hold them down. She was very good and fast and unpanicked and when Roberto came up we dug out gauze and tape and made a tournequet alongside the left eye.

Very gory story. Ought to sell it to TRUE. If Roberto hadn't been there I probably would have bled out. But vision ok now and on three dressings she has been clean and today hurts hardly at all. Wanted them to take out stitches today but they said it was too deep. Am always bored shitless when am hit or smashed up. Never like to be in bed without a woman or a good book or the Morning Telegraph (Telegram?) so this time decided to not go to bed at all except very late at night.

Now to get to business:

1—about the ballet and Anne-Marie [Lacloche]. I think she should come to N.Y. in the fall and you two people discuss all your differences and reach an agreement. I want her to have top billing, you second and me third. All in the same type. I want her to have 50% of the money the ballet may earn and you and I will split the other 50% thirty to you and 20 % to me. If it is sold to Movies or television I think I should have 50% and you two should split the other 50%.

If this does not seem just we can discuss it. All I want to be is just and good friends.

2—I am sending the sketches made by Adriana to submit to Ted Patrick to illustrate the Good Lion and The Faithful Bull. I do not wish to publish The Great Black Horse. But I have enclosed a story or fable by Count Carlo Robilant which is in the best traditions of the Venetian Fable. You can explain to Ted that there is an entirely new school of Venetian writing and that the Conte Robilant and myself are the heads of the movement. We are going to pass Jean Paul Sartre and all other movements as though they were anchored. Ted can run the two fables by me and the one by Carlo together and Adriana can illustrate them.

You can edit and copy Carlo's fable and have ten per-cent when you sell it. Carlo has four more absolutely formidable fables already delivered to me.

We have another member of the Movement Gianfranco Ivancich (Adriana's brother) working on a novel now out in the Little House which Scribner's want to publish. It is damn good. We have a couple other members of the movement under wraps and they will surprise the public like Bataclan did.

Incidentaly that filly that we liked so much (Lady Nigel) won the Grand Steeple.

And I write books in stiff covers. I wrote Charley Scribner to bet her and he won with her in her last tune up race.

Am made up with the Kraut [Marlene Dietrich].

What are you doing about Mitri and Lamotta? I have 250 on Mitri with no gen. Kid Tunero, here, says it all depends on how big a percentage Mitri has given Jackson's mob of his contract.

Never lose your faith in the honesty of sports boy.

Dick Berlin was very chic and payed my money after [Herbert] Mayes tried to foul out. I would like to see a fight between Mayes and Greb if they were sisters to each other. When I was bleeding out I thought if I could give this old North Cheyenne blood to Mayes how much happier he might be.

Please let me know promptly about the sketches and what you think of the parable by Carlo di Robilant. You might tell Ted Carlo was a great flier in both wars and a naval officer and related to most of the royalty in Europe. Also a founder of the Venice School of writing. Co-Founder with me. We have no

Academic backing but everybody reads the fables aloud in bars and taverns which was where the writing was when it was good.

Would you send a copy of the paragraph of this letter that concerns her to Anne-Marie? I can't find her address and, actually, I can't even lean over to look good.

Give my love to Jerry and I hope the child is fine.

Best always

Papa.

busier than a one-armed South Korean: On June 25, President Truman had ordered U.S. troops to support UN forces in Korea.

Tin Kid: Auxiliary craft that accompanied the *Pilar.*

TRUE: Subtitled "The Man's Magazine," this monthly featured stories about crime, sports, and hunting.

a story or fable by Count Carlo Robilant: Remains unlocated.

(Lady Nigel) won the Grand Steeple: EH may have been thinking of another race, because the Grand Steeple-Chase de Paris was won by Meli Melo in 1950.

Mitri and Lamotta: On July 12, 1950, Jake LaMotta won a 15-round decision over Tiberio Mitri, retaining his world middleweight title.

Kid Tunero: Evelio "Kid Tunero" Mustelier, a Cuban middleweight boxer who defeated Ezzard Charles in 1942 and went on to become a trainer.

after Mayes tried to foul out: In the earliest surviving typescript of *Papa Hemingway,* AEH quotes EH as saying, "Did I ever tell you that after you left [*Cosmopolitan*] Mayes wrote me that the book had not lived up to his expectations and as consequence he was slicing twenty Gs off the contracted price?" Aaron E. Hotchner Papers, box 1, p. 201, John M. Olin Library, Washington University, St. Louis.

Greb: Harry Greb, middleweight champion from 1923 to 1926 with a reputation as a dirty fighter.

{38} EH to AEH
13.10/50 [October 13, 1950] (TLS, 1 p., LOC)
FINCA VIGIA, SAN FRANCISCO DE PAULA, CUBA

Dear Ed:

Glad to hear from you kid. Like getting a new left wing or something.

Here it has been rugged. Mary believes Louella Parsons etc. and the lovely stories relayed, possibly to Louella, came from a girl you met, I believe, just a kid that I have never written a letter to in my life; not vicious nor knowing the terrible damage they can do; but only little girl fantasies. For instance she tells people that she has been in Cuba twice with me; that my daily letters are all she has except that wonderful time we spent in Paris where we won millions on the horses. It is all harmless except to me and maybe two other people. But anyway she is a nicer looking child than the dame that shot Eddie Waitkus. She got her pan on the Cover of the local LIFE. End of situation report on womenies. Gentlemen, I would rather do slow rolls all night long with no altimeter and the needle jiggling in a P51 than be mixed up with crazy womenies.

Beware Hotchner: YOU HAVE BEEN WARNED.

Book goes. 97,000 copies first week. Doubleday-Doran ordered 5000 and sold them out and re-ordered 5000 as of Sep. 13. Another jobber the same and another the same. Critical reaction hysterical both ways. One ex-member of Parliament wrote that I should be hanged. I wrote back offering to have his head examined, free, and to send him, free, to any approved elemental school if he could pass the entrance examinations. Later got a slow burn and called him out quite formally. Naturally he will be a no-show. But have never killed an ex MP and we might have him mounted or dried or something and hung in the garage. Many letters from 8th army blokes who agreed about Monty. Only one unfavourable letter. Most people shocked by the reviews. Maybe we win.

Please give me Gigi [Viertel]'s address. Know nothing about the Salsberg sequence. Also Marlene [Dietrich]'s if you have it. Will write about her if she wants it and it can do her any good. She is in London I know; but not at which hotel. She cabled last from the George V in Paris on the day there was loose talk of amputating my right leg saying she was worried about me.

Also I appreciate the aid you gave me and the good advice in editing the book. Jige's was good too. But I wanted to make the Colonel exactly as a regular army Col. should be with his grave faults. You and Jige showed me the things I should omit. I miss you both very much and we all had a lovely time didn't we? I didn't think Peter [Viertel] behaved too well; but I know <u>wunderkinde</u>. Please tell me too exactly the situation with Ann-Marie [Lacloche] and the ballet.

If she had been around, she would know Rome was not built in a day. Or at least they say so. Maybe it was.

Please ask a price from Collier's on the Marlene piece and keep ten per-cent of it. She was a great hero, truly, and if she wishes me to write about her she has only to furnish me the exact data and I will write it.

Best always and keep better contact unless it is too much trouble.

<u>Papa</u>.

Glad to hear from you: AEH's letter remains unlocated.

Louella Parsons: Hollywood society columnist who had announced on her radio show in early October that the Hemingways were separating because of his involvement with an Italian contessa (*HIW,* 316).

a girl you met: Afdera Franchetti, who said in an interview with *Europeo* that she and Adriana were the models for Renata, that she and EH were in love, that she had visited him twice in Cuba, and that they had spent a month together in Paris (*Story,* 486).

the dame that shot Eddie Waitkus: Nineteen-year-old Ruth Ann Steinhagen critically wounded Waitkus, first baseman for the Philadelphia Phillies, on June 14, 1949. An unflattering photo of Steinhagen, who was judged to be insane, appeared in the *New York Times,* June 16, 1949, p. 23.

Book goes: Across the River and into the Trees was published on September 7.

Monty: In *Across the River and into the Trees,* Col. Cantwell criticizes Bernard Law Montgomery, commander of the British Eighth Army in North Africa from 1942 to 1944, for being overly cautious in seeking vastly superior numbers and firepower.

Salsberg sequence: This reference remains unidentified.

loose talk of amputating my right leg: EH's fall aboard the *Pilar* on July 1 caused encysted metal that had been in his right leg since his wounding in 1918 to travel and rest against a nerve, producing pain and swelling (*Story,* 486–87).

You and Jige showed me the things I should omit: According to AEH, Jigee Viertel joined him in encouraging EH to eliminate passages that might be considered anti-Semitic.

{39} AEH to EH
Nov. 7, 1950 (TLS, 1 p., ViU)
A. E. Hotchner/415 West 21st Street/New York 11, N. Y.

Dear Papa:

The U.S. mails recently brought the enclosed which possibly mystifies you as much as it did me. Perhaps you'd like to know anyway that Marlene is at the Plaza Athene, Paris, as far as I know.

I have heard from Gigi [Jigee Viertel] whose current address is (unless I've confused it with a cheese wrapper): Chesa Grishuna, Klosters, Switzerland. She asks how you are and from the tone of her letter I can tell that a note from you would be a major pleasure. She says, "Peter will be off to Paris soon to begin work on the book, and I will stay here in Klosters to be near Vicky until November. Then a small whirl in dear Paris and back here for Christmas and then until Spring. I think we're going to rent a house here as it will be cheaper than the hotel, and we'll have an extra room. It's magnificent weather here now, bright hot sun and the mountain air and the remote sound of cows bells indicating bovine enterprises on the high meadows. I would trade it all in a minute for Paris natch, but motherly duties keep me here."

I am back in this frigging city and I wonder why. What looked so good ten years ago either isn't here any more or I'm not looking out of the same part of my eyes. It's pushed and flat and the bars that used to be good now have signs on the mirrors to discourage the homos. There seems to be more antique shows, flower shows, met openings and cocktail parties for W. Somerballs Maughm to celebrate the opening of his Tintair Television show, than anything else, and I hear that the fighters at the Garden now use pancake make-up for television. The latter is strictly hearsay and I would not like to be credited as authority for same. So I am working out a Big Plan, note capitalization in lieu of italics, whereby the Cherokees can <u>have</u> the goddam place.

I keep pretty well back from the lit'rary discussion groups but I have read Mr. Schulberg and I think it's a fucking shame. I hope you find time to work and without being crowded but I know that's a lot to ask. I hope it anyway.

Best as always,
hotch

the enclosed: Bill Emerson of *Collier's* wrote to AEH: "Due to circumstances I could not forsee . . . we will not be able to ask Mr. Earnest Hemingway to go ahead with the Marlene Dietrich story." Bill Emerson to AEH, October 4, 1950, ViU, 6250f.

Vicky: Ten-year-old Victoria Schulberg, Jigee's child from her first marriage. AEH, phone call with DeFazio, June 15, 2005.

W. Somerballs Maughm: Author W. Somerset Maugham hosted weekly radio and television series.

I have read Mr. Schulberg: Probably *The Disenchanted* (New York: Random House, 1950), Budd Schulberg's fictionalized account of his collaboration on a screenplay with F. Scott Fitzgerald.

{40} EH to AEH
15/11/50 (TLS, 1 p., PC)
FINCA VIGIA, SAN FRANCISCO DE PAULA, CUBA

Dear Ed:

Thanks for the mysterious missive from Collier's. I suppose it had something to do with that editorial they wrote with the lovely drawing of me. Or maybe they had a surreptitious opening of that famous corner stone and found my message. Anyway would have tried to write something very good about Marlene for them.

This [typewriter] machine, the one you brought, is being used by a number of people, all of them extremely nice, but each time I meet it again something new has been lacking. There's a cat too, named Sun Valley, that can hit five keys at a time.

I'm glad your tennis turned out so well. It's always more fun to come back than to never have been away.

I wrote Jige to the Paris hotel address she gave when I heard from her last. But never heard.

Mary still gives me hell day and night about Jige and to hear the story now you would imagine Jige and I lived in a state of complete and perfect sin in Paris, always, of course, WITH THE DOOR LOCKED.

Have gotten to the point now where I wish the hell it all were true. But anyway we did have lovely times raceing didn't we? And we were a good fast double play combination talking too: J to H to H [Jigee to Hotchner to Hemingway] aided or un-aided by that ancient Calvados.

Have knocked blood pressure down to 140 over 70 and don't have to take any medicine. But legs went bad after that spill on the flying bridge of Pilar (newly varnished deck and wet in a squall. Me comeing over the rail to relieve Gregorio). Got to really hurting bad; really bad. Somebody around the joint referred to it as my imaginary pains so demanded a Court i.e. X-ray and the photos showed 7 pieces of shell fragment in right calf, eleven and parts of a bullet jacket in left calf. One piece was resting on a nerve. Will have to cut it all out. But the one on the nerve was travelling and has hung up for the moment and they think it is encysting again in a good place. All the calf of your leg is a good place to encyst in if you ever want to encyst. Offer this as thought for today.

So-long Ed. I miss see-ing you.

Papa

that editorial they wrote with the lovely drawing of me: An unsigned editorial in *Collier's* (November 18, 1950, p. 86) challenged John O'Hara's positive assessment of *Across the River and into the Trees* (*New York Times Book Review,* September 10, 1950, pp. 1, 30–31). O'Hara declared EH the most important writer since Shakespeare, and in a caricature that accompanied the editorial in *Collier's,* Al Hirschfeld depicted a rotund EH holding a giant pen with which he had presumably slain numerous literary greats.

found my message: EH claimed to have put a note in the time capsule in the Collier's building cornerstone saying "that I hoped that Mary and my three sons were all well, that my friends had prospered and that the world was at peace. I also said that I hoped by then the guy who had been my editor, whom I named, would have gone out and hanged himself by the neck to save everyone else the trouble" (*PH,* 105–6).

would have tried to write something very good about Marlene: EH eventually published an article about Dietrich; see "A Tribute to Mamma from Papa Hemingway," *Life,* August
  18, 1952, pp. 92–93.
Calvados: Spirit originating in northern France, twice distilled from cider.

{41} AEH to EH
Monday [December 4, 1950] (TLS, 2 pp., JFKL)
New York [*tw*]

Dear Papa:
  You sound more black-ass than I have ever known you to be, and it breaks
my heart since I know how much you like to be up on the balls of your feet,
feeling good. I can understand how you feel about the leg thing. Even if the
hurt stops, just being slowed down is a pain in the ass, but so is waiting
around for doctors' cuts to heal up. If you decide to let them take out the iron
works, I hope you get a really good man or else you can wind up with the
limps. As a matter of fact, I wish you'd give some thought to having it done
stateside—I know there are good men there but I don't think the talent and
facilities can equal what the U.S. has to offer. Dr. Hotchsmear will release other
bulletins within the hour.
  A guy called me last week—from what I could gather in the twenty minute
thumbnail he gave of himself he is a very important mouthpiece for N.B.C.—
and asked me if I knew how you'd feel about a television project involving
your short stories. What they have in mind is a weekly program that would
run over the course of a year, each program presenting a dramatization of a
short story. Of course, those stories tied up by the movies would be omitted.
I think they would pay very good dough. The guy said the dramatizations
would be of high caliber and that you could retain supervision of the scripts
through an emissary. He had a lot of other detailed stuff to suggest but I told
him to hold off until I got word whether you had any initial interest.
  Last week seems to have been Hemingstein week. On the train to Philadelphia I ran into Bob Fuoss who is managing ed. of The Saturday Evening
Post and during the course of trading talk (he is a fine guy and you would like
him very much) he asked about you. He said he could not understand why
you had never appeared in the Post which is the most logical place for you to
be and he asked me to tell you that he would very much like to print your
next story. I agree, Papa, that the Post's dignity and coverage is such that it is

the ideal place for your short stories. They are all honorable men who go by their word, respect their writers, pay them good and as promised. Unless you have prejudice against them, please let me send them your next short story, if it's right for them, and I cannot imagine that it would not be.

Another event in Hemingstein week was a visit I had with Dan Mich who is now managing editor of McCall's. Mich used to run Look—a really good guy whom everybody likes. I was in to see him about an article I'm doing, and while I was there I told him that I thought I could interest you in doing an article on Marlene. (It's really too good a thing to drop simply because of the Collier's jerks.) Mich thought it was great for them and he'd like to call it, "The Most Fascinating Woman I Know", thereby enabling you to write the kind of appreciative essay I know you have in mind. I left it at this—I said I'd sound you out on it. Marlene was due back here this week.

Papa, I hate to put you to the trouble and I've hesitated doing it, but I would very much like for you to write in your book [*Across the River and into the Trees*] for me. I'm sending down my copy. I hope you don't mind.

A year ago today we were all in Paris and I was having one of the best times of my life. I think we were all up. I did not see any tears except when we hit the cashiers at Auteuil. That was the last fun I had and it's lasted clear through to now. But I'm running thin, and so are you, if I read right. This is no state of affairs, men. Got anything good in the third? Wish to hell you were around—even this shit hole would be bearable.

Ed Hotchner

Have you read the three-part Shor in the New Yorker? From the little I know him I'd say Bainbridge, whoever he is, was on the junk. But you know Shor lots better. Is the piece true? I mean the overall piece, not the parts.
Have you read Budd's book [Schulberg's *The Disenchanted*]? I thought he was over his head in all but a couple good spots.
Want to buy some Dodger stock? It's up for sale.
Good gal I know named Pat Coffin may be down your way. She drinks very fine + talks splendidly so you may want to pass a couple hours with her to break monotony.

black-ass: EH's term for depression.
the three-part Shor: A profile of restaurateur Bernard "Toots" Shor (John Bainbridge, "Toots's World," *New Yorker,* November 11, 18, and 25, 1950). Toots Shor's Restaurant in midtown Manhattan was frequented by celebrities, sports figures, and politicians.

Want to buy some Dodger stock? In October 1950, Walter O'Malley became president of the Dodgers by purchasing 25 percent of the team from Branch Rickey.

{42} EH to AEH
7/12/50 [December 7, 1950] (TLS, 3 pp., JFKL)
FINCA VIGIA, SAN FRANCISCO DE PAULA, CUBA

Dear Ed:

Thanks for the letter and the gen on the various periodicals. Tell me one thing will you? Mary had a piece ordered and accepted by Flair. What does she do now? When they fold they are still committed aren't they? Let me know about that.

Marlene would have to help with the story and it would be her story as she wants it. I might make a few observations.

Sorry about the Black-Ass. I carefully manoevered myself up shit creek without paddles and it's nobody's fault. A. [Adriana] her mother and brother are here and nights if M. [Mary] has nothing else on her mind she gives me hell about Jigee. You would think Jige and I had been liveing in a state of sin over a period of several centuries and that I was a worse character than Henry the Ate. Everytime we ever went to the races now rates as triple space adultery. Am thinking of doing a few of the things I get accused of nights. It isn't such a bad program.

Want to go over for the raceing when Auteuil and Enghein open in the spring? George will have kept track of the form and we can do the field work and I will brain and watch what happens and we can split the work. Am down to 206 and knocked pressure down to 160 over 70. Had it down to 140 over 65 but Doc claims that too low. The iron re-incysted ok. Am ok if don't ride, or ski. Can fish and shoot.

Going around with your heart sort of a dis-placed person is not much fun but it is damn sight easier than being in Korea and I have no kick and feel ashamed to think of personal things. Worked a big cat 5 ½ years old when the trainer quit on acct. cat was getting bad and now grown up and did o.k. Takes your mind off things. They offered me the job with the two cats (one is easy and the same ones I knew before last year. But thought I should probably stick to book writing.) Circus (the big little one of John R. North's that they bring over here to polish up) is in town and opens tomorrow. Think I'll hang around a while and might do a story. The animals I understand pretty good. Think could maybe write a good story. John North is down here but Buddy North, who with Mike Burke, used to form Hemingstein's Junior Commando's (our specialty was out-stareing the falling buzz bomb after the engine cut out) is up at Sarasota. But I think I can get him down.

The Korean thing takes all the fun out of kidding.

A. and her mother like it here and it is wonderful for her mother. We rode out that big storm down at Escondido. Spray comeing over the hills of the harbour and whirlwinds from where the wind would bounce off the hills like a pelota court. I can't say how hard it blew, trew, but going home, in a hole in it, there was a 1700 ton Italian Freighter high on the rocks like a child's plaything.

Gregorio's and my seamanship (mostly Gregorio's) was so good it didn't show and nobody knew what they had been through (except us) until they read the papers. It had hurricane force without being a hurricane. Caught a fish box full of good mackerel running home and got in just ahead of the 2nd echelon of the storm.

Well the book Mayes thought he had been sold a pup on held 1st place in the Best Sellers for ten weeks in spite of the gang up. What I want to do now is throw with the stories and then bang them with the long novel. Had only <u>one</u> unfavourable letter on it. Some guys have read it 4 and five times and I am truly grateful for you helping me when I was too angry or wrong. The damn Col. was angry often; but you helped me see where to take out the parts that would be misunderstood and make a bigger gang up.

I wonder what they think of their Mac Arthur's and Willouby's now. Sir Charles Willouby the boys used to call him. Phony, a passed-over-liar that nobody would take and really a failed Kraut with an American taken name. There is no reason for a Kraut to change his name. There was no racial persecution nor descrimination when he changed his name. He did it for his advantage.

Bonny Prince Charles; and the people he and the other character got into it; trying to fight their way out to the coast for the eff-off.

Wrote the whole damn thing to three different pros as it began to build and wrote it to Newsweek for their information. Have a carbon. Maybe can get a job thinking for the Guatemalan 3/Eye Military League.

That's part of the Black-Ass. The hell with the personal part.

Buck Lanham wrote me and he has worse black-ass than me. But he always had. It is sort of an occupational disease in the last ten years; only bad when it hits cheerful people. Was always a cheerful and will be again. But this is the first time my country ever fought and I was not there and food has no taste and the hell with love when you can't have children etc.

Thanks for telling me about the Post and the others and give them my best. Especially the Post.

Best to you, Ed. And best from everyone here.

Write anytime you feel like it. Will be here certainly until the first of the year.

Thank you very much for getting Adriana the Holiday work. She will write Ted Patrick a letter thanking him and I will write him too. The Post are good people and always have been. Collier's have been bitches, un-truthful and never complying with their obligations since that one good editor they had died. I've had no dealings with other magazines except Cosmo who were always straight and good until Mayes. Still trust and am friends with Dick Berlin and know Young Bill [Hearst] and get along ok because he knows I always level. It seems as though some of the magazines have gotten over-extended in their egos and try to make a mystique of Success. Esquire, naturally, I know from the start and it was like liveing [in] a cave with cheap thieves without a sense of humour. Dave Smart would steal the pennies from his dead mother's eyes and then gild them and try to pass them as ten dollar gold pieces.

Let me know anything about the CBS. deal or, if too much detail, pass it to Rice. Better that way. What they want; what they will do; what they will pay. Rights to any story for Television to be for one year only. There are many that have no moveing picture tie-up. Also I am doing more. Have five that are checked out. Four more, unpublished, that am checking out. These all unpublished in book form. Also there are the sporting stories. Enclose an uncorrected carbon (you can see where you would have edited it) that TRUE is paying $2000. for. That is not much money with the tax bite, but it is easy to write a straight story. This maybe a little too much laying it on the line. But they wanted me to write a story of a famous shot and I get sick of being called a braggart and played the shot down; but tried to put meat in. They publish under the name of TRUE too.

Am trying to make a good career for A. But it is like handling any colt. Infinite patience.

But we know where we had and have true fun and I always think of you as my soundest and truest friend and am sorry for any bad luck I made you and always ready to fight our way out of anything we get into.

No excuses and no alibis and you can tear the broken nail off your meat hand when the liner hits it wrong; and I never went into second, if they crowded the bag, without trying to cut his legs off. He gives you the ball. You give him the elbow in the mouth.

Not good. But as Giggy said, "They don't have fathers on a ball field."

Best always, Ed.

<u>Papa</u>

You be a good boy and not worry too. When our duty is clear it will be quite clear and we will do it

Papa.

Flair: Mary published "Life with Papa: A Portrait of Ernest Hemingway" in *Flair,* January 1951, pp. 29, 116–17; the magazine folded that same month.

Auteuil and Enghein: Parisan racetracks.

George: Georges Scheuer, barman of the Ritz.

John R. North: John Ringling North, nephew of John Ringling, one of the five Ringling brothers. North owned and directed the Ringling Bros. circus after his uncle's death in 1936.

Buddy North: Henry W. R. "Buddy" North of Ringling Bros., whose circus EH and AEH visited. Buddy North was John R. North's brother (*Final,* 220; *Story,* 387).

Hemingstein's Junior Commando's: Buddy North, Mike Burke, and EH caroused together in London during World War II, calling themselves "Hemingstein's Bearded Junior Commandos," and observed numerous buzz bombs, pilotless V-1 missiles used by the Germans (*Story,* 387, 395).

held 1st place in the Best Sellers list for ten weeks: Across the River and into the Trees actually held first place for seven of the twenty-one weeks it was on the *New York Times* best-sellers list; Budd Schulberg's *The Disenchanted* bumped it from that spot on December 3.

grateful for you helping me: AEH persuaded EH to cut passages that might be perceived as anti-Semitic, offensive to individuals or religious groups, or too sexually suggestive. See Albert J. DeFazio III, "The HemHotch Letters: The Correspondence and Relationship of Ernest Hemingway and A. E. Hotchner," Ph.D. diss., University of Virginia, 1992, 79–96.

Mac Arthur's and Willouby's: Gen. Douglas MacArthur, commander of Allied powers in Japan and UN military forces in South Korea, and Maj. Gen. Charles Andrew Willoughby, MacArthur's Chief of Intelligence G-2 in the South West Pacific. Willoughby changed his name from Weidenbach in 1910 when he became an American citizen.

since that one good editor they had died: Refers to Charles Colebaugh, who edited *Collier's* from 1943 until his death in 1944 (*Final,* 90–92).

Dave Smart: Publisher of *Esquire.*

a story of a famous shot: Ernest Hemingway, "The Shot," *True,* April 28, 1951, pp. 25–28.

as Giggy said: See letter 13.

{43} AEH to EH
18 December 50 (TLS, 3 pp., JFKL)
[New York City]

Dear Papa:

The good letters from you mean a lot to me because you are one of the very few people in the world I really care about and the letters are always exact and tell me how you honestly are. The things that come second-hand are always distorted with the teller's point of view who cares more about himself than the person he's telling about. Anyway, I would say that you are now re-grouping and that G-3 has it all on the boards and that is just fine.

Here attempt is quite similar but there are so many elements that can't be figured. As you know, I'm a major in the Air Force active reserve and I've already received a couple of questionnaires. My trouble is that the outfit I served with-Antisubmarine Command of the U.S.A.A.F.—and the only one I really knew about and became a specialist in, was dissolved as a result of a brilliant political coup by the navy. Navy was always jealous of our command because we were the only air outfit, from Pearl Harbour on, that was locating and sinking U-boats. We flew these incredible airborne coffins, the B-18s, and later B-25s, neither of which was intended for anything even remotely resembling anti-submarine patrol, but we fitted them with depth bombs and flew them. I have a 16-mm. movie which I made for our outfit from strikes and training and I would like to show it to you some time. You will see why the navy was jealous. So we came into headquarters one morning and General Larson walked into the room, or should I say tottered, and his face was white with defeat and he said, "We've been fucked by the navy, men. I trusted them and I was wrong. I'm sorry but you'll all have to be re-classified. Me with you." It was a hell of a sorry speech for a General to have to make but he was not a very able general and he had it coming to him. I pissed around with a couple of heavy bomb groups after that but I wasn't useful so toward the end I switched to Air Force Magazine which was a good move because I went where the tough stuff was and met good guys like Arthur Gordon, Ed Wallace and Mark Murphy. But now when the thing is here again, it's hard to figure the move. At 33, I'm an old, but I told them that if they find the slot where I'll do good, I'll go up right now. Meanwhile, I'm talking with guys I know. Europe is still the vital zone, of course, and where I want to go. Col. Clarke Newlon was in New York last week and we had a big talk over a bottle. He's going to be a wheel in the United Army on the continent and from all he told me, that's my outfit <u>if I can be useful.</u> The time to get that set is before or else you will find yourself sitting on your twat in a Paris garage allocating badminton rackets for the recreational periods of the boys on the line.

So, Papa, Auteuil next Spring (if this all subsides and they do not want me) is the only good thing I have heard for a long stretch. When you think of what we did to them as first season investment team, imagine what will happen with all that experience. Run for cover men, H & H are at the windows! I will bring my fine binoculars which Jack [John Hemingway] very kindly purchased for me, and we will keep the calvados at an even flow and beat them the same way, for they have not learned.

Magazine talk: about Mary and Flair [see letter 38]. There is nothing deader than a dead magazine, as you know, unless it is a dead newspaper. If Mary has already done work on the article and especially if she has finished it, then she should send the material or finished piece and say that she is sorry to learn of the demise but the work has been performed and payment is expected. They are obligated, to the extent of work actually done at the time Mary learned they were out of business. I do not know them nor whether they are honorable but if there is anything I can do you know I always stand ready. Please call on me. You forgot to enclose the TRUE carbon—won't you please send it to me because I would like to see it very much. And I must tell you, for I am your friend and I talk out whenever I think your best interests are involved, that $2000 pay for you is quite bad. TRUE's prices are first line. They pay such eminent journalists as Maurice Zolotow and Ted Shane $1500 and I know that they have paid $1750. I know your value very well. A minimum price for them should be $3000 and $3500 would be better. Of course, I tell you this not to influence this deal which is consummated and must stand but for future deals. I know that you do not wish to get involved in price-setting; however I am more than glad always to handle these things for you if you'd like it. The ease with which you can do the article is not the real measure of the pay— I think a more accurate measure is—what is the value of the property to the magazine for which it is written. Tell me if I'm off on this. Great news that you have several short stories written and it sounds like you have written them when you wanted to write them. I could not tell from your letter what plans you had for them. Again I will talk up and you poke if you think I'm being a guardhouse lawyer. Everything considered, I'd place these at good intervals in the POST, or wherever else they're suited. I think you should do this before they come out in book form. First, because they will bring good dough. Second, because they will have impact on a whole new audience. Third, because the hacks who merchant opinion deserve to be treated to occasional fine writing. I will happily officiate if you'd like. This is my advice and you may forthwith tell me to slip it vertically up my ass and I will make room. As for the Marlene thing, I thought perhaps a short account of what you think about Marlene, how you observed her during the war, a short essay of appreciation, rather than anything that resembles a profile, might be effective. It just seems a pity that other people cannot share the wonderful stories you told me about her. Would you like me to drop her a note and ask how she feels about the project?

Still on the magazines, have you heard about our esteemed friend, H. Mayes, the honorable and trustworthy? As Cosmo's circulation got worse and worse so did Herbie's health—that is, his psychosomatic health—and his imaginary ills finally got so bad that his doctor has ordered him to cease and desist. A young, "personality" advertising-agency-type fellow, talentless, has been made editor and the talk is that it is only a death watch. No advertising guarantees have been met. I feel sad that this once proud magazine has come down this far and that it will most likely die. This is only trade talk but generally it is accurate.

Working the cats must be a hell of a challenge. It is something I do not identify with, however, because I have never been around them and I do not understand them or the men who work them. Also, I have never had the feel necessary for skiing, mostly for the same reasons. For me, the feel I get from a tennis overhead, or waiting, crouched, as safety man to make a tackle with the runner coming full speed—head on, or gloving a fly ball that is beyond and to the right or feeling a home run ball hit the fat of the bat—that kind of feel gets me inside the sport. But that is not to say that watching the cats work or seeing a fine skier does not excite and thrill me. You are right, though, that making words is your business and leave the cats for the men who cannot meet the challenge of stiff covers.

The Gigi [Jigee Viertel] thing is incomprehensible since we know how matters really were. Gige holds high and good in my book. She uses both hands very well for a girl and she holds her head straight. She is the only person I know whom I would vote for if we decided to expand the H & H syndicate. Have you ever seen a better girl at a race track? She has shown some inconsistency but then who of us hasn't? She has been squeezed badly and for this we make dispensations. All in all, she rates fine. And I'll never forget what she did to those strings in the shooting booths.

Thank you very much for the kind things you say about my help on the book. The things I brought up you would likely have edited yourself on the re-writing, but I wanted to talk them out so that the Colonel, angry and army-bigoted though he was, would not give the Opinion boys anything for their distortion mirrors.

I went to see Al Rice last week to talk about Television. I have been finding out everything I can about the situation. I have re-read all of your short sto-ries—at least, those which are in the Modern Library anthology. You know me well enough to know that I do not excite easily. But I am excited about what could be done at this time. Al and I agree that the property could bring a re-ally good price and that on the basis of it being for one performance only, it would retain all of its future TV value. I have not yet had the talk with the CBS people because I first wanted to talk it out thoroughly with you. Here I go shooting off again—the series should be identified in your name. Al suggested that the first deal should be for thirteen stories (then on the next thirteen, if all goes well, we can increase the price). I would try to make this the best thing TV has seen and I think I can do it. Frankly, I was not interested in TV until I re-read the stories and realized what could be done on TV with them. I'd like to produce them myself—by that I mean that I'm pretty sure I can get fine di-rectors like [Elia] Kazan and [Garson] Kanin and others each to undertake one program. Also, on one program bases, I'd like to get Arthur Miller, Sidney King[s]ley, Clifford Odets and the like to do the adaptations. I've sounded out a few of these people just to sample their interest and when I outlined the proj-ect they were not only interested but enthusiastic. I figure if we're going to show in this medium let's show good, the way The Killers came through. Maybe if this thing goes the way it could go, we might put some stuff on tape for you to say, because I think you've got more God damn drama in your voice than all the Greek choruses the Theatre Guild can muster. I don't know. The more I think of it the more of a challenge it becomes. Of course, any part I play in this would have nothing to do with the purchase of the stories them-selves—that would be the best price that Al and I could get. When I did the ballet adaptation of The Capital of the World I got a taste of what could be done in dramatizing the basic, emotional patterns set up by your stories and after I got to thinking about this TV suggestion I saw that this was something I was really interested in. We would give them the best thing they ever saw on their sets, Papa, and maybe the best things they'll ever see. Christ, I'm be-ginning to sound like Aimee S. McPherson. I thought that in addition to CBS, I'd talk to NBC and Dumont. There is no reason why you should not get the advantage of the best offer in this highly competitive field. I would of course have Al in on the money talks and then send to you the best offer and you would be able to tell whether there was enough dough in it to justify a TV deal at this time.

Last year, this time we were in Paris and what a good time we had. Next Saturday morning we pile into the Packard at the Ritz and leave on the best God damn trip anybody could ask for. And if you examine Hemingstein's inside pocket with the flap buttoned you will find it like an extended accordian. I still have half bottle of the good calvados I brought back and tonight's just the night to put an end to my hoarding. Merry Christmas, Papa, and to Mary and Adriana and her mama. And I wish you, all the best possible things in the new year to come.

Your pal,
Hotchsmear

G-3: General Staff, operations and training.

A young . . . fellow . . . has been made editor: David Brown, a motion picture producer, was named managing editor of *Cosmopolitan* in the 1950s. In 1965 his wife, Helen Gurley Brown, became editor and recast the magazine for a new audience of young women.

The Gigi thing: According to Mary, EH informed her around January 1950 that Jigee Viertel had attempted to ensnare him (*HIW*, 290). EH does not seem to have shared this information with AEH.

the way The Killers came through: *The Killers* (Universal, 1946) earned four Academy Award nominations, including best director (Robert Siodmak) and best adapted screenplay (Anthony Veiller).

Aimee S. McPherson (1890–1944): U.S. evangelist.

Adriana and her mama: Adriana Ivancich and her mother, Dora, visited the Hemingways in Cuba from October 28, 1950, to February 7, 1951 (*Final*, 365).

{44} AEH to EH
December 31. [1950] (TLS, 1 p., JFKL)
[New York *pmk*]

Dear Papa:

I guess it is the old lawyer in me that I can't let go a thing until I've heard straight talk from all the people who know. Since I wrote you, I have put together the gen from good guys who make sense: network executives, agency men, packagers, producers, and I think that if the TV thing is handled right it will be a good deal for you.

All hands think this is best time for TV deal because with controls that have recently been put in effect, there's not going to be much change in the situation for several years.

After talking around, I have worked out an idea for you—as far as I know it's unique. The program we would offer would be called "The Ernest Hemingway Theatre" or "Ernest Hemingway Presents" or any other suitable title. For the first 13 weeks it would offer dramatizations of your stories. After that, it would present stories you have liked, with an occasional story of your own included. You can see the great advantage of this arrangement. It allows you to use your own stories sparingly. It provides you with a good income, 52 weeks out of the year. As for the income: I have talked with the advertising men who handle the big accounts: Ford, General Motors, Dupont. I'm enclosing an ordinary cost estimate. You can see how expensive TV is. But I think it's safe to estimate that on weeks when your own stories are presented, you will get around $3000, on weeks when other stories are presented your take will be $1000. Of course, this amount would be definitely set by contract. Over the course of a year, this is good dough. It is understood that the first 13 stories are given for one year only, and only for television. You will note that for an ordinary drama, story rights <u>and</u> adaptation go for $1000, so you can see that I've got them up to a healthy level. Also, there is a strong possibility that in selling a block of stories like this it can be regarded as a capital transaction which means that tax can't disturb it. I'm going to see Al [Rice] today and give him this gen. I hope this appeals to you, Papa, because I think we can hit them with the first real thing they have seen. I can promise you that you will not be bothered by any details, although it may be fun for us to put you on tape or on film and use it at beginning or end of program. Advantage of this would be that I would have to confer with you over cock-fight or at Auteuil.

I received a letter from George Antheil who says he has written you enthusiastically about the ballet. Apparently, he was not aware that I was handling this for you and I have written him to that effect today. No contract has yet been signed—Al is coming with me when it is . . . I mean a contract with the ballet Russe.

If we work out this TV thing would A. [Adriana] be interested in set design. It would be a weekly wage and perhaps it's an artistic field in which she'd be interested.

Papa, '50 was rough but maybe '51 will go good—you know that if ever there was a guy who wished it for you—I'm that guy.

Ed

One Hour	35 stations	63 stations
	$24,600	$36,050
½ Hour	$14,760	$21,630

Figures for CBS and NBC

Cost your program would be $52,890 (hr.)

                              38,470 (½ Hr)

DRAMA (60 min.)

Average cost break-down for programs of this type.

Rights and adaptations	$1,000	
Cast	3,000	
Sets, Props, Costumes	2,500	
Sound Effects, Recorded Music, Art, Film	500	
Producer	500	
Director	250	Too low—plan to pay $750
10 Hours Camera Rehearsal	2,250	
	$10,000	
15% Misc. Station Overhead	1,764	
	$11,764	
15% Agency Commission	2,076	
Total	$13,840	
add 3000, your fee	3,000	
	$16,840	

George Antheil (1900–1959): American composer and acquaintance of EH. Reynolds, *Hemingway: The Paris Years,* 226–27. In 1927 his experimental *Ballet Mécanique* caused a stir in the music world.

the ballet Russe: AEH's friend Alfred Katz, a Broadway press agent, had contacted Sergi Denham, director of the Ballet Russe de Monte Carlo, about "The Capital of the World." Denham presented the script to Antheil, but Denham's slow pace prompted AEH to approach Lucia Chase of the Ballet Theatre, which produced the ballet. See A. E. Hotchner, "Hemingway Ballet: Venice to Broadway," *New York Herald Tribune,* December 27, 1953, sec. 4, p. 3.

DRAMA (60 min.): This is a preprinted form to which AEH added a comment about the director's fee, EH's fee, and retotaled the figures.

On his first visit in June 1948, Hotchner photographed Mary, Ernest, and Black Dog in front of Finca Vigia.

Hotchner on an early visit to the finca.

FINCA VIGIA SAN FRANCISCO DE PAULA, CUBA

June 27 1948

Dear Ed :

        Thanks for the letter ,the enclosures and the two
stories . They came the morning we were shoveing off in boat
for Cay Sal and Double Headed Shot Keys in Bahamas with the
kids who were here on ten days vacation . That was why didn't
answer sooner .

        Enclosed is the contract . So he TOOK the fifteen
thousand dollars .My lawyer is haveing prostrate gland trouble
in Philadelphia and his assistant lawyer doesn't know his prostrate
from a hole in the ground so I haven't heard from them yet .But
if law still same as it was pieces contracted to write by a
bona-fide non-resident written while out of country are tax
free if non-resident out of country over six consecutive
months . Maybe now it is changed but if my prostrated lawyers
find that is so I can give the monies back or just write the
piece and the stories and take the loss same as always .

Will you now please send me tear sheets (tear as in tear

paper not tear as in eyes) or mss. of what any of your other
master minds have written on the Future of Everything so I
get the pitch . You and Arthur both know that I do not know
a shit about the future of anything but will write a good
straight piece about what I think and will try to xxxxixxkxxxxxx
straighten up and think as good as I can .Also tell me minimum and
maximum length .

        It was swell knowing you ,Ed. This isn't
the old craperoo between the writer and the editor . You're very
welcome any time you can ever come down . Please give best
to girl .

        Wish you had been on this trip . We caught
around 1800 pounds of game fish , turned three big turtles ,got
lots of crawfish and had wonderful swimming .That water is
almost virgin fishing and the kids had a wonderful time .I got
down to 210 which is about as low as should go . We have
enough turtle meat to feed the cats for ten days and enough
white eggs to justify opening a whorehouse here in San Francisco
Have the deep freeze full of everything . On four days , fishing
five hours a day we averaged a fish every four minutes . The
Malabar Farm of the Seas and we didn't even have to use manure .

        Give my best to Arthur ;also Mary's . Everybody
tired from trip but feeling wonderful . Would like to take
you there sometime if you would go . No insects ,lonely island good
sanddunes , African vegetation , sandy beaches, salt pond in the
middle ,make a lee with almost any wind , water so clear you think
you will hit a rock when you have thirty fathome over it . Awfully
good life if that is what you like and that is what I like .
        Write me the gen .

Best always

Hemingway's first letter to Hotchner, June 27, 1948.

Hotchner remembers taking this photo of Ernest and Mary in the living room of the finca shortly after their return from Italy in the summer of 1949.

Hemingway and Adriana Ivancich, the inspiration for the young contessa of *Across the River and into the Trees,* at the Bridge of Sighs in Venice, winter 1949–1950. (Photo by A. E. Hotchner)

Hemingway and Hotchner fishing off the pier at the French port of Grau du Roi, 1949.

Hemingway and Jigee Viertel in the Garden of the Popes, Aix-en-Provence, March 1950. (Photo by A. E. Hotchner)

Hotchner's photo of Mary and the cats (see letter 51). The bottom of the White Tower was reserved for the cats, with a separate maternity section.

Hemingway at work on *The Old Man and the Sea* in his study at the top of the White Tower, 1952. He used this study for editing, not composing.

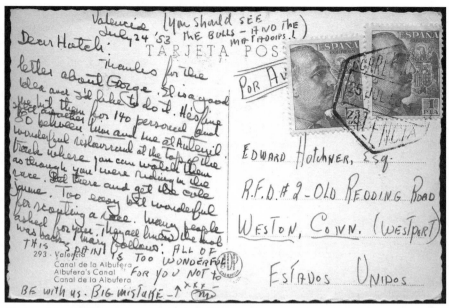

Postcard from the Hemingways to Hotchner, July 24, 1953.

Hemingway and his driver, Adamo Simon, beside the Lancia in which they and Hotchner drove across Spain and the Riviera in May 1954. (Photo by A. E. Hotchner)

During that trip, Hemingway demonstrated his capework for Ava Gardner and Luis Miguel Dominguín at the latter's ranch in Madrid. This is one of the photos that Hotchner says he "snapped at the tienta" in letter 72.

The pigeon target that Hotchner described in letter 59 and enclosed with letter 79.

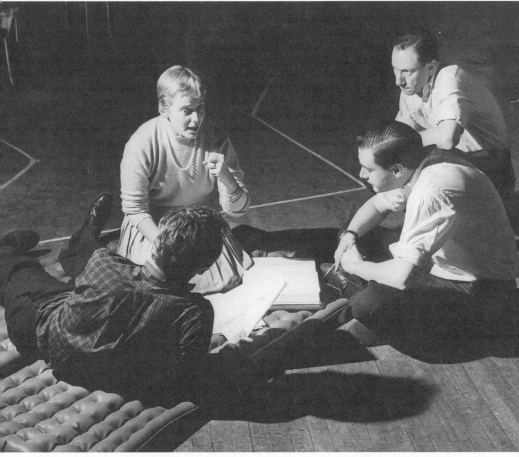

Jason Robards, Jr. (reclining), Maria Schell, director John Frankenheimer, and Hotchner rehearsing the sleeping-bag scene for the *Playhouse 90* production of *For Whom the Bell Tolls*. (CBS publicity photo)

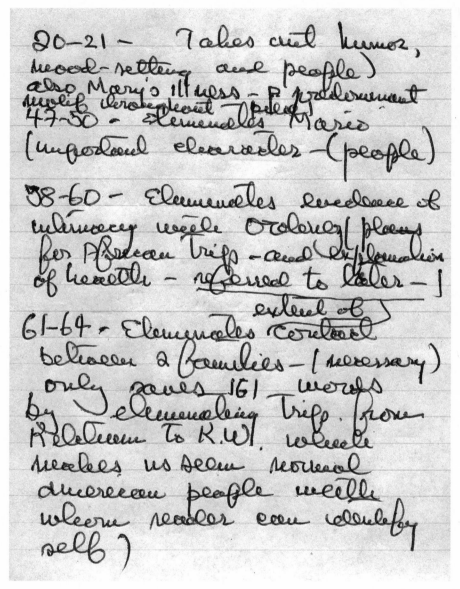

A sheet of the notepad on which Hemingway responded to Hotchner's suggested cuts in the *Dangerous Summer* manuscript; summer 1960 (see appendix, pp. 311–12).

1951

{45} EH to AEH
5/1/51 [January 5, 1951] (TLS, 2 pp., PC)
FINCA VIGIA, SAN FRANCISCO DE PAULA, CUBA

Dear Ed:

Thanks for the two good letters. I would have answered sooner but was jamming on the book. Finished first volume Xhmas Eve. The sea part. But will do the other parts before I publish it. But it's a property already. Not just a piece of un-finished business. I could break it into three books because this one is self contained. But why do it? I have not told anyone a god-damned thing about any part of it and am not going to serialize it either. But Mary read it all one night and in the morning she said she forgave me for anything I'd ever done and showed me the real gooseflesh on her arms. A. [Adriana Ivancich] read it and rated it the same. So have been granted a sort of general amnesty as a writer. Hope I am not fool enough to think something is wonderful because people under my own roof like it. But you'd like it I'm pretty sure and Herbert Mayes isn't ever going to see it until he pays the three dollars and takes his chance.

Let's not talk about the war. I've been training hard and good to be in good shape for it. Plan is to work as hard and as good as I can until it is time to go to it. Then go where you are most useful with whoever will take you. Meantime am not going to get caught in any war of nerves.

Yesterday was A.'s birthday (21). It is hard to believe I have had the luck to know her in 48, 49, 50, and 51. Pretty soon Hemingstein and Ivancich (Bookmakers) will be as old a firm as Lloyd's or Thomas Cook and sons.

Mary is fine and happy. Mouse [Patrick Hemingway] was down here with his wife and Gigi [Gregory Hemingway] showed up with a seventeen year old opera singer with her father who started caseing the joint. Tell Al Rice to brush up on statuatory rape just in case. She is built like an elephant act but sings wonderful in a pure levantine voice. She reminds me a lot of an Armenian tomatoe who was once my night nurse in Billings, Montana. She has a good heart.

The Television deal sounds very good. I wrote Al Rice (who seemed to be sore at me in a letter. But I tried to clear it up. He ought to get out to the track with us more and see what sound people we are) to work with you and put the deal in a presentable form so that everybody knows exactly what they are getting into. Then we could work out details or I could give a straight yes or no on anything.

Don't say anything to Al about him seeming sore at me. You know me better than he does and you know I have defects etc. But I can always get in shape if I can get out of it. And I can pitch double headers when I'm out of shape and love nothing as much as a really impossible situation. This sounds like awful bragging. But you know some of it is true from what we did together. And what I want to do now is write.

So you work hard and let me know how it shapes. Whenever you come down is fine. But let me know plenty ahead.

And we'll be at Auteuil in the Spring.

Flair paid up and the agent's check bounced. Then we are waiting on that next check to see if it bounced. The son of a bitch is bounceing checks in the wrong League. But maybe he just got caught at Christmas. Many have been. TRUE paid $3500 instead of $2000. and claimed they liked the piece. About Marlene: I better lay off it. She doesn't need it now and is rideing high and very beautiful. If you ever see her tell her it was to say how lovely she was; not to make dough for me.

I hope Mayes hangs and rattles. Sorry about the magazine [*Cosmopolitan*]. What became of [David] Brown; the comeing man?

Working cotsies is foolish, of course. I only do it to show off in front of some woman or for straight fun. The fun is to see how they react to discipline without provocation. They are fine, proud animals and will do anything they have been taught until their dispositions are ruined by the people who have to make them snarl and make theatre. I try to go in; make friends with the cotsies; command with a folded newspaper (which you can slap across their eyes if they don't understand we are friends) and not be afraid of them. If you've known lots of cotsies it isn't hard. It is an act that ruins the actual trainers and you can't work more than two at once because it is dangerous to let them get behind you.

I share your views on Jidge [Jigee Viertel]. Let's not talk about it.

We did have a lovely time that year with the track and the trip and the lovely town at the end of it. Thank you very much for the good work in the Television thing. I think we ought to do it.

Enclose uncorrected TRUE script. You will see the corrections I would have made. But only corrected the original. Please don't show it to anybody as I do not know what the ethics are on this.

My own ethics are only to attack on time and never leave your woundeds except to pleasant auspices.

We can get somewhere in this television I think and I could keep on writing as long as we can do that honorably.

Anyway should send this now and get it to you. Mary and I send you and your wife our love and best Christmas, New Year (that Bitch) greetings. We'll fight our way out of this one the same as every other one and on our Television thing, since the year shapes bad, let's work fast and good.

Papa.

The sea part. . . . the other parts: EH's sometimes confusing references to his post–World War II writing are deftly explained by Rose Marie Burwell. Of "the land sea and air book" (see letter 47), the land portion appeared in *Across the River and into the Trees;* the sea portion became *Islands in the Stream;* and the air portion, about flying with the Royal Air Force, never developed into more than a fragment. When EH began writing *The Old Man and the Sea* (New York: Scribner's, 1952) in January 1951, he envisioned it as part of the sea portion. EH often made reference to a three-part "big book"; other material from this project was later published as *The Garden of Eden* (New York: Scribner's, 1986). See Rose Marie Burwell, *Hemingway: The Postwar Years and the Posthumous Novels* (Cambridge: Cambridge University Press, 1996), 51–52. *they liked the piece:* "The Shot"; see letter 38.
Enclose uncorrected TRUE script: This was not enclosed.

{46} AEH to EH
[9 January 1951 *pmk*] (TLS, 2 pp., JFKL)
[New York City]

Dear Papa:

I am so glad you are going good on the book and I think you are absolutely right in holding off until the whole work is finished and in no case going in for serialization. Let everybody play the three dollar window this time. I received another letter from Antheil who seems to think that if he composes the right music this will be the greatest thing ever to hit a ballet stage. Did you know him way back in Paris?

I am delighted that you share my enthusiasm for the television thing, and I hope that I can nail it down fast and solid so that 1951 can be resolutely told to go shit up yon creek. You have no idea how many ends, all loose, have to be pulled together; this is a new field and this is a unique deal but I cannot see but what it will come out pretty nearly as I indicated. In order to give myself some kind of authorization that I may show the Big Wheels at the networks and advertising agencies, I have drawn up an agreement which I think you will find okay. If not, please type up something similar. All I need is something that will show you have authorized me to negotiate for you. Of course, final approval of any kind of deal rests with you. And naturally I will be consulting Al [Rice] along the way. Would you please get this statement back to me soonest? I'd like to move on these guys while their interest is hot. The carbon is for your files.

You once told me that babies should not be seen until they are strong enough to throw their weight around and now that the kid is almost a year old I can see plainly that you are right. She is real fun now and begins to show promise that she will not be a Mongolian idiot. But New York is a bum situs for her—and for me.

I saw J. Louis last time out, on television, and I couldn't believe my eyes. I had seen him both against [Ezzard] Charles and [Cesar] Brion and what the sports boys said was true. That poor paralyzed right hand that stuck against the chest—I've never seen such frustration on a fighter's face as the way Joe looked against Brion, wanting so badly to throw that right when the big openings came, but not able to get it off his chest. But the last fight, Joe must have had a large shot of joy juice because the reflexes were there, almost as before, and the right was working and hurting. Have you ever known it to be, Papa, that the legs held and the reflexes came back and the punch sustained? Ezzard is a good competent fighter but I do not think he would have survived the left hook and the right chop Joe showed. It is really too bad that you do not get the fights on TV—I think it is even better than the movie coverage on the fights I sent you. If the Louis-Charles thing comes off, and if Joe looks as good his next two outings, I shall cover some Charles money.

Please give my love to Mary and A. [Adriana] and I do hope that the coming year will be pleasant and reasonably rewarding for all of you.

hotch

You forgot to enclose the True carbon. Please send it next chance—of course, I'll keep it confidential.

Best,
Ed

I saw J. Louis last time out: After losing to Ezzard Charles on September 27, 1950, Joe Louis defeated Fred Beshore on January 3, 1951.

True carbon: EH eventually mailed an inscribed carbon of "The Shot" to AEH (ViU, 6250f).

{47} EH to AEH
7/2/51 [February 7, 1951] (TLS, 2 pp., ViU)
FINCA VIGIA, SAN FRANCISCO DE PAULA, CUBA

Dear Ed:

Please forgive me for not writing. First I had it in my head that you and Al Rice were comeing down around Jan. 15. Then I began to work like a bastard and went 800 to 1200 to sometimes 1400 words a day and was dead-house pooped afterwards. Plus other alibis that could make and won't. Have jammed straight through and we win.

Anyway that is it. I was working as hard as we ever worked together. Have the sea part of the land sea and air book done (within a week's work) [what became *Islands in the Stream*]. I had it done on Xmas Eve and then saw it needed this third part [*The Old Man and the Sea*] and am in the stretch on it now. It will break the first book of the long book into three separate books, each independent, and each publishable. Am trying to keep my work finished and publishable for whatever comes. On account when it comes we have to go and in the meantime I want to write as well as I can. The whole long book can break into three big publishable books.

Your television deal sounds fine, as I wrote you. But I do not want to quit working for any N.Y. appearances.

News: Mary, Adriana and her Mother Dora left this morning for a trip through Florida, the Gulf Coast and then the Ivancich's leave Jacksonville on February 14 for N.Y. Adriana and her mother, who is a hell of a nice woman, will be at the Barclay from Feb. 15 until they sail on the Liberté on Feb. 23. I wrote Ted Patrick of Holiday that if he was in town I wish Adriana could meet him and he could meet her. He wrote that they were very happy about the fables and the illustrations. Adriana has done much better on this new book.

Mary is comeing back down here the 16th. Charley Scribner is due the 18th to be here until the morning of the 20th.

I'd like to be finished to shoot in the International Championships 21st through 27th. Plenty dough to be made but you have to shoot with the eyes of over-work. Maybe not worth it. Could you and Alfred Rice come down after the 27th and we know what is more or less what by then?

All the news you hear about me makeing deals is shit. I clear everything with Alfred. But they come down and you say the answer is no. But they all want their dime's worth of publicity and say they have you under contract. While they talk to you a guy like this Condon is sweating and jerking like a hop-head who is without it.

Ed would you take Adriana out a couple of times and show her what I would have showed her and keep her name out of the papers as anything but an illustrator? Enclose cost of same, (i.e.) what I would be spending and wish you would spend for me. There is some scandal around Paris and Venice that she is the girl in that book we all wrote. You know this is impossible. However she was over here for several months but she and her mother were visiting Mary and myself and other friends and not spending all their time here. Also she and I are business partners. Bookmakers.

Also give her the true gen on the ballet so she can tell Anne-Marie. I do not like Antheil, nor his music and his name is true box office poison (not that that would matter if his music were good enough. But I don't want him in.) Correct me if I am wrong.

Enclose the two papers. Alfred Rice can execute them for me if he approves. But I have to centralize all this and he writes me he has three mutually exclusive deals. From what he writes and you write I like yours much the best. But I want to hear the whole god-damn thing. Meantime if you need something to show as credentials he can draw it up. Am only trying to protect everybody all around in this.

Wish we did not have to write business. Louis looks good and as though he had sharpened up to beat Charles. You know what Sam Langford said that you could sweat out eating too much and you could sweat out beer and whiskey but nobody could sweat out women. But first, Louis, to get his speed and timing back had to quit eating like a pig. That he seems to have done. Fighters legs go from womens. Ball players from the sudden stops.

What else? Think Adriana should see Metropolitan Museum, Museum of

Natural History, (the African and American halls and if she likes it as much as she can take includeing the fish) 21, Stork, etc. Hope the damned enclosed will cover this. Also one good show anyway. Also Museum of Modern Art and maybe some of the old film shows. If you have to get show tickets contact The Hat Al Howrwits's friend and old fellow member of the Unione Siciliano.

Get a dispensation from your family and give them my love. Tell Jerry I will do the same for her if she hits foreign parts.

Glad baby is in good shape. Will be able to see the famous character in the spring I hope.

Now have to work.

I appreciate everything and I know my true obligation to you.

Papa.

the fables and the illustrations: "The Good Lion" and "The Faithful Bull," with Adriana's illustrations, were published in the March 1951 issue of *Holiday.*

Mary is comeing back down here the 16th: Mary was traveling with the Ivanciches on their way to New York (*Final,* 238).

a guy like this Condon: Richard Condon, publicist in the film industry who later wrote best-selling novels, including *The Manchurian Candidate* (1959).

Sam Langford (ca. 1880–1956): Heavyweight boxing champion of Mexico, 1923. Retired in the 1920s after fighting more than 300 bouts in every division from lightweight to heavyweight.

21, Stork: The 21 Club and the Stork Club, popular nightspots.

The Hat: AEH recalls that movie publicist Al Horwits wore a gangster-type hat, earning him his nickname. AEH, fax to DeFazio, November 29, 2004.

Unione Siciliano: Originally a fraternal organization of Italian immigrants, eventually corrupted into a branch of the Mafia.

{48} AEH to EH
21 Feb 51 (TLS, 2 pp., JFKL)
[New York City *pmk*]

Dear Papa:

I think Adriana and her mama are having a good time. Adriana is worried that she has not heard from you but I explained that you probably are out on the boat. Last night I took them to the Stork for dinner and after to see Ray Bolger in "Where's Charley?" In the past five years Bolger has developed into a comic of true Chaplain [Chaplin] strain and A. and her mama enjoyed him immensely. We have gone to the Museum of Modern Art and Museum of

Natural History and we take the Met by storm tomorrow. I was embarassed at the showing at the Museum of Modern Art. All the good things I wanted to show were out on loan. I've never seen such a piss-poor collection in the years I've been going there. If it hadn't been for the Lembrooks, an early Dali, the Guernica, and a couple of novelties—a tree of babies by some character named Tchelichew and Levy's green Mussolini—I could just as well taken them window shopping at Gimbel's. A. had a fine time, however, at Mr. Roosevelt's memorial and since it had been several years since I had been there, I enjoyed it too. I think she was most impressed with the crustaceous dinosaurs. They have been to see "Kiss me, Kate," a musical version of Mr. Shakespeare's "Taming of the Shrew", with music by Cole Porter who composed it on a lyre to preserve the mood, and this afternoon, with the help of the Hat's friend, I got them tickets for that Manhattan gold mine, "South Pacific." Tonight, they will round out their theatre-going with "Guys and Dolls," which is a fine musical based on a Runyon story. Afterwards I will take A. to some chic boite that I'm sure she'll enjoy—like Le Ruban Bleu. She wants to see New York Cafe Society and that should do it nicely. Ted Patrick is going to take her to lunch at 21 Friday. The reason for all the musicals is that that seems to be what A. enjoys best. I wish, Papa, that I would not have to use the money you sent and that I could manage this, but, unfortunately, I am operating in close quarters and I have almost no room to move around. I get by fine but that's it. However, I am keeping accurate count.

My plan is to fly down the night of Feb. 28th and I'll phone you the next morning. I think Al [Rice] plans to arrive late that day—he's going to fly over from Florida—and then we can take accurate readings and plot the course. I think it all shapes good. In the past two months, I have talked to most everybody in the business and I have kept Al closely briefed. So you know the lode has been worked here's the people I've had dealings with: James Caddigan in charge at Dumont, Carl Stanton of N.B.C., Charles Barry of N.B.C. radio (it ocurred to me that I could make simultaneous deal for radio and I have a good one), Underhill at C.B.S. (his inquiry started all this, if you recall), Rosenthal at M.C.A., packagers: Lester Cowan, Robert Souvain, Het Mannheim, Jeff Jones, Weenolson & Ryerson, Mannie Reiner, Ted Ashley Assoc., an independent producer named Martin Stone, Arthur Pryor at B.B.D. & O., Riéber at J. Walter Thompson, and Chet La Roche at La Roche and Co. The two or three that sounded right I had Al meet to get his reactions and I think we're on solid ground and that we will keep the name okay with healthy payments to Dr.

Hemingstein. Anything you or Mary want transported? God-damn but it'll be good to see you again. Too bad there isn't a local track that we can punish. Very best always,

Ed

the Lembrooks, . . . the Guernica, . . . a tree of babies by some character named Tchelichew and Levy's green Mussolini: Sculptures by an artist named Lembrook; Picasso's *Guernica* (1937); Pavel Tchelitchew's *Hide and Seek* (1940–1942); Peter Blume's *Eternal City* (1934–1937), which portrays Mussolini as a green-headed jack-in-the-box. Julien Levy was a New York art dealer who exhibited surrealist works.

Mr. Roosevelt's memorial: Reconstruction of the Manhattan brownstone where Theodore Roosevelt was born.

{49} EH to AEH
Easter Sunday 1951 [March 25] (TLS, 1 p., ViU)
FINCA VIGIA, SAN FRANCISCO DE PAULA, CUBA

Dear Ed:

Thanks very much for your letter. Am so sorry everybody was so sick in the family and that Al's mother died. Am writing him; not that anything you can write about such things is worth anything.

After I got your letter made three wire reels on three days straight and the first two were worthless. The third I sent off by air-mail yesterday. In the first my throat wasn't sore but the soft-palate swollen and sort of a hang over from the really choked up sore throat I had; when it was so sore you couldn't swallow. Then I did 4800 words week before last and 4900 this last week and I was pooped.

I'm spooked about the whole thing, Ed. If there was some way you could sell the stories without me talking or mugging I would give anything. I'm going so damned hard now and in a real belle epoque and every morning I wake up worrying about TV and all its angles.

For instance: The Fifth Column, that you wanted me to read the introduction to on this wire, is a subversive play now. It wasn't when it was written. But I don't want to be a TV personality in a probe of TV and explain to some committee, that wouldn't believe me, that I love my country and would fight for her against all enemies anytime anywhere. (Doing this when I should be writing a novel.)

Then I start to worry that I might get a recurrence of that skin condition when we have to work takeing pictures or my throat be bad and that I would let you down that way.

I worry bad, and I'm not a morning worrier, and I have to start working before it is properly light to quit worry.

So I work until I'm dead and that kills the worry and me too. But it isn't much of a life.

Then I worry about the City of Venice and whether I have harmed anybody there with scandal that they do not deserve to have. This handles my afternoon worrying and leads into my night and before daylight worrying which is this deal. Hell if we could only make some money and me not have to photograph or talk. Isn't there any such deal?

It's not, I hope, that I am yellow on this but I truly hate to take on something that I've never been checked out on. A guy like Don Ameche who was down here has poise, clarity, naturalness and charm and it would be no strain at all on him to do such work because he is a pro. I could write what he had to say because I am a pro at that. Cooper could do it. But it ties me up in knots.

So write me what you think. They might pay more dough for people like that. I agree it would be a fine thing for the program to have me if I was good and it did not destroy my other work. But I still think you could have a hell of a program with someone else if I wasn't there to maybe louse it up.

Please let me know what you think. Mary sends her love and we are both truly sorry everybody was sick and hope all better.

Best always

<u>Papa</u>

your letter: AEH's letter remains unlocated.

made three wire reels: AEH recalls: "I asked Ernest to record a few paragraphs on his Webster wire recorder to demonstrate to the network executives how he would introduce 'Ernest Hemingway Presents.' When I visited him in Cuba, during our discussions he seemed perfectly willing to host the series, but obviously he had changed his mind." AEH to DeFazio, September 27, 2004. AEH preserved some of these recordings on long-playing disks (ViU, 6250f, phonodisc 520–25).

skin condition: erysipelas; see letter 9.

Don Ameche (1908–1993): Film actor who served as master of ceremonies for radio programs and as co-host of television's *The Frances Langford–Don Ameche Show* (1951–1952).

Cooper: Gary Cooper (1901–1961), star of *A Farewell to Arms* (1932) and *For Whom the Bell Tolls* (1943), joined EH on hunting expeditions in Idaho in the 1940s.

{50} AEH to EH
April 10, 1951 (TLS, 2 pp., JFKL)
A. E. Hotchner/415 West 21st Street/New York 11, N. Y.

Dear Papa:

I asked a friend of mine at N.B.C. to listen to the wire with me and there's no doubt that with a couple of minor suggestions you could go against any radio pro and give odds. My friend said it was one of the best sample takes he had ever heard.

Now I have done some preliminary digging on the problem of making a deal without your participation. The chances are slim. If only your own stories were involved, it might work, but when the program gets around to presenting a Guy de Maupassant story that you like, that's when it becomes unfeasible. And, of course that's the only way that the program can have any longevity. Another point: Al [Rice] was counting on your pay as "actor" to up your take because it is tax-free, since it is performed in Cuba.

But I have put the Don Ameche-Gary Cooper thing before the Thinkers and it is still up, but interest, I can tell, is way down. So I'd say, it looks like if we drop the participation, then we must revert to selling an occasional story to various dramatic shows. One compromise might be left—we might be able to work out a radio deal (for less dough, of course) that would require a little talk participation. Since this is done way in advance I don't think you would have any worry about throat, work, etc., do you? However, radio is like the model A now and nobody is buying new programs—thus, I don't know whether such a show would have a market.

So I'd say to beat the worry rap, better forget the whole project. If an offer of any kind should come through, I'll send it along and you can re-consider it. I can tell you this: I edited the film I took and ran a section of your wire (I've transferred it to tape) in back of it; I had four guys I know (advertising agency, network, 2 producers) watch it and I only wish I had taped their enthusiasms and sent them to you. But I certainly respect how you feel and, as I have said right along, how you feel is all that counts. I'll keep on figuring it and maybe come up with a solution.

I've got tickets for the Dodger opener and I certainly wish you were here to come with. Looks like the Yanks have a real winner in Mantle. I try to follow the fortunes of my old love, the Cards, but no can do any more without bottle of ipecac. Saigh sounds like number one on the jerk parade. Saw their boy Poholsky pitch last year and he certainly looked like he had it. Great control and change-up. The part of the new stuff you read left no doubt why you don't want to fuck up your work schedule with TV; it's right in the same vein as the old man and the sea and, having heard just that little section, I feel like the guy who went off his nut because the second shoe didn't drop. It's a hell of a section, Papa, and from the bottom of my heart I hope that they don't break in on you and they give you this stretch all to yourself so you won't have to brake at all on this ride.

Clan healthy; I'm putting in the Conn. crops this week so we can eat out of the ground all summer. We dug for soft shell clams and came up with 94 which provided the biggest orgy since O'Dwyer fed off the Fire Dept.

Love to Mary.

Ed

Saigh: Fred Saigh and a partner purchased the Cardinals in 1947.

new stuff you read: Probably the "Sea Chase" section of *Islands in the Stream* (Burwell, xxi).

O'Dwyer: William O'Dwyer was elected mayor of New York in 1949, but poor health and scandal—he was accused of accepting money from the Uniformed Firemen's Association—prompted his resignation in 1950. James A. Hagerty, "Crane Testifies to O'Dwyer Gift; Jury Record Used," *New York Times,* March 22, 1951, pp. 1, 25.

{51} AEH to EH
[mid-April 1951] (TLS, 2 pp., JFKL)
[New York City]

Dear Papa:

Please strike the TV worry off the list. You and I have been partners in several ventures now and what we do in stride we do, and what we have to break stride to do we don't do. Before I set this TV up in the form we discussed, I gave a lot of consideration to the possibility of having a Cooper do the actual appearing and talking. I know you pretty good and I knew from the start that the performance part would be a pain in the ass. Trouble was, anyway I figured it a Cooper would have two drawbacks: (a) whether you believe it or not, E. Hemingway is much more of an attraction for this kind of program than a hybrid of Cooper and Gable (and Grable too for that matter); (b) when you bring a Cooper into the deal you have to pay big dough; since the whole point of the deal was dough, it seemed illogical to take a big bite out of what I wanted to get into your coffers. However, maybe I can fix some kind of deal that will fetch you enough money and keep you out of it. I'll do my best, Papa, and, as they say in "Guys and Dolls," more you cannot ask. Seriously, we have the basic appeal of the very best short stories and novels that anybody has between covers and that is the best equipment you can ask. Maybe I can work out some kind of rotating appearances in the introduction spot.

As for "The Fifth Column", I'm sorry that I didn't explain that the wire is for presentation use only. If "The Fifth Column" is included in the series, I am well aware of the dangers you set forth and I do not aim to put E. Hemingway on limb with Hotchner sawing. However, in my judgment, the play can be so adapted to television that none of its dramatic value will be lost, although all controversial (and I use that term in its broadest sense) stuff will be eliminated. But that's something for much later. The wire is for a totally different use.

By the way, the film (movie) I took came back yesterday and it's fine. I ran it off last night and all I can say is that G. Cooper and C. Grant are lucky you took to the typewriter. Also, said he modestly, the color I took of Mary is great. I'm enclosing prints but of course color prints are so poor compared to the original. And I'm very pleased with this picture of Mary and the cats. I've done a 11X14 enlargement and it's quite exciting.

I manage to keep quite busy doing all variety of shit. I've been working on my hound along the lines you suggested and he's better. Please keep well and think only about what a really great book you are writing and accept my apologies for having worried you up with the TV thing. However, you know that I meant well, as I always do, and I'll do what I can to lay off our bets.

My best love to Mary.

Ed

Gable (and Grable too for that matter): Film actor Clark Gable; film actress and "pin-up girl" Betty Grable.

the film (movie): AEH's footage of EH and Mary at the finca and aboard the *Pilar* survives, as do several photographs of Mary taken at the time (ViU, 6250i).

{52} EH to AEH
April 13 '51 (TLS, 2 pp., PC)
FINCA VIGIA, SAN FRANCISCO DE PAULA, CUBA

Dear Ed:

Thanks for the two fine letters and the beautiful prints of Mary. There are a lot of womens in this highly disorganized world. But Miss Mary is a lot of woman in a handy and readily available package and she never had to hit any couches in her lifetime which compensates, and not only financially, for her carefree, spendthrift ways. (Am so fucking tired of writing like me, or like writing, putting everything on every ball and being my own re-lief pitcher that am now writing to you in the style of the late, and was he late, Henry James.)

I feel like a heel about not going through with the Television now and also loseing a chance according to your rateings to be the Ezio Pinza of the Poor. But if I interrupted the way I'm going now I ought to be taken out and hanged by the neck until dead. I know you know about it and you are so damned straight and good about it.

Here is a possible solution: Couldn't we make a deal for the fall of 52? I'll stay in shape and between now and the summer of 52 I will write my guts out. I don't think I will have a change of voice and I already had a change of life in Hurtgen Forest.

Couldn't we do that so all your work wouldn't be loused up? They could insure me with Lloyd's. Blood pressure was down to 140 over 70 on the check up night before last and I would truly keep in shape; fish two days a week and work five. I'm a good writer and I will work at it good and I don't think will be less valuable then than now.

Last week I wrote 2361 one day and 2142 and 1081 and 1157. Then I knew I was bearing down too hard but I ran around a thousand a day all this week. It has been blowing a gale from the south all week and we couldn't get out to fish. Now it is straightened out and the glass is riseing and the wind will go into the North and then we should get the trades. There is a big purple current and the stream is full of fish. Maybe we can get out tomorrow.

Are you eating o.k.? I wish there was some way we could postpone this and still eat. Maybe we can work one out.

I don't want to chop it up but keep it as one big deal. But at the same time it would be nice as hell to eat. But as long as I am hitting around 1000 words a day of the really good it is ok to borrow to eat from Charlie Scribner. I pay him interest and there is three and a half times as much book as I would be justified in borrowing on.

He, Charlie, has a 876 page book by a 135 pound writer named Col. James Jones who went over the hill by his own publicity in 1944 (not a vintage year for that) and it recounts the Colonel's sufferings and those of his fellow in-mates in the Army of the United States to such a paranoic degree that it gets almost sad if you are a type who saddens up easy. I don't believe Col. Jones will be around for very long. But maybe he will be with us forever. Maybe you could cover by obtaining the services of Col. Jones to say exclusively fuck on

Television. Anyway it is Charlie's idea of a book next to something by Taylor Caldwell. But I will just write on as good as I can. There is an old Spanish proverb that says if you have a twenty dollar gold piece, and it is gold, you can always get change for it.

If any of this is too metaphysical knock me on the head with your own mallet.

Mary sends her best. It is good to know you are all well. Ed please write me absolutely frankly and tell me if you think I am being a shit or a coward about any of this. I am a pro and I will understand completely. The thing is that I live absolutely and completely in this book and I do not care about anything else. I would much rather be shot than not do it as well as I can; and doing it perfectly gets longer and longer.

Alfred [Rice] wrote me about the Antheil thing. It is o.k. to go ahead with Antheil since you made the commitment (one T missing) as in Notre Dame. I don't want to louse up everything in the world. Maybe Antheil is better now and maybe he really learned his stuff scoreing things. You have my o.k. to go ahead with him. OK. EH. I am sure he was a better musician than I gave him credit for always. But he was such an opportunist and a letter-down of his friends that I could have cramped my judgement on him as a musician. What is it the old White Owl cigar ads said, "Spit is an ugly word. But it's even worse on the end of your cigar."

Always rated that with "Drink Schlitz in brown bottles and avoid That Skunk Taste."

But I am probably unjust about Antheil and if it is so that he should do it let him go.

Maybe the horse can win once. He should have always won.

Ed, would you mind showing this letter to Alfred. I am writing him formally about his mother's death. But this will save time on business while I can get back on the book.

Haven't been able to follow the ball teams. The draft act. makes it difficult and then all the virus infections and injuries incline you to lay off. I don't see a solid Team. Maybe a couple; but big maybes. Horses are simpler so far. Fights I can't figure. Gavilan rated to beat that Chicago boy. But then maybe I am being patriotic. I wouldn't bet on any animal that can talk except myself.

Have to work.

Best always and to your family. Your daughter is really beautiful. Please tell Jerry.

Papa.

Ezio Pinza: Star of opera and Broadway who hosted *The Ezio Pinza Show* on television (1951–1953).

a change of life in Hurtgen Forest: In November 1944, EH accompanied Colonel Lanham's Twenty-second Infantry Regiment during a two-week battle in the Hurtgen Forest on the Belgian-German border; 87 percent of the men were casualties (*Final,* 117–18).

Lloyd's: Lloyd's of London, a British insurance market.

a 876 page book by . . . Col. James Jones: From Here to Eternity (1951). Jones belonged to the new generation of writers with whom EH was competing.

Taylor Caldwell: Best-selling author of popular fiction.

the old White Owl cigar ads: The slogan was apparently used by Cremo cigars, which claimed that some "other cigar makers . . . would spit on the end of the wrapper leaf to make it stick." David Westheimer, "Words to Live By," http://www.senior women.com/articles/david/articlesDavidWords.html (accessed May 2, 2005).

draft act.: In June 1948, President Truman signed an act requiring men aged 19–25 to register for military service.

that Chicago boy: Kid Gavilan would defeat Chicago's Johnny Bratton at Madison Square Garden on April 18, 1951, winning the World Welterweight Title.

{53} AEH to EH
May 1, 1951 (TLS, 1 p., JFKL)
A. E. Hotchner/415 West 21st Street/New York 11, N. Y.

Dear Papa:

Of course I don't think you are chickening in any way on the TV thing. You are first and always a writer and all matters that might interfere with your trade are to be resisted. We both recognize the importance of dough in the scheme of things, but I don't think either of us has ever let a buck get in the way of good living or friendship or kicking a son of a bitch in the ass or side-stepping the ulcer or knocking down on what we consider the proper level of operation. I have called off the TV dogs, however, there is one deal that has developed to such an extent that we would all look like jerks if I were to say that the word is to back off. There is a good chance that this thing won't jell and then we are all clear. If it does, I will grab the arm lock and wrestle it. The TV brains tell me that the effect of withdrawing and holding until '52 will be bad because the word will go out that there were no takers, which, obviously, is not the case. I do not accept their brainpower or their prediction. I will guide this thing best I can and if a way develops to make a deal and not bother you I will move in on it.

I have been working hard on the Conn. fields, putting in the assorted green life that will fill assorted guts for the summer. If only they had a seed that would thrive in solid rock life would be much easier. I have put in enough strong young asparagus root to warrant fresh hollandaise by the hour. The farmer next to us up the road is a good guy about his equipment so I've been able to farm up a good area. I did find time last week to stand in the Aspetuck which has a nimble current and is only a couple of minutes away, and I hooked into a fine fat bass that was Spring sweet. Local carpenter is providing me with another little shack—that makes four—because the Hotchner tribe is expanding, maybe this time a boy, but it isn't very important to me. I happen to be a set-up for little kids right now.

The hysteria over MacArthur has given me a permanent upset stomach and I want to run hide and be a French or an Italian.

Hope the work goes good and steady. Give Miss Mary my love—glad you liked the pictures.

As ever.

Hotchsmear

The hysteria over MacArthur: MacArthur's differences with Truman about how to pursue the conflict in Korea led to his being relieved of command of UN military forces in South Korea on April 11, 1951.

{54} AEH to EH
10 Oct [1951] (TLS, 1 p., JFKL)
A. E. Hotchner 415 West 21st Street New York 11, N.Y.

Dear Papa:

This has been a shit summer, up and down the line. Now I hear you have had it too and so has Mary and I am sorry as all hell. Has it cut into the work? If it has then it is doubly awful because I know the beautiful way you were going and the old man alone in his boat making his catch and then losing it to the sharks is as clear and powerful in my mind today as it was when I first read it. To know that you have this section all done and locked away must be like 100 Gs in the safety deposit box. If it were mine, those typed pages, I would be the richest goddam guy in the world.

A friend has sent me an article from the Sept.–Oct. Partisan Review that describes Lillian Ross' visit to Hollywood. Have you seen it? If not please tell me so that I can send it to you. I would like you to read it so that I can discuss it with you, but on a closed circut.

[Paragraph omitted]

Too bad you weren't around for the baseball finish. The whole town was up for it, and I was at Belmont the afternoon Thomson won it. Never saw a track crowd less interested in the nags, only radios, and the roar that went up on Thomson was something to hear. I went to see Counterpoint run and he looked damn good. The steeplers were only fair, but that is surely an attractive course. I wound up with a little win money but without Dr. Hemingberg figuring the sheets I didn't expect to go any too good. My love and sympathy to Mary and my best always to you.

Ed

Lillian Ross's visit to Hollywood: The *Partisan Review* piece grew into *Picture,* "the first piece of factual reporting ever cast in the form of a novel"; it traced the difficulties encountered by John Huston as he filmed *The Red Badge of Courage* (1952; reprint, New York: Modern Library, 1997), v.

[Paragraph omitted]: Restricted by the John F. Kennedy Library, Boston, MA.

the baseball finish: Bobby Thomson's three-run homer gave the Giants the third and final game of the National League playoff series against the Dodgers at the Polo Grounds.

Counterpoint: Winner of the 1951 Belmont Stakes in Elmont, New York.

1952

{55} AEH to EH
Thursday [January 17, 1952] (TLS, 2 pp., JFKL)
[Washington, DC]

Dear Papa:

Thanks for the good Christmas card. We sent no cards at all this year although we thought about it. It was one of those projects on the right hand side of the ledger that never got done. In fact, I don't think the ledger has even got a left hand side—or maybe it just seems that way.

I have been running my ass off for a couple of weeks on an assignment that involves, God help us all, the Congress of the Yewnited States of Amurrrrica. I am now ready to throw in what's left of my sponge and settle for any place you care to mention. I defy anyone to hang around these bird brains for one week and not wind up playing Russian Roulette—solitaire. Maybe it's just that I'm a senile now but it seems to me that these servants of the peeepull have gotten a hell of a lot worse since the last time I came here and got nauseated. But a man must work at these things if he is going to keep up his installments on his A & P bill and I should be philosophical about it but I'm not.

I went to the Uline Arena last night to watch the Golden Gloves semis. Big local favorite, a 148-pounder named Quattacchi, got cut up and dropped to his knees twice by a lithe colored boy named Thomas who has pro class. On the whole, though, the boys looked less good than the last card I saw three years ago (I've had it, I guess—living in the past the way I am). Only two white boys on the card—both novice and senior, about 25 matches. Now when the coloreds start to go I suppose Chinese laundrymen will start training in droves. Never has been a yellow champ (pun utterly accidental and would erase it if I could.)

Please tell Mary that This Week saw the picture I took of her and all the cats and is going to run it. They are going to run a couple of paragraphs of innocuous copy with it. What ever happened to the article she did for Cosmo? I've given up reading anything but the Congressional Record so I may have missed it.

I have not seen Peter Viertel's movie, Decision Before Dawn, but it has received very good reviews in the New York press. I have not heard from them since they were in Switzerland, which is a long time back. Have you?

Although I have always been most interested in editing work, as you know, I have decided that since I am in this free-lance status I had better make the best (term used advisedly) of it. So I took two fast left hooks at the short story, and although I was uncomfortable and they are not very good, I sold one to the Post and the other to the Journal. When and if I ever write one that shows at least a little ground speed I would like to send it to you. Now to go from the ridiculous—I do hope the book is working your way and pounding into the shape you want. I have not seen Rice or Scribner for a long time and I am all out of touch. But of all the guys you've got up in the stands yelling themselves hoarse, you know I'm the loudest, and that's the way it will always be.

Please give my very best love to Mary and know that I want you to have a fine year.

Yours,

<u>hotchsmear</u>

Christmas card: Three undated Christmas cards survive among the correspondence between Mary and AEH (ViU). One features the *Pilar;* inside, Mary writes, "OOO XXX," next to which EH writes, "Very criptic. But I'll sign. OK EH." Under the card's printed message "Merry Christmas - Happy New Year," EH writes, "Should we just say merdre this year? Am writing Hotch." Another features the three wise men and the manger in Bethlehem; inside, EH writes, "So glad that show was good. Very proud of you. Writing Papa." The card signed by Mary alone features the Eiffel Tower.

an assignment that involves . . . the Congress: AEH remembers that the assignment was to write an article for *This Week,* a Sunday supplement.

This Week . . . is going to run it: A. E. Hotchner, "Hemingway's 50 Cats," *This Week,* January 20, 1952, p. 14.

the article she did for Cosmo: Probably Mary's article about the Havana Marlin Tournament, "Girl at Sea," *Cosmopolitan,* January 1952.

Decision before Dawn: Adapted by Viertel from George Howe's novel *Call It Treason.*

sold one to the Post and the other to the Journal: "What Happened to My Little Girl?" describes the conflict that ensues when a girl turns seventeen and quits accompanying her father to Dodgers games. *Saturday Evening Post,* September 29, 1951, pp. 34–35, 98, 100, 102, 105. In "Till Death Do Us Part," a man who believes his wife and daughters have been killed in a plane crash discovers that they missed the plane and are alive. *Ladies' Home Journal,* April 1952, pp. 42–43, 106–9, 111–12.

{56} EH to AEH
July 21 1952 (TLS, 2 pp., ViU)
FINCA VIGIA, SAN FRANCISCO DE PAULA, CUBA

Dear Hotch-Maru:

Thanks ever so much for finding that opening for Miss Mary to write a piece. You are so god-damn loyal and thoughtful and I am so sloppy and bad about writing.

There was a big pile-up of merde last year with everything that went on with Pauline's death and I would have needed street sweeper equipment to write for a while. Didn't want to write you gloomy letters and gloom was thicker than [Rocky] Marciano's ankles.

Today am 53 and so start turning over a new leaf to write you and tell you how damned much I appreciate your friendship and your old fast double play loyalty.

Hope we win with this book [*The Old Man and the Sea*]. The B.O.M. [Book-of-the-Month Club] will straighten me out on the tax money I had to borrow from Scribner's and get me off the hook here. The LIFE will pay the taxes and straigjten me out (old Holland spelling) and then if it sells with Scribner's poor old Papa will emerge into the clear. The good thing is what is already on paper and re-written once and gone over again to back this one up. I thought it was stupid not to bring The Old Man out since it was complete in its-self. Hope you agree.

Read about the Snows of Kilimanjaro yesterday and how there was only one minor alteration. The man lives instead of dying. We must look on that as a very minor change don't you think? Now all we need is to have that poor bloody Colonel get out of the back of that Buick car and walk back to Venice and walk down the middle of the canal (this is a symbol) and into Harry's Bar dry shod. A minor change, Hotch. Or should we say a clever bit of editing?

Didn't you think that Lillian's pieces on Hollywood were excellent? I mean superior. It was such a damned sad story and a hell of a lot better than most novels. I'm glad she has come along so well and was very proud of her.

How are you really, kid? I wish we could see you. I miss you very much. If we can make it I want to get over to France. Mary wants to go there and to Italy too. I don't think I should go to Italy and if I go to France and don't get in touch with Venice it is as bad, and if I do it is worse. Who said a dilema had only two horns? He must have been fooling around with little dilemas before they were of age. A real dilema (spell it yourself) has between eight and ten pairs of horns and can kill you as far as you can see it and vice versa.

What do you hear from Peter and Jige [Viertel]? Did they have a baby? Somebody told me Peter had written a book about Houston. No, I read that.

George [Scheuer] wrote me despairingly about the horses he had that would have to win and couldn't be put off any longer. We probably just wasted a year at whatever we were doing. That was a lovely fall though wasn't it?

Am trying to be so good now for such a long time that I stink. You get a sort of ropy odour of sanctity. When we all used to be in an absolutely impossible situation everything was much simpler. Give me a reading on this. You sound as though you were being pretty impossibly good yourself.

I miss Charley badly. Who is left that ever stuck together when things were really impossible? You are who is left.

Adriana writes. She is very loyal and loveing and remembers the wonderful times you gave her in New York. She is 22 now and I wish she would make a brilliant marriage.

Hope Matthews beats Marciano. But Marciano is an awfully strong boy. The word I hear down here is that times are really bad for the boys and that no favorite can win. An awful lot of the boys are down here now due to the hot weather Dr. Coonskin televised. It was heartening to know that Ruby Goldstein recovered from his heat prostration and that honest Sugar Ray also will live. Well Hurley used to win with Billy Petrolle. Maybe he can win with Mathews. But watch the switches in the betting. Marciano really is strong too and always in good shape and he can ruin anybody he can hit. Anybody can be hit. Mathews is no great hitter. But he is a good boxer and a sharp hitter and he likes to fight. Marciano doesn't like to fight and only likes the money. If Mathews could keep from getting hit and work Marciano over really I think the hit would go out of him. Marciano has short arms too. But Savold showed that, as of then, he didn't know how to fight a short armed fighter's fight. I can't imagine a guy pulling back his hands the way he does and not get clipped. But as they say he is a terribly strong boy.

How is your tennis doing, Ed? I haven't done anything but swim and fish. Had one run of luck when hooked and landed 14 out of 15 marlin strikes. Usually you are doing good to get three out of five. Very good actually. Was in awfully good shape but then the weather went bad a week ago. There was an undeveloped storm here that never could get going. I think it made a lot of your heat up there. Today the weather is straightening out.

Blood pressure was down to 130 over 65 on June 24th the last time they took it. This is without any medication. Haven't used any medication for it for nearly two years now.

Mary is healthy and fine and quite happy. You would be pleased to see her.

Bumby [John Hemingway] has decided to stay in the Army and will go regular army. He has had superiors for the last two years so it is a good deal. No chance of a career in civil life at his age as a reserve officer liable to call. Good chance of career in the Army. He is at Ft. Bragg now and was down here two weeks ago for the week-end.

So long, Ed. Thanks so much for thinking of the thing for Mary. If there is ever anything I can do ever let me know.

Your friend

E Hemingstein alias Mr. <u>Papa</u>

that opening for Miss Mary to write a piece: Eventually published as "Living with a Genius," *Modern Woman,* September 1953.

everything that went on with Pauline's death: EH's ex-wife Pauline Pfeiffer died on October 2, 1951, after a disturbing conversation with EH about their son Gregory's personal troubles.

old Papa will emerge into the clear: The Book-of-the-Month Club would publish 153,000 copies, which earned EH $21,000, enough to repay Scribner's the money he had borrowed to pay his taxes. The September 1 issue of *Life,* which carried the story in its entirety, sold more than five million copies and earned EH $40,000, of which $24,000 was relegated to a special tax account. Scribner's first edition of 50,000 copies sold out in ten days and the book remained on the *New York Times* best-seller list for 26 weeks (*Final* 258; *Story,* 504).

one minor alteration: In the movie *The Snows of Kilimanjaro* (Fox, 1952), the character of Harry Street, who dies in the short story, is allowed to live. EH ironically suggests that Colonel Cantwell, who dies at the end of *Across the River and into the Trees,* might as well be allowed to live, too.

Lillian's pieces on Hollywood: Lillian Ross, "No. 1512," *New Yorker,* May 24, 31, June 7, 14, 21, 1952. The title of the series came from MGM's production number for John Huston's film of *The Red Badge of Courage.* The articles were collected in book form as *Picture* (New York: Rinehart, 1952).

Peter had written a book about Houston: Viertel's *White Hunter, Black Heart* (New York:

Doubleday, 1953) was a fictionalized account of working with John Huston during the filming of The African Queen (1951).

I miss Charley badly: Charles Scribner III died on February 11, 1952.

Hope Matthews beats Marciano: Rocky Marciano would defeat Harry Matthews in a second-round knockout at Yankee Stadium. New York Times, July 28, 1952, p. 22; July 29, 1952, p. 24.

Ruby Goldstein . . . Sugar Ray: Sugar Ray Robinson suffered from heat prostration in his June 25 championship bout with Joey Maxim at Yankee Stadium, losing in the fourteenth round by technical knockout. Ruby Goldstein, the referee, succumbed to the 104° heat in round 10. New York Times, June 26, 1952, p. 34.

Hurley used to win with Billy Petrolle: Jack Hurley, Matthews's manager, managed Petrolle from 1922 to 1934.

Savold: Lee Savold was knocked out by Joe Louis on June 15, 1951, and lost by TKO to Marciano on February 13, 1952. James Dawson, "Louis Knocks Out Savold in Sixth and Gains Chance for Another Title Bout," New York Times, June 16, 1951, p. 10.

{57} AEH to EH
[**August 1, 1952**] (TLS, 1 p., JFKL)
A. E. Hotchner RFD 2, Old Redding Road Weston, Connecticut

Dear Papa:

The phone rings yesterday midnight and it's Mickey Murphy to say in that flat too-controlled way that Mark is dead. The clip that appeared in the morning paper gives you the details. I know you did not know Mark very well, and only met him briefly, but he liked you enormously and I thought you'd like to know about him. Whatever it was that got him, I mean really got him not the medic label, was always there to see and so was the quick finale because he was burning himself up with deliberation. Last time I saw him we had lunch at Costello's and he had been drunk for four days. He made no sense and I was sad for a week after. He entered the hospital on July 4th for a "mild liver sclerosis" and then it complicated into hepatitis jaundice, oxygen tent, transfusions, boom. I've had the jaundice, London style (you, too) and I would not like to have to fight it in a rummy condition. So Mark is gone and so is another good friend. Died on his 40th birthday.

What I have to tell you about the Viertels has to be rated against the source for accuracy. I got it from Ted Patrick, the Holiday guy, who knows both of them well. But it's hearsay, nonetheless. Gigi, according to mine informant, gave birth to a child about two months ago. While she was still in the hospital, Peter announced that he had fallen in love and was divorcing her to remarry. This is now in the process of being accomplished and I presume Gigi will turn up on these shores fairly soon with an infant. With that good clear eye of yours you called the shot on that guy and he's performed for you right to the wire. Our mistake: we should have let him go back and take that hot bath.

Can't tell you how glad I am that the new book has shaped financially the way it has. Guy on the Reader's Digest whom I know quite well was over last night and I told him thought Old Man was fine for them and he is going to bring it before editorial board if they have not already considered it. Said I didn't know whether you wanted it to go there but that you always liked to consider offers. They pay fine dough for that book spot and you might like to pick that up, too. Artistically, the book is a better shot than Bataclan II. It hangs with me real good, all the power and details, and it's been a couple of years—well, almost—since I read it.

Sorority here is in good shape, although dog met face on with skunk last night and it's either him or us. Please give my best love to Mary and remember me to Roberto, Sinsky et al.

Hotchsmear (Bloody)

The clip that appeared in the morning paper: AEH enclosed a clipping of Murphy's obituary. *New York Times,* August 1, 1952, p. 17.

Peter announced that he had fallen in love: Viertel identifies the woman as Bettina Graziani, a French model. Peter Viertel, *Dangerous Friends* (New York: Bantam Doubleday Dell, 1992), 155–61.

we should have let him go back and take that hot bath: Alludes to Viertel's unwillingess to join EH, Mary, and AEH on a sightseeing trip in December 1949 (see letter 61). AEH, phone call with DeFazio, June 14, 2004.

that book spot: Reader's Digest Condensed Books were omnibus volumes, each containing several condensed best sellers.

Sorority here: The Hotchners had had another daughter, Holly.

{58} EH to AEH
August 4th 1952 (TLS, 1 p., ViU)
FINCA VIGIA, SAN FRANCISCO DE PAULA, CUBA

Dear Ed:

Am awfully sorry about Mark [Murphy]. I knew him in a very concentrated way because I met him the night we had the gen that put us in the Death

House for that river crossing opposite Trier that was to be made with the support of 2,000 heavies bombing through the over-cast. This was a combined dream of [Gen.] Georgie Patton and [Brig. Gen.] Orville Anderson. I used to go out to report back to Buck Lanham on various aspects of the development of this project and then go into Luxembourg in the evening to get drunk so as not to think about it dureing the night. I would see Mark then and naturally I could not tell him we were in the Death House. But after it was called off I told him and he was very understanding and loveing the way people are who really understand such things. He didn't drink too much then and I was very fond of him. He was working on that Air Force magazine then. Did he quit eating at the end? They say that is what brings on the cyrhossis (mis-spelled). But they say so many things. I never learned to spell cyhrossis figureing that by the time you had to spell it that it would be too late. Poor Mark. Scott [Fitzgerald] took the same way out no matter what they tell you. It seems to be an Irish ending. I wish I'd known Mark better because he was an awful good guy.

We picked a winner in Peter [Viertel] didn't we? What do you suppose he divorced Jige for? Because he was anti-semitic? I'm glad there is one guy left that I can make a joke like that with.

You ought to get your copy of Der Alte und Das See this week. Hope it stands up. Don't know about Reader's Digest. But thank you, kid. That is a second serial right which means a split and if it came too soon it could hurt the regular Scribner sale and that is the one I declare to win with. The other monies just get me off the hook.

Christ I wish we were going raceing again. The old Hemingstein to Hotchner to Chance was the best double play combination I ever had anything to do with. Do you remember when the poor touts were comeing to us for the word? And the man who said one sees that Monsieur is of the metier.

Did I write you about some of those of the metier I've met down here due to the great Television inspired exodus? Imagine if you and honest Alfred [Rice] and I had gone into Television and then somebody had dug up that I had been honorary president of the Chicago chapter of the Unione Siciliano. We certainly would have given an adequate explanation I know. But it would have been awkward to keep on explaining up at some place like Dannemora.

Have been trying hard to keep within the framework of my new semi-Christlike dignified character. But Hotch I am afraid it cannot last. Last Friday night a character so over-grown that he looked like a side-wise Primo Carnera came up to us at the Floridita and picked one. I nailed him with two left hooks and a right chop and turned my back and never looked at him. Bar room fights are stupid as we both know. But this one would have made a funny slow motion picture because I didn't spill my drink, turned away without looking to see what happened, and went on talking to the character on my right. Busted the second knuckle on the left hand though, bad, and raised a long sort of leech-like blister on the right from the way a chop glances. Sorry I hit him. Glad they can still be over so fast nobody sees them.

Hope you'll like the book in stiff covers. I'm waiting to get mine here to write in it for you instead of sending one with a card, since you read it before.

Love to your family. Mary is working very hard on her piece and eyeing me clinically. If you want a fast book with a card in it instead of a written in book let me know.

<u>Papa</u>

that river crossing opposite Trier: **Campaign to cross the Rhine and capture the German city of Trier, January–March 1945.**

Hemingstein to Hotchner to Chance: **A takeoff on the Cubs' famed Tinker-to-Evers-to-Chance double-play combination.**

the great Television inspired exodus: **Many television writers blacklisted in the McCarthy era left the filmmaking centers of Hollywood and New York.**

Dannemora: **New York State prison.**

Primo Carnera: **1933 heavyweight champ who was six feet six inches and weighed 260 pounds.**

{59} AEH to EH
22 Aug [1952] (TLS, 2 pp., JFKL)
A. E. Hotchner RFD 2, Old Redding Road Weston, Connecticut

Dear Papa:

Mary's editor just phoned me and for 15 minutes told me how splendid he thought Mary's article was. I am so glad. Of course I take Miss Mary's proficiency with typewriter for granted. I hope sitting for the portrait was not too much of a pain in the ass for you. The plain fact is that the peoples want to know and if they want to know it's certainly better that they be told straight and good rather than with chi-chi and distortion and the other tricks.

Papa, I'd love to have the written in Old Man and would vastly prefer it to the card in. The advance page in today's LIFE certainly sets it up, but no matter how high they are prepared for it, it is going to rock them and leave them with the pit of their stomach hurting, the way mine did and still does when I think about it.

Last week I visited where the types were of the country club, and along with some c.c. tennis I found myself involved in a shooting contest. I have not had a gun in my hand since the brave team of Hemingsling and Hotchplotch roamed the land, annihilating pigeon eyes. (I'll never forget the look on the face of the old woman in Nimes who watched with dismay while the cardboard flew from her pigeons' eyes, only to have you present her with the champagne we had won with the request that she drink to the health of Auteuil's finest marksmen). But here I am at the c.c. paired off with some arrogant son of a bitch who is still disgruntled about MacArthur. He's got the costume right out of Esquire and a specially tooled gun. I've got on what I've had on for the last five years, and a gun mine host hasn't had out of the closet since the Civil War. But my opponent has had his martinis and I have had only two gins with tonic so I shoot like it was with the pigeons and he is no problem. Next two matches never shot better but in shoot-off with the club champ I unsteadied and lost. So they hand me a silver dish thing which is just fine for the baby's teething problem. I wish Mary had been there for the women's moving clay target; she could have shot over her shoulder. And with good light you could have spotted the champ three targets. He was damn good, though.

I guess it's too pat, but certainly one of the contributing causes to loveable, laughable Peter's behavior is his desire to preserve himself in a young, bohemian, artistic state, whatever that may be. Gigi, of course, was responsibility. And maybe too much female for him. But you stuck the label on him when he was two days off the boat and the shot was as you called it. Very rough on Gigi. Whatever Peter's trouble, he should have had enough decency to hang around long enough for her to get her bearings. But we don't have all the facts, so the sermon may be cock-eyed.

I have a couple of magazine jobs offered but prefer to limp along like this with the hope that I can work out way to transport this sorority to France October 53 to live for a year or more. Plan to get house with lots of room and can't think of anything more appealing than to have you and Mary in residence, especially during the races. The New York-Conn axis is something I would gladly not turn on for a good long stretch. The going, men, is dull . . . something which Paris and the environs knows not the meaning of. Have you travel plans? I suppose lots depends on the money end of the book.

My dog Pango has just come up to the door with a much-bloodied wood-chuck in his mouth so I'd better give him the praise he wants. The first wood-chuck he ever met up with last summer bit the shit out of him and the vet had to stitch him and shoot him with the penicillin. But he knocks them off now like the critics will go on the book and I think he has rather distorted ideas of his hunting prowess. But I encourage him. Nothing wrong with a distorted idea kept within bounds.

My love and congratulations to Mary and best luck to you on the book. It's surer than Bataclan.

Ed

sitting for the portrait: In June, Alfred Eisenstadt had come to Cuba to photograph EH for the *Life* issue that would feature *The Old Man and the Sea.* The afternoon heat had bothered EH (*Story,* 502–3).

the advance page: A week before featuring *The Old Man and the Sea, Life* ran quotations from EH's letters and an endorsement from James Michener. "From Ernest Hemingway to the Editors of *Life*," *Life,* August 25, 1952, p. 124.

the cardboard flew from her pigeons' eyes: EH and AEH were shooting at cardboard targets of pigeons.

1953

{60} AEH to EH
[February 25, 1953 *pmk*] (TLS, 2 pp., JFKL)
A. E. Hotchner/415 West 21st Street/New York 11, N. Y.

Dear Papa:

Out of nowhere, a letter from Jigee [Viertel]. I know you're still interested, though the stock fell pretty low, and it is damn sad. She is in Switzerland, a joint called Haus Masura in Klosters. She writes: "Around Christmas time I found myself thinking about that peculiar but fine Christmas we all had in France. These have been strange years since then. There have been separations, good times, violent times, trips to the hospital in disservice to the race, also trips to the hospital in service of same. There was even two months in Africa, in Papa's old territory, which I fell in love with, in spite of obvious spoilage. The well known material truly hit the fan last March a month before I was to have the baby Peter finally agreed to, when he decided he was in love with someone else and departed. I had a grim Caesarian, then had to go back and have it done all over again as they had left nondissolving stitches inside. A capital affair all around. I was in bed for three months, not feeling quite at peace with the world. However, there is now a splendid new citizen, Christine. A fat, healthy, terribly funny small edition of Peter. I am living in Switzerland again because we've lived here for two winters, and Vicky loves the school and speaks German well and it's fine for the baby, and Paris is too expensive (I've had to batten down my hatches considerably) though natch I would prefer it there. Hard, though, with a new baby to live with gaiety but no heat. There was no point in going back to what is no longer home since I cannot work. The Committee and all that. In the spring I'll have to decide where to go, how to live, etc. But this winter I'm still planless and bleeding more than a little. I feel like an elderly, worthless egg in jelly. I guess I will stay in Europe. Where else is there? I have been set adrift, but like Papa's brother have a strong desire to weigh my sea anchor. I have to pull myself together, but so far I've been dwelling mostly in Martiniland which is perhaps the best country after all. I finally met Papa's friend, Buck Lanham, in Paris, at a terrible party given by the Goldwyns and Zanucks. I got quite loaded sitting between these gentlemen who were trying to convert me to the Eisenhower group. Lanham began to press a bit, sort of a flushed flirting, and I got a bit testy with him. I could see where he would have been fun with Papa, though. Do you write Papa? If you do, give them both my love and tell them whatever you think they may like to know about me, if anything. My, how I would love to hear from them. Papa's book is great—now if only he would write some of the stories about his childhood that he told us. God, do I wish we could all be together again now for a short burst."

A guy just back told me he saw Peter who talked like he was on the verge of returning to his role as family man, so this is the gay little fuck-up we all got to know so well. But Jigee I shall always like, her failings noted, and it grieves me to know she's beat like this, as I'm sure it does you. After all she was a charter member of the only worthwhile track syndicate I have ever belonged to.

I hope Mary relayed to you all the good reactions I had on re-reading the book. You ruined fighting for them, and now they can't touch the sea without debt. I'm so very glad that Charley [Scribner] got on this one before he died. It made him very happy.

I am going down to do a round-up on the Florida ball camps and I plan to wind up in Key West and spend a week or so floating. I've rented a little cottage near the water—always wanted to spend a little time there because you've told me such good things about it. Any chance that you and the Mary might be on the water and would put in for a visit? I'd love to see you. I leave Sunday and figure to be in Key West around the 4th. Mary seemed so damn happy when she was here it made <u>me</u> feel happy. I don't know anyone in New York as happy as Mary. Or any one I'm as fond of. All my love to both of you.

<u>Hotchsmear</u>

The Committee and all that: The House Un-American Activities Committee and its blacklist.

Papa's brother: Leicester Hemingway built a boat and sailed it across the Gulf of Mexico

in May 1934, arriving in Key West just before EH's *Pilar* was delivered. He crewed
for EH aboard the *Pilar* and also went on his own expeditions. Leicester Hemingway,
My Brother Ernest Hemingway (1962; reprint, Greenwich, CT: Fawcett, 1967), 131.
Mary seemed so damn happy when she was here: Mary mentions going to New York "on
September 25 [1952] for a week" (*HIW,* 354).

{61} EH to AEH
March 10 1953 (ALS, 1 p., LOC)
FINCA VIGIA, SAN FRANCISCO DE PAULA, CUBA

Dear Hotch-Maru:

Thanks very much for the letter and the word on Jige. Made me feel awful.
I guess there is not much to be done. I'll try to write her a comic letter. With
the luck and bad management she has it's a good thing she never got mixed
up with, say, airplanes. She would have been dead in 1937. But we did have
a fine time right up to Aix en Provence. I started to lose a little faith the first
time when we couldn't get them out of the car to see the Maison Carré in
Nimes that beautiful morning. You know for a dime they wouldn't have seen
the arena and Aigues Mortes was a place to make a picture to Peter.

Probably all those 18 month non tax guys will be the founders of the next
great American Fortunes. The former ones were founded by the people who
didn't fight in the Civil war (1861–1865).

Down here we just hurry up and wait on, of all peoples, Leland Hayward
and Spencer Tracy. Have installed a giant bulldozer to serve me the shit I have
to eat each day. Everyone in the high jerk off notch about 3D pictures etc.
Haven't seen as much panic since I used to hang around Italy as a boy. Hope
to get the hell away and to Africa soon.

You didn't give me any Key West address so this probably won't reach you
until you get back. Wish you'd have come over here instead. If you get this in
time, by luck, and feel like it fly over. It's lovely now and you know how we'd
love to see you.

Evan Shipman came over and nearly died on us but is odds on to live today.
Any day he lives you can bet on him to work the next.

No news. Book goes unbelievable in foreign parts. Steady at 800 a week in
U.S. Everything ok in Italy but I'm a sad son of a bitch if it isn't a long way away.

Mary well and happy and sends her love.

Best to you kid.

Hemingstein.

Leland Hayward: Broadway producer and friend of EH who convinced him to publish *The Old Man and the Sea* in *Life* (*Story,* 499) and took an option on the film rights (*Final,* 260). Spencer Tracy would star as Santiago.

Hope to get . . . to Africa soon: On May 12, EH would sign a contract with *Look* editor William Lowe providing him with $15,000 in expenses for a safari and another $10,000 for a 3,500-word article (*Final,* 263). *Look* hired Earl Theisen to photograph the safari.

Evan Shipman came over and nearly died on us: Shipman was ill with pancreatic cancer (*Story,* 495).

In June the Hemingways spent a "few days in New York to verify shipments of rifles, shotguns and ammunition from Abercrombie's to Africa" for a safari (HIW, 370). On June 24 they embarked aboard the Flandre, docking at Le Havre on June 30 (Story, 511). They spent most of July in Spain, attending the bullfights in Pamplona and touring. On August 6 they boarded the Dunnattar Castle in Paris, bound for Mombasa, Kenya (Final, 266).

{62} AEH to EH
Saturday [July 11, 1953 *pmk*] (TLS, 1 p., JFKL)
A. E. Hotchner R. F. D. 2 Westport, Conn.

Dear Papa,

I had a fine time seeing you and Mary, as I always do, and the joint seems to dull up when your boat pulls out. I am sorry you did not see a better ball game the one chance you had, but I have no confidence in the American League. I would like some day to sit with you and watch the Brooklyns and the Cardinals—that is my idea of a ball game, no matter what the score. I have seen them tangle many times and I have yet to see a flat game.

Today I got a letter from Jigee, saying how she had phoned the Ritz on the outside chance and there you were and how good it was to talk to you again, so good she cried a little. There was talk in her letter about being roughed up on passports and how the kid was coming back to summer in the U.S. alone. It sounded like she was trying to act content. How did it come over the phone?

The This Week mob asked me if you would write a short article for them and I said that if the subject was one you would like to write about, and the price was equivalent, roughly, to what we won on Bataclan II, you might. So they asked me what you might like to write about and I said that was like trying to guess three daily doubles in a row, but they finally thrust their stilettos against my belly and I told them that maybe a short piece about George [Scheuer] might interest you. I said, though, that you'd have to get around a buck a word for such efforts, thinking that would scare the shit out of them, but the enclosed letter shows they don't scare easy. So, if at some point, Papa, you would like to produce this article, or any other, all this gold awaits you.

I pulled a giant charley horse in my left thigh yesterday and I am now hobbled while a perfectly good tennis day goes to waste. I have been playing better than ever before in my life and it is enormously satisfying. I hope this leg thing doesn't throw me off.

I hope you and Mary have a great time; I certainly envy you. Next year, so help me, I'm going to get over and stay. Love to both of you,

Hotchsmear

I am sorry you did not see a better ball game: On June 23, EH and AEH watched the Yankees lose to the Chicago White Sox of the American League. In a piece written later that year, AEH remembered attending a "Yankee–White Sox game at the Stadium last summer" with EH and seeing Yankee pitcher Allie Reynolds "absorb a terrific pasting." A. E. Hotchner, "Hemingway Ballet: Venice to Broadway," *New York Herald Tribune,* December 27, 1953, sec. 4, p. 3.

the enclosed letter: From C. B. Roberts of *This Week,* dated June 30, 1953: "We all like the idea of Mr. Hemingway doing a piece on George of the Ritz—the man who can arrange anything. . . . from 1500 to 2500 words would fit us nicely. . . . will pay $1,000 for a look at such an article, and an additional $2,000 if it works out for us."

{63} EH to AEH
July 24 '53 (ApostcardS, 1 p., ViU)
Valencia [hw]

Dear Hotch:

Thanks for the letter about George. It is a good idea and I'd like to do it. He's fine. We hit them for 140 personal and split another 80 between him and me at Auteuil. Wonderful restaurant at the top of the track where you can watch them as though you were riding in the race. Bet there and get the cote jaune. Too easy but wonderful for scouting a race. Many people asked for you. They all knew the mob was back. Mary follows: All of this Spain is too wonderful for you not to be with us. Big mistake—X X X—M. (You should see the bulls—and the matadors!)

cote jaune: Odds sheet.

Mary follows: The rest of the card was written by Mary. On the front of the card, which features a man polling a masted skiff along a canal lined with houses, Mary writes: "Like Venice—But it's Valencia."

{64} AEH to EH
12/1/53 [December 1, 1953] (TLS, 2 pp., JFKL)
A. E. Hotchner R. F. D. 5 Westport, Conn.

Dear Papa Hemingstein;

I hear bits from Counselor Alfred [Rice] about your Safari and where you are and what a fine time you are having and it makes me extremely sad ass not to share this one which I am sure is even better than our celebrated assault on Paris and points south and east with Venice as the last battlement to fall before our deadly pigeon (cardboard and clay) shooting. I miss you and Mary very much, and the little stretch I see you, impresses on me all over again what good friends you are.

I have give up the city, and the city me, and bought a big joint with lots of ground—about six acres I think—in a section knows as Greens Farms. I know you rate this area shit low on your chart but as long as I have to stay in the vicinity of N.Y. I honestly don't think I can do better. There was a beautiful young deer standing in front of the house yesterday evening and it stood there long enough for my kid to hop out of her skin with delight. So that's fine. Although now she goes outside every ten minutes or so and waits for the deer to re-show. That's like playing Bataclan a second time. But now I have this joint—me and the bank, that is—I am trying to scheme and plan a way to spend the year in France or Italy that I've been promising myself. I would rent the house, of course. Well, that's the Big Plan, Colonel, and we ain't even checked out on the Semi-Big Plan.

The Tee-Vee boys, may they all have chronic dropsy, (whatever became of Dropsy . . . or Eva, for that matter) are finally coming around after a couple of years of more conferences than I ever hope to have again. I got the Ford Foundation Omnibus program to do The Battler for $2500, which is about the most anyone has ever paid for any source material on The Medium (this is said in a hushed voice with violins behind) and now after three years we've finally brought off The Capital of The World. It's been a long grind but Ballet Theatre is doing it with Eugene Loring (he did Billy the Kid) doing the choreography.

It will first be done on Omnibus on Dec. 6th and then will have its world premiere at the Met Dec. 27th. Big, fancy occasion, boys say. Ford will pay or has paid $3000 for this one. I have several other stories that I'm sure will go now—Gambler, Nun & Radio, Today is Friday, couple of others. By the way, what do you want done about Ann-Marie [Lacloche] in relation to the $3000? I have hopes I may lead this into a movie sale, so that should be borne in mind. The script they are dancing is mine, not Ann Marie's, but I believe you had some basic thoughts on the subject which you may have relayed to her. At any rate, please pass me word so I can tell Alfred [Rice]. Sorry to trouble you with vexious item while on your holiday, but I didn't want Ann Marie to make the first move. Thought you'd like to make it.

Couple of nights back I edited the film I took of you, Mary, Roberto etc. (movie) in Cuba, and some of it is okay. Maybe on your way back, if it's through here, you'll have time to see it. Have you plans for the return, or are you just floating? Last letter to Gijee, no answer. Peter, I see, is doing a new script for Huston which, on the heels of the book, leads a man to speculate.

On the whole, here, all the wrong ones continue to die. Please give my fondest love to Miss Mary, carefully preserving hunk of same to yourself.

hotchmareo

Dropsy . . . or Eva: Topsy and Little Eva are characters in *Uncle Tom's Cabin.*

I got the Ford Foundation Omnibus program to do The Battler: Omnibus broadcast an adaptation of "The Battler" on October 11, 1953. AEH's own adaptation of the story would be broadcast on NBC's *Playwrights '56* series on October 18, 1955.

on the heels of the book: White Hunter, Black Heart (Garden City, NY: Doubleday, 1953), Viertel's fictionalized account of his experience working with Huston as the screenwriter of *The African Queen.*

It will first be done on Omnibus . . . and then will have its world premiere at the Met: The ballet was jointly commissioned by Ballet Theatre and the Ford Foundation TV Workshop. George Antheil wrote the score; AEH's script is housed with the Hotchner Papers, box 6, Washington University. One reviewer found the stage version "immeasurably superior to the television production. . . . Not that the Hemingway ballet is now flawless, for it is not." Walter Terry, "Ballet Theatre," *New York Herald Tribune,* December 28, 1953, p. 14.

{65} AEH to EH
14 December 53 (TLS, 2 pp., JFKL)
A. E. Hotchner R. F. D. 5 Westport, Conn.

Dear Papa:

The way Capital of the World finally worked out on television was in two versions, dramatic and ballet, one right after the other. Two separate contracts were drawn, and Al [Rice] arranged for most of the fee to go to the dramatic version, so that condition will prevail against whatever you decide re Ann Marie, who of course has nothing to do with the dramatic version.

I cannot tell you much about the ballet on TV, since I threw up after two minutes and departed. The adaptation I wrote was very simple, as I believe a ballet line must be, and close to the original story. But the little dancing master who choreographed it, one Eugene Loring, famous for a ballet named Billy the Kid which, like most ballets, I have not seen, switched the locale from the Luarca to a tailor's shop. What this achieved I can't say since, as I said, I was compelled by gastronomic upheavals to turn the whole thing off. Perhaps the world premiere at the Met, however, will correct this small discrepancy.

Mildest winter, or I should say fall, in anyone's memory and I have been doing considerable hacking away at various under and overgrowths around the house. To keep up these grounds I'm going to need a small tractor, the best of which I think is the Beaver. They do everything, including taking a lot of jack out of one's pocket, but I hear the tractor trust needs donations. The papers (speaking of donations) are currently full of information about a national charity "The National Foundation for Kids Camps" which, with Bing Crosby and Mrs. Bob Hope as co-directors, collected a million and a half bucks last year, only ten percent of which actually went to charity—the rest of the dough was for "administrative expenses." They've been able to find a congressional committee to investigate that, some little group, I presume, that happened to be between communists. By the way, CBS and I have had a preliminary talk about Across the River and Into the Trees for television and they informed me that both you and I have been checked out and cleared as loyal Americans, thereby qualifying our names to appear on the Columbia Broadcasting System. I told them that now you and I would have to clear them on our loyalty list. So, Papa, check through your mobile files and send me the word. The initials might just stand for Communist Broadcasting System; we better play it safe.

All of us here wish you and Mary a merry and happy Christmas and further wish you were here to share ours with us. The kids are now at the only age when Christmas is right and wonderful and I enjoy them very much. So will you when you meet them. Love,

Hotchstein

{66} EH to AEH
22/12/53 (ALS, 3 pp., LOC)
Kimana Swamp Camp [*hw*] [Kenya *pmk*]

Dear HotchMaru

Thank you very much for the wonderful letter with all the good news. I split with you on any terms you name. Anne-Marie should have a very tiny piece and only as a present. I have never carnal-ed her in any way and she is entitled to only what she is given. The Volpi family has 800000 times more money than you or me and you could even weigh in Alfred Vanderbilt. Please ask Alfred [Rice] to secure an absolute release from her on picture, television, sodomy in 3 dimensions and all action past and future rights for the payment of a certain token cash sum. Say 200 dollars. Am sure that is more than her sainted mother ever received at one time when she came from N. Africa and met Volpi. On presentation in theatre cut her in for 1% repeat one percent unless this seems excessive. The name is Hemingstein and the Horse's name is REMORSE in the 7th at Enghein. Or call the horse Jige.

This god-damned country is <u>wonderful</u>. Somebody ought to write about it or put it in the films. Kilimanjaro is right outside our back yard. Kilimanjaro means in the local dialect Papa's Big Money Hill. We are plowing back the money fast with a Cessna. It does only 180 on the deck but you can drive it fast and it will not stall at 40 using flaps right. It is really wonderful Ed and Miss Mary loves the deck which was always my home town. It is not as much the elevation you get as the lasting friendships you make as I discovered when chose Austin Business college over Harvard.

Miss Mary has shot an without white hunter lion and many beasts with good heads and the food. We are stripped down to 13 feedables so you only have [to] get a piece of meat every 3 days. Yesterday she and her trusty gun-bearer Charo aged over <u>80</u> and the same height as Miss Mary were photographing buff[alo] with the wind perfect toward us and steady and a beautiful approach made. In back and backing up like the Unione Siciliano (and invisible) were Mr. Papa and N'Gui my gun bearer who is about 30 and my bad and wicked brother. While Mary was photographing (I bought her a

Hasselblad with a 14 inch lens that looks like a 60 mm. mortar and cost a little less than a Jaguar), N'Gui and I see a pack of hunting dogs under the same
tree as Miss Mary and Charo. Miss M. and Charo are photographing[;] the
hunting dogs are counting the buffalo calves. Neither group have seen each
other but the hunting dogs hear the click of the camera and seeing Miss Mary
and Charo decide they would just as soon take them as buffalo calves. It was
really something to see a wolf pack work. But Miss Mary kept on photographing the pack <u>and</u> the <u>buff</u> and N'Gui and I broke it up with our powerful old Vincent Coll approach without shooting or spooking the buff.

Miss Mary is <u>wonderful</u>. We all get the shots etc. But with terramicin (which
I won't use on acct. wish to keep my friendly bacteria) there is no real problem knock on wood.

So far have shot one rhino that tried to join our group and carried it past
where he should have and one buff that Mary can tell you about and lions,
leopard, (one in a real western gun fight in the dust) and turned down about
everything. Am trying to learn a new medium, the spear. Charo thinks I can
kill anything but elephant with it and kill elephant if I learn. But have to work
hard in the gym. So far have wild hunting dog, hyena and leaping hare for
speed. Ed you use it like a boxer's left hand and right and you keep punching
and get inside right away. There are a dozen places where she will go in (anywhere not bone) but the place to punch is under the armpit or kidneys forward. It slips in like into butter and is much more deadly than a rifle. Have 4
spears now. All blooded. The boys, our pals, love it but I should not do it in
front of Mary as it makes a bad impression when you are running as a good.

But Mary has been so <u>damned</u> good and she likes me bad. But spear throws
womens off. Good womens anyway. Local womens it appeals to.

Don't pass any of this around as someone will steal it and I have to write
what I've learned to make a living.

Am down to 190 and the reflexes are so that I truly think I could juggle
throws and let the runner be safe and still have it look ok. We do the god-
damndest things Ed and will not mention them. Can't get pictures of the really fast ones or the funniest ones. Christ I wish you were here to photograph
and participate. Yesterday took Miss Mary (who had been in Nairobi with the
Cessna Xmas shopping) on a fine evening hunt (she is after Gerenuk) and to
a neighboring village where we have good friends of the same tribe I threw in
with 21 years ago. They have a really lovely farm. The corn nearly 12 feet up
with this rain.

The Game Ranger left me in charge of the District (this area) and it is the duty to protect crops but kill nothing that is not a real destroyer of the necessary to live. Liveing has been very rough with the two year drouth and marauders and predators make bad trouble. Am honorary Game Ranger gazzetted and commissioned as such.

Look is publishing the pictures and short piece with captions on Jan. 16— Hits the stands Jan. 26. Think you'll like the colour. Runs some 15.

Ed could you do me one more favour? Call Alfred [Rice] or better see him and tell him I have not written because every time I start to write some character comes in and says "Bwana the elephants are destroying my shamba (plantation or planting or home)" or the Police Boy (22) who runs the area and does not know his ass from adam and is full of too much zeal arrives, completely destroyed, and says "Bwana we must block the passes. They are coming through running arms with Masai donkeys. How many men can you commit?"

I know it is 10/1 to be bull shit but I always know there is that 1. So I say, "I have six fighting men with service in K.A.R. [King's African Rifles] or in the Scouts (not Boy Scouts) who I can arm and 4 spears. How many passes are you blocking?"

"Four," he says. "I'll brigade my men (12) with yours."

"Who will block the 2 unknown roads to Amboselli?"

"You."

"Shit maru," I say, having my pen in my hand to write to Alfred. And he doesn't get written to. This type of operation takes all night. Three non arm carrying donkeys are intercepted. But I do it for our Queen.

God bless our queen. God bless Miss Mary. God bless you and Alfred.

The men stand at attention. Cut to the next incident when not writing to Alfred but exhausted and in bed with Miss Mary. We hear the noise of the Land Rover of the police, he is beat up, confused and over-disheveled, "Bwana there is a lion terrorizing Laitokitok!"

"How many lions. Sex of same?"

"A single male lion but he has just killed a goat 1/2 mile from town."

"I will pay for the goat."

"No Bwana. You must kill the lion."

I buckle on the equipment and we go. We fail to kill the lion due to him, naturally, having fucked off. But <u>maybe</u> he would have stayed. That's the trouble.

Let Al read this so he understands. Yesterday Miss Mary said "Papa do you know you have not taken any rest since August 27th?" I do not know what type of rest I took on that specific date. Probably packing to get off the Dunnottar Castle. Shit maru.

Anyway for an old alleged non-rester will you do me one <u>more</u> favour. Please subscribe for me to Romeike the clipping outfit for clippings on Mary Hemingway <u>and</u> <u>Papa!</u> [last two words inserted by Mary] to 2000. <u>No duplications of syndicated or press service stories.</u> Clippings to be <u>air-mailed</u> to Mary Hemingway Barclay's Bank-Queensway-Nairobi-Kenya-B.E.A.

Them to bill me through Guaranty Trust Co. of N.Y. 4 Place de la Concorde Paris.

Mary would like any <u>back</u> clippings they have, if any, on her Vogue piece published in October or November.

Guess that's it. Best to any of the mob. Love to you from us both. Love to your wife.

Papa

[inserted by Mary] Darling Hotch—it's great about your house, but here I'm all mixed up in greats. You have to get up before dawn to go for lion to get the idea of great. No place and nothing we've done compares with this life of Safari. Papa's in greatest shape. We're coming home via Venice and Paris, leaving here early March. Best love to you all, and next time, come here with us. [inserted by Mary on verso] Merry Christmas

The Volpi family: Anne-Marie Lacloche was the stepdaughter of Sen. Giovanni Volpi, First Count di Misurata and founder of the Venice Film Festival.

Enghein: Parisian racetrack.

Vincent Coll: Vincent "Mad Dog" Coll, Irish gangster who was shot down in 1932.

We all get the shots: Antidysentery injections.

terramicin: Terramycin (oxytetracycline), an antibiotic powder used in treating infections.

The Game Ranger: Denis Zaphiro, a 27-year-old Londoner who ingratiated himself with EH by inviting him to kill a rhino that had been wounded by another hunter.

Look is publishing the pictures and short piece: "Safari," *Look,* January 26, 1954, pp. 19–34, a photographic essay of the safari with text by EH and photos by Earl Theisen.

her Vogue piece: Mary Hemingway, "My Father in Minnesota," October 1, 1953, pp. 138–39, 182, 184.

1954

{67} AEH to EH
Feb. 10 [1954 *pmk*] (TLS, 2 pp., JFKL)
A. E. Hotchner R. F. D. 5 Westport, Conn.

Dear Papa:

I didn't go for it and I was fine and knew you and good Miss Mary could overcome any AP voodoo, but when I went to sleep that night it hit me and it was a bad night. But the morning papers were like uranium, gold and geysers struck in the back yard. I stumbled into town and honest Al [Rice] and I found a bottle of admirable cognac and sat around his desk holding a wake for those shit sheets that ran the obits like any hop head runs when he hears the pusher's in the neighborhood. A half dozen magazines called here to ask how they could get the story of the crashes and I said by buying the book he puts it in, if ever. But I referred them all to Al who gave them your address. May I say, Papa, I am not a praying man, but that night you made me pray.

The ballet, as it was presented at the Met in front of the fanciest audience you ever saw, had some good things about it, many bad, and when you come through here again I'd say it would be one of the things you could pass up and feel no loss. Basically, it was all there, but when the fairies descended on it and flitted all over it and poked at it with their dainty fingers they left it like the locusts. Antheil's music, however, was surprisingly good, as the enclosed clip by Virgil Thomson will attest. And the boy, Roy Fitzell, does as good by the cape and by the Spanish dances as you could hope for. So I learned it the hard way—ballet ain't for me. However, the Omnibus-Ballet Theatre presentations netted $3000 for the coffers and that's on the plus side. I took no part of that payment—Ballet Theatre paid me a couple hundred for doing some work for them. As for Ann Marie [Lacloche], gave Rice the gen, he will act accordingly when and if she ever shows up.

I have had great enjoyment proving to these great minds that control TV that they don't know their ass from a splendid story. I wanted them to do Gambler Nun and Radio but The Minds said it couldn't be done, no way to make a play of it, so I sat down and wrote them one, taking it right out of the short story, and now they all want it, saw that it had it in it all along, etc. etc. The phonies are rampant. Best offer came from Omnibus, good cast, director, the works. I don't think they can hurt this one—you wrote it indestructible. The more I work in the dramatic form, the more I see this is what I like best and do best. The Theatre Guild did a drama of mine last December that the critics liked, for whatever that's worth.

Publisher I know phoned me to make suggestion that sounds good on the surface and think is worth referring to you; I checked [Scribner's editor] Wallace Meyer on it, just to get his off-hand opinion, and he agrees it's something you might like to consider. Of course it would be a Scribner's project— my friend just gave forth the idea. He pointed out that the reading public was largely unfamiliar with the non-fiction you have written over the years. In his opinion, among the Esquire, Ken, Transatlantic Review, Collier's, Holiday, True, etc. articles, are wonderful pieces which should be brought out in book form. He suggested that I might collect all the articles and serve as editor for such a volume. What do you think? If you think it bears consideration, I can dig up some of the articles and when you come through we can give it some further thought.

Papa, I have a couple of very good friends who want to take a trip through your Africa country. Could you please send me the name and address of a good guide whom they can contact? They have dough, they are hardy and courageous.

Really enjoyed your letter—almost like having you on the bar stool next to me, swapping good stories about the war and no war. I am going to Paris second week in May. Any chance you may land there for a while on your way back? Enghein would be running and we owe it to them to let them try to get even.

Give my love to Mary—I hope she is all mended. And you, Papa, all I can say is that you're my good friend and brother.

Hotchschmeer

The snow around here is waist deep, thermometer a steady zero. I've been playing basketball on a local team + averaging 24 points per game. It's a rough sport for a guy my age but I enjoy it + it doesn't take too much out of me.

AP voodoo: On January 23, with Roy Marsh piloting their Cessna, the Hemingways crash-landed near Murchison Falls, Uganda, on their way to Entebbe. Initial reports by the Associated Press and others asserted that they had died. In fact, they were picked up the next day by the steamboat *Murchison* and attempted to reach Entebbe by air again with another pilot, but his de Havilland burst into flames upon take-off. Subsequent accounts did not suggest the seriousness of EH's injuries (*Final*, 272–73).

the enclosed clip: Virgil Thomson, "Music and Musicians: In the Theatre," *New York Herald Tribune,* January 3, 1954, sec. 4, p. 3.

Roy Fitzell: Performed the lead part of Paco in the ballet.

Best offer came from Omnibus: AEH's adaptation of "The Gambler, the Nun, and the Radio" was eventually broadcast on *Buick Electra Playhouse* in the spring of 1960.

The Theatre Guild did a drama of mine last December: "The Vanishing Point," a television play coauthored by AEH, was broadcast December 22, 1953, on *The U.S. Steel Hour* (ABC), produced by the Theatre Guild.

{68} EH to AEH
14/3/54 (ALS, 7 pp., LOC)
~~off Mogadisu~~ (?)
<u>SS Africa</u> [hw]

Dear Hotchsmear

Sure wish you were aboard. It can get dull sometimes. What I drew as cards when we pranged [crashed] in the 2nd kite was ruptured kidney, and the usual internal injuries plus full upstairs concussion, double vision etc. Now the left eye has cut out and we had a very bad brush fire down on the Coast which I had to fight and burned the shit out of the left (the good) hand and because I was weaker than I figured I fell once and so burned belly etc. Genitals ok. But Hotch times are just faintly rough now.

Did the fucking piece through the good luck of running into a girl who used to be RAF [Royal Air Force] and knew all of us characters and used to have to take down what I would say on the intercom when we coming in or stacked up. So dictating with her was easy and I just show-boated as always. I figured to go for a shit but am better than even money now.

Miss Mary loved the deck. Roy Marsh is a lovely pilot and we had much fun. As you know you can do anything with that Cessna 180 and anything you can do we did or I hope we did. You would have liked very much. Who started all that stuff about Papa fearing the aircraft? All I was was grounded for keeps in 1944 after having been through CNAC [China National Aviation Corporation] in China, etc. etc. CNAC in China the worst. But also have flown in and navigated for B 25, Mosquito, Lauc. Hausa and Hurricane gliders and various other kites. This you must tell <u>nobody</u>. Because Roy and I have been cleared clean by local Gestapo. You can tell Alfred [Rice] under complete pledge of secrecy between 1 Indian and 2 Jews.

Miss Mary discovers the joys of the deck and doesn't know that if you live on the deck you die on the deck. I tried to explain this to her but just considers Roy and me the conservative type. So you know how that type of opinion can make old fly characters feel. So for any amount of hours you would wish to name we show Miss Mary the deck she loves. Naturally it catches up.

For a couple of months 30th November–Jan 20 had been functioning as ½ of the Law West of the Pecos as the other ½ is a boy police officer 22 years old who calls me Governor. You can say maybe we are ¾ of T.L.W.O.T.P. They should have had great sherrifs like Cooper to play the part. I am down, then, to 185 so maybe I could even play the part myself. Wish old Jige [Viertel] could have seen we gave them justice without rancour. Keep everything clean. No torture. Nobody guilty who isn't guilty like with the old Irregulars. Hotch I know it is a sin but christ it is lovely to command and by that sin fails always [*indeciph.*] Hornsby.

I get the Cessna 180 because, as you probably know, one needs observation and an unexpected mobile striking force. We have more fun than goats. If I wrote it nobody would believe it. So will omit. Have 2 wonderful Wakamba outfits. One worthless Masai. One wonderful Masai mob known as the Honest Ernies. Each one has a bottle cap from a bottle of Tusker beer which I have shot the eye of the elephant out of while he held it in his hand. If I hit the hand of course I think the honest Ernies would have more or less disbanded. Anyway we have good luck and don't hit any hands. But I would have liked to have you doing the shooting when the Honest Ernies are enrolling. They could then have been the Royal Most Honorable Honest Hotch-Ernies. We have, as yet no Regimental crest but 2 Slogans—Kwenda Na Shamba (Let's go home) and Na N'auua (Let's kill everybody). I may misspell these slogans.

Miss Mary having gone to Nairobi and the district being confided to me by a man we call The Gin Crazed Ranger [Denis Zaphiro] I take a Wakamba bride and inherit her sister, a widow of 17, this is a rather considerable occasion and is referred to [by] us in the tribe as The Great N'Goma Preceding by ½ of the Moon the Birth of the Baby Jesus. I am very happy with my lovely wives with their impudence and solicitude and stacked better than M. Monroe but with good hard palms to their hands and smell wonderful. Obviously so as not to be lonesome we sleep on a bed about 14 feet wide and everyday I shoot them a little something. My father in law is a jerk but am very stern and won't speak to him. He can come to me and I grunt and tell Deba in Spanish what to tell him. Have been teaching her Spanish since we met. She understands it ok now but can't talk in it. Understand Kwamba.

I always want to do slow rolls over our Shamba but restrained. However we want to buzz it properly and we succeeded in cutting the flag off the Police Boma at Laitokitok on 2 occasions and we were not truly, I assure you, the completely conservative type. Neither were we Arthur Godfrey. Were engaged in putting the Fear of God into Mau Mau and potential Mau-Mau with a Cessna 180. One time in the back room of Mr. Singh's joint in Laitokitok LAITOKITOK (wonderful town) and Mr. Singh fine man with 8 children by a Turkana wife (that's the way Laitokitok is and the drink is free because one can shut Mr. Singh up with a [4 *chars. indeciph.*] to the DC.) But we don't take advantage of this and one time when I was forced to arrest Mr. Singh on the road after curfew he said he had never been arrested gentler or prettier in his life. Anyway on this day a chickenshit Mission boy in hard shoes (that's one thing get from religion. Wear hard shoes and not be respected. Maybe they go to Heaven) came in and said "You must be one of the richest men in the world, Sir. How many Ngeges/birds or aircraft do you have?"

Never at a loss for a false answer I say, "Eight and fuck off."

"Thank you Sir," he says. "But when will [they] be back to make the marvellous things over Laitokitok again?"

"My Ndeges are all in Nairobi with Memsabib Miss Mary and in the North. But one of them, the smallest, may return at any moment. I am sitting here reading and listening for the sound of motors."

"Thank you Sir," he says.

"Have a drink of beer?"

"No Sir Mr. Shaeffer (the missionary) might hear of it."

Outside some of the Honest Ernies are give[ing] the old Na N'uua and warming up on Mr. Singh's Golden Jeep Sherry. The Masai are supposed to drink only milk and blood mixed but many have switched to Golden Jeep and there are some converts to an Anhauser Busch lithography of Custer's Last Stand of which I modestly finally admitted I lead the assault.

The Honest Ernies have a copy of Life the one that shows all the prehistoric animals etc. Pressed I admit to bagging 84 Saber tooth Tigers before I was 19 all, naturally, with a spear. After this I was allowed to be circumcised and take the first of my 12 wives Miss Mary runs 12th. I am reticent about how many Mastodons I have killed. I do admit though to haveing been the King President of Idaho Mountain and Wyoming and to the destruction of the US army to the last man.

We all nod solemnly and grasp one another's thumbs. Na N'auua. We have killed them all.

A group of M'Zees, elders of the tribe check in. Tony, one of our drivers who was the only Masai Sergeant [in the] Tank Corps has told them how he personally has seen me kill over 324 men. All I believe armed with flame throwers at the least. Many I killed with the spear. The M'Zees call [me] Mr. Papa (Supreme Governor Mr. Papa) Drink quite a little and exchange deep grunts reminiscent of Miss Marlene Dietrich.

After this I go to see if my Wakamba fiancee has purchased the material for her Xmas dress and pay my respects to Miss Rosie Rochau at the dubba. I purchase a chicken for camp and release it in the street and shoot it's head off with the pistol.

Our group now loads into the vehicle and proceed down the hill (the big hill Kilimanjaro) to Kimana dropping off friends, partisans and adherents at the five shambas where booze is made and proceed to camp where a group of informers are waiting.

At this moment in a cloud of dust drives the local white police officer. I say "How are things?" "Not good." "14 have escaped. All murderers or 3 time oathtakers."

"Where did they escape from?"

"Machakos."

"When?"

"Yesterday."

"Take it easy kid," I say doing logistics. "They can't be here until tonight or tomorrow. Put your post in a state of defense and I guaranty this area."

I figure that these M.M. [Mau Mau] being captured near Machako on acct. of getting drunk and boasting they were going to Na N'auua everybody will if they are at large make for some place where there is to drink. Just as I say should be sought by the police in the Ritz Bar or at Auteuil.

So post a Wakamba each to all the shambas and if any Wakamba speaking characters arrive to send a girl with the word. Then I send a roving member of the honest Ernies to circulate in a drunken manner and bring the word. Then post guard on the road etc. and start ammo and spear count. Also established a curfew on the area. Send notice of the curfew to Laitokitok camp.

Well the 14 characters brake the other way. The head man sums it up by this "These are Wakamba Mau-Mau Not Kikuyu Mau-Mau." Wakamba are hunters and poachers.

Well Hotch will you please keep this letter for me carefully so I can use it for a story? There is an excellent chance Miss M. will beat my brains out and as we approach Venice the odds on this shorten. Intrepid Miss Mary is not fun to be with when you are wounded. In lots of ways she reminds me of Leo Durocher. In others of Eddy Stanky. In others of Johnny Miebane—and a French fighter named Francis Charles.

If you want rare and interesting experiences be her white hunter for a few months. She can also be lovely. But I have never seen her be kind except to servants and I have never seen her in a good temper in the morning. Sharing a small cabin is rough if you are the one confined to the cabin. I beat the rap by staying on in Nairobi where even if you had to crawl on your hands and feet to the toilet it was better than some things. I guess being an only child known in the family as "Lamb of God" is not the best training for a barracks life. But she was lovely 4 months on Safari really wonderful and most of the time quite brave and very indulgent with me. When she started to get vicious was after the first kite pranged when she decided Roy could just as well kept on flying and not crash landed. The only thing wrong with the air craft was, of course, the prop shot and a length of telephone wire around the tail assembly.

She didn't think very much of the landing and she refused to believe in the elephants when I could tell the males from the females by the smell. She doesn't think that lions are dangerous and that the really bad fight we had with a leopard where I had to crawl on my face into bush thicker than Mangrove swamp and kill him with a shot gun is bull shit. He was hit bad and I had a piece of shoulder bone in my mouth to keep <u>my</u> morale up and would fire at the roar. Too thick to see. So that's bullshit. You know how they get. Actually nothing of this is against her because she is in a state of shock. But she doesn't know about shock nor believe in it and she thinks when I am removing impacted feces from a busted sphincter I am dogging it. Then she will be loving and wonderful. But I wish she had some Jewish blood so she would know that <u>other</u> people hurt. But you can't have everything. Anyway I've been bad enough. And I want Miss Mary to have fun and until she got enamored of the deck she had a lovely trip. She'll sort out OK. But I married a womans ½ Kraut ½ Irish and that makes a merciless cross but a lovely woman.

Anyway now we go to Venezia. When we were [reported] dead in Venice A. [Adriana] took it rough. Her final decision was to leave for Cuba and burn the Finca so no one would ever sleep in my bed, sit in my chair, nor ever go up into the White Tower. She was, seriously, going to destroy the swimming pool. Poor damned blessed girl. Something to be said for Venice.

In Cuba we run now as Saints according to reports. Prio cabled. Batista cables all my known relatives. They closed the Floridita. My old Fascist pal The Diario de La Marina had 3 pages when we were deads including an elegy that would move us all to tears. Manolo Asper who runs and owns Ambos Mundos Hotel announced to the press that I was a devout and practicing Catholic. True. This according to the Havana Post gave me faith when the horses were off.

What makes them give such mystic importance to a couple of kites pranging? But they do. I guess it was getting all the characters out ok. plus the animals etc.

I guess it is the speed maybe. When she burns it has to be faster than a triple play in the big leagues.

Anyway Miss Mary is fine now and we[']re due at Suez day after tomorrow about off Port Sudan now. Still in bed. Had first real movements yest. and today. Shitted about ½ my weight in it. 64 movements in 20 hours. All spasms. Couldn't piss for last two days on acct. of plug somewhere with that kidney cell material. Passed it ok (looks like quill toothpicks) and urinate fine. Arm and hand burns from the brush fire OK. They cut away the dead stuff (not cut—just scissored). The Dr. is very capable and good and we split a bottle of champagne once a day.

Miss Mary has a good time I think and has met Lord Portland and old Nol Wallop's grandson from Sheridan Wyo and has made other nice friends and is up now for the cocktail hour. It is a nice boat with a good crew. Everybody fought; the Capt. (who was in today with the Dr.) had his destroyer cut in two off Tobruck. The Dr. fought on the Russkie front and was in my old regiment. Several guys from Spain. So we rate all right.

Hotch I shouldn't run on so long but I get lonesome and you know my problems and I can see all the freckles on your funny face and remember all our problems and the fun at Auteuil and on the trip and how you liked Venice and stayed better than any brother.

I think I have the rap beat. Maybe get up day after tomorrow. Probably better mail this from Brindisi as Egypt they might take a month to censor.

Better knock off and get it in envelope. Give my love to Alfred and please ask him to be patient with me under the circumstances—Today's check up shows there was:

rupture of kidneys

collapse of intestine

severe injuries liver

major concussion

severe burns legs, belly, right forearm, left hand, head, lips

paralysis of sphincter

large blood clot left shin outside above ankle

dislocated right arm and shoulder etc.

Love Papa

With all this shit I dictated 16,000 words and I hope I kept it funny EH. Wish I had a ghost writer.

Everybody will be okay.

off Mogadisu: Beneath the date, EH wrote "off Mogadisu" (Mogadishu, Somalia) but then put a line through it and added "(?)"

Sure wish you were aboard: The Hemingways left Mombasa on March 9 on the SS *Africa* bound for Venice, arriving on the 23rd.

the fucking piece: "The Christmas Gift," with photos by Earl Theisen, ran in two parts in *Look* on April 20, 1954, pp. 29–37, and May 4, 1954, pp. 79–89 (*Final,* 276).

great sherrifs like Cooper: Gary Cooper had played Marshal Will Kane in *High Noon* (1952).

the old Irregulars: While a war correspondent for *Collier's,* EH had functioned as a liaison between divisional controls and an "irregular" outfit of Free French Fighters (*Story,* 408).

Hornsby: Possibly Rogers Hornsby, who managed ball teams for many years but could not tolerate interference by the front office and for that reason was frequently dismissed.

a bottle cap from a bottle of Tusker beer: One of the founders of Kenya Breweries was killed by a charging bull elephant; the lager he created was named Tusker and the labels and bottle caps feature a bull elephant.

Miss Mary having gone to Nairobi: The Hemingways' safari was supposed to conclude with a fishing expedition, but EH's injuries prevented him from leaving with Mary on February 13; he joined her on the 21st (*Final* 278; *HIW* 447).

Kwamba: Another name for Amba, a Ugandan language.

Laitokitok: Principal town on the northern slopes of Kilimanjaro in Kenya, extending to the surrounding savanna and including Amboseli National Park.

Arthur Godfrey: Radio and television personality who buzzed a control tower while piloting a small plane. "Godfrey Is Accused of 'Reckless' Flying," *New York Times,* January 14, 1954, p. 31.

the DC: Possibly district commissioner.

Mau Mau and potential Mau-Mau: The Mau Mau conflict was both a civil war and a war for independence waged by a coalition of Kenyan tribes, comprised primarily of Kikuyu, against the white settlers. Beginning in 1947, the Mau Mau took oaths of loyalty and conducted guerrilla strikes that escalated into full-scale war in 1952. By 1953 the insurgency had abated but not ended, and the British enlisted counter-insurgents to inform against the Mau Mau.

"These are Wakamba Mau-Mau Not Kikuyu Mau-Mau." Wakamba are hunters and poachers: The Wakamba of EH's acquaintance were less radical than the Kikuyu Mau Mau, whose agrarian lifestyle was devastated by the loss of land to white settlers.

Leo Durocher . . . Francis Charles: Brooklyn Dodgers Durocher and Stanky were cantankerous and hard-nosed on the field. Johnny Miebane could not be identified. Francis Charles boxed in the 1910s and 1920s.

the White Tower: Constructed in 1947, the tower was designed by Mary to house the family cats and to provide a place for her to sunbathe and for EH to write; it had "a commanding view of the sea and the distant city" (*Story,* 462–63).

Prio . . . Batista: Gen. Fulgencio Batista ousted Cuban president Carlos Prio in 1952 and took control of the country. Prio fled to the United States.

Diario de La Marina: Havana newspaper.

Lord Portland: Lord Portsmouth, who had a ranch in Kitale, Kenya. Mary wrote that he had "studied in depth the colony's economy and political and racial problems" and that she "hoped the British government would have enough sense to pay attention to his formulas" (*HIW,* 452).

I dictated 16,000 words: Refers to "The Christmas Gift."

On May 2, AEH arrived at the Gritti Palace in Venice, where EH had been staying since late March. Together they traveled to Milano in EH's Lancia with Adamo Simon, his driver, and then to Madrid for the San Isidoro festival. There they visited Luis Miguel Dominguín's bull ranch and met Ava Gardner, who had starred in The Killers *(1946) and* The Snows of Kilimanjaro *(1952) and with whom Dominguín was having an affair. During a stopover in Madrid, EH consulted Dr. Juan Madinaveitia, a friend from Spanish Civil War days, who treated him for several of the injuries he sustained in the crashes, as well as the second-degree burns he received from the brush fire. On June 6 the Hemingways boarded the* Francesco Morosini, *bound for Havana (Final, 280; Story, 524–25).*

{69} AEH to EH
29 May [1954] (TLS, 2 pp., JFKL)
A. E. Hotchner R. F. D. 5 Westport, Conn.

Dear Papa,

What a fine trip it was. Venice, which is more real to me now than St. Louis, Mo., and never as hot; the unbelievably beautiful country we travelled; the good talks and companionship all the way; and then, Spain, Madrid, and the bullfight. I thought I knew something about the bullfight, I mean I thought I had some idea what it was like. But there is no way to be prepared for it, I guess—the tragedy, the triumph, the courage, the brutality, the suddenly delicate texture of it, my God, what an experience it is. It's not just two hours of the late afternoon, is it? It's the whole day, and days before, and certainly, as I now know, days and days after. Last night, I reread Death in the Afternoon all over again. How different it is to read it after you have seen some good fights. It seems impossible that you could have learned so much and written so brilliantly about an intricate art that is so foreign to your basic culture—meaning Oak Park, Ill. But then I guess nothing is really foreign to *your* basic culture, which, as far as I can tell, extends to wherever I've been with you and a helleva lot further. Christ, this is turning into some specie of fan letter, but I've just put down Death in the Afternoon so you'll have to excuse me. And I've just spent three good weeks with a guy who tops my list. It did my heart good to see you get progressively stronger, not all at once, for you had a rough couple of days along the way, but that day out at the farm, when you reached out and effortlessly held off that plunging cow and turned her away, I knew that a good deal of the strength was back and you had it beat. Take care now, and I'll bet you'll be fit enough to fish again before the summer is gone.

As you predicted, the jewel was more than Gerry could cope with. She is still speechless from it, and I think she feels that it should be placed on exhibition with a Brinks' man guarding it rather than be worn. She says there is no way adequately to thank you for being my partner in the giving, and I agree with her. It was such a goddam nice thing to do, but still I shouldn't have let you do it, and I'm sort of embarrassed about it.

Wasn't Pete [Viertel] a good guy? So changed from our last meeting, I really can't get over it. I envy him his trip to India. Maybe he and I can work together on a project someday—we discussed it. I am bent now on moving this group over to the continent for a good stretch. I could rent this big joint for something more than its basic cost. I'm confused, however, as to where I want to establish base—so many good places. (This typewriter has suddenly gone out of its mind . . .) Paris is so goddam expensive I guess it's out of the question. Where would you go now? I mean if you were me. I <u>know</u> where you would go.

People here spend most of their time glued in front of their television sets watching the McCarthy-Army hearings which are televised every day, all day long. That dignified American, Roy Cohen, is on the stand now and you can tell at a glance that he is composed in the guts somewhat differently than Mr. Chicuelo II. I have dismissed the whole nauseating shit heap and I spend all my spare time practicing with my muletta. How did my boy Cordoba perform? Did you save any newspaper clips? I hope I can work out the Mexico trip—that's my plan, as of now, but the best laid plans, friends, sometimes complain.

I want you to know, Papa, how much I enjoyed our trip and how much I appreciate sharing it with you. I hope we are not so long a time seeing each other again. Get strong, work good, and have as much fun as you can.

Please give all my love to Mary.

Yours,

Hotchbloor,

de Monte Carlo

---

the jewel: According to AEH, EH helped him purchase an emerald for Geraldine in Italy.

(This typewriter has suddenly gone out of its mind . . .): The paper in the typewriter carriage had advanced only half a line space, causing one line to overlap another. Thereafter, the carriage return operated properly.

I <u>know</u> where you would go: Implies that EH would go to Italy to be near Adriana.

McCarthy-Army hearings: The first nationally televised congressional inquiry, airing April 2 to June 17. A consultant on the staff of Sen. Joseph R. McCarthy had been drafted and Roy Cohn, McCarthy's chief counsel, had sought special privileges for him; when the request was denied, McCarthy accused the army of harboring communists.

Mr. Chicuelo II: Bullfighter Manuel Jiménez Díaz, whom EH described as "braver than a badger or than any animal and most men." Ernest Hemingway, *The Dangerous Summer* (New York: Scribner's, 1985), 90.

Cordoba: Jesús Córdoba, whom EH described as "the Mexican bullfighter who was born in Kansas, speaks excellent English, and had dedicated a bull to me." Hemingway, *Dangerous Summer,* 51.

{70} EH to AEH
21/6/54 (ALS, 3 pp., ViU)
On board "Morosini" 3 ½ days out of/La Guira (Venezuela) 15 days out/of
Genova—[hw]

Dear Hotchmanship:

Thanks for wonderful letter to the boat. In St. Jean de Luz we saw Pete [Viertel], John Huston and Paul Kohner of Kohn, Kohner and Kohnest. I thought he was Huston's money but it turned out after he was gone he was Huston's agent.

Peter was to get hold of you on his arrival in N.Y. and explain it all. He said you knew about it. This came out at the end when I said in all the talk I hadn't heard your name mentioned and Peter said you and he had talked it all over. Anyway, no matter what anybody says to you nor how mysterious anybody gets: Papa is not going to double cross you even 1/100th of 1% and not single cross you either. As left by me they were to A—Peter get in touch with you at Wesport. B—They decide what they want to do and put it in writing to me. That is where it stands.

You let me know what Pete told you and I'll forward you what he told and tells me.

Huston made a good impression. He was in very good shape. Pete should have told you before now everything they were thinking about. If not then things aren't right. Let me know and I'll let you know all about it.

Al [Rice] had not deposited my Look money. He was "holding it for me." Consequently my guaranty account was $522.$\underline{00}$ and over drafts had been covered by Scribner's. That would account for Scribner's being a little upset. If they were. This dead confidential. The Abercrombie bill I'd ordered paid hasn't yet been paid and I've never seen it. How is a character supposed to keep his credit good when sums that should be automatically deposited (The deal was between Bill Lowe and me) are held for you. Don't say anything of this to Alfred nor anybody. He probably did it for some excellent reason such as tax position or to have tax money. But since I'd spoken about it this was how it was.

You're boy Cordoba got tossed on his head, looked like a terrible cornada [goring] but the horn slid up his belly between cloth and the skin. He was bleeding from nose and mouth and unconscious. Went to see him in bed at the hotel and he had a bad headache but fought a day later and was not good. Shouldn't have been allowed to fight anymore than a fighter who has been knocked out two nights before. I saved you clippings, pictures and the bull fight magazines complete. Chicuelo II got a bad horn wound in the thigh on June 4 in Madrid. Out for 3 weeks. We saw him once more in Aranjuez May 30 before he was wounded. Hot as in Madrid in the first bull—cooled out and didn't try on his second. Antonio Ordonez very good in both.

Rupert [Bellville] slipped one day on the booze but I got him off and he made it back onto the wagon solid and OK. Juanito [Quintana] rode up with him to St. Sebastian and he was OK. He wrote from London OK.

We saw the Pyrenees as clear and beautiful on our right going home through all that country you and I ran from Carcassone to Bayonne with mist and drizzle. It was as lovely as the Alps that day from Torino down to Cuneo. Remember the dammed autographs in Cuneo? And that shakedown at French border? They never cracked a bag at French border coming back nor going out nor at Italian.

A. [Adriana] and her mother came down to Nervé to surprize us and they went home with Adamo [Simon].

Think will beat this rap ok if kidneys straighten out. The right one was hurt bad. Have had 4 drinks of whiskey and water in 15 days. None from Naples to Lisbon—Then had a couple in Funchal—a couple yest. 6 in all. No gin. It is a lousy bore for everybody else and for me.

I had a fine time with you Hotchmaru. You were Epic at Monte Carlo. You did see some damned good fights though and it was fun when we could go to the country. After you left we went out one day and picnic-ed at the bridge.

Excuse such a dull letter. Very dull people on the boat including me. I liked Cadiz very much. Might be a good place for you. Cheap, clean, nice climate, fine beaches. Take a look some time. The one nice town on the Italian Riviera going back was Alassio (will check this). A. sent you her love.

Papa

Miss Mary said she was writing you. I got good 12th Brigade Dr. in Madrid and good kidney anticeptic medicines. Believe they are good.

Paul Kohner: Worked for Universal Pictures before founding the Paul Kohner Agency.
explain it all: AEH remembers this as a discussion about adapting *Across the River and into the Trees* for film. AEH, fax to DeFazio, November 29, 2004.
Look money: EH earned $20,000 for "The Christmas Gift" (see note to letter 68).
Antonio Ordonez: Son of Cayetano Ordóñez, who was the prototype for matador Pedro Romero in *The Sun Also Rises*. EH described seeing Antonio fight in 1953: "I saw that he had everything his father had in his great days. . . . I could see he had the three

great requisites for a matador: courage, skill in his profession and grace in the presence of the danger of death." Hemingway, *Dangerous Summer*, 49–51. EH traveled with Antonio's entourage while in Spain and invited him and his wife to Cuba and Idaho.

Rupert [Bellville]: Englishman who met EH on board a ship to Spain in 1937. On this 1954 trip, he met Mary in Paris to drive south to the spring ferias (*Story*, 512).

Juanito [Quintana]: Owner of the Hotel Quintana in Pamplona until the Spanish Civil War, friend of EH since the 1920s, and prototype for Montoya in *The Sun Also Rises* (*Story*, 148, 512).

Remember the dammed autographs in Cuneo? AEH recalls: "As we went over the Alps from Italy to France we stopped for coffee in the Italian border town of Cuneo where Hemingway was swamped by a tidal wave of townspeople all seeking his autograph. Ernest was so shaken from the experience that when we checked in the Hotel Ruhl in Nice, Ernest went to the barber and had his beard shaved off." AEH to DeFazio, September 27, 2004.

You were Epic at Monte Carlo: AEH remembers "the night I played roulette at the casino (Ernest stayed in the bar because of back pain) with our pooled capital and came away with ten-fold winnings. Ernest invested most of his loot in tins of Capitaine Cook's mackerel in white wine along with purchases of pate de foi gras, bottles of Cordon Rouge champagne and jars of pickled mushrooms and walnuts, none of which he ever ate or drank." AEH to DeFazio, September 27, 2004.

12th Brigade Dr. in Madrid: Juan Madinaveitia, who "advised continued rest, a careful diet, and a greatly reduced intake of alcohol" (*Story*, 525).

{71} EH to AEH
9/9/54 (ALS, 3 pp., LOC)
FINCA VIGIA, SAN FRANCISCO DE PAULA, CUBA

Dear Hotch:

You have no obligation to do that reserve job. I wouldn't even think of it.

Please forgive me not writing. I started working and finished a short story and well into another when Bill Lowe came down with a proposition to make a documentary in Africa in 1955. I made a tentative agreement saying I couldn't do it until Sept.–Oct. 55. They got out an announcement on coast I was going to write, <u>act</u> in, etc. an original full length feature. No mention of making a documentary which is a perfectly dignified thing to do. So I called the deal off. That sort of announcement does me bad damage as a serious writer. But have come through other things. But Hotch the god damned people coming down here has been murder.

Right after Bill Lowe comes young Ava [Gardner]. Behaves very well. But is an interruption. Winston Guest shows up. Also Dave Shilling the flyer. The airforce brings out some enlisted personell who have won an award as aircraftsmen of the month in which visiting us is part of the tour. Then Luis Miguel Dominguín shows up and has been here 9 days. Sinsky turns up for 3 days and later 4 days (drunk). I go into my bed-room and work no matter what. But it is murder. Roberto, my secretary gets sick. He is now convalescing on a voyage on Sinsky's ship. Sinsky never drinks at Sea. Only at our house.

I am a son of a bitch who needs to be let alone to write. Can also write in Venice.

But characters come here like Mme. Tussaud's wax works. Every son of a bitch has turned up except Marthe Richard. She's in jail. A tramp newspaper man even figures it is a good publicity scheme for him to want to fight a duel with me. This I refuse.

It is getting to be no good Hotch. Mary is fine but it is getting her down. She has been <u>exemplary</u> though. Have her folks settled in a good nursing home on the beach outside of Gulfport that they like and are very happy in. She's happy and healthy except for the damned people.

I'm going to have to be ruthless about people coming here. Will be once Miguel leaves.

Wish the Christ you were here for what is funny of it. It is about as resting and favourable to the production of literature as Hurtgen Forest. But have started the counter-attack. A. [Adriana] won't take any phone calls from anyone. Long distance neither.

If we had any brains we should have been killed at Murchison Falls and come back under some other names and continued to write posthumously.

Everything I should write you about I haven't written about. I wish the Christ some jerk like Scott Fitzgerald or who likes to be notorious had ours. But will fight out of it ok.

Have all the bullfight stuff on that Kansas wetback fighter [Córdoba] for you when you need it.

Hope the hurricane didn't hit you too badly. Any at all is too badly.

Mary sends her love.

Will write a sensible letter soon as I get the joint cleaned out. Hope they don't clean me out of it first.

Am 37 pages (typed) along on the 2nd story. This letter just to let you know why haven't written. Did you ever read a shittier book or books than [William Fain's] The Lizard's Tail or [William Faulkner's] A Fable? Wish I could read good book to cheer me up on writing.

How are you doing kid? How does everything go, really? Please write and forgive my sloppiness about letters.

Best always
Papa

that reserve job: AEH recalls this as an assignment for the Air Force Reserve.

They got out an announcement: Thomas M. Pryor, "Hemingway Signs to Appear in Film: He Will Also Write Story of Big-Game Hunting in Africa for Two Independents," *New York Times,* September 2, 1954, p. 18.

Winston Guest: Met EH while on safari in 1933 and served as first mate aboard the *Pilar* during its sub-hunting missions (*Final,* 65).

Dave Shilling: Third-ranking ace of the Fifty-sixth Fighter Group during World War II.

visiting us is part of the tour: A photographic essay describing this event appeared in *Look,* April 19, 1955, pp. 105–8.

Luis Miguel Dominguín: Top Spanish matador who met EH in 1953. EH had referred to Miguel's father, also a matador, unfavorably in *Death in the Afternoon.* In the Spanish Civil War, Dominguín's father, Domingo Gonzáles Mateos, had sympathized with Franco and the Nationalists, while EH had sided with the Republicans.

Mme. Tussaud's: Madame Tussaud's Wax Museum continues to be one of the most highly visited attractions in London.

Marthe Richard: Pilot, spy, and prostitute who mounted a successful campaign to close down many French brothels following World War II (*Choice,* 87).

A tramp newspaper man: Ed Scott, columnist for the *Havana Post,* challenged EH to a duel over comments Mary had made to him at a party (*HIW,* 467–69).

the hurricane: Hurricane Carol had struck the Northeast on August 25.

{72} AEH to EH
Nov. 4 [1954 *pmk*] (TLS, 2 pp., JFKL)
A. E. Hotchner R. F. D. 5 Westport, Conn.

Dear Papa:

Goddam but I'm glad about the prize. You and I have kidded about it, pretty rough some times, and God knows it's not to be taken too seriously, but when you actually got the damn thing I felt like I was boozed up, that glad I was. For the dough, of course, which insures that you won't have to take in wash for awhile, but also for the honor. Of course if those thick Swedes had an ounce of sense they'd give it to you every year, but then I'm prejudiced.

I have finally got around to sending you prints of the photos I snapped at the tienta that day. That girl Ava [Gardner] photographs great no matter where you hit her. But I saw her the other night on one of my rare visits to the movies—I was in Detroit doing an automotive story and what the hell else is there to do in Detroit but go to the movies—and she didn't come off too good; however she really gave it a struggle but Mr. Mankiewitz strangled her every time she opened her mouth. The Barefoot Contessa, yet. The hero of this piece, see, (I don't mean Ava, I mean the movie) has his rocks all steamed up over our girl and he's the most manly critter you ever saw and he finally marries her and she's elated as hell and there's the scene in the nuptial bedroom, she all decked out in a flimsy nightie, and he comes in and says, Honey I'm crazy for you but it's got to be kissin' only because—yep, you guessed it—because I was in the war and I stepped on a land mine and the same thing happened to me that happened to a guy in a book I read by chance entitled the Sun Also Sets or something like that. So Ava is Lady Brett if she's anything (and I had my doubts about that) and the hero is our boy. I left about half way through and went to the bar next door where they had a television on; it is a giant 24-inch screen which gives you a big, perfect image, and that's unfortunate because the image I get is what is billed as a championship fight between the Kid and a tiger of a man named Saxton. From the way they carried on hugging and caressing each other I fully expected them to go down on each other. It made me wish I had stayed for the end of that lovely cinema. So that was Detroit. But Ava's a good girl and she's not to blame if they slip her a Mankiewitz hot-foot.

Pete Viertel checked in on his way back to his ski and horse preserve, and he seemed pleased with the movie he did—Frank Harris' Reminiscenses of a Cowboy. He has a new stint to do for Huston and another for [Anatole] Litvak so I guess he can be rated as in the bracket of the full dinner pail.

If you can put your hands on them without too much trouble, would you send me the photos of Cordoba?

Papa, True has been after me to do a piece for them about you, mostly about your interest and participation in sports (now there's a broad word for you). When they first asked me a good while back I said I wouldn't want to do anything until the Nobel thing was out of the way, but now they've started with the phone calls again. How do you feel about my doing it? At first I said

I didn't think it was a good idea, but as they point out if I don't do it they can get someone else who probably would have no background for it. If you think it's okay, would you read the thing for accuracy? True is eager to send me down to talk to you about it, but I've told them you'd like to write a little, which you might do if the stream from the north ever abated. They are also slightly concerned that I don't have enough information about the specifics they want, which is one concern that does not have to be posted on the big board, men. But let me emphasize that I am at present flourishing with projects—I have three sures and a probable for the Post, Digest and Redbook—so this is something to do <u>only</u> if you have no anti feelings whatsoever. I'd appreciate the quick word on this so that I can get these jokers off my tail, one way or the other.

I think it's good sense not to make the trip for the awards. Let it all knit solid. I'm glad you told them how it really was. Most of these Madison Ave. Commandos think guts is a four letter word invented by Mickey Spillane.

Give my love to Mary, that lovely girl, and tell her that the sangria got us through the summer very well. But now we're back on the French stuff.

Your fellow matador,

El Hotchnaldo

the prize: It was announced on October 28 that EH had won the Nobel Prize for Literature.

the photos I snapped at the tienta: EH defines *tienta* as "the testing of calves for bravery on a bull-breeding ranch" (*Death in the Afternoon,* unpaginated glossary). The photos are housed at the Alderman Library, University of Virginia, Charlottesville, 6250i. Some appear in *The Dangerous Summer* and *Papa Hemingway.*

Mr. Mankiewitz: Joseph L. Mankiewicz, writer, producer, and director of *The Barefoot Contessa* (MGM, 1954).

So Ava is Lady Brett: Ava Gardner would in fact play Brett Ashley in the film *The Sun Also Rises* (Fox, 1957).

the Kid and . . . Saxton: Kid Gavilan lost the welterweight title to Johnny Saxton in a controversial decision on October 20, 1954.

Mickey Spillane: Author of a popular series of novels featuring Mike Hammer, a hard-boiled detective who is sexy and sexist. Spillane's clipped prose provided returning veterans with a taste of the language and adventure they had left behind.

Seeking a respite from the furor surrounding the Nobel Prize, the Hemingways spent December 3 through at least the 12th "incommunicado aboard the Pilar at Paraíso" (HIW, 477–78).

{73} EH to AEH
December 7, 1954 (ALS, 3 pp., LOC)
FINCA VIGIA, SAN FRANCISCO DE PAULA, CUBA
On board "Pilar" [*hw*]

Dear Hotch:

Your letter came just as we were leaving the Finca last Friday. Am writing this anchored in the lee of Megano de Casigna down off Pinar del Rio in a big norther.

Am so ashamed I did not answer your first letter. It was chicken not to and there is no excuse. But these are circumstances. I was writing maybe better than I ever have (after 2 months of trying and failing every day) and had 35,000 words done and was going wonderfully. The Prize thing began to build up and I still kept working until the day they sprung. Had no chance to enjoy it, if any of it is enjoyable, just photographers, people mis-quoting you and yammer, yammer, yack, yack and my book, all I gave a shit about, and which I had been living in day and night being knocked out of my head like clubbing a fish (if any of this sounds nuts am writing with the [*Pilar's*] battery charger running into one ear and maybe not out of the other. It has same cycle rate as a V1.)

Well for 2–3 days there are photographers etc. and then I say there won't be any more and I get back into the book. Then characters come down anyway no matter what you say and that you are writing a book means nothing. Bob Manning said he had to write the thing (haven't seen it and it is Time's past anyway probably murder) whether I would see him or not and I got conned into seeing him. He seemed like a very nice guy and I liked him. But christ knows what the piece will be. Then London Times man showed up without giving me any address where I could tell him not to come and a Swede with a Magnum photographer and interrogated (and probably got answers wrong) and photographed for 6 hrs. and 50 minutes and the Japanese Charge D'Affairs who speaks a little basic English plus an elderly Japanese journalist who he is the interpreter for, along with a delegation from the Rotary Club of Guanabacoa, then more Swedes flown from Sweden and I won't try to fill you in on all of it. I am still trying to write through this but am going nuts fast. At same time problems re investing money called 6% preferred in children's estates, checking on the 5% debentures offered in exchange being stole from myself etc.

So when I got the children's end straightened out I thought I better get the hell out before I blow up. So we left on Friday. No good part is am not fit yet to fish in The Tin Kid. I'd forgot how sound you have to be.

Hotch this all sounds like one long blab of Crybabyismo but when I get interrupted when I'm working good it really ruins me.

Now I've got so sick of myself, of answering questions, of photographers, of making God damn pronouncements, of pieces for and against me, I don't want to ever hear about or think about myself so I can get writing clean and fine the way I was going.

I had it written down to write you to ask you to stall True and then finally, in the end, get them to lay off that piece. Nobody takes as an excuse that you want to work or that you don't want any piece or that you've gotten pathological about pieces about you and one god damn more and you'd never write another bloody line. I talked too bloody much about myself on that trip we made to Europe but I was relaxing and drinking and talking after having written a book and I never thought of it as stuff that would be printed. Was just kicking the shit around as I talked too much from Venice to Madrid trying to keep from thinking about how I felt.

Hotch I will pay you whatever True will pay you to write the piece to <u>Not</u> write the piece. I can do that out of the Nobel dough. That will all be gone anyway and I do not know a better way to spend it or one that would make me happier. This is true not True.

I have your Jesus Cordoba pictures and the bull magazines and clippings for you that I will send as soon as get back. Am a shit for not having sent them before.

About Jige [Viertel] I think the simplest way to put it is that Mary does not want to see or hear from Jige. Mary has put up with a hell of a lot from me. I do not want to cross her up on this. It is something she feels strongly about. If she has never spoken about it to you she probably will. You and Jige and I had a wonderful time racing that winter. But after aix en Provence that night nobody had any fun anymore and it is better to remember the fun we had. This stuff is easier to talk about than to write about, and it isn't too easy to talk about. Better just remember what a lovely winter it was racing.

Would certainly like to be heading out to the track with you now. I hated that we missed auteuil last year, hell no, it was this year. But you did see Venice again and you saw the bulls.

Hotch if you can forgive me for being so difficult and know it comes from being beat-up and also from being spooked of destroying what I write with through all this publicity. It really makes me sick, not the phrase, truly sick.

Lillian's thing was my fault. I never should have allowed her to do it. I shouldn't have let Cowley either. Nor have seen Bob Manning whether he writes good or bad. I'm never going to have another piece about me if I can help it. Will move to Africa or stay at sea. Can't even go into the Floridita now. Can't go to Cojimar. Can't stay home. It can get on your nerves really badly Hotch. I know some of it is my fault but some of it isn't too. If I had had any brains once Miss Mary was out I should have stayed in that 2nd kite [airplane] at B'utiaba. Anyway that's how I feel today. But if I had to do it again would play it just as I did. I miss you and I wish we could talk. Gregorio cooking wonderfully. Love to your family.

Hemingstein.

Your letter: Remains unlocated.

writing maybe better than I ever have: One of EH's stories "expanded so steadily under his hand that he thought it might become a novel" (*Story,* 526). Portions selected and edited by Ray Cave were serialized as "The African Journal," *Sports Illustrated,* December 20, 27, 1971; January 2, 1972. The manuscript was later edited by Patrick Hemingway and published as *True at First Light* (New York: Scribner's, 1999).

same cycle rate as a V1: The V-1 missile, or buzz bomb, was a pilotless monoplane with a pulse-jet motor.

Bob Manning said he had to write the thing: Robert Manning, "An American Story Teller," *Time,* December 13, 1954, pp. 70–77 (cover story).

Lillian's thing was my fault. . . . I shouldn't have let Cowley either: Refers to Lillian Ross's *New Yorker* profile (see letter 35) and Malcolm Cowley's *Life* article (see letter 7).

{74} EH to AEH
December 22 1954 (TLS, 2 pp., LOC)
FINCA VIGIA, SAN FRANCISCO DE PAULA, CUBA

Dear Hotch:

Will not attempt to organize this letter properly as just got in from the ocean. Very big N.W. storm; cold and rough and the room still moving. Arrive to find large stack of mail, everything to be done for xmas, boat must be unloaded stuff put in deep freeze, checks to be written etc. We were three days overdue having to wait out the storm. It was the type of storm which breaks over the Morro.

Got in last night and at the club Mary told me that a Mr. Kennedy of TRUE had called her to tell her I had cost you $6,000. by cancelling the piece about me; or rather by my letter asking you to do so. Mary said Kennedy told her you had worked on the piece for a month. That I had written you to go ahead on the piece. That it was the special annual fishing number and that he, Kennedy and you were planning on comeing down to consult with me on the technical fishing part when I had suddenly and inexplicably called this off. We have no tape recorder on our phone but this is what Mary told me and what I have just gone into her room to have her confirm.

That's the first thing I heard when I got in.

Getting home I found your letter about Manning.

This is the true gen on the Manning deal. He phoned Mary and said he had to write a cover story for Time and that they would make it whether I saw him or not. He said he wanted to see it was good instead of bad and would I call back. I talked to him on the phone and said I would give anything if they would not write a cover story on me but he said they were going to do it anyway. I agreed to see him if he did not bring a researcher with him nor a tape recorder and if all questions on wars, religion, personal life, wives etc. were barred. I said that I was working hard and it was murder to interrupt and I remember saying that to interrupt a man while he was writing a book and going well was as bad as to interrupt a man when he was f——-ing. He agreed on this but said the thing had to be done and they were going to do it anyway and he wanted it to be a good piece rather than a bad one.

I finally told him that I would work as hard as I could until he came down in two weeks time and then would lay off two days and fish. I usually try to get out in the boat at least once or twice a week to keep in shape. But I had been working so hard I had not been out in nearly two months.

Bob Manning came down on a late plane and was obviously a good and straight guy. I took him out in the boat two days and he caught a lot of fish. I caught a few watching my back and using every trick I knew not to use it. For your own information it still hurts badly enough when I swing it wrong to bring the sweat out. For your own information I have not been without considerable pain ever since I saw you last. I try to be good about this and I ignore it to the limit of my abilities but I think it would get on almost anybody's nerves. It gets on mine anyway. I can make it and my head feel better by taking a drink. But if I took a drink every time I hurt or felt bad I could never write and writing is the only thing that makes me feel that I am not wasting my time sticking around. That and reading which I do all the time to keep from thinking when I am not writing and to forget about a lot of things. Please forgive me for explaining this at length. I am not in good shape Hotch but I am trying to fight my way out of it. O.K. let us skip my condition which requires exercise to keep my blood pressure down and where exercise is not an unmitigated pleasure. Also let us skip the fact that I do not like to hurt bad and feel bad in front of people.

To resume Manning stayed here in the little house the first night fished the next day, stayed in the little house the next night and fished the following day. We talked about writing which, after all, is the trade a writer is supposed to know something about. I liked him which is not really a disloyalty to TRUE which is not after all my Alma Mater. I would rather say For God For Country and For Keeps than for Yale or for TRUE. But would rather omit such slogans. Anyway Manning slept the end of the second day at the Hotel Nacion and went back to N.Y. and wrote a piece where he kept all his promises and anything snide was inserted by the management. If that seems to you like I was seeking publicity Hotch that is the way it will have to seem I guess. He said Time was going to do something whether I liked it or not and he would try to keep it straight if I saw him. He kept his promise. To continue this disorganized attempt to get some of the shit out of the electric fan. I had your first letter about True wanting a piece and intended to answer it every day but because you had said it was not urgent, that you did not need the jack etc. I did not interrupt my work (Did 45,000 words on new book) to write anybody. I owe Pete [Viertel] a letter. Have not written A. [Adriana] in two months. Was only writing checks and business letters and my own stuff in some sort of race against I cannot tell you exactly what. You could call it trying to keep from going nuts I guess. Think of it this way: injuries to the brain and spinal cord, the kidneys and the liver which is the seat of valor don't clear up by snapping your fingers and saying "Clear up." You have to take it slow and easy and you can do so much a day. I opted for writing which cheers me up and takes me out of whatever hell I happen to be in. So as a worthless son of a bitch I did not answer your letter but instead took it to the boat to answer. On the morning we were shoving off your other letter about having come to a decision on TRUE was in the mail and I took it to the boat. From the boat anchored inside of Megano de Casigua I wrote you a letter which evidently flang the shit into the fan.

So now we have poor TRUE bitched by me. The editor of True had written me and I had answered him, early on in this book that still would like to be allowed to write, that I could do no pieces because I could not interrupt my writing. This letter should be proof that I am a liar if not much worse and as I do interrupt my writing. I also saw Bob Manning, seeking, obviously, publicity. Actually laying it on the line for poor bloody Ezra Pound knowing all the trouble I will get into for it. If you heard something called Meet, E.H. (probably publicity I sought,) the Editor of TRUE should know he is dealing with shit.

So now we should seek a solution. Publish anything you have written. The only sports I was ever outstanding in were fishing and shooting. You would have to get that from people who have seen me do it, I do not know who you would know that could give you the true gen on those. It should certainly not come from me. I have had long strings of shooting in the field and on big game hotter than Willie Mays in baseball. But am I the son of a bitch to describe them? The guys who know about these things are inarticulate, reserved and would think someone was trying to frame Ernie.

What you can do is publish whatever you have written and put this in a box.

"Quotes. As regarding sports I was a mediocre ball player; a slightly better foot ball player; a worthless tennis player and a contemptible performer on the violincello and tuba. Boxing I learned the really hard way and I had a certain aptitude for it. Anything about boxing or fighting is my own business and I could always be broke and wish to write about it myself. I deplore the tendency that any literate man should have everything that he knows about and has personally experienced written about by someone else who neither knows about it nor has experienced it. This is especially true about fishing and shooting which were the only things I was ever good at. These are sports which are not performed in public nor in stadiums and so those who are any good at them, if they tell about them truly are almost invariably regarded as liars.

"Now the field of Big Game hunting especially has become the province of the professional liar. There are even entire magazines devoted to the exploits of these dubious characters. A man who has done anything worth doing should keep his mouth shut and if he writes write only for those who know what he is writing about." Ernest Hemingway

Hotch publish whatever you have written with this (correct spelling) in a box and your and TRUE'S troubles are over.

Visits by Mr. Kennedy are out repeat out. You and your wife are always welcome here.

Will send this today and call you to let you know it is enroute.

Best to all for Christmas Papa.

Papa

the Morro: Morro Castle, at the entrance to the Havana harbor.

Mr. Kennedy of TRUE: Douglas Kennedy, editor of *True.*

your letter about Manning: Remains unlocated.

laying it on the line for . . . Ezra Pound: Pound (1885–1972) was a friend of EH's since the 1920s. For making Fascist broadcasts during World War II, he was tried for treason, declared insane, and institutionalized. EH sent him $1,000 of his Nobel Prize money and supported the effort to free him. Pound was finally released in 1958 (*Final,* 296).

Meet, E.H.: "Meet Ernest Hemingway," a critical and biographical introduction to the author prompted by his winning the Nobel Prize, aired on NBC radio on December 19, 1954, narrated by Leon Pearson and featuring John Mason Brown, Max Eastman, Charles Fenton, Sidney Franklin, Leonard Lyons, and a dramatic reading by Marlon Brando. In a passage excised from *Papa Hemingway,* AEH describes EH wittily exposing inaccuracies in the commentary as the two listened to a long-playing record of the broadcast. Hotchner Papers, box 2, 347–69, Washington University.

publish whatever you have written: A piece was eventually published as "Who the Hell Is Hemingway?" *True,* February 1956, pp. 14–19, 25–31, 68. It was a disjointed collage of photos, recollections, reviews, and rumors, most of which had been previously published. Contributors included John Peale Bishop, Robert Capa, Malcolm Cowley, Marlene Dietrich, Sidney Franklin, John Groth, Mary Hemingway, Jed Kiley, Leonard Lyons, John O'Hara, Leon Pearson, Lillian Ross, Edward Scott, Charles Scribner, Jr., Toots Shor, and Philip Young.

{75} EH to AEH
December 31 1954 (TLS, 2 pp., LOC)
FINCA VIGIA, SAN FRANCISCO DE PAULA, CUBA

Dear Hotch:

Mary had a letter from Douglas Kennedy of True, very nice letter, and speaking highly of you and on the last page it says this

"With the understanding that your husband had no objection, Hotch and I had agreed to that $6000 package price; we had already made our reservations to Cuba; and True had planned its whole April fishing issue around this one story."

The italics are mine.

Mr. Kennedy has probably shown you the letter. I hope I handled the matter of Bob Manning comeing down here in my letter to you but Mr. Kennedy's letter says also—

"I know your husband is fed [up], that he wants to get back to work. I have just one telling question: if your husband will submit to the Bob Mannings (and the Swedes and the Japs <u>et al</u>.) why won't he sit still for an old friend and for a magazine he likes?"

It is quite true that I like True as a magazine and have it sent to Patrick in Tanganyika. It is also true that you are an old and valued friend.

I think you might make it clear to Mr. Kennedy though that in your first letter to me you said the matter was not pressing and that you had plenty of work ahead and did not need to write the article. I was wrong in delaying an answer but I was absolutely swamped with correspondence and I did not think it was the most urgent of the letters pending and took it with me on the Pilar to answer it when I could enjoy the fun of writing you. Your second letter came when we were leaving the house to go aboard the boat.

I apologize to Mr. Kennedy if he had the impression I had invited him down here or agreed to the article. But I do not know how he could have received such an impression from me when I had been writing my closest and oldest friends asking them to please omit visits they had planned to see us as I was working and in not in shape to see people. In the same mail sent off to you from the boat I wrote Alfred Vanderbilt, for instance, asking him to please not come down on a visit he had planned and I have known him since 1933 and 34.

Some of the angles on this thing are very hard for me to figure. I had never been offered more than $4000 for a piece or long story by True and I had no idea you commanded such prices. I thought you were probably getting at most $2000. I can't afford to pay even some one I am as fond of as you $6000. not to write a piece about me that you said was neither necessary nor urgent to write. But I feel badly to be made to feel a shit for not doing something I had never promised to do and for costing you a huge fee.

In case Mr. Kennedy still thinks I am seeking publicity while pretending it is harming to me and an interruption to me can I tell you that this week, so far, I have turned down the chance of a piece by J. P. McEvoy Reader's Digest; some six different journalists who have wanted to come out to the house, a man from Argosy who, according to his Air-Attache at the Embassy would pay $1000. if I would let him come out and make some pictures and just now finished writing a letter to Bob Edge turning down a proposition that would have been very attractive to anyone who wished publicity.

Every day there are letters, phone calls and brutal interruptions. It is getting on Mary's nerves and it hit mine a long time ago. I do not want to be driven out of here in the good working months. It is my home and my work place and I love it. But I am not a public performer, nor am I running for office. I am a writer and I have a right to work and also a right to make a fight to stay. I like True and have always had good relations with them. But I should think that they could understand how it is to write under really bad handicaps when you have something and are going good and have to stay in it for the whole 24 hours and not be interrupted. Should a guy be asked to throw away and lose a book that is as much a part of his life as anything can be to help any magazine get out any given issue?

Hotch I explained to you privately that my nerves are shot to hell with the pain and that is not a thing I would tell anybody. You know that a first rate writer has to have a delicate writing mechanism. You don't write with a club or a hatchet. You can't use junk. You have to take it cold turkey. You look awful and the lousy pain shows on your face. So they take photographs of you. During that hell time after the prize somebody told me that one photographer boasted at the Floridita after he left the house that he got 425 shots of me. The guy shooting all of the time even crowding into the pantry when I was talking private on the long distance. Then the outfit that made them sent them all to me as a present thinking I'd like to have them. Some 414 of them looked more or less like Chinese Torture shots. They had even thought of taking a picture of Blackie lying in front of my empty chair just in case.

Well a cable has just arrived this morning New Year's day mail addressed to Robert Ruark care of Ernest Hemingway Finca Vigia San Francisco de Paula Cuba. I guess Mr. Kennedy will never be convinced I didn't invite Mr. Ruark down.

Felt pretty cheerful this morning until I saw the cable. Went to bed at ten on New Year's eve and didn't eat supper, didn't drink anything, washed and scrubbed, put the new stuff the Skin Specialist gave me yest. on the chest and on the face (had clipped off the damned beard for Xmas) and in four days my face broke out with something a little handsomer than jungle rot. Mary had been dressing another special gift item on the trip that I won't bore you with. But the face makes impetigo look like The Skin You Love To Touch. It is sort of comic to have this all outside while you are making your main fight inside. Don't know whether it's the anti-biotics' revenge or whether somebody sticking pins into a piece of wax in Africa.

Anyway good luck, Hotch. New Year's resolution not to pay any attention to any physical troubles but just follow Dr.'s orders and try to train good and get my work done.

Hemingstein

Alfred Vanderbilt: Alfred G. Vanderbilt II (1912–1999) met EH in 1934 on a fishing expedition to Malindi, on the northern Kenyan coast (*Story,* 256).

J. P. McEvoy: Editor of *Reader's Digest* who lived near Havana.

Bob Edge: CBS sports commentator.

a cable has just arrived . . . addressed to Robert Ruark (1915–1965): Ruark traveled extensively in Africa in the 1950s, writing journalism and fiction about the continent; EH owned five of his books. On November 3, Ruark wrote to EH to congratulate him on winning the Nobel Prize and to express his hope that he might see him around the first of the year. When a cable for Ruark arrived at the finca on January 1, the Hemingways forwarded it to him along with a letter saying that they were sorry to have missed him. He replied that he had decided not to call after seeing a sign posted on the finca's gate to deter visitors. Robert Ruark Papers, University of North Carolina at Chapel Hill.

The Skin You Love To Touch: Slogan introduced by Woodbury's Facial Soap in 1911.

1955

2/21/55 (ALS, 3 pp., JFKL)
Orange Court Hotel/Orlando, Florida

Dear Papa—

I am sorry to have signed off for a while, but I have been battling class A shit on the home front, + you know how rough + destructive this can be, so I figured what you probably needed least on a long list of things you need least, are letters from me steeped in black ass, which is what we are currently steeped in—three shades of Black Ass, ranging from black to blackest. But I'm away from it for now, I am doing a baseball story here with old Clark Griffith + enjoying it. The old man (he is 85) talks baseball past + present, wonderfully, + although he may drop dead tomorrow, he's got everything as of now—ears, eyes, energy—an inducement to be old, I guess, but from the way I've been looking at it—the Life Span, that is, respectfully capitalized—I'm ready to check out any time. I'll swing around down here, a few more training camps, + then face what some idiot once called the music. Music, shit!

What a horseshit business all that True ruckus was, the way those guys stirred it. $6000 package deals, fishing issue, big conferences in Havana, TIME is getting preferential treatment, + on + on + on. I think I squared it all away finally, with only the loss of four or five of those life years I care nothing about, but I wonder if the TRUTH as distinguished from TRUE ever got through to you? Kennedy had been after me for a long time to do such a story—I guess since last July or so, but I said I couldn't possibly be [doing] anything until after Nobel, if + when. Then pressured after the Nobel, I said no, he said we'll get someone to do a re-write of Lillian Ross + other such sources, I said I would ask you if okay + if you'd read it + correct, but your time was valuable + <u>you</u> <u>had</u> <u>to</u> <u>be</u> <u>paid</u> <u>as</u> <u>well</u> <u>as</u> <u>I</u> if you cooperated, + to remember your time was valuable. (You recall our revered Auteuil slogan, don't you, made up in the heat of winning "Share & Share Alike"?) So this is the "package deal", I presume. As for it being a fishing issue, this was never mentioned to me—I was to write a simple, declarative piece about you, shorn of shit, + against my better judgment. I know nothing about fishing, don't pretend to, don't pretend anything, never have. As you know, when I heard about the fishing issue I dug up the Holiday piece + induced them to buy that. But, they said, we still need your piece because although it is a fishing issue yours was to be the only non-fishing article in a fishing issue. So how's that for the fried turds right off the griddle? Six phone calls a day—count 'em six, meantime I talk to you, get letters containing box complete with coffin nails, so I finally try to hold on to whatever sanity I've got left by writing the goddam article + making it so bland they are forced to go with the Holiday piece & we have put me off to the vague future, Lady Future, the foul whore who acts like a Duchess. Rice offered me some money, but like I said, dough had nothing to do with this; I thought, in the beginning, I was acting in your best interests, wound up at the other end, glad you at least salvaged a few bucks out of the wreckage. As for the grand descent on Havana, Kennedy was all booked on his own to storm Finca Vigia + I knocked that off + said if you wanted to see him I'd let him know. Whatever he said to you, I can't be responsible for. I know only what I told him. As for me, I was going to Jamaica + I said I would stop <u>if</u> <u>you</u> <u>wanted</u> <u>to</u> <u>see</u> <u>me</u> <u>about</u> <u>the</u> <u>article</u>. Quite different from what was told to you.

Well, you can bet I know how to handle the situation from here on out. I have had two magazine inquiries since, + a phone call from Sam Boal, asking how he should go about something or other for Good Housekeeping, the magazine of that sterling prick, Herbert Mayes, + my answer to one + all is uniform: I have no advice, I have no information, I know nothing, see nothing, hear nothing, + and anybody implicates me in any way will be ball-less within the hour. Before all this TRUE shit hit the revolving door, I had helped Marlene [Dietrich] with her answer in the THIS WEEK series; but you know she writes very well, for an actress, + only needs a little editing. I have gotten her a researcher for her book, which she seems set on doing. It has nothing to do with you—I have queried her closely on this point.

I make plans to live abroad. I am sick + sour of this life + Conn. + TRUE +

the Squeeze + all that can come of this is the ultimate destruction of the few things I care about. I have always ridden my own horse but it's gotten rough now with the Certified Creeps trying to steal the saddle out from under. If you ever get a few minutes from the book which I am delighted to hear, moves so well, give me a few words on that Latin bitch, Status Quo. My mail gets to me from the Westport address. I am sorry to be so cheerless, but thinking about the kids is what makes me that way. How do you reconcile it about kids? Lovely kids who break your heart even when you are around them all the time. That's what moves around inside + tears you. And ruins your sleep which was already half-ruined. But I'll put this together + straighten up the old crate + maybe brighten the picture tube next time I write.

To Miss M. my fondest love. Are you any better? The back thing worries me. Is it still as bad? If so, maybe you should get a couple of hot specialists M. D.s to take a look. Wish I could give you a couple of my vertebrae—you think they can transplant vertebrae?

Yours,
Hotch

I've come down to Daytona for the speed races. First time here. Helleva beach, isn't it?

---

the home front: According to AEH, the Hotchners were having marital difficulties.

Clark Griffith (1869–1955): Pitcher in the 1890s, the first manager to draft Cuban players, and ultimately the owner of the Washington Senators. AEH remembers writing a piece about Griffith for *This Week*.

Auteuil slogan: In December 1949, when the Hemingways and AEH won their bet on Bataclan II, EH tossed the winnings on a bed and, using a walking stick, divided them into three equal piles (*HIW,* 288).

I dug up the Holiday piece: Ernest Hemingway, "The Great Blue River," *Holiday,* July 1949, pp. 60–63, 95–97 (see note to letter 2).

box complete with coffin nails: The quotation that EH provided in letter 74 with the request that it be run in a box.

Sam Boal: Colleague of Mary when she was a correspondent in London during World War II and the Hemingways' occasional house guest and traveling companion (*HIW,* 285). Boal had published one article about EH ("I Tell You True," *Park East,* December 1950, pp. 18–19, 46–47; January 1951, pp. 36, 48–49), and was planning another.

I had helped Marlene [Dietrich]: Dietrich's article, "The Most Fascinating Man I Know," was about EH (*This Week,* February 13, 1955, pp. 8–9).

{77} EH to AEH
March 14 [1955 *pmk*] (TLS, 2 pp., LOC)
FINCA VIGIA, SAN FRANCISCO DE PAULA, CUBA

Dear Hotch:

Terribly sorry about the Black Ass and cause of same. The only negative satisfaction is that I don't think Europe would have been any fun last year. They never had a day of Spring and it was wet, cold, over crowded and expensive as hell and summer never came at all. Not just a bad British summer: everywhere.

This winter has been miserable with floods and in the Spring it will be so over-run with Tourists. When you get homesick for it remember the Autobahn with the signs on both sides from Mestre to Milano and Milano to Torino. You can remember that lovely day and how the Alps looked to have something to hold on to. That stretch below Turin to the border. But I can get black ass about going anywhere when I remember those autograph people in a remote town like Cuneo.

Hotch one thing you have to remember is that the economics of people having busts-up maru is almost fatal. You not only loose childrens no matter what you're promised but you go straight into economic slavery and what's left unless you hit jackpots is never enough to satisfy anybody else. Maybe I just read all this in an article by you. But from what I remember any sort of Modus Viviendi if you can keep from fighting can be better. The last time with Miss Martha it was a break to break up on acct. no children, no love, she was making more money than I was and convinced she had a much better future without me and was probably right since our interests and tastes were not the same and I liked to write and could not match her in ambition. Nobody can advise anybody. I don't want to try. But I believe I did read some of the economic stuff in a piece by you.

Am sorry that True business was all so screwed up. When I'm working I have no sense of time but I do think the True editor had less and didn't know how far into it guys get when they are working. Am on page 321 [of what became *True at First Light*] now typed. Been carrying a certain amount of weight and poor Mary more with her father so bad up in Gulfport and then having to commute back and forth from there. He died finally and she had to get her Mother settled and handle her. It was all an awful job for her and I have been trying to help her back in best shape, help with income tax (was a complicated year to keep track of) and write on book every day. Am writing this in the morning early before I start because if I don't will never get it written. Forgive anything I skip, miss, state improperly etc. Was only trying to bring in my end of contact.

About health am much better all the way around and should get better all the time because can swim now that the water is warm enough again. Taking lots of exercise. Been out twice in the boat this year. Both times loosened up and made me feel better. Don't worry about my health. As soon as can get normal exercise regime will be better all the time. Mary is very healthy but took a bad beating up at Gulfport. Thanks very much for the vertebrae. But the back is going to [be] absolutely o.k. On writing have been averaging over 4000 words a week since the first of the year. That's too much for me. But it is the 7 day week on the 0700 to 1330 duty. Too rough at 55 and you shouldn't have to do it. Am going [to] pace myself better now.

Thanks about Marlene and the piece. She wrote me you were helping her so I could trust it.

Mary scratched the Sammy Boal thing. She likes him and would have liked to help him out but with the Gulfport business and having to come back here straight into the income tax thing. She couldn't do it. Sammy drives me nuts having him around and she was kind about that.

Hotch reading your letter I can see how worthless this one is to you. About kids I don't know. With Bumby (Jack) everything worked out fine. The other boys it was fine for a long time. Then Pauline started deliberately to turn them against me and made a hell of a conflict in them where there wasn't any. After Patrick's long siege down here where we had him out of his head for three months and had to feed him rectally for nearly two and did the damndest job of nursing. Probably or maybe never told you about it I can't remember now what year it was and whether knew you then or not. Anyway. after this was all over and we'd won Pauline who'd seen it and come and helped and lived and claimed to have the greatest admiration in the world for what we'd done and really had too told Patrick and her relatives I'd abandoned and neglected him. Everything that we had done here she transferred as having been done by her back in Key West and even collected for from her Uncle Gus. Actually Patrick had come over here to take his examinations for Harvard from Key West where he'd had a concussion when his brother drove an MG into a tree. Patrick had played five sets of tennis afterwards with the pro. Pauline had let him lay out all night on the grass because as she said she thought he was drunk. (He'd never been drunk). He hit here the day after and I told Mary after he had talked at the table that he was out of his head. Went with him to the University where the exams were given stayed to pick him up and have lunch with him and for the afternoon session. Brought him home and that night he went out of his head. Had to stay with him and hold him to keep him from harming himself. Taylor Williams was in the Little House but he is almost stone deaf and I carried P. over my shoulder there to try to wake Taylor with P. having bitten through my hand. Would rather skip all of it if it is the same to you. Anyway he was violent until he got too weak finally but had to be nursed by Sinsky[,] Roberto Herrera, Ermua the great pelota player and me. You could not have hired people to do what we did for him and nor have taken the beatings without hitting back[;] in an institution (any in Cuba anyway) they would have let him die or kill himself. But with three good doctors, one average Dr. and one poor Dr. we pulled him through. I have the daily log and from late Spring until Fall I averaged less than four hours sleep a day and two months averaged 2½ hours. Anyway we saved him and he went to Harvard and graduated magna cum laude and is now in Tanganyika. When it was over my blood pressure was 225 over 125. But the point of this is that after that, which was the biggest fight I ever made ever, the boy's mother, when he has no memory of what happened, (skip all therapy) when you are divorced will tell him that his father abandoned him and she saved him. This is only to tell you that you can't figure on retaining much of children these days if you split up. I skipped all the really horrible part.

Let's skip all the gloomy stuff now should we. I was not trying to prove anything. I don't know anything. That story isn't a normal one because in Pauline's family the children, and there is a long history of it, tend to blow at adolescence and when women's have any feeling of guilt they tend to get rid of it by slapping it onto you. P. probably would have blown anyway and the concussion just set it off.

Would it do you any good to go down and live in the Key West small house with the pool? You can have it for a month if you want it. Mary put it all in shape and the pool (sixty foot, regulation, fills and empties over night semi-salt wonderful water.) House really lovely and charming place. You can have it for longer if I know to arrange the time.

The enclosed letter from Bill Roeder came Saturday. I called him at the McAllester Hotel and told how you had been writing a piece on sports and me and had laid off it so as not to interrupt and that I had already told you the story Billy Herman had told him probably (It was about the fight with Hughie Casey and the other stuff you could check with Billy if you ever did a piece and the fun we all used to have in the old days) and he said he understood and would lay off. I haven't seen anybody nor given any interviews nor nothing since I wrote you no matter what you may read.

Had better knock off and send this. Worthless news from all over including Dark Continent. I better get back to writing on book now. Excuse lousy letter. But after I work am too pooped to write and I was spooked about writing on subjects you mentioned. All children gen absolutely confidential. Not as in Confidential. Things are really filthy with those outfits aren't they? Lots of no good things going on. Juan [Sinsky] is going to town so will mail this.

Love from us both.

Hemingstein

an article by you: A. E. Hotchner, "You Cannot Afford a Divorce," *This Week* (*Choice,* 119).

Mary scratched the Sammy Boal thing: Despite this, Boal later published "The Hemingway I Know" (*Gent,* December 1957, pp. 7–10, 55–57) and "The Old Man and the Truth (Ernest Hemingway)" (*Escapade,* August 1959, pp. 53–54, 56, 58–59, 70).

Patrick's long siege down here: Patrick arrived at the finca in April 1947 with an undiagnosed concussion, the result of a car accident; he became violent and required constant care into July (*Final,* 155–57).

Taylor Williams: Chief guide at Sun Valley, Idaho, and friend of EH since 1939.

Ermua the great pelota player: Félix Ermúa, "The Kangaroo," technically a jai alai player and a member of the *Pilar's* sub-hunting expeditions. Norberto Fuentes, *Hemingway in Cuba* (Secaucus, NJ: Lyle Stuart, 1984), 199.

The enclosed letter from Bill Roeder: Remains unlocated. Roeder was a sportswriter for the *New York Journal-American.*

the story Billy Herman had told him . . . about the fight with Hughie Casey: Herman and Casey were among the Brooklyn Dodgers whom EH met during their spring training in Cuba in 1941 (see letter 11). One day, after drinking and shooting at the gun club, the group returned to the finca for more drinking. EH challenged Casey to a boxing match and was beaten, whereupon he challenged Casey a duel. The players left and EH went to the ballpark the next day to apologize. Donald Honig, *Baseball When the Grass Was Real: Baseball from the Twenties to the Forties Told by the Men Who Played It* (New York: Berkley, 1976), 139.

Confidential: Scandal sheet with a circulation of 4 million in the mid-1950s, more than any other magazine in the country.

{78} AEH to EH
22 Mar. 55 (TLS, 4 pp., JFKL)
A. E. Hotchner R. F. D. 5 Westport, Conn.

Dear Papa:

Such a damn fine letter you wrote me, like the whole thing is blowing when in comes the guy from the bullpen and throws one in there and the whole team steadies down. Sure, the economics is something I know only too well from lawyering and sure I wrote about it, but like the doctors who kill themselves doing precisely what they warn their patients not to do, I was somehow figuring that all this couldn't happen to me. But don't ask me how. However, as you know, when the situation becomes unbearable, you barter off anything deluded by the momentary stress. But to hear how it was with you and how you felt inside was exactly what I needed: I am a strong boy with a good back and I can take a lot—certainly, on quiet reflection, I am a far way from my tolerance point. The travel was very good for me. I had time to think and to reassess. I think I have it clear and straight now. It was the first real boil up in me that I can remember, and a boil-up is good for the Spring blood—or so I'd like to think. But I cooled down in the hot sun and the baseball atmosphere. Christ, I enjoy baseball! Going out to the field I still get as excited as when I played second base for the Kennard Grammar School in South St. Louis (where you live by courtesy of Augustus Busch), or shortstop for Soldan High where I learned to switch-hit and not get suckered any more by right-handed curve-ballers, or pitched for Washington U. where the coach taught me to throw what in those days was called an inshoot but now is called a slider. I guess going out to the mound to pitch was the most excitement there was, and the first pitch always felt so fucking strange you wondered if you had ever thrown a baseball before. Well, that's how the feeling still is, in a way, especially when I'm around the Cardinals. The cards have a rookie named [Ken] Boyer at third who's sensational—Christ, what a glove man! I was there on a story that involved [Stan] Musial; it was at the start of training and one morning, before regular practice started, Musial put me in the batter's box and let me try to hit a few. A tall new boy named [Bobby] Tiefenauer was throwing them, but not hard since it was still too early, but I was way off until Stan moved my feet and told me a few things and son of a bitch if I didn't belt one 14 miles on a hot line. That was the most fun, but any and everything about baseball is fun for me, as you have discovered—I could listen to your baseball talk around the clock, and the thing is that you know about the players better than anybody else. But how come, Papa, you've never written a baseball story? You know so many wonderful ones. As a matter of fact, am I mistaken in thinking that besides Lardner's classic about the midget, there is no really good baseball story? How can that be?

It's so goddam nice of you to offer me the Key West small house, which I am sure is a perfect place to be right now, but I shot back up here because one of the little girls fell quite sick with temperature around 105 day after day and nobody knowing what the hell was causing it, and now she is much better but

I'd like to keep an eye on her; but, also, there is a lot of work to do that I must do right here. I am now at that happy time when I have to turn down magazine assignments because there are too many; I do all that This Week asks me to do because they are such a splendid bunch of guys to work for, and they stand by me and they are as loyal as if I were a member of the staff; I do all I can for the Post because they are the best of the big ones, in my opinion. They all pay very well—magazine prices have increased quite a bit (for example, last year Fawcett paid me $3000 for a straight piece on Barbara Hutton)—but a straight diet of magazine articles becomes dull and you get the feeling of being in a job if you don't mix it up—that's why I have tried my hand at a few television plays, and surprised the hell out of myself with how well they have gone. I guess Al [Rice] told you that I turned The Battler into a drama that is going to be done on NBC's big May spectacular. Such wonderful characters in that story, Papa, it would be hard not to make a spectacular out of it.

I'm very excited over what we can do with the touring company idea that Al discussed with you. I feel that a woman who is attractive, talented, and a big name is an essential part of the offering, along with an equally qualified man, and I have talked to Marlene [Dietrich] as the number one candidate (for the woman part, although for my dough she could play all the parts.) She is overwhelmingly for it, and I'm sure that it will please you to have her in the company. It might also be a way for me to ease her off the authoress kick, which I think she'd be happier without. She's told you all about this fucking book commitment, I know, and now McCall's wants to print four chapters in advance of publication as independent articles and will pay good dough for it, but why is it that everyone thinks that this word racket is such a pipe? Why can't they see what a big backbreaker a book is, and that it's like building a pyramid, and that it demands everything, especially from the inside. Not that Marlene isn't serious and able, she is, and I am only too happy to help her, as I have been, with advice and guidance, but I feel that she is doing this because she is not in a position to pay back the advance Doubleday gave her, not because she wants to write on beauty; so, if she comes in on this project she will have all the money she needs and can easily pay back her debt, so that the writing of the book will become something she <u>wants</u> to do not <u>has</u> to do. I am very hopeful that the project will turn out well for everyone concerned.

I was sorry as hell to hear about Mary's father dying—I can imagine what an emotional and physical wallop that was for her. I feel badly that on top of that and trying to get yourself back in shape and trying to work on the book, which sounds like it's coming on wonderfully, I had to weigh in with my own pound of troubles. I usually contain my troubles pretty well, but I was at that point where I needed to talk and you are the only guy with whom I am close enough to discuss these things and know that the discussion is as between brothers. But I am truly sorry to have piled on more stress when just the opposite was needed. But I'm so glad to hear that you are mending and swimming a little and rounding into good shape again. Perhaps by the time the filming of Old Man and the Sea begins, you will be able to fish it. Pete [Viertel] should be showing up pretty soon to start on the screenplay, shouldn't he? I still can't quite get over how much I liked Pete after the Madrid period, as compared to how I felt after the '50 trip. He is very talented in movie writing and I'm sure he will do well by your book.

By getting away from here, I realized that one of the chief factors in my pile-up was this fucking Westport; this community with its chi-chi shits and Madison Avenue pushers just ain't the right place for me. It's a great house we live in, big and French and on six acres surrounded by good woods, but the people around here make you keep your fingers in your throat most of the time. So I've got to move myself out of it, maybe not full time because to keep going with the magazines you've got to be in the environs occasionally, but for sizable stretches. This summer I plan to head north, toward Maine, and stop off to live wherever it looks good; the kids are very pliable and adventurous so no problem there. And then next year I'll transplant the outfit to Europe somewhere, as I once discussed with you. Paris, if I can afford it. I can rent this house for pretty good dough and that will help. I would like to go back to Spain, to see more bullfights and to see some of the country to the south and more of the Basque country which was so very attractive; that would be a fine place to live with a family, I think. Whether I could produce as much and as easily I would have to find out. A chance to go to Palestine to do a piece there has just come up, and I'd like very much to go, but I must stay here for now to get our tour project in shape and work on a few pressing assignments. I can probably pick up on the Palestine thing later. If I go, I'll also spend some time in Istamboul which, since boyhood, is a city that has intrigued me.

Papa, I thank you again for offering the house; I liked Key West very much the time I was there and I would surely like to return—maybe at some future time, if the house happens to be empty, I can have a rain check. And maybe at some future time, we can have another pleasant stretch abroad. Yes, the Alps were as lovely as anything of nature's I ever hope to see, and so were a couple of stretches of the non-billboarded french country, and certainly from Biarritz down; and what about the drive to the Escorial to watch Dominguen?

You're right, let's check the gloom; we always have; we have always believed in the best of times, we have been right often enough to justify a good win bet right now.

Please give Mary my fondest love and sympathy, and ask her if there isn't some New York doo-dad or other that would cheer her that I could send down to her. I know that you have almost all the buyable niceties available right there, but I thought there might conceivably be some item that escaped the merchandising dragnet.

Best as ever,

Krotchner

Our ballet Capital of the World—being performed at the Met again in a series of big galas. Did you receive a recording of the music? If not, I'd like to send you one. Do you have a Long Play machine?

Suggested to Al that he incorporate our venture as Vigia Productions, Inc. Although, on second thought, maybe Bataclan, Inc. would be a better bet.

South St. Louis (where you live by courtesy of Augustus Busch): August A. Busch was the son of Adolphus Busch, founder of the Anheuser-Busch beer empire whose roots lie in St. Louis.

[Stan] Musial: Played 22 years with AEH's hometown team, the St. Louis Cardinals, earning seven batting titles and being named to the All-Star team 24 times.

Lardner's classic about the midget: The story of a midget who is hired to pinch-hit is not one of Ring Lardner's baseball stories but James Thurber's "You Could Look It Up" (*My World—And Welcome to It* [New York: Harcourt, 1942], 85–110).

Fawcett paid me $3000 for a straight piece on Barbara Hutton: The Fawcett publication in question was probably *Redbook.* AEH, phone call with DeFazio, June 14, 2005.

The Battler . . . is going to be done on NBC's big May spectacular: The drama ultimately aired on October 18, 1955.

the touring company idea: Plan for a series of dramatic readings of Hemingway texts that was never carried out.

book commitment: Dietrich's book was eventually published as *Marlene Dietrich's ABC: The Wit and Wisdom of One of the World's Most Wonderful Women* (Garden City, NY: Doubleday, 1962).

Mary's father dying: Tom Welsh died on February 17, 1955 (*HIW,* 481).

{79} AEH to EH
25 May 55 (TLS, 2 pp., JFKL)
A. E. Hotchner R. F. D. 5 Westport, Conn.

Dear Papa:

I unfolded an old Paris map last night and look what fell out. Now if there is any who doubts the hotness of our hands that season let him step forward and take close note of the condition of this destroyed pigeon's eye. Is it any wonder the poor old lady in that stall at Nimes was pee-ing in her pants that night when we knocked off six cards like this one, each for the grand prix of a bottle of champagne, and only two dusty bottles were on the shelves? I have never seen a more beautiful look on anyone's face than on the old lady's when, at the conclusion of our shooting when her moment of catastrophe had arrived, you said, "Madame, will you have the kindness to accept our champagne as a token of tribute to the excellence of your guns." They were, in fact, damn good guns for a shooting booth, but the fact that you found a positive way to unembarass the old lady has always been high in my admiration book. It is a neat eye we cut, though, isn't it? We were shooting against each other that night for ten dollars and we took turns destroying the eyes until finally we called it a stand-off because the cries and bleatings from the dining room across the way—where there were non-shooters with iced feet—interfered with our concentration. But we were happy.

Also enclosed is a newspaper picture which, as a bullfight expert, puzzles me. The caption says that the matador is dropping his cape, as indeed he is, to help a gored banderillero. But how could he make a quité without his cape? Or would he be concerned only with pulling the banderillero off the horn? Seems to me the bull would just hook him again if he were not distracted.

Lawyer Rice says you look fine, work good (discounting distractions) and appear to be in good spirits—which, for Christ'ssake, is all a man is entitled to ask. He gave me your typed paper on Dietrich and I'm very glad that you are going to read a section to see how it goes. One of the pivotal selections will be Kilimanjaro, and I shall send you that shortly and we can discuss it by letter or any way you wish. It is a wonderful reading piece, and my problem is only that I must cut its length; these cuts will most likely be in the flashbacks. Selection of material is very difficult, for everything I re-read, and I am re-reading everything, I would like to include. However, two hours being what they are, I have chosen, in addition to Kilimanjaro, Cat in the Rain, Hills Like White Elephants, A Farewell to Arms, Death in the Afternoon, and For Whom

The Bell Tolls. Of course, I use only selected passages, but I think these give good variety, lend themselves to reading, and I think that a program such as this that did not include A Farewell to Arms and For Whom the Bell Tolls would be regarded with some disappointment by those who came to the the-atre. Also, these particular things are rather good for Marlene.

I know you are busy with your book and soon now with [the filming of] Old Man and the Sea, so I'll try to keep your time spent on this to a minimum. As I understand the agreement, you will read [the adaptation of] Kilimanjaro, and if approved, I won't have to involve you any further.

I have just tried to read Mr. Robert Ruark's definitive novel about Africa, a continent which he discovered, but had to put it down after the third vomit. You have a much stronger stomach than I so maybe you can finish it. Mr. Ruark belongs to a school of writing that can best be described as early Mickey Spillane.

Swimming, lots of tennis at which I am going very good (age will wilt me, like Jackie Robinson, when the summer heat catches up), other outdoor pur-suits—I am in best shape been in for a long time. Have rented a joint on a small offshore island for part of this summer—would like to stay there for good. Give Mary my love and affection.

Your devoted wing shot,

<u>Hotchelmer</u>

look what fell out: Cardboard pigeon target (see pp. 108, 138).

also enclosed is a newspaper picture: AP photo with the caption "Portuguese matador Jose Rose Rodrigues (right) drops cape and runs to help banderillero being gored in the thigh by enraged bull in corrrida staged in Manila. Rodrigues suffered a dislocated shoulder, but helped banderillero escape with his life." A *quité* "is the taking away of the bull . . . by the matadors armed with capes and taking their turns in rotation." Hemingway, *Death in the Afternoon,* glossary.

your typed paper on Dietrich: AEH recalls this as an introduction that was to accompany Dietrich's dramatic reading of EH's work. AEH, fax to DeFazio, November 29, 2004. EH's revisions to AEH's script survive (ViU, 6250f).

busy with your book: By May 11, Mary had typed 404 pages of *True at First Light;* by Thanksgiving the manuscript had grown to 694 pages (*Final,* 289–90).

Mr. Robert Ruark's definitive novel: Probably *Something of Value* (1955), about the Mau Mau uprising.

age will wilt me, like Jackie Robinson: In 1956, after a ten-year career with the Brooklyn Dodgers, Robinson was traded to the Giants and then announced his retirement.

{80} EH to AEH
June 2̶0̶ (22) 1955 (TLS, 1 p., ViU)
FINCA VIGIA, SAN FRANCISCO DE PAULA, CUBA

Dear Hotch:

Mary sent off the Mss. this morning. I'd wanted her to let me add a ps. but she had it all wrapped up. I wasn't conning about the phone. Called at noon Sunday and then until 1230 pm your time. Again on Monday from 2000 to 2330 and left it open for in the morning.

If I sounded brusque or anything on the phone am sorry. The Gen is Alfred [Rice] came down and fucked my work up (necessarily) in May. Leland [Hayward] and Peter [Viertel] took June 1st to June 14th. I got going good when Peter left. Thought I could cut corners by talking with you on phone but failed on that.

Should go to K.W. [Key West] to size up rental situation there and look after children's interest. Children concerned do not answer letters, never help in any way, do not contribute, but always have a feeling they are being bitched. Patrick very nearly did not meet me in Africa because he had a feeling that a proposal I had made to buy up house furniture and give it to him so that the estate could be settled without a destructive auction was a plot. End of talk about children.

Key West place is pleasant with sixty foot salt water pool and ideal conditions for necessary reading and talking. It might be simpler for you to fly direct here. Four hr. something. National flight leaves N.Y. two something pm. or later and is non stop and you fly that on Thursday June 30th arriving here and staying Little House that night. I will work on Thursday and knock off on Friday and we can go out fishing on July first (Friday), and then fly over to Key West at a convenient time on Saturday July 2nd. All that would be good for me and I would pay your flight expenses down and to Key West and then to N.Y. and you'd live here in the house in K.W. and have none otherwise. I am o.k. on cash and can charge it off as a legitimate expense as will have to pay tax if the readings make any money.

We would love to see you here. I always miss you and you are a good friend and I have to make this K.W. trip on acct. of my conscience with my kids worthless or not and I am sure I can do it and not become confused like Willie Mays. Have not been reading my publicity like Willie has and Durocher have. Maybe it has been terrible.

I think it would be nice if you came down here. The aircraft is usually half empty and highly deluxe. Leland made it without even bleeding internally. Alfred [Rice] suffered but Came Through. I think for people like us it would be relaxing.

Have not heard from Marlene [Dietrich] since early May. She was sound about me seeing the stuff. I agree on that. But she certainly crowded you on the 5000. word business. For people who argue for the privelege of laying it under the baserunner's ear when he has to come down bringing his previous history with him both you and I put in a hell of a lot of time being God's Little Gentlemen to people who would regard cutting off our balls as merely a regrettable incident.

· When you come down we will have fun as always and I will be as helpful as I can.

Best always

Hemingstein of Harrow.

H

the Mss.: Probably AEH's adaptation of "The Snows of Kilimanjaro."
Leland [Hayward] and Peter [Viertel] took June 1st to June 14th: The two men talked with EH about filming *The Old Man and the Sea*.

{81} AEH to EH
25 June 55 (TLS, 2 pp., JFKL)
A. E. Hotchner R. F. D. 5 Westport, Conn.

Dear Papa:

Thanks very much for phone call and good letter. I want to be the world's last guy to intrude on your work time and I can't figure why, with all the characters around this fucking joint, there was no one to answer the goddam phone and spare you the re-phoning business. However, when they do catch the phone, the messages usually read like something the British have been trying to decode since 1942, and I have taken to working them instead of crossword puzzles. I've got one on my desk now that I've been at, off and on, for three days, waking sometimes during the night to take a whack at it, and I'm happy to say that I've just cracked it. Message reads: "R. Third Gurd on Cost Tellyos Five O'Clock." The only part of the message I regard with suspicion is the five o'clock. All the rest makes sense. I interrogate the keeper of the message pen, one Rose Mae Collins, age 20, attended cryptology school in New

Orleans, can get no further information of helpful nature despite a few sound ones across the rump with a Louisville slugger, which I figure, should feel familiar to her. Anyhow, like I said, I broke the thing wide open just after breakfast this morning: "Arthur Gordon Costello's Five O'Clock." I phoned Arthur, who has now moved his collection of females [wife and daughters] to Princeton, and he said he understood okay, and that a couple of hours at Tim [Costello]'s at the bar is nobody's loss.

Listen, Papa, I feel very badly about having to come in with the reading scripts at this time. I wish it could have been set aside until you were all squared off on the book, because the book, as we both know, is all that really matters. But the way things work out, we've got to make our move now, and I hope I can come in fast and clean and with a minimum of intrusion—but I realize that having to turn your mind to something other than the book is major intrusion. However, I am not, and hope never to be, like other of the Northerns, Mr. L. Hayward et al., who have to be guested. You were fine on the phone, and I knew about Alfred's necessary visit and the Hollywood contingent stretch. But I am the one guy who resents the disturbance he causes when a book is working, more than anybody you know, so please just let me fit into whatever the routine would be without me. It's damn nice of you to want to give up a perfectly good work day to take me fishing on Pilar, but Key West, I'm sure, is going to be interruption enough without having to give up a perfectly good workday. I will feel much less an intruder if I meet up with you at Key West where we can read and talk at whatever time you are finished working and feel like it. I plan to leave here Sunday, July 3, the airline willing, and will fly or bus to Key West depending on what is available. Mary sent me your address so I'll have no problem. Offer of transportation dough is very much appreciated, but I'm okay. I'm still considerably beholden for a huge pile of past generosities—like the trips and the Venice jewel [see letter 69]. Getting away for a couple of days right now will be a fine thing, the pressures being what they have been.

I am looking forward to seeing you and Mary again, eagerly as hell, but it will ruin the enjoyment if you extend in any way; I'm old family by now, ain't I?

All the best,

hotch

Hotch de Ner of East Passaic

This Week just phoned + asked me to do a thing on Thursday so it works out fine that I don't come Cuba but see you Key West Sunday.

Hotchner flew to Key West on July 3 for a three-day visit with the Hemingways at 907 Whitehead Street; the two men discussed Hotchner's possible dramatizations of several of Hemingway's short stories (PH, 155). EH made numerous interlineations on the script of "The Snows of Kilimanjaro" and objected to the ending, writing, "Fix end. Otherwise OK EH" and, at the end of the manuscript, adding, "OK EH. July 5 1955." The project was ultimately produced in 1967 as The Hemingway Hero.

{82} AEH to EH
14 July 55 (TLS, 2 pp., JFKL)
A. E. Hotchner R. F. D. 5 Westport, Conn.

Dear Papa:

Gerry took off for Canada as soon as I got back—her mother figures to go very quickly—and I have had to smooth out the joint. I finally seem to have established a little order—no law—and have my first opportunity to write to you. As always, being with you, and with Mary, is being with special people, and you are my good friends and I enjoy being with you very much. I hope that having to work on the readings was not too large a pain in the ass for you. I think that we really have a good program shaping up now, thanks to the straight way you worked on them—the way you have always worked with me. Marlene [Dietrich] has asked to see the script before she signs the contract, and I'm getting one ready for her. The contract gives her right of approval, but she prefers to read it first, which is certainly an okay request. I think you and I are going to go very well with this, at least as good as we did with Bataclan II. But I will hold any further details about it, material, etc., until at some future time you have a brief break in your work, and I will try to get Alfred [Rice], Marlene and the other characters to do likewise.

The turtle steaks preserved beautifully and were consumed with cold Tavel and nothing, repeat nothing, can go up against that. What makes Tavel so much better than any other rosé? Just the soil or is there some other secret like a special bee, indigenous to that area, who shits on each grape. I keep thinking about your story about the cat you shot to put it out of misery, and every time I do, I laugh out loud. Probably funniest story you ever told me. And, in a way, the saddest. That's a splendid house and pool, and it's real waste for it not to be rented. I'll tout it around up here—I hope a couple of the pictures do it justice. I should know the rent, however, since that is virtually the first question these money mad characters up here ask.

I cannot really tell you how much I enjoyed seeing you again and sharing the relaxed and hospitable atmosphere of the junior finca. You are in much better shape than when I last saw you and that made me very happy. Naturally I shall guard our various confidences as just that and I'm sure you will too—especially in re (the lawyer re-emerging in me) Marlene. Love to Mary,

Yr Obedient Frnd,
Hotchcock of Banbury Cross
<over>

Marlene's attorney, who just came back from London, tells me her success this year was even greater than last. Some dame, eh?

H

Dear Mary—All vegetation survived, good shape. Gerry in horticulture heaven. Got everything into pots prior to departure. I water. Pls/send Betty's address so I can thank her. As for you, you are the nicest gal ever hostessed, + I thank you from the bottom of my black heart. H.

Hotchcock of Banbury Cross: Play on the nursery rhyme that begins "Ride a cock horse to Banbury Cross."

Betty's address: Betty Bruce was the wife of EH's friend and handyman, Otto Bruce (see note to letter 28).

{83} AEH to EH
30 Aug. 55 (TLS, 2 pp., JFKL)
A. E. Hotchner R. F. D. 5 Westport, Conn.

Dear Papa:

Alfred [Rice] says you have been fishing and hooked on to some really big stuff which beat the hell out of you—but left you happy, I'll bet. We have all been living on the ocean in a little joint where we ate the local catch (mostly flounder, striped bass and lobsters) and spent most of our time swimming in the heavy surf or on our asses. The girls are nut brown, their red hair redder from the sun, happy as two porpoises (and who says porpoises are happy? Half the porpoises this side of Canarsie Straits are getting group therapy.) Geraldine, who was trained from the crib in icy Banff waters, daily scares the shit out of everybody by swimming off beyond the horizon, but she is equipped with flares in her belt so I don't worry. There are very few people. The hurricanes did not actually hit here but the outer winds did and it was a helleva blow. The sand came at you like somebody was firing straight pins out of a machine gun. It was a fine storm.

But now I've ducked back to straighten up this Dietrich thing. Since she left for London, as I told you in Key West, Marlene suddenly became Grand, God knows why. Wouldn't answer letters, so forth. Now she suddenly sweeps in, but I could smell the Big Negative on its way before she got here, because I think Marlene, as she has done on all stage projects all her life, has gone scared. She has a very bad reputation on this count, and I've been expecting this nervousing. Big Beefs about the way she is introduced, that the selections which we prepared are not dramatic enough (that includes Kilimanjaro), that the material should be adapted and not presented straight, that I am not a ster-ling NAME, (I presume like Truman Capote or Christopher Fry who seem to be of her stable), tra la. I explained (1) that this is a reading so we would read it as it was wrote and not have any changes, (2) that I can bring her on any way she chooses, with tits akimbo à la Vegas or not, (3) that the material is not all set—some of it, in fact, only suggested—and would she please stop being so fucking actressy. She calmed, and I think understood, and I am sending her a script with a new introduction for her, which seemed to be her most vehe-ment objection. But she is running very scared, taking wild pot shots, and I think despite what's done that she will in the end happily avert and we will cast in some equally big names. I write you this just as general briefing and suggest if she writes that you say you understand I am sending her new stuff and so we'll all hold off and see. Last night I had a fine professional actor and actress who are friends of mine read Kilimanjaro and the other stories you and I worked on and I can tell you that they read powerfully and beautifully and I have not the slightest reason to doubt they will go fine on the stage. So please, give all this no thought, we are under control for now, despite the huffing and puffing.

Alfred read me your think on The Battler adaptation which, be assured, is faithful to the story. It is virtually the same version that was to have been used on the spectacular, for it is one of the interesting Truths about television (prob-ably the only one) that on an hour program the play only runs 48 minutes (we gotta sell them Pontiac automobiles with their chartreuse fenders, don't we?) Of course, if you'd like to read the script, I'd be happy to send. Only problem involved is one of time, since they are trying to sign Jimmy Cagney and James

Dean but can't because they don't own anything yet. But that's their problem. So, Papa, please give me the word on how you want me to play this—walk up two flights, I aim to please.

I located some fresh turtle steak, did everything Mary told me to do—fiasco. Thus, learned elemental life lesson—don't trust the turtle steak unless you know the man who owns one.

The color pictures of the Key West house turned out fine and I have exhibited them to those I feel are likely candidates for the Key W. stretch—I have a couple of interested people in the balcony, Doctor, but inevitable question is: what is rent, so please give me some idea.

I suppose this is movie time for you, isn't it? I hope it goes well and fast. My best love to Mary.

Yours for the return of the Monarchy,

Sir A. E. Hotchbatten IV (of the Queen's Bath)

[Here AEH sketched a whiskered seal and wrote "His Seal (trained)."]

living on the ocean: The Hotchners were summering in a beach house in Nantucket, MA.

who seem to be of her stable: Possible reference to Dietrich's gay following.

if she writes: Deitrich had in fact already written to EH on August 25, 1955, calling AEH's script "as untheatrical as can be" and objecting to her planned introduction. Fuentes, *Hemingway in Cuba,* 411–12.

James Dean: According to AEH, Dean, whose performance in *East of Eden* (1955) had made him an icon of restless 1950s youth, "read the script and consented to make this his first live television performance" (*Choice,* 177). After Dean died in an automobile crash on September 30, 1955, the lead was played by Paul Newman on the October 18 broadcast.

unless you know the man who owns one: Alludes to the 1929 Packard slogan "Ask the man who owns one."

movie time: EH was involved with the script and filming of *The Old Man and the Sea* (*Final,* 289–90).

Sir A. E. Hotchbatten IV: Allusion to Louis Mountbatten, First Earl Mountbatten of Burma and British naval officer in both world wars.

{84} Mary Hemingway and EH to AEH
[**15 December 1955** *pmk*] (ACardS, 1 p., ViU)
[Cuba *pmk*]

> Hi fellas—much love—M.
> Best love to all—
> Sorry not written—been laid up
> Papa.

Except for this Christmas card, no letters written between August 1955 and September 1956 have been located, although letter 85 indicates that some were written. The paucity of correspondence can partially be accounted for by an extended illness that kept EH in bed for forty days; his involvement with the filming of The Old Man and the Sea, *which took him to Peru; and by a wealth of visitors to the finca (Story, 532).*

1956

The Hotchners moved to Rome in the summer of 1956. On June 18, EH cabled him on board the Ile de France: *"GOOD LUCK KID HOPE SEE YOU SOON PAPA." On September 1, the Hemingways boarded the* Ile de France *and stayed in Paris until the 17th, when they motored to Spain.*

{85} EH to AEH
14/9/56 (ALS, 1 p., ViU)
[Paris *pmk*]

Querido Hotchmaru:

Thanks for the fine letters. Here is the gen. We leave here Monday Sept. 17 for Chantaco—St. Jean de Luz. Then to Logroño to see a couple of fights (Antonio [Ordóñez]) Sept. 23–25 (must check on this). Proceed to Escorial where will set up shop for a month or so. Think Mary is much better with change in temp. and have good hopes change alt. and temp. will be big help. She was down to 3,200,000. which isn't funny. Eisenhower has 5,000,000. Black Dog 5,200,000. Have slightly bigger Lancia and a good new chofer [chauffeur] from Udine.

George [Scheuer] will work on the [racing] form and we can activate the old firm around the 3rd week in Oct. George very good. Sends best.

Saw honest Alfred [Rice] and he said The Undefeated project going ok. I refused to have old friend and gambling partner fucked in any way which is always regarded as an amiable weakness by A. [Alfred] rather than as a basic principle.

This town full of beautiful dames as you probably know.

Am rushing this off. Guaranty Trust 4 <u>Place de la Concorde</u> <u>not</u> repeat not Vendome will forward mails. Keep in touch and best love to all. I will be happy to see your honest, intelligent, freckled face.

Love to all. Mary sends love. Weather filthy.

Best

Lord Hemingstein of Tel-Aviv.

Mary is much better: A series of blood transfusions had temporarily alleviated Mary's life-long anemia (*HIW,* 500). EH says her red blood cell count was down to 3.2 million; the average for females is 4.7–6.1 million.

The Undefeated project: AEH's adaptation of EH's story "The Undefeated" was never produced; according to AEH, no one could figure out how to induce a bull to follow the script. AEH to DeFazio, September 27, 2004.

Guaranty Trust 4 <u>Place de la Concorde</u> <u>not</u> *repeat not Vendome:* AEH apparently misaddressed an earlier letter.

{86} AEH to EH
18 Sept. 56 (TLS, 2 pp., JFKL)
La Residnza/Hotel Pension/Via Emilia N. 22/Tel. 460.789–487–480/Indir. Telegr.: Residenza—Roma

Dear Papa:

Like old times, both of us back on home grounds. Each time I think, this is the most fun it can be—the Paris-Nice trip of 1949, the races, the first time to Venice from which I have never fully recovered and I may never; but Venice in 1954, that fine drive all across to Madrid where also first time and first time bulls and first time Prado and isn't that positively the best there is? And now I am sure there will be things to top that, which is the grand part of being on one's home grounds, rather than in St. Louis, Mo., where they trade off Virdon, Schoendienst and Haddix.

Was very concerned about Mary because only reports I had were second-hand and magnified; much relieved to get true reading on her and to hear she is heading okay. Please give her my love and tell her how much I look forward to seeing her again.

Letter from Rupert [Bellville] arrived day before yours, suggesting that we convene for some of the bulls, but as I wrote him, I think perhaps the Spain crowd might grow a little too big for comfort by the time you hit dig-in territory, and as we always deal very straight with one another, it will be best to hear from you as to good cut-in time and place. We have settled in here very good and quickly. Kids are already going to school, Geraldine has embarked on an ambitious project involving various ruins (me excluded), and there are no abrasives in the gears. I am okay on movement and I still go to my left pretty good although, like Jackie Robinson, I have slowed up a good two steps on the right side. This summer I have not had as much physical life as I am accustomed to—and need—and I feel it. The month in Normandy was very good, but not after. However, there were some fine places and many enjoyments.

I am puzzled about your reference to Honest Al [Rice] and The Undefeated project, but we'll go into that when I see you. The Honest One never writes me beyond two-sentence notes that say "another installment of your income tax is due" or something of that nature, and I have nothing to go on.

Why the hell I put the Guaranty Trust Co. in Place Vendome is something I will have to leave to my analyst who fortunately is travelling with me with his portable couch. I'm sure it is closely bound up, in his opinion, with the fact that as a boy in St. Louis, on summer days I used to poke my finger into the sun-softened tar surface of the streets, gauge out a wad, and chew it like gum, which I couldn't afford.

All best,
Elvis Hotchley, Street singer

Virdon, Schoendienst and Haddix: Players traded by the Cardinals to other teams during the 1956 season.
like Jackie Robinson, I have slowed up a good two steps: After the 1955 World Series, Robinson confessed to having lost "a step and a half."
Elvis Hotchley: Elvis Presley's first record album was released in 1956.

{87} EH to AEH
30/9/56 (ALS, 2 pp., JFKL)
Hotel Felipe II/El Escorial [Madrid, *pmk*]

Dear Hotchmanship:

We had a good trip down to here. It is a very nice place and only 32 minutes from town by Lancia. Climate ideal for Mary and we are forted up good.

Rupert [Bellville] was completely off the sauce and couldn't have been better company in Paris nor at Logroño where saw two fights. Antonio [Ordóñez] wonderful. Giron very good and a Mexican named Joselito Huerta did the damdest faena for exposure and variety and sheer balls I've ever seen in a bull he dedicated to us. He and Giron both dedicated bulls and laid it on the line like one Indian to another. Huerta cut both ears, tail and a foot in a tough Plaza where they know bull fighting.

Antonio wants to dedicate the best one he draws in Zaragoza and will really put out. We have been hanging around together and he is the same loveing, unspoiled kid. But Christ how he can fight bulls.

The fights at Zaragoza are the 13th, 14th, 15th 16th Antonio fights 3— Joselito Huerta and Giron 2 each, two new kids, one a friend of ours Jamie Ostos, the other will see this afternoon, and Litri, who, for me is a bum in spite of Kenneth Tynan who wrote a book on it after 14 fights. The bulls are good. If you cable me here I can get seats from Chopera the Impressario who is an old friend of Juanito Quintana's. Rooms at the Gran Hotel are harder to get but if you cable in time can swing it for a single room or have you bunk in with Peter Buckley who has a double.

They look like the best possible fights and we would have fun. Will hold our rooms here and return after the fight. Then maybe you could do your business with Ava [Gardner]. (Sounds sinister)

Look Hotchmaru my head is quite sharp now and not banged to hell like the last trip. Have worked out something I think will be good. Keep it between us. All of it. Did you hear of Capt. Alister MacIntosh (Ali Mac Intosh?) He has been ADC. to more Royalty than we know spit ball pitchers. Married Constance Talmadge once, knows everything inside out. Is a great gent and a good friend of mine for many years. Will be dead in a year or so and is now staying at the Balmoral in Monte Carlo. I talked him into writing his reminiscences which are wonderful from Royalty through Valentino's funeral and up to now. I told him how to write them and offered to go over them. But he needs professional help and I'm sure you and he could make a good deal. I told him about you.

If you could stop off at Monte Carlo and see him it would be fine. Going or coming from here. You could size things up or if you did it on the way back you would have my gen. It would be nice if you wrote him and said I asked you to get in touch. You don't have to touch it if it does not appeal to you.

Capt. Alister Mac Intosh
The Balmoral Hotel
Monte Carlo

Now about Alfred [Rice]—If you haven't the gen on the deal he is handling for you and me on The Undefeated write him so you will have it in writing. It sounded like a good deal. But you were to submit your treatment by a certain date which I haven't in my head.

Al is very difficult for me sometimes. He told me not to be a fool and pay the regular rate for francs. He could buy them legally at 384. I had already bought them legally from the Guaranty at 422.$\underline{96}$ (2 g. worth). He also wrote me he trusted I had remembered to have my passport in order. Having had one since 1917 I fortunately had thought of that. So check on your deal on The Undefeated.

Antonio fighting today at Nimes. He has a chalet just down the road from us. When he gets back he and I are going to call on Pio Baroja.

Haven't seen any press in Paris, nor here yet. We've been going good. Wrote six short stories when I quit fishing for the picture and want to write some more here. Shooting season starts the 14th Oct.

Will give you all the Venetian gen and other gen when I see you.

Will be waiting to get a cable on what you want me to do about Zaragoza.

We should do good at Auteuil. Have made a preliminary recce [reconnaissance].

Love to all

Papa.

Mary says we're looking forward to you just like Xmas.

Giron . . . and a Mexican named Joselito Huerta: Curro Giron dedicated his second bull to the Hemingways and, according to Mary, "worked with it extensively and beautifully." Mary remembered Huerta as a "little-known Mexican matador [who] dedicated a bull to Ernest and thereupon executed a succession of passes of a virtuosity that awed us" (*HIW,* 504).

Jamie Ostos: "[A] boy from Ecija . . . as brave as the wild boar of the Sierras of his country. Like the wild boar he was almost insanely brave when angry or wounded." Hemingway, *Dangerous Summer,* 77.

Litri: Bullfighting name of Miguel Báez, whose showy maneuvers "contrasted sharply with Manolete's sober, economic classicism [and] seemed to herald a new era in bullfighting." Miriam Mandel, e-mail message to DeFazio, November 23, 2004.

Kenneth Tynan who wrote a book on it: EH owned a copy of the critic's *Bull Fever* (New York: Harper and Brothers 1955).

Peter Buckley: Writer and photographer who became part of EH's entourage; described by Mary as "our dear semi-giant friend" (*HIW,* 505).

Alister MacIntosh: Alastair Mackintosh, aide-de-camp to the Viceroy of India and equerry to Princess Beatrice.

Constance Talmadge (1897–1973): Silent film star whose marriage to Mackintosh in 1926 lasted only a year.

I talked him into writing his reminiscences: Eventually published as *No Alibi: The Memoirs of Captain Alastair Mackintosh* (London: Frederick Muller, 1961).

Valentino's funeral: The body of silent film star Rudolph Valentino was viewed by enormous crowds in New York City in 1926.

Pio Baroja (1872–1956): Basque novelist. EH visited him on October 9 and attended his funeral three weeks later (*Story*, 535).

Wrote six short stories: Carlos Baker identifies five of these as "A Room on the Garden Side," "The Cross Roads" (also called "Black Ass at the Cross Roads"), "The Monument," "Indian Country and the White Army," and "Get a Seeing-Eyed Dog" (*Story*, 534).

when I quit fishing for the picture: EH unsuccessfully attempted to land a giant marlin to be used in the movie (*Story*, 531).

AEH joined the Hemingways in Zaragoza for the bullfights. After EH's appointment with Dr. Mandinoveitia on October 22, 1956 (Final, 401; PH, 188), AEH traveled to the United States to attend to some business and then returned to Rome. On November 19, the Hemingways began a stay at the Ritz Hotel in Paris. That same month, Mary became ill with gastritis and colitis.

1957

{88} AEH to EH
10 Jan. 57 (TLS, 1 p., JFKL)
[Italy]

Dear Papa:

I have meant to write sooner but I have been distracted by a great deal of activity signifying nothing. It makes me sad to realize that you are only 13 days away from departure and that there is no chance of seeing you again for a long time. I was delighted to hear that you whacked them a good one across the knees at Auteuil; it figured that you would. I was sorry to duck in and out like that, because it is a poor way to play the horses; you need the continuity of going regular and getting a little rhythm and method, the way we did the time before. Well, we'll plan a better session together next time.

Mary's news from the medical front is very cheering, although I imagine the fucking regime is a great bore by now. But what the hell, you can't win them all. (A regime of fucking would be more like it, I guess.) The news re mama certainly sounds ominous, but if ominous sounds from the hills haven't engulfed us before, I guess we can consider ourselves pretty ominous proof by now. Maybe by the time Mary gets out there and checks, the situation will have righted itself.

I am going to Athens on Monday for four days, and then maybe a brief return to Vienna. The problem abroad for me is that I have to do a lot more for a lot less but considering where I'm doing it, it is worth it. It is callous of me not to be filled or half-filled with nostalgia for the wilds of Connecticut, but then I never was very sentimental about money or split-level ranch houses.

The last letter I got from the States (and believe me there aren't many from friend or publisher) was from a guy I know who spent three pages complaining about the high cost of installing heating pipes in his swimming pool. So you see, men, there are hardships in Westport like unto Ruark among the Mau-Mau [see note to letter 79].

I will stay on at this address until May sometime, then go back to France, spend July and Aug. in Spain, and then reluctantly but of necessity take a boat back beginning of Sept. Please let me know where you are and how you are whenever you can, and I will do the same. Zaragoza, Escorial, Paris were splendid. Thanks for all of them—we had a fine time as always. Ali [Mackintosh]'s ms. seems hopeless to me. Maybe Mary can send it on to some type in England where it might have a chance. I see no U.S. chance for it, as is or with any amount of labor on my part. Writing, I guess, is a pretty tough racket.

I'm going on a wild boar hunt next month—any advice for the conquering of the savage boar? Have good trip + a good year ahead.

All best

Alfredo Hotchcock

Finally got straight on that strange business in Hungary. Magazine had nothing to do with it—the Vienna newspaper man had slipped me some of his stuff to carry in to a contact in Budapest. So I guess I wasn't as hot (as with heat on) as I thought.

you are only 13 days away from departure and . . . there is no chance of seeing you again for a long time: AEH visited the Hemingways in Paris; the dates of the visit remain unknown. The Hemingways would depart Europe on January 22 aboard the *Ile de France* while the Hotchners remained in Rome (*Final,* 367; *PH,* 169).

I was delighted to hear: Probably refers to an unlocated letter.

I imagine the fucking regime is a great bore: EH's high blood pressure, cholesterol, and unhealthy liver prompted Dr. Madinaveitia to put him on a diet, reduce his alcohol intake, and preclude sexual intercourse.

the news re mama: Mary's mother, Adeline, was ill in a nursing home in Minnesota (*HIW,* 507).

Alfredo Hotchcock: Alfred Hitchcock released two movies in 1956; his television anthology series was in its second year.

that strange business in Hungary: AEH had been assigned by *This Week* to cover the Hungarian uprising against the Russians in Budapest; at first the Russians appeared to depart, only to double back for a three-day assault. AEH wrote about the incident in "The Night I Got Caught in the Hungarian Revolution" (*Choice,* 119–29).

Taking with them two trunks containing manuscripts, the Hemingways sailed aboard the Ile de France *for New York on January 23 and arrived in Cuba on February 14 (Final, 298–300).*

{89} AEH to EH
17 March 1957 (ALS, 2 pp., JFKL)
Hôtel du quai Voltaire/19, Quai Voltaire/ Paris (7^e)

Dear Papa—

Today at Auteuil I had two of George [Scheuer]'s horses, First Guard in the 4th who ran 3rd at 3–1 money, and Torrigiano in the 5th who was never in it. However I recouped pretty good with Orage in the 6th who came in at 8–1. He had two wins in an otherwise nothing record, but I figured that once a horse tastes front-running he might like the flavor again. He ran a beautiful race, coming up from dead last on the back + catching the leader on the last jumps. It was a good day but I missed you.

I am here on a story about the Lafayette papers that were found at La Grange last summer. One of the richest caches of historical books, letters, papers + possessions, + who comes into possession of it?—M. Pierre Laval's son-in-law + daughter, Count + Contess René de Chambrun. Chambrun was one of the Vichy top-rank ass-kissers, + wouldn't it just be that he is the one, as Lafayette's great-great-grandson, to become owner of this treasure house. That is the apotheosis of Vichy. Well, the shits will inherit the earth + we both know it.

The weather is warm + sunny + Paris has never looked more beautiful. I think I'll move the troops back here in June for about six weeks, then go to Lake Garda [Italy] or perhaps a lake in Austria I've heard about—The Worthersee, a town on it called Velden. Do you know it? My only fear is that being up in the mountains, it will have a lot of rain. The thing I like about Garda is its nearness to Venice. I wish we had all made Venice this time— maybe next time around, the air will have cleared. I give up on all French + Italian coast line during the summer, after last year's experience. I may find that the lakes are just as overrun. Everything is beginning to look like Deal, N.J. I've booked us on the Flandre, Aug. 27th, to arrive back in the Land of Tums on the 3rd. The thought of Westport drives me to the ipecac bottle but now that I've mapped this out, I think I'll adopt it as a regular alternate year procedure. But I've got to go back to keep the $ well from going dry.

Papa, how are you? Are you still on that goddam regime? And is it effective? And I wonder too about Mary, whether she's keeping the blood count up. I had a hopped-up letter from Pete Buckley (what else), followed by silence—I like Peter as you like him, within the same limits. Ava [Gardner] is in Rome + either she or Bee [her sister] are on the phone a couple of times a day. They are both stark nuts. Last time I saw her, she carried on weepfully about how much you disliked her. I assured her it was otherwise, + that she had mistaken your passion for pique. Ain't that right, Massa—you got passion fo' all dames, aintcha? Anyway that's what I read somewhere about you. Passion for dames + death. Very good think piece. I should have saved it—that's the trouble with me—no sentiment. I head back to Rome tomorrow. Would love to hear a word from you, general briefing. All my love to you & good Miss Mary.

La Hotchfoncied

the Lafayette papers that were found at La Grange: Count René de Chambrun, a descendant of Lafayette, purchased his ancestor's chateau, La Grange, in 1956 and discovered an extensive cache of valuable documents. "Lafayette Papers Found in Castle," *New York Times,* June 19, 1956, pp. 1, 31.

Pierre Laval: Prime minister of France under the Vichy government; after the war, he was found guilty of high treason and executed.

{90} AEH to EH
13 April 1957 (TLS, 2 pp., JFKL)
Viale di Villa Massimo 33/Rome, Italy [*tw*]

Dear Papa:

Mary's letter splendid, gives me a very good reading; must be shit for you not to drink anything at all, because hot climate, cool drinks in the evening almost a necessity, but Mary says the blood tests show up improved so I guess you have to credit the medicos with a good enough batting average to stay in the line-up. And speaking of that, the spring-training news filters over here, with the names so changed I feel like an aged Roman soccer fan. It certainly looks like no one can come six city blocks near the Yanks, but the National should be a good battle. I think the Brooklyns will be hit hard by Robinson's going and what looks like another bad Campanella year, and I expect the Milwaukees to take it. But then my crystal ain't no better than Toots Shor's, and he don't pick 'em either. How they look to you? I have those old

St. Louis blues for the Cards, even yet, as they say on Broadway, because the Gas House Gang was out of my boyhood and any team that once put together those nine guys, deserves eternal allegiance—but there isn't much there to be allegianced to. Frank Lane [Cardinals' general manager] should clean latrines.

I just did a circuit, Viterbo-Siena-San Gimignano-Florence-Arezzo-Cortina-Perugia-Assisi-Todi-Roma (I had an article to do on some new Etruscan discoveries) and, Christ, how beautiful it all is this time of year. The vineyards are all crisp and manicured, and the fields are a hundred different colors of new green. The variety of wines is really astounding—how can the Orvieto white and Est Est Est be grown within a few kilometers of each other? I have now been to Florence three times but I cannot see how any one man in his lifetime can reasonably be expected to look at, much less assimilate, the art in any one of its galleries—the Pitti, for example, where there are ten repeat ten Raphaels in one room. My eyes, head and heart aren't strong enough.

Has Alfred [Rice] been in touch with you about the television project for CBS? I'll be a son of a bitch if I can understand Alfred. As you know, I have always backed him but I really think he's hit the menopause. He's like the chauffeur of the Rolls Royce who speaks of it as "our car" and assumes everything except the financial burden of the master. Well, at this point Alfred, who's never <u>been</u> on the line much less put anything on it, has written everything from The Sun Also Rises on, and has knocked off all the television adaptations for good measure . . . CBS phoned me from New York about a new program of high promise that will begin in the Fall; the man in charge is John Houseman who produced the Julius Caesar with Brando, other Broadway classics, a man of taste and good imagination. He wanted to know whether there was any of your stories that you would okay and that I would like to adapt. I told him that you and I had briefly discussed the possibility of doing 3 or 4 Nick Adams stories, but precisely as they appear in the book—that is, no attempt to join them, just presenting them, The End of Something, The Three-Day Blow[,] The Battler, as distinct pieces, with the little chapter paragraphs read between; maybe The Light of the World, as you suggested, if we can get it by censor, if not, Now I Lay Me—in other words, Nick Adams as these few stories reveal him. He was immediately taken with the idea, and excited about it. I told him that if he could work out financial arrangements with Alfred, I would then re-check with you to see if the project was okay. I then wrote Alfred, gave him the details. I have received no word since then from Alfred (who nevertheless takes his ten percent from me with alacrity) but I receive a letter now from CBS saying that Alfred has pronounced that The Battler cannot be included and that he was going to write or phone you to convince you not to allow The Battler to be done. And no word to me. Well, I'm a sad son a bitch, if ol' Alfred isn't sittin' there with his feet up and the Havana in his mouth buying and selling us foreign cattle like goats. With no understanding of the dramatic or artistic problems involved, nor attempt to understand same, ol' Alfred is wheeling and dealing. There seems to be a small oversight that the two times The Battler has been done, I'm the guy who did all the work and who knows what the problems of putting the short story into dramatic form are. That we can do The Battler a third time now, and on our terms, so that the other stories build to it just as they do in the short story collection, this should be regarded as a splendid development—but ol' Alfred views it as a calamity. Well, to assuage his feelings somewhat, I have suggested to CBS that in addition to what they have offered for the rights, they now pay a sum to be earmarked just for The Battler—that will bring the amount up to a hefty total and may slack Alfred's thirst.

From my own point of view, this is a chance to do these pieces with complete honesty—a rarity for television. It is also a chance to develop these stories which I feel will in a further step, be eventually done as a motion picture. Of course, if you have changed your mind about wanting to have them done, then we just cancel out, but I would like to ride with you on this, not with the seer at 630 Fifth [Rice].

The weather continues fine, and the life slow and appealing, the rewards anywhere you want to look. I'm going up to Venice in a week or two, and that's when the crop is really reaped.

All love to Mary and you.

Hotchorama, the only man in Italy not yet accused of having done in Wilma Montesi—(you should have seen the little bubbles come out of her nose when I shoved her head under the water!)

Mary's letter: Mary had written that she and EH were resettled at the finca and that doctors had restricted EH's drinking to four or five small glasses of wine a day. Mary Hemingway to AEH, April 4, 1957 (ViU, 6250f).

another bad Campanella year: Roy Campanella, the Dodgers' catcher from 1948 to 1957, battled nagging injuries that affected his batting average in some seasons.

a new program of high promise: The anthology series *The Seven Lively Arts.*

John Houseman: Executive producer of *The Seven Lively Arts* and producer of stage and screen productions including *Julius Caesar* (Warner, 1953), with Marlon Brando as Marc Antony.

which I feel will . . . be eventually done as a motion picture: AEH did eventually adapt these stories as a screenplay, *Hemingway's Adventures of a Young Man* (Fox, 1962).

Wilma Montesi: Woman who died mysteriously on a beach near Rome in 1953. Several suspects were tried; all were acquitted. *New York Times,* January 21, 1957, sec. 5, p. 1.

{91} AEH to EH
9 Mayo 1957 (Cable, 1 p., JFKL)
Roma

HAVE CBS UP TO SIXTEEN THOUSAND FOR RIGHTS PLUS DRAMATIZATION FOR
ONE HOUR LIVE TELEVISION BASED ON NICK ADAMS STORIES I MENTIONED MY
LETTER STOP CAN WE GO ON THIS AS WE DID ON UNDEFEATED PLEASE INFORM
LOVE TO MARY BEST.

HOTOSADODLEDO—

AS WE DID ON UNDEFEATED: An undated document titled "A Motion Picture Development of Ernest Hemingway's 'The Undefeated'" is marked "only copy—never
produced—AEH." Hotchner Papers, box 7, Washington University.

{92} AEH to EH
22 May 57 (TLS, 1 p., JFKL)
[Italy]

Dear Papa:

Letter from Alfred [Rice] two weeks back relating phone call from you:
"Ernie said he had received your cable asking whether he will agree to split
the total received 50–50." And then on and on about 50–50 and 60–40 and
so forth. Well, I'm a sad son of a bitch if the Italcable people haven't gone into
creative writing because when cable left here had no splits, up, down or side-
ways. I have not ever, nor <u>will</u> I ever presume to get into the dough thing. I
simply asked whether we could go ahead as we have in the past. What the
dough thing is, is for you to tell Alfred, as always, and Alfred to take the action and that is fine with me. If you want to make it 70–10 with 20 for the Joe
McCarthy Memorial Fund that is okay with me too. I only push these things,
which I never seek, because it's the only way to get the characters off my back,
as you know only too well. This time I had three overseas phone calls from
CBS, each requiring me to hang around the house, seven cables and several
letters, all requiring replies. I asked for patience, but did I get patience? Do I
hear a thunderous NO!? These are very good men and I understand the pressure under which they work and appreciate their enthusiasm, which is based
upon the previous dramatizations I did of your stories. But they can sure be a

pain in the ass. I handle these things as best I can but Alfred in N.Y., you in Cuba, not easy. However, since somebody has to, I am glad to do it, but if you have suggestion please say—you know I would be happy to do or not do whatever you say in this goddam "business" area that occasionally crops up. I had a call last week from NBC about Fifty Grand as a "spectacular" (Christ, what a word that is!) but I pretended the connection was bad and anyway I spoke Italian. I figure the CBS thing, with Alfred making high-money demands, is enough to recover from for now.

I exchange letters with Ali [Alastair Mackintosh] pretty regularly. The book has been read and rejected by the Beaverbrook people, and I got it one stateside reading with a fast rejection. I am afraid it is utterly hopeless but I am very considerate with Ali in the letters and trying to ease him very gradually toward the pain of reality.

I have been working hard, this is a good place to work, but I think over my head; however, I figure that is the only way, to drown a little, to find out my depth. I'm going to stay on here in Rome, now, until end of July, then will motor back to Paris, then to Britainy, Normandy, [and boarding] the Flandre [in] Le Havre end of August to arrive Sept. 3 in time for kids to get to school. I will spend a year in the Westport wilds replenishing my all but disappeared capital, then return to Europe to live until again scrape pebbles at the bottom. I hope it again coincides with your Europe plans, for Zaragoza and Paris visits were wonderful fun. I shall never be able to appreciate another view after what we saw from the windows of the Escorial. Those golden mornings. God!

Mary's letter was wonderful—I will write her very soon. She is such a splendid female—tell her for me, will you?

That troubador of the Roman sewers,

Enrico Hotcharuso

(di La Scala) naturally

Joe McCarthy Memorial Fund: After the senator died on May 2, 1957, a fund for his wife and infant daughter was proposed by radio commentator Fluton Lewis, Jr. "Commentator Proposes Memorial Fund for Late Senator," *Tablet,* May 11, 1957.

a call . . . from NBC about Fifty Grand: AEH's adaptation of the Hemingway story "Fifty Grand" aired on NBC's *Kraft Television Theatre* in April 1958.

Beaverbrook: Canadian publishing firm owned by William Maxwell Aitken, Lord Beaverbrook.

Mary's letter: Remains unlocated.

La Scala: Opera house in Milan where Enrico Caruso made his debut in 1900.

{93} EH to AEH
May 28 1957 (TLS, 1 p., ViU)
FINCA VIGIA, SAN FRANCISCO DE PAULA, CUBA

Dear Hotchenroll:

Awfully sorry you got into Alfred's 60–40 dollar question program. You'd been having some difficulty getting action of any kind from Alfred you wrote so when you cabled I called him. He claimed the same as always referred to 50–50 split. I didn't think so but said I thought 60–40 was fair on this one if you did. He said, later, that you did, etc. He claimed first it was better than just. But the hell with all that. It was what I offered if you thought it ok and just. I didn't have any of the details of past or present in my head but remembered I had insisted against Alfred on splitting Fifty Fifty on that last thing whichever it was (The Undefeated?) on acct. I wanted to average out money I had cost you on the True piece deal [see letters 72–77].

If this inaccurate am wide open to be countered. Only let's you and me not ever get sore or split up because of business through Alfred which as you wrote is very difficult to do. Alfred claims he had sale for Battler (which I included in the Nick Adams package to you) for 15 G for Battler alone. But since I remembered it was you who had done good with Battler (hope I'm right again anyhow if it wasn't you it should have been by God) and not some fairy From A Small Planet (I think he was Farewell To Arms) anyway. I figured if that represented 15 and I enclosed it in a package for which I would get 12 as my share I wouldn't be bitching my old Hotchmaru the uncrowned King of Nippon. But then I could have been wrong as often am at the races track. But I wanted action from Alfred and thought the monies were better in your hand than up some bush not to mention my own hand which is practically palsied from not receiving any monies while cinemas bearing my name are being filmed everywhere.

I figured if it were a matter for the saliva test you would let me know. Am not really a very big shit about monies; or maybe I am and nobody has told me.

The reason before I didn't write and Mary did was that was working over the ears and writing has been difficult. Had last drink of hard liquor on March 5th. Will not bore you with details. It is about as much fun as driving a racing motor car without lubrication for a while. A good car that you know well and just what it takes to lubricate and just what can do with lubrication. Well skip it. Wish I could skip it. Actually that's just what I do.

Thanks about Ali [Mackintosh]. It was always hopeless but you were lovely about it and I appreciate it. It was much more than Ali deserves but thank God we don't have to hand out the exact measure of what anybody deserves including us. Would rather be happy once in a while.

I am awfully damned sorry you had so much damned work and annoyance on the CBS thing. I called Alfred the hour your cable came and thought I made it clear and as fast as possible. The best thing in future is cable me what you want me to say to Alfred. Also let me know clearly if money figures are not right. I'm not trying to rack rent anybody.

Mary is fine and healthy. I have blood pressure down to 140 over 68. Weight, this morning, 210. Hope you have a good summer Hotch and that the family are fine. Until I started this was working since early morning on a letter to Peter Buckley. He doesn't realize that there is a certain discipline in pro writing and that he has to work on it until he gets it in shape.

Reference to his bull book. God save us from amateurs. They kill you. Wish we were some place where we could talk instead of write. We never have any difficulty if we can see and speak to each other.

Papa

60–40 dollar question program: Play on the name of the television quiz show *The $64,000 Question* (CBS, 1955–1958).

True piece deal: See letters 72–77.

some fairy From A Small Planet: Refers to Gore Vidal, whose *Visit to a Small Planet* was a television play in 1955 and a Broadway production in 1957. Vidal had adapted an episode from *A Farewell to Arms* for *Climax Mystery Theater* (CBS, 1954). His homosexuality probably bothered EH less than the fact that he had published a novel about World War II (*Williwaw*, 1946), encroaching on what EH considered to be his turf.

not receiving any monies while cinemas bearing my name are being filmed everywhere: Possible reference to David O. Selznick's production of *A Farewell to Arms* (Fox, 1957). Selznick purchased the rights from Warners, which had bought it from Paramount Pictures, the producer of the 1932 version, and said he would compensate EH if the new film was successful. AEH recalls EH's telling him "that he sent Selznick a cable to the effect that if his film did make money, which he doubted, Selznick should take Hemingway's share, change it into nickels, and stuff it up his ass." As EH predicted, the film was not a success.

his bull book: Peter Buckley, *Bullfight* (New York: Simon and Schuster, 1958).

{94} AEH to EH
26 June 57 (TLS, 2 pp., JFKL)
Viale di Villa Massimo 33/Roma [tw]

Dear Papa:

I have been to Vienna again on a long and rather involved and ultimately dull story. Your letter came while I was away. It is such a goddam good letter, but I feel badly you take your good work time in the morning to make explanations to me who long ago stopped needing any explanations where you and I are concerned. You have always been more than fair whenever the demon cash has reared its frightening face, and certainly to split with me 60–40 on the CBS thing is generous as hell. My ass was simply griped at Alfred [Rice]'s touting me as a boy who's writing the book now on how the money goes. I leave that role to that austere Hollywood statesman, Mr. David O. Selzprick who, according to the enclosed dispatch out of Mr. A. Buchwald's treasury of facts, may throw you a little something or may not, depending on his financial whim. Someday you and I are going to run into Darling David and we will hit him guard-and-tackle high-low and leave him for the vultures. At any rate, I do not assume the Selzprick mantle despite Alfred's reading, and I just want you to know that I too hope we never get scuffed up or sore over businesses conducted by third parties. Like you say, if only we were some place where we could see each other and talk, we always settle whatever there is in a few minutes and have our time for important things like baseball, the bulls, and the track. I do not at all like the anti-Hemingberg crack about the races. It's true we had one negative day, but hell, what about the good ones when we finished front-running thanks to the skulling of the aforementioned Hemingnagle? Leave us always drink to the memory of Bataclan II.

At any rate, to strike a final chord (maybe the lost cord for all I know) on the CBS thing, I doubt Honest Alfred's 15 G claim for The Battler, but what he forgets is that interest still continues in the television play because previous version I did hit pretty good and got a couple of awards and what not, and as long as you go with the few good guys who are working in TV there is a chance of doing something pretty good, whereas if you do it just for the dough and with no feeling for the material involved you are likely to wind up with the Small Planet version of A Farewell to Arms, complete with the swivel wrist. It is possible to do movies and television plays that honestly project what is in the original story but it has to be done in a special way with special people. End of deep, penetrating observations.

On my way back from Vienna, I stopped in our town, Venezia. It was a very sad experience. I only stayed one night. The town was completely overrun with German tourists who travel in bus-packs of 200 or so. They carry canvas bags full of wine bottles and foodstuffs, they wear kahki shorts with cuffs on the legs, colored shirts that hang over them, and leather sandals. They all need haircuts. They either do not have the price or the inclination to sit down at one of the cafe tables in the Piazza, but instead sit in enormous clumps all around the bottoms of things—campanile, statues, lights, buildings, etc. They toss their garbage right where they eat, and if you can imagine St. Mark's littered with glistening banana peels and orange halves then you'll have a good picture of what I saw. I went to see Cipriano but he was out tending his place on Torcello which apparently is going okay. His daughter was there, however, and we talked; she said Cipriano was disgusted with what the Germans were doing to Venice and he was building a new joint on one of the islands, between Venice and Lido. Showed me photos. Big joint, combination hotel and restaurant. The daughter said that Cipriano had hoped very much that you would have been able to make Venice this last trip, and had half-expected you, but I made very polite explanations for you and said how much you always wanted to see Cipriano. I phoned A. [Adriana Ivancich] and later went round, but everyone there is away. So I got the hell out, not wanting to damage the beautiful things you and Mary established for me in Venice on my two times there. I know now to go only in the off-months, and, if possible, only when you and Mary are there to share enjoyment with.

I had the signal honor to encounter the Hon. Oiwin Shaw whilst he was sitting at a table on the Veneto, eating a Doney chocolate ice cream. He had descended to Cinecittà in connection with a movie script he had written, and during a lull in his ice cream spooning, he informed me that he was building a <u>big</u> house in Klosters and Pete Viertel was building a <u>little</u> house right next door to him. (Emphasis indicated Oiwin's, not mine.) I presume that Oiwin is building a big house so that it can hold <u>all</u> his money, and that Pete is locating next door hoping for some of the overflow. The latest poop on Bettina [Graziani], Pete's ex-girl, is that she and the Aly [Khan] will be married up by September, but do not rely on this, if you have started to rely on it, because my hot items are about as authoritative as Mr. Earl Wilson's.

A sirocco has brought African desert heat to Rome but despite a good deal of mid-afternoon gasping it beats anything the 5:02 can bring from New York to Westport. But come 1 Aug. I will move the caravan north, pausing in Garda, then unhurriedly through France to Paris to Normandy, a few days on the

Trouville beach, then the Flandre back on the 27th. I look upon the return without relish (or onion) but there is only 12 months on the native rock pile then the plan is to hit the trail back. I hope your distant plans bring you back about the same time. We still have so much to do.

It's wonderful to hear that you and Mary are fine, and getting finer; I know what a pain in the ass it must be to stay on the temperence trail, but you've got to trade back and forth for the things you want. With pressure at 140 over 68 and weight at 210 that's a helleva reward. But I know that doesn't make the evening, when it would be pleasant to have a glass in the hand, very good.

Thank you very much for being so good and decent about saying what you did re the televisions, but then if I ever got started on all the thank yous it would be a very big project.

Ibn ben Hotchsand, Rex

Saudia Arabia (Semitic Division)

the enclosed dispatch out of Mr. A. Buchwald's treasury of facts: Syndicated columist Art Buchwald did a two-part report on Selznick's production of *A Farewell to Arms.* Art Buchwald, "Farewell, Farewell, Farewell," *New York Times,* June 30, 1957, sec. 4, p. 4; "Getting a Point Across," *New York Times,* July 2, 1957, sec. 2, p. 1. (The columns appeared earlier in Italy than they did in the United States).

Cipriano: Giuseppe Ciprani, proprietor of Harry's Bar in Venice.

the Hon. Oiwin Shaw: Irwin Shaw, author of *The Young Lions* (1948), a popular novel about World War II, introduced EH to Mary in 1944. "Oiwin" mimics Shaw's Brooklyn accent.

Cinecittà: Major movie studio near Rome.

Bettina [Graziani]: After her brief affair with Peter Viertel, Graziani became involved with Pakistani playboy Prince Aly Khan.

{95} AEH to EH
6 July 1957 (ALS, 1 p., JFKL)
[Italy *pmk*]

Dear Papa—

The dulcet tones of Twentieth-Century Fuck-Up have been wafting this way over that favorite Hollywood instrument, the overseas telephone—Beverly Hills eagerness being what it is, I send you this dispatch from the front to give you actual gen. As you may recall, about four years ago I did a television adaptation of The Gambler, The Nun + The Radio, + ever since then, about every two months, a character named Jerry Wald has been phoning me to see what could be done about doing a cinema version of Across The River + Into The Trees. I invariably say that you do not wish to sell it to the movies. This last phoning he was more gizzed up than usual, however, + wanted to discuss an offer (astronomical, of course) with you by phone. I <u>hope</u> I beat him off this phone kick—but I can't be sure. I told him to write you instead because you could give the matter more weighty consideration, although I tried to convince him that he was on a pursuit that should be tabled (Tabling the Pursuit is an old St. Louis maneuver in case you don't know). At any rate, I do not wish to be mis-quoted to you as one is likely to be in the heat of Hollywood pursuit. I said (a) last time Across The River was mentioned (I told you of Wald's interest) you said "no go for the time being;" (b) there was no harm in Wald writing you of his interest; (c) no, I did not know if you were writing a new book; (d) yes, the weather was hot here, how was it there, well I guess it's hot all over.

Love to Missis Mary + all best.

Cecil B. de Hotch

about four years ago I did a television adaptation of The Gambler, The Nun + The Radio: The version that survives is the one produced by CBS's *Buick Electra Playhouse* in the spring of 1960. Hotchner Papers, box 7.

Jerry Wald (1911–1962): Screenwriter and producer whose production company, Wald Productions, released films through Fox.

Cecil B. de Hotch: Cecil B. DeMille had most recently directed *The Ten Commandments* (1956).

{96} EH to AEH
20/8/57 (TLS, 2 pp., ViU)
The Finca [*tw*] [Cuba]

Dear Hotch:

Called Alfred [Rice] last Thursday and Friday but no can get officewards. Finally nailed him at his home to put a few queries Sunday and got load of double talk and a promise of wiring your address from the office on Monday and the address actually came through—as follows—hotchner hotel roches noir trouville frances august twenty first trough august twenty sixth stop enroute paris trouville august eighteen twenty first regards ALFRED.

Just how he expected me to contact you enroute I don't know but all other gen. One of the reasons I called was on acct. the CBS [payment] never showed up in my accounts and he told me on phone he had just received payment but not yours and I could not understand any of it. So if there is anything you don't understand know it that I don't understand either and we will get together in N.Y. some time in Sept. and you and me try and understand anyway. I had been worried about a letter he had said on the phone he'd sent on some tax matter and I hadn't received and now it is two weeks and damned funny I never received it.

Hope you have fun in Trouville and a good trip back. Can't be as bad weather there this year as it was last. Maybe the heat will still be hanging on. Must be lonesome pulling out from Europe. Hope nothing happens with strike on French Line. They've had a terrible year all around.

This has been the year of The Corn Cob here. Am ½ way through the 6th month of no liquor. Haven't touched since March 5. Worked on the diet and exercise and have weight steadily under 205 and for two weeks just over 203. Cut the Cholesterol from 428 (deadly) to 204 (normal). Dr. says nobody ever did it before. Liver not cured yet but tests show improving and will heal up if allowed to. Then will be o.k. Blood pressure down to 136 over 68 and if keep that down and the cholesterol down ticker is not under strain and arteries good. So must stick to the two glasses of wine with the meal in the evening. Plan to come to N.Y. to see Robinson-Basilio fight and you. Not in that order. Robinson figures big for Basilio; too big. But many other angles.

Won't be able to stay long as must fight it out with the diet and the not drinking to get the liver all healed good.

The corn cobbery has been mostly poor Mary's mother steadily bad and crazy bothering Mary all the time and writing to all her friends how she is mistreated etc. while getting wonderful and top expensive care. Bumby [John Hemingway] with extravagant wife problems. He's had close to 5 G in eight months. Then poor Bum got sick bad with flu he didn't stay in bed with and it turned into jaundice. Gig now in hospital with very big expenses and nobody knows how long go on. Lots of worries. Thought I would go loopy myself for a while. Difficult when you could always take a drink and cheer up about anything not to be able to take the drink. But haven't had one since March 5 as said. Not the rummy type of offlay with the sn[e]aked ones etc. The damned cold turkey.

Hotch you always write such good letters and I was so glad to hear about Venice the two different times and the other trips and the good jokes. Mary always loves your letters too and they cheer her up. She says she would rather have you around with us than anybody. Me too. Remember when we rode into Madrid from Escorial with that Kraut journalist at speed and me afterwards in the Prado feeling I was dying and we went over and got a drink and cheered up and a few days later Dr. Madinaveitia explaining that I had been dying? That is the sound type of Hemingstein Hotchwald joke that is always fresh and clean. No forced gags there men.

Have lots of things to talk about beside weights, blood pressures and Hangar tests.

No matter what Alfred has done we will fish it up.

Let me know when you get this. But don't interrupt your fun to write a letter. Just keep in touch.

Thank you for writing me about Jerry Wald. I never did anything about it but I will write and thank him for his interest. There is nothing I can do about selling that now. Will tell you rather than write.

Best to Jerry and hope the kids are fine. Am down to having to declare to win with Patrick [Hemingway]. He is doing very well and is very well liked and has a fine future. I don't want to upset him with any news about Gig. Nobody knows about Gig so bury it. I put off and put off writing you on account nothing but bad news but wanted to write so you'd know how much appreciated the splendid letters and how much it has meant to hear from you. For a while was working like a crazy trying to bury everything in work. But you just over work is all like a pitcher not working his regular turn but using the arm up. Maybe it is ok if you have an easy enough motion.

So long Hotch. Have a lovely time and a good trip over and I'll see you when you get settled and we'll plan some big coups.

Love from Mary and me.

Hemingstein

august twenty first trough august twenty sixth: EH circled *trough* and wrote in the margin: "Does he believe you are a cochon [pig] to employ that word trough?"

the year of The Corn Cob: Possible reference to William Faulkner's *Sanctuary* (1931), in which the impotent Popeye rapes Temple Drake using a corn cob.

Robinson-Basilio fight: Carmen Basilio and Sugar Ray Robinson were to compete for the World Middleweight Championship on September 23.

Gig now in hospital: For a discussion of Gregory Hemingway's physical and psychological trials, see Valerie Hemingway (née Danby-Smith), *Running with the Bulls: My Years with the Hemingways* (New York: Ballantine, 2004), 226–97.

He is doing very well: Patrick had become a white hunter and since 1955 was running his own company, Tanganyika Tour Safaris, near Mount Kilimanjaro. Jeffrey Meyers, *Hemingway: A Biography* (New York: Harper and Row, 1985), 497–98.

{97} AEH to EH
26 Aug. 1957 (ALS, 4 pp., JFKL)
Hôtel des Roches Noires/Trouville [France]

Dear Papa—

The sun just dropped and I am feeling shit miserable because this is the last night where I have had good times and been happy since June, 1956, when the frayed boy who poses as the chausseur taps on the door and hands me your letter. Kind of spooky—me feeling shit miserable and lonely and there's your letter—such a goddam good letter. With you and Mary it is always home, it's like relatives, or like we were boys together and lived on the same block. So now to know that in September you'll come up makes the whole return okay, and we'll have the good times we always have. I'll be back on the 3rd, the Flandre willing, and maybe we'll talk on the phone if I can set things for you in any way—fight tickets, where to stay, etc. We should see some baseball, which looks like Yankee-Braves without mystery. Oh, Christ, I'm glad you're coming up.

I gave up solving Alfred [Rice] about a year ago, when he wrote me a rough letter that would have landed him on his ass if I had been 3000 miles nearer. But I worked it out and held it in and we get along with nothing going back and forth. I guess he's got his problems but I just like to keep them out of my life which has problems enough. No, I've seen not a penny of the CBS dough, which gets paid in two shots—$16,000, and then $5000 when script is delivered in final form. The 16 Gs were supposed to be on signing of the contract, but I guess from what you say, Alfred just now got the money on that. But, as I say, I have no information on subject. I have finished the script ["The World of Nick Adams"] which I will deliver to CBS as in the contract on Sept. 5th. Then they give us rest of dough—with, I presume, another healthy delay.

I have not had much heart for the Casino, one play only, with 35,000 fr. profit, not much, but almost pays out the hotel here. Seven and red, with a few intuitive variations, and I couldn't help but remember that crazy night with Adamo [Simon] who had never been in a Casino before, + when he saw my stack of winning chips he said, "Oh, Monsieur Hotch, now that I see how easy it is, could I try?" I gave him a stack + he went through them without a win, and as we walked out, he said, "There must have been something you did which I did not notice."

Poor Adamo.

And poor Bumbi, what a lousy stretch. I was three months in a closet room in the Shelton Hotel in 1947 with the jaundice eating me right through the gut, so I know. And you surely know. Please give Bum my regards. I liked him a lot + I'm sorry as hell he's having such a shit time.

And I know how rough it's been for you—I really admire what you've done, + God knows the results are unbelievable. But then, if we don't produce unbelievable results, who will? Kiss Mary girl for me.

Love,
Aly Khanotchner III

looks like Yankee-Braves: These teams did indeed meet in the 1957 World Series.
Aly Khanotchner III: Alludes to Aly Khan (see letter 94).

{98} AEH to EH
11 Sept. 1957 (TLS, 1 p., JFKL)
A. E. Hotchner R. F. D. 5 Westport, Conn.

Dear Papa:

Trip back pleasant, but Flandre a dull and badly built boat. How the hell could the French build a boat only five years ago that has so many mistakes in it? I only hope the new <u>France</u> doesn't repeat them. Scuttlebutt on the boat was that the U.S. was going to sell the <u>America</u> to France next year when the Ile goes out of service.

I hope your plans for coming up haven't changed. What can I do as advance man, now that am on scene? How are you coming up, plane or train? Please give me exact word on arrival so that, if you don't have other plans, I can meet you with car and ease you into the city. Anything I can do about (1) quarters (2) fight tickets (3) baseball tickets (4) passing word to any one you want to see—or anything else? I would phone you but I know the glitters of the long distance operator is disturbing especially if you happen to be working. However, I'm just unpacking trunks and pushing junk up and down stairs so please phone me anytime if you have any special requests. <u>Phone: Capital 7-4453. Otherwise,</u> if you will brief me on arrival and any other matters in letter or telegram I will follow up. Christ, but it will be good to see you.

The word on [Sugar Ray] Robinson is very high. Spoke to a guy who spent two days at his camp. Says physical condition really extraordinary, and he's hitting very hard with both hands with solid reflexes. No word on Basilio.

I want to get this in the mail, so will hold all discussion items. Give Mary all my love, and send me word as soon as you can.

John Foster Hotchess

John Foster Hotchess: **John Foster Dulles was President Eisenhower's secretary of state.**

Later in September the Hemingways and their houseguest, game ranger Denis Zaphiro (see letter 66), flew to New York, where EH and AEH watched Carmen Basilio's victory over Sugar Ray Robinson in Yankee Stadium (Story, 538). They returned to the stadium for the first two games of the World Series on October 2 and 3. On October 4, EH joined Mary in Washington, DC (HIW, 514).

{99} AEH to EH
16 Oct. 57 (TLS, 1 p., JFKL)
A. E. Hotchner R. F. D. 5 Westport, Conn.

Dear Papa:

It is really too bad you were not able to find some important Yankee money but we do have this small indication that we knew the blow of the wind. At 8–5 we got 65 for our 25. I thought they warmed up quite a bit over the first two games, and although, as we agreed, there weren't any immortals out there, there were some fairly exciting stretches and at times some first-rate defensive ball. For a guy who was supposed to have a minor league ceiling on his fielding, I thought Mr. Covington held up pretty good, didn't you? That bounce off the wire fence to grab the home-run ball is the kind of thing you see in the Sally League every Sunday afternoon.

I had a feeling, after you left, that there were a pile of things I should have planned out for us to do, but the time burned off before I ever really got into anything that resembled motion. I seem to have been in a kind of zombie state since I came back, which is the part of living abroad that I forgot about. So please tell Mary that I usually field the position with less lead in my ass, and can guarantee more satisfactory results on future visits. Aftermath of Dennis' [Zaphiro] fuck-up on the classy girl: seems girl had planned to go to Easthampton for day but I had made Dennis sound so fascinating she cancelled out for his phone call and rendezvous which never came, so you know what reaction this set off in girl. However, I excused him as unpredictable bush character. Girl (who is really splendid girl to look at) has returned to London where she could have been good contact for Dennis. Very classy girl. Wish I were going to London. That classy.

But only travel plans are to Washington, D.C., where I uncover big scoop on juvenile delinquency, which seems to have overtaken sex as the major preoccupation of the U.S. mind, and then I fight my way onward to the University of N. Carolina where I shall uncover some dark secrets discovered by a psychiatry outfit there. So you can see, I do nothing but make significant contributions.

I have twice been summoned to smoke-filled rooms to discuss BIG (Upmann cigar) deals relating to the New Medium. If and when any of these check out wholesomely I'll send them along for you to consider.

How nice it would be if we all lived in the same area all the time. Well, we do the next best thing, which is to cross paths as often as we can. You know how much I enjoyed having you and Mary in the Big City.

Thanks for all, + much love.

Hotchnik

It is really too bad you were not able to find some important Yankee money: According to AEH, he and EH had bet against the Yankees, who lost the Series to the Milwaukee Braves. With the letter, AEH enclosed a check with EH's winnings.

Mr. Covington: A catch by the Braves' Wes Covington ended a Yankee rally in game two.

Sally League: Minor league baseball's South Atlantic League.

Upmann cigar: Renowned Cuban cigar.

Hotchnik: The Soviet Union launched Sputnik I on October 4, 1957.

{100} AEH to EH
14 Nov. 1957 (TLS, 1 p., JFKL)
A. E. Hotchner R. F. D. 5 Westport, Conn.

Dear Papa:

I think we hit pretty good with the television thing and showed the peoples if what you got is true at the source and you do it honest you wind-up with something that works—whether for the New Medium, the Old Medium or Mr. Zanuck's crotch works. What worked best was The Light of the World because we had two great whores. I enclose a couple of the pile of clips which CBS sent me, all of which were okay. We are not scrap book boys but you are pretty far away and this is just about the best second-hand information to get. As a result of the television show, much interest now in stage and movie. What I would like to do, if okay with you, is to do a stage version using Nick Adams material. Just done stark and literal, the way handled on television. If can do a good stage version, then movie thing becomes that much more valuable and desirable. At any rate, with much of the work already done for television, would not be much more work to convert into stage play.

We are having just about the greatest Fall weather I can remember. You can see your breath at night but the days are warm and the leaves are beyond anything I ever saw. This is the compensation for being back. I have been outdoors a lot and never felt better or stronger. I played in two tennis tournaments and luckily won them both—which for an old fart of 40 is a testimonial to cunning over agility. Like using the laces and only throwing a right when you know it can land. I saw the Knicks play Boston and I wished very much you could have been there. I know it's been a long time since you've seen Pro basketball, and you've never seen anything like this. It is so beautiful to watch, so graceful and deadly to watch. All giants, but not like the clumsy web-footed giants of former pro ball; now the giants have all the speed, coordination and fakiness of the little forwards, and they can hit from anywhere. I guess as it is now I would rather watch pro ball than any other sport. Surely what we saw as the best in baseball ain't no corpuscle racer. And the ring . . . Pro football, they tell me, also has it, but I have not been to any games. There is a big one coming up, Giants and Cleveland, and I will try to see that. Those boys you met at Toots', Gifford and Conerly, are having good seasons and are the pistons of the team.

I finally got around to seeing THE SUN ALSO RISES. I have been under sedatives ever since.

I have done nothing about the Indian thing because I felt that you were uncertain about your plans + would rather wait. But if you want me to get soundings will do discretely whenever you say. Everybody here sends love to Mary + you.

Hotchenheimer

Read The Atlantic stories—simply splendid A Man of the World hits like a bulldozer and the other works all the way—splendid stories.

---

we hit pretty good with the television thing: "The World of Nick Adams" aired November 10, 1957, on CBS's *The Seven Lively Arts,* earning favorable reviews.

two great whores: The whores in the "Light of the World" segment were played by Vivian Nathan and Olive Deering.

the pile of clips: One reviewer called the production "one of the first shows I've caught in years which assumed that the audience had reached the age of reason." Jo Coppula, "The View from Here," *New York Post,* November 11, 1957, p. 17. Other complimentary reviews included R.F.S., "Hemingway's Adams," *New York Times,* November 11,

1957, p. 51; "Tele Follow-Up Comment: *The Seven Lively Arts,*" *Variety,* November 13, 1957, p. 36.

Gifford and Conerly: EH had met New York Giants Frank Gifford and Charley Conerly at Toots Shor's Restaurant.

I finally got around to seeing THE SUN ALSO RISES: Released by Fox in August 1957. Produced by Darryl F. Zanuck and with a screenplay by Peter Viertel, the movie starred Tyrone Power and Ava Gardner.

Hotchenheimer: John Frankenheimer was a television director who would direct several of AEH's adaptations, including "The Snows of Kilimanjaro," "The Fifth Column," and "For Whom the Bell Tolls" (*Choice,* 201–13).

The Atlantic stories: "A Man of the World" and "Get a Seeing-Eyed Dog" were published in the *Atlantic,* November 1957, pp. 64–68, under the umbrella title "Two Tales of Darkness."

{101} EH to AEH
December 7 1957 (ALS, 2 pp., ViU)
FINCA VIGIA, SAN FRANCISCO DE PAULA, CUBA

Dear Hotchnick:

Was delighted with your letters—(the one with the check) and the one about the TV. going well (with the clippings).

Wanted to write at once but Alfred [Rice] had just given me a real bajonazo and it was so bad that had to write full out everyday, then Gregory [Hemingway] had to go to hospital again and Mary and I both got bad dose of flu and were busy being laid up in the two different ends of the house.

You remember how often I protested about Alfred keeping income for me that came in for me letting me get over-drawn at the bank when we were in Venice that time, not paying K.W [Key West] taxes and having property offered for tax sale and etc. [see letter 70]. Well what he was doing for his benefit was illegal, for tax purposes it seems. (He just found it out after 10 years and him a tax lawyer) and because one year him keeping his six months' collections over the year end on his 6 month accounting system made my income less for that year it is going to cost me between 35,000 and 50,000. He had the dough for his own use. Piled up all the Foreign rights as fast as he could get them. So he had the money to use in a bull market and now I have to pay. Plus all sorts of other trouble and insurance. <u>Don't mention this to anyone or to him</u>. He probably was doing the same thing with other people.

He said he wanted to set up a corporation for the readings. I told him he was not to set up any corporations of any kind for me. Told him to tell you

Bataclan a bad name as is name of a Indian Fakir. Probably belongs to the Fakir.

I have to send him a cable to get anything in writing from him. He wants only to talk on the telephone.

When I remember how I told him always to pay every possible tax, to never cut corners and then for him to have used my money for himself and kept it illegally and then me be stuck with [*indeciph.*] taxes on account of what at best could be overall ignorance by him. I could have paid easily and without a thought at the time and now have to put myself out of business to pay. I doubt now if he even ever kept my money in a separate account.

No answer except for me to get to work and not worry which have been doing. Have written 750 to 1200 words a day since Nov. 5 when got his letter. (He's written once since on cabled demand.) This is just to explain why I have not written you as I should. Worrying about how he's gypped me or seeing he is punished would not help.

Have been 2 days without fever now and worked twelve hours yest. So laid off this morning to write you as it was getting on my conscience.

Mary's much better now. She had it harder than I did but I had to be careful as did not want it to hit kidney or liver. She still runs fever in the afternoon.

It is important not to let Alfred know you know this as it would start him throwing up various smoke screens <u>at the least</u>. Have to stop now to quit thinking about him. Fixed charges Gregory $150 a week (non deductible) plus treatments. Mary's mother 420 per month (plus extras). Bumby's [John Hemingway's] rent $140 a month. But he's starting to get going good now and that may not be permanent.

Hope things go well with you.

Will fight my way out of this one same as out of every other one. Best always old Hotch,

Mary sends love

<u>Papa</u>

(*the one with the check*): Since EH left New York after game two of the Series, AEH collected their betting winnings and enclosed a check with letter 99.

bajonazo: "[U]sually a deliberate sword thrust into the neck or lower part of the shoulder by a matador who seeks to kill the bull without exposing himself." Hemingway, *Death in the Afternoon,* glossary.

Indian Fakir: Possibly refers to a music hall act. EH likely knew of the Bataclan, a 2,500-seat theater in Paris.

1958

{102} EH to AEH
MAY6 58 (Cable, 1 p., ViU)
Cuba

THANKS FINE LETTER BEFORE SHOW AND CONGRATULATIONS ON YOUR PER-
FORMANCE STOP WE JUST READ CROSBY REVIEW AND HAPPIEST YOU GETTING
DESERVED RECOGNITION LOVE=MARY PAPA=

FINE LETTER: Remains unlocated.
CROSBY REVIEW: AEH's adaptation of "Fifty Grand" aired in April 1958 on NBC's *Kraft
Television Theatre.* John Crosby wrote that it "caught the breathless, raw authenticity
of the Hemingway dialogue about as well as I've ever heard it." "End of Studio One
and Kraft," *New York Herald Tribune,* May 5, 1958, sec. 2, p. 1.

{103} EH to AEH
August 26th [1958 *pmk*] (ALS, 1 p., ViU)
FINCA VIGIA, SAN FRANCISCO DE PAULA, CUBA

Dear Hotch:
    Hadn't written also on acct. book.
    You must know about book as you'd warned me. But was against Naples
story transplanted to Venice where gangsters don't come from. Using Gritti for
your gangster to live. (They would not permit this and I didn't think it was

231

very chic repayment of their many kindnesses to us.) Fight was O.K. Only mention this to get it out and forget it.

Was upset by the Town and Country pieces i.e. Pres. Theo. Roosevelt who went to Africa in 1910 returning from there to Ritz Bar which did not then exist—many others. But that the worst since you should have caught it. Also Carpentier can sue George [Scheuer] and Town and Country for the matter on him. Hope to hell it was overlooked. I hate to go back now to either Gritti or Ritz Bar. Nothing to do about it.

Alfred [Rice] was told to split with you on whatever you considered right. He said you were completely satisfied. But since latest developments I know I can believe nothing he says. So let me know if that was fouled up too. He did with me <u>exactly</u> what I told him not to do and put that shit in my mouth.

Sorry to have mentioned the book and The Town and Country pieces but was not writing on account of them and I want to keep in touch. Hope things go well with you.

Rice ruined my book which I was finishing as well as ruining everything else I gave a damn about. So what to do? Come out for the next round. Don't mention to him that you've heard from me. He'd find some way of double crossing on it. Christ knows what people like that are made of.

Best always
<u>Papa</u>.

Hope your Preminger business ok. and everything else.

---

on acct. book: AEH's first novel, *The Dangerous American: A Novel of Suspense* (New York: Random House, 1958), traces the fortunes of Johnny Cella, who is deported to Italy because of his association with racketeers.

the Town and Country pieces: The two-part article about the barman of the Ritz, Georges Scheuer, "as told to A. E. Hotchner," reported that Teddy Roosevelt visited the Ritz "in the twenties," though Roosevelt died in 1919 and the Ritz opened in 1921. AEH also reported Scheuer's recalling that boxer Georges Carpentier claimed in his memoir that many of his bouts were fixed. "The Secret of George of the Ritz," *Town and Country,* April 1958, pp. 56–57, 112–13; May 1958, pp. 104–5, 134, 136.

put that shit in my mouth: EH sued *Esquire* in an attempt to prevent the reprinting of three of his Spanish Civil War stories, "The Denunciation," "Night before Battle," and "The Butterfly and the Tank," in *The Armchair Esquire*. Rice said that reprinting would result in "great personal injury and irreparable damage," implying that EH was concerned about the political implications of the stories. Layhmond Robinson, "Hemingway Brings Suit to Stop Reprint of Spanish War Stories," *New York Times,* August 6, 1958, p. 1. EH responded: "Those statements were made by my lawyer, . . . and I have just called him up and given him hell for it. . . . [I]f anyone thinks I am worried about anyone reading political implications in my stories, he is wrong. My only concern is that my stories are straight and good." Layhmond Robinson, "Hemingway Says He Will Drop Suit," *New York Times,* August 7, 1958, p. 27. Only "The Butterfly and the Tank" was reprinted in the anthology.

my book which I was finishing: EH was at work on *The Garden of Eden* (Final, 311).

your Preminger business: Director Otto Preminger admired AEH's original teleplay "Last Clear Chance" (*Playhouse 90,* CBS, 1958) and asked AEH to adapt Pierre Boulle's novel *Other Side of the Coin* (1958) for the screen. (The film based on Boulle's *The Bridge over the River Kwai* had won the 1957 Academy Award for Best Picture.) AEH's screenplay was never produced (*Choice,* 261–70).

{104} AEH to EH
2 October 1958 (TLS, 1 p., JFKL)
A. E. Hotchner R. F. D. 5 Westport, Conn.

Dear Papa:

I gave Alfred [Rice] the word and presume he has moved ahead on it; I mentioned nothing beyond the bare facts, as you wanted. Although the accompanying letter to Mary is full of work gloom, actually I had one great redeeming project of adapting For Whom the Bell Tolls. That was like picking apples in the warm sun. Seems okay to me. I felt terrible that you felt shut out on the Gritti and the Ritz, and I was having a hard time writing to you because of that—I hope our phone talk put a little of that straight. The situation on deportees is unique, has nothing to do with the prevailing situation where the mobsters are in the Genoa-on-south area. As I explained, the ones I spent time with were in Venice and there is another, even larger group, in Milan. But, as you pointed out, even though the top guy I saw in Venice was staying at the Gritti, I should have switched it—that was stupid. However, since I restricted the book to one printing, and that a small one, I really don't think it has had any damaging effect so far as Gritti reaction is concerned; what's more, I was there on my own, and this was totally unrelated to our visit. I just hope to Christ I haven't loused anything as good as your relations there—I really don't think I have. But I feel very bad about it, just the same. As far as George [Scheuer], Ritz & Co. are concerned, letter I had from George after the pieces indicate he's happy about them. I explained to you about the checking, no sense going into that again. George and Emil both checked out on T. Roosevelt's having been there in 1918, and I went with that <u>plus</u> Town & Country's assurance that they would run a check on all names, dates, etc. Of course, now

I see they didn't. At any rate, this has been a big year for the Learning of Lessons. Amen.

I was very sad yesterday, watching the first game and realizing that a year had passed without seeing you. We have passed very few years in the past ten without seeing each other at least once. It was a good game, better than anything we saw, and the cameras at [Milwaukee] County Stadium are beautifully placed, especially one that puts you right on the pitcher's box and lets you follow the pitch on a line into the plate. Spahn's screw ball to right-handers was a beauty. I think they'll cream Turley today. I have a very good bet down on the Braves, and would have got some for you but it only developed yesterday morning, and I figured you were probably down already, or I would have phoned.

Would be wonderful if we could cross paths in the west—so please let me hear from you when you light somewhere.

All best,

Chiang Kai-hetchk

the accompanying letter to Mary: **Remains** located.

adapting For Whom the Bell Tolls: The production aired in two parts on CBS's *Playhouse 90,* March 12 and 19, 1959.

T. Roosevelt's having been there: Writings about the Ritz still perpetuate the claim that Roosevelt visited the bar: "The Bar Hemingway began as the Petit Bar in 1921 and was frequented by the likes of Winston Churchill, Theodore Roosevelt, and Noel Coward." Review of *The Cocktails of the Ritz Paris,* by Colin Peter Field (New York: Simon and Schuster, 2003), Globe Corner Bookstores, http://www.globecorner.com/t/t36/18351.php, accessed June 28, 2005.

the first game: The 1958 World Series was a rematch between the Braves and the Yankees. On October 1, AEH watched on television as the Braves beat the visiting Yankees 4–3 in game one. Warren Spahn pitched for the Braves and Bob Turley for the Yankees, who went on to win the Series.

Chiang Kai-hetchk: In 1958 Chiang Kai-shek, ousted president of China and leader of the Chinese Nationalists in Taiwan, said he would seek to retake China by political rather than military means.

In late September, Mary and Betty Bruce flew by separate routes to Chicago while EH and Otto Bruce drove the Bruces' station wagon north from Key West. They picked up their wives on October 4 and all four drove to Ketchum, Idaho (HIW, 521–22).

{105} EH to AEH
[**November 5, 1958**] (ALS, 1 p., ViU)
[Idaho *pmk*]

Dear Hotch:

Don't let the year go by without us getting together. Classy shooting—fine country and people—next best thing to Spain and very like it—we have guns and gear for you—of all kinds—also can fix transport—Have car here and am driving—Hope you make it. Would be swell to see you. Best to Jerry—

Papa

getting together: This note appears on the verso of Mary's letter of the same date inviting
   AEH to visit the Hemingways in Ketchum (ViU, 6250f).

*AEH's visit was occupied with hunting and tending to a pet owl. EH gave a talk to
schoolchildren and AEH later published an edited transcript; see "Hemingway Talks
to the American Youth,"* This Week, *October 18, 1959, pp. 10–11, 24, 26. AEH was
adapting several Hemingway stories for a dramatic reading, but EH had another
project in mind for him: adapting Maj. Frederick Russell Burnham's 1926 memoir*
Scouting on Two Continents *for television. Burnham (1861–1947), a frontier and
Indian scout in the American Southwest, volunteered to serve the British in southern
Africa and distinguished himself in the Boer War.*

{106} AEH to EH
(**12/19/58**) (AEH's parentheses; ALS, 1 p., JFKL)
[Connecticut]

Dear Papa—Here's a copy of the Burnham report, for your information. Have a good tracer at work on this now, hope to have quick results. Am getting other information etc., so we can move when ready.

Best

Hotcho

the Burnham report: This note was attached to a letter from Johnson & Tannenbaum
   Attorneys, dated November 28, 1958, explaining that the U.S. copyright for
   Burnham's *Scouting on Two Continents* had expired in 1954; the British copyright, how-
   ever, was still in force.

Hemingway asks for copies
of these photos in his post-
script to letter 128. The
portrait of Hemingway was
taken by Hotchner in Le
Escorial.

LA CONSULA
CHURRIANA
MALAGA

Dear Hotch:
19/6/59

Just thought of 2 things you could bring if not too bad trouble — a light weight shooting jacket 44-46 — with leather patch on shoulder — For shooting trap or live pigeons - from Abercrombies. They know my size - and a pair of Levis or else those faded blue boat pants size 38 - Horse or something for the real country or unpressed getting on horse - They mean much here than a couple of friends — 4 at least and will pay the excess - You can get the coat in the gun dept + it's the same coat Mary has to shoot with.

Weather wonderful here. Think you will find wheat place along the coast where would be what you've always been looking for for summer and winter. Some terrible ones I want to show you + lots of places like the Riviera was before they ruined it.

wonderful to be seeing you so soon.

Mary sends love to
Jerry and the girls. They wrote
her nice letter.

Best Luck
Papa

Hemingway to Hotchner, June 19, 1959.

Hotchner attending his first bullfight with the Hemingways in Alicante, June 28, 1959.

Hotchner with Rupert Bellville and his companion, Polly Peabody, at the bullfights.

Hotchner and Hemingway seated in the bullring before the start of one of
the mano a manos.

Hemingway often presided over lengthy luncheons during his stay in Málaga in the summer of 1959. *From left:* Hotchner, Pat Saviers, unidentified man, Annie Davis, Hemingway, Valerie Danby-Smith, George Saviers. (Photo by Cano)

Hemingway's sixtieth birthday party in Málaga, July 21, 1959. *From left:* Hemingway, actress Beverly Bentley, Hotchner, Annie Davis at far right. (Photo by Cano)

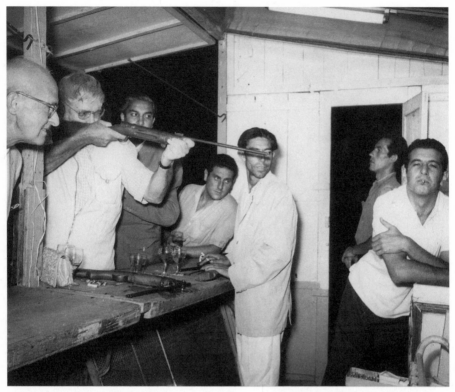

At the party, Hemingway shot a cigarette from the lips of Antonio Ordóñez. Hemingway is flanked by Col. "Buck" Lanham and the Maharaja of Cooch-behar. (Photo by Cano)

The last photograph Hotchner took of Hemingway, standing in the entranceway of the finca before souvenirs of his two great passions: the bullfight and the hunt.

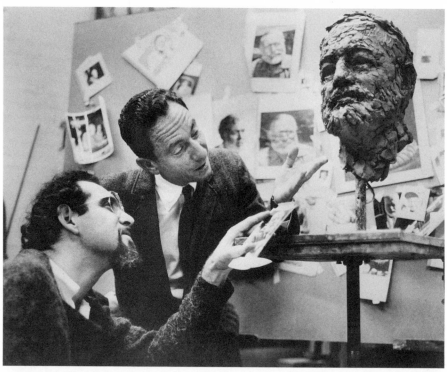

Sculptor Robert Berks shows Hotchner the bust that was used on the *Buick Electra Playhouse* series; see letters 137 and 138. (CBS publicity photo)

Antonio Ordóñez displaying the style that Hemingway admired.

During Hotchner's visit to Ketchum in late 1960, Hemingway schooled him in shooting duck and pheasant.

Hemingway, Bud Purdy, and Gary Cooper hunting duck in Ketchum. Purdy was an Idaho rancher and friend of Hemingway. (Photo by A. E. Hotchner)

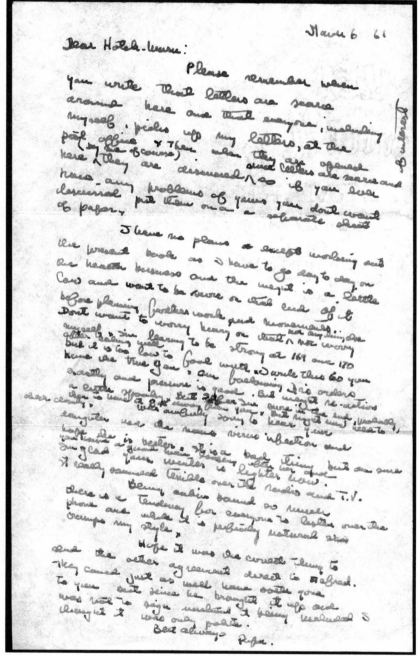

Hemingway's last letter to Hotchner, March 6, 1961.

The cast and creators of *Hemingway's Adventures of a Young Man* (Fox, 1962).
Left to right: Eli Wallach, Susan Strasberg, Ricardo Montalban, Richard Beymer,
director Martin Ritt, and Hotchner. (Fox publicity photo)

1959

AEH returned to Ketchum on March 16 to help the Hemingways drive south. On the 19th, in a motel in Phoenix, they watched part two of AEH's television adaptation of For Whom the Bell Tolls (HIW, 529).

AEH parted with the Hemingways in New Orleans (PH, 202). They went on to the finca but stayed only three weeks; on April 22 they flew to New York, meeting AEH briefly. In a document dated April 23, 1959, EH granted AEH permission to proceed with his adaptations: "I hereby grant to A. E. Hotchner, in consideration of his services, the right and authority to present a theatrical program based on my writings, this authority to include all forms of 'live' performances in any place of his choosing" (JFKL).

From New York, the Hemingways sailed for Algeciras, Spain, and drove to La Consuela, the estate of wealthy expatriates Nathan "Bill" Davis and his wife, Annie, on the Costa del Sol near Málaga. EH began following the fortunes of Antonio Ordóñez and his brother-in-law, Luis Miguel Dominguín, intending to publish an addendum to Death in the Afternoon (Story, 544).

{107} AEH to EH
13 May 1959 (TLS, 1 p., JFKL)
A. E. Hotchner R. F. D. 5 Westport, Conn.

Dear Papa:

Went to the Stadium last night and watched the Yankees lose another ball game, this time to Cleveland which certainly doesn't look like a first place team. But the Indian outfielder, Rocky Colavito, is a beautiful ball player, big, moves like a cat, and has an easy swing that reminds you of DiMaggio. But I really couldn't get worked up over what anyone was doing, including Mr. Y. Berra who made his first error in 180 games or some such figure. The crowd was around 35 or 36 [thousand], though—I know you'll be relieved to know that the sentimentalists who own the team are still making out okay.

I had a fine time the few days you were here. I was very sorry not to be able to make the boat, but it was noon before I got the mob in. I have really never seen you or Mary look as well, even a step up from our recent celebrated passage from Ketchum.

I go out to that nameless city in California tomorrow for the final push on Mussolini (June 4). Since you left, CBS, Buick and I have been back and forth over the program of specials and I think it will work out okay. I thought, in light of what you indicated about number, that it would be best to limit it to four—they will probably be done October and December this year, Feb. and March next year so the income will be split. At any rate, the project is approved and awaiting a meeting of the GM Board of Directors on May 19. If that checks out, then I will have them put their proposal in writing and fly over with it to wherever you are in Spain so we can go over it. CBS has time clearance problems, so in fairness to them I would like to do this as soon as I can, probably end of June. I have eased the Burnham down but there is still considerable pushing on it, and alternatives, but we can talk about that when I see you. I enclose a couple of clips, just in case you were uncertain as to what you'd be working at for the next year or so. I think Mr. Castro's cinematic demands are refreshingly modest, don't you? As for the ABC thing, where they want you to wander into bizarre areas, the only bizarre areas I can think of, if you walked in with a TV camera you'd be shot between the eyes. So maybe that's a more limited employment than it seems.

Mrs. Henahan's jacket arrived and I really look like the freckled white hunter of Fairfield County. It's a great jacket, fits perfect. I'm ready for Ketchum, 1959–60.

Kiss Mary for me. Hope the [bull]fights are good and exciting. I hate to be here when the fun is there but I guess there are stretches when acting like a responsible citizen is mandatory. I'll write again soon.

Louis M. Hotchminguin

Mr. Y. Berra: The Yankees' Yogi Berra had no errors between July 28, 1957, and May 12, 1959, setting a record for a catcher in consecutive games. In the game AEH describes, the Yankees lost 7–6 to the first-place Indians.

the final push on Mussolini: AEH's original teleplay "The Killers of Mussolini" aired on CBS's *Playhouse 90* on June 4, 1959.

Mr. Castro's cinematic demands: Jerry Wald had acquired the rights to film the life of Fidel Castro, whose guerrilla forces had caused Cuban dictator Fulgencio Batista to flee the island on January 1, 1959. Castro, it was reported, "would like Ernest Hemingway to do the script . . . Marlon Brando to portray him and Frank Sinatra as Brother Raoul." "Castro Biopic via Jerry Wald," *Variety,* April 29, 1959, p. 1.

Mrs. Henahan's jacket: According to AEH, Mrs. Henahan, a professional seamstress in Ketchum, had mailed him a jacket made from the skin of a mountain lion, a duplicate of one she had made for EH. AEH, phone call with DeFazio, June 14, 2005.

Sports Illustrated *persuaded EH to provide an account of the mano a manos, but Edward Thompson, managing editor of* Life, *and Will Lang, the magazine's Paris representative, intervened, cabling EH to ask for "*THREE TO FOUR THOUSAND WORDS DESCRIBING BOTH MEN PERSONALLY AND COMMA BACKGROUND OF CURRENT RIVALRY AND LASTLY COMMA OF COURSE COMMA THE EPOCAL FIGHTS THEMSELVES.*" "Transcripts of Correspondence between E.H. and* Life *re* The Dangerous Summer *1959–1960," ViU, 6250f, 2–3. EH suggested a 4,000- to 5,000-word piece and, in the ensuing months,* Life's *editors were remarkably flexible regarding price, which increased from $30,000 to $100,000 (PH, 247), and deadline, which shifted from fall 1959 to fall 1960.*

{108} AEH to EH
[May 26, 1959] (Cable, 4 pp., ViU)
Hollywood, California

DEAR PAPA CBS-BUICK SITUATION NOW COMPLETED FOUR LIVE SHOWS TO BE DONE TWO IN 1959 AND TWO IN 1960 AS YOU REQUESTED FOR DIVIDEND INCOME PAYMENT TO US FOR BASIC RIGHTS PLUS FOUR ADAPTATIONS TO TOTAL DLRS240,000 (TWO HUNDRED FORTY THOUSAND) AT RATE OF SIXTY THOUSAND EACH SHOW YOU AND I WILL MAKE FINAL SELECTIONS OF STORIES WHEN I COME TO SPAIN WITH WRITTEN CONTRACTS FOR YOU TO APPROVE AND SIGN BUT CBS WOULD LIKE THE KILLERS AND MACOMBER AS FIRST TWO IF OKAY HAVE CHECKED THEM OUT WITH RICE AND LEGALLY OKAY THINK THIS GOOD CHOICE WE ARE GETTING BEST PEOPLE AND BIG BUDGETS PLEASE CABLE ME WHETHER THIS BASICALLY OKAY OR PHONE IF YOU WANT TO DISCUSS CABLE ADDRESS CBS-TELEVVION [sic] HOLLYWOOD TELEPHONE OLIVE 1-2345 EXTENSION 727 PLEASE ANSWER SOON AS POSSIBLE SO I CAN ACT ON THIS WHILE HERE HOPE ALL GOES WELL BULLS GOOD ANTONIO BETTER LOVE TO MARY ET AL. HOTCH.

{109} AEH to EH
June 12, 1959 (TLS, 1 p., JFKL)
A. E. Hotchner R. F. D. 5 Westport, Conn.

Dear Papa:

The Buick-CBS deal has all been worked out now, with the usual number of horse-shit conferences, re-conferences and un-conferences, and I am waiting for the lawyers to finish all their fee-justifiers. On close look, as Alfred [Rice] probably informed you, it seemed best not to do this as a corp. because of the nature of the thing—I'll explain when I see you.

I will also have to hold up a few days longer than I had planned because the 20th-Century Flux has another project, more long-term, involving rather good amount of realm money, and so, to oblige their interest, will have to fly to Hollywood quickly, get papers, bring to you.

I will get out of here, projects or no, (and the Iberian Airlines being more cooperative than they are at this minute), end of June, the 26th being target date right now. Where will you be from the 26th through lst week in July? I realize Pamplona is [July] 6–14, but beds and tickets being what they are (or, rather, aren't) I will pass on to some by-way and mark time and re-group with you on conclusion. In other words, please do not regard me as a Pamplona liability (or any other, I hope). But I will fight to the death to worm my freckled ass onto a bench at Valencia and following. Where can I count on being hoteled on arrival in Madrid? Is [Hotel] Suecia okay as you thought?

Can you or Mary drop me a note at The Chateau Marmont, 8221 Sunset Blvd., Hollywood 46 Calif.—where I'll be next week, giving me your whereabouts? It will be fine to be all together again in Spain, having fun as we always do at everything.

Juan Hotchmonte
(anything I can bring?)

Juan Hotchmonte: Alludes to matador Juan Belmonte, who came out of retirement in 1925 and fought poorly, as reflected in EH's unfavorable depiction of him in *The Sun Also Rises.* He fought better in 1926–1927, earning him praise in *Death in the Afternoon* (243). Miriam Mandel, *Hemingway's* Death in the Afternoon: *The Complete Annotations* (Lanham, MD: Scarecrow Press, 2002), 77–78.

{110} EH to AEH
18/6/59 (ALS, 3 pp., ViU)
Apartado 67/Malaga [*hw*] [Spain]

Dear Hotch:

Got your letter giving me Hollywood address and last night your cable from N.Y. giving arrival in Madrid as morning June 27th. Send this in duplicate to the Chateau Marmont and Westport.

Here is the gen—Antonio [Ordóñez] fights Zaragoza 27th, Alicante 28th[,] Barcelona 29th, Burgos 30th. Zaragoza is the first fight after the big wound. Bill Davis and I will drive from here to Madrid on 26th. Be at Suecia. OK joint. Maximum protection.

If you could get to Madrid by 26th it would be wonderful. If you can't you can't. It is 6 hrs. drive to Zaragoza. We can wait until 1030 on 27th before taking off for Zaragoza. If your plane doesn't get in on time will gen out how you can meet us and where in Alicante on 28th and leave it at desk of SUECIA. These rides are a hell of a lot of fun and easy to do (comparatively) when you don't have to boat womens.

Bill's wife and Mary will drive to Alicante from here for the fight on 28th. Maybe we'll all drive to Barcelona. Depends how tired they get.

After Burgos you and Bill and I will drive back down here and then go up for Pamplona. Will get your accomodations and tickets. We have good mob for these. Antonio is going with us. He is not fighting on account of a contract mix up. But some <u>actual</u> crazies are fighting and it will be fun. Bulls terrific. George [Saviers] will be there from Ketchum too.

After Pamplona we can have a cool out period and then hit Valencia. Antonio fights three times there. Luis Miguel the same. Then the feria here. Eleven fights in small ring—Best bulls—Antonio 4 times—Miguel 4—Juan Ostoes 3—The rest build up from what crazies survive Pamplona—Wizard ops in prospect. All we need is George Plimpton and Mac Mullen. Bill Davis is about the best guy you've ever known. For the 21st we have joint birthday party of Carmen, Antonio's wife and my 60th. We have to survive it men because we have to push on to Valencia. Antonio has bulls on the 19th and 20th at Dax but will fly in the afternoon of the 21st and can rest here 2 days after the party before we all go to Valencia.

Hotch there never was such a summer in prospect and I hope we can see you on 26th. But if not then the 27th. All expenses we charge to the firm and this new stuff for the new edition of Death in the Afternoon. All Antonio wants, except to be the greatest matador that ever lived, is to be with us guys. We are just back from his bull ranch. Had wonderful time. Wound is healed good. Love to all. See you soon. Write and give the exact gen on ETA.

Best love from all
Papa

If you could bring smallest practical tape recorder it would be good.

the big wound: On May 30, 1959, Ordóñez was gored in a performance that earned him both ears, a hoof, and the tail Hemingway, *Dangerous Summer,* 87–104.

George [Saviers]: Sun Valley Hospital physician who treated EH in 1958 and became his friend while continuing to serve as his doctor (*HIW,* 523).

George Plimpton: Editor of the *Paris Review;* interviewed EH for "The Art of Fiction, XXI: Ernest Hemingway Interview," *Paris Review* 18 (spring 1958): 60–89.

Mac Mullen: Forrest "Duke" MacMullen, hunting companion from Ketchum and EH's "man Friday." Meyers, *Hemingway,* 517.

{111} EH to AEH
1959 JUN 18 (Cable, 1 p., JFKL)
Spain

IF CANNOT MAKE MADRID ON TWENTYSIXTH AND IF WE NOT AT AIRPORT TWENTYSEVENTH COME DIRECT TO SUECIA AND WE DRIVE TO ZARAGOZA FOR ANTONIO'S REAPPEARANCE TWENTYSEVENTH SIX PM WILL HAVE EVERYTHING SET FOR PAMPLONA VALENCIA ETC. LOVE :=PAPA=

{112} EH to AEH
JUN18 1959 (Cable, 1 p., ViU)
[Spain]

JUST CABLED GEN TO CHATEAU MARMONT LETTER ENROUTE SEE YOU TWENTY-SEVENTH SUECIA LOVE FROM ALL=PAPA MARY=

{113} EH to AEH
19/6/59 (ALS, 1 p., ViU)
LA CONSULA/CHURRIANA/MALAGA [Spain]

Dear Hotch:

Just thought of 2 things you could bring if not too bad trouble—a light weight shooting jacket 44–46—with leather patch on shoulder—For shooting trap or live pigeons—from Abercrombies. They know my size—and a pair of Levis or else those faded blue boat pants size 38—Have nothing for the real country or [*indeciph.*] getting on horse. They won't weigh more than a couple of pounds—4 at most and will pay the excess. You can get the coat in the gun dept. It's the same coat Mary has to shoot with.

Weather wonderful here. Think you will find place along the coast where would be what you've always been looking for for summer _and_ winter. Some terrific ones I want to show you. Lots of places like the Riviera was before they ruined it.

Wonderful to be seeing you so soon.

Best luck

Papa

Mary sends love to Gerry and the girls. They wrote her nice letter.

{114} EH to AEH
27th 0900 [June 27, 1959] (ALS, 1 p., PC)
HOTEL SUECIA—MADRID [Spain]

Dear Hotch:

We'd figured out all combination of waiting and still making Zaragoza. But then got your word departure delayed. Here's gen.

Fight at Alicante is 6 pm June 28th. We will meet at Carleton Hotel—(Biggest there) will have tickets.

To get to Alicante you can fly to Valencia and take taxi from there But Bill [Davis] says best take taxi from here via Albacete. ALBACETE. Six hours. Hotel concierge can get good taxi. Cost 3p. Kilometer—800 (aller-retour [round trip]) 2400 pesetas.

Leave stuff you don't want for trip here. We will be back here July 2nd after Burgos.

Guess that's about all. Terribly sorry you missed today's fight. Am sweating it out. Antonio [Ordóñez] in fine physical and mental shape. But this is first fight with Luis Miguel [Dominguín] since L. M. retired and it is rough to make that your comeback fight after such a bad wound.

Am also sweating but not heavy [about] the Swede, I bet a grand on him at 4/1 and think he should make it. [Toots] Shor bet it for me. I called from Malaga before we came up.

See you soon Hotch.

Wish we were meeting you and driving together.

Love

Papa

We have a Salmon Pink English Ford with Gebralter license plates.

EH.

the Swede: Boxer Ingemar Johansson, who beat Floyd Patterson in New York on June 26, 1959, winning the heavyweight crown.

On the back of the envelope, EH wrote: "Paper just came and the Swede made it. Menos mal [not so bad]," having just learned he'd won $4,000 on his bet. There is a six-hour time difference between New York and Madrid, and the fight ended around 1 or 2 a.m., Madrid time.

On June 28, AEH met EH in Alicante and they joined up with Mary, Annie Davis, and Juanito Quintana in Pamplona on July 6. Other companions included George and Pat Saviers and Valerie Danby-Smith, a writer for the Irish Times *whom EH subsequently hired as a secretary. On July 21 the group held a birthday party for EH and Carmen Ordóñez. At the bullring at Ciudad Real, AEH donned a* traje de luces, *the matador's suit of lights, and joined Antonio Ordóñez and Luis Miguel Dominguín as a* sobresaliente, *presumably prepared to substitute for an injured matador.*

AEH departed in mid-August, having spent nearly two months with EH (PH, 206; Story, 547). In the August 17 issue of Sports Illustrated, *both Hemingways had pieces about Ordóñez and Dominguín recovering from horn wounds: Ernest Hemingway, "A Matter of Wind," p. 43; Mary Hemingway, "Holiday for a Wounded Torero," pp. 44–45, 48–49, 51.*

{115} AEH to EH

28 August 59 (ALS, 2 pp., JFKL)

A. E. Hotchner R. F. D. 5 Westport, Conn.

Dear Papa—

I've just touched down and am very sad to be back to this—not so much being back to this, as being off from our happy cuadrilla. It was a fine time! An unceasing fine time. There was what we always have (only this time in spades with diamonds set on the spots) plus the emergence of Le Negro [Bill Davis] and Miss Annie [Davis] and, for me, getting to really know Antonio [Ordóñez]. Christ, what a summer! And I don't even check list assorted prisoners and various other stalwarts. But now I must adjust from this feeling of being lost and out of it. There are wheels + grindstones here to which shoulders + whatever else must be put. I was asked by Bertin [Ritz barman] in Paris if the toros tour had been educational, to which I replied that any summer in which a man learns how to correctly position his prick in matador pants is highly educational.

Monday I begin the production work on The Killers—also, will see Chas. Scribner [IV], Alfred [Rice], and look into the Speiser + Leicester matters. Letter from Rice received in Paris says our corp. is already set up + we can operate out of it. So therefore I will let H+H Ltd buy the Burnham book as its first activity. For this we must furnish it some capital + get stock in return. I suggest we both put in $2500—I know your situation re cash right now, so I'd be glad to put in $5000 + you can pay me your share later. At any rate, it should be done very shortly—The Burnhams have returned from vacation + I can buy the book at any time.

I could not get copies made of the Paris material in Paris because everything was Shut for August—but I'll take it into N.Y. Monday + return it right after that. I am having the poems copied for you.

Please give my love to everyone—kiss Annie, Mary, Valerie [Danby-Smith], Nicole + any new females for me + give my best to Bill.

As ever,

Hotchulin, Baron of Pecas

Le Negro: Antonio Ordóñez thought that EH's handwriting was bad and joked that Bill Davis, who had beautiful handwriting, was EH's "negro," or ghostwriter, and the nickname stuck. "The Dangerous Summer Part II: The Pride of the Devil," *Life,* September 12, 1960, p. 66.

assorted prisoners: Out walking one evening, EH, AEH, and Antonio Ordóñez "captured" an American tourist, Teddy Jo Paulson, and escorted her to her lodging, where they met her roommate, Mary Schoonmaker. Thereafter, the two women joined the group, attending the birthday party for EH and Carmen Ordóñez on July 21.

the Speiser + Leicester matters: EH's brother, Leicester, claimed that the late Maurice Speiser had given him rights to certain materials belonging to EH, which he wanted to include in his biography of his brother (*PH,* 231; AEH, fax to DeFazio, November 29, 2004).

Chas. Scribner [IV] (1921–1995): Took over the publishing firm after his father's death in 1952.

The Burnhams have returned from vacation: Refers to Roderick Burnham (Major Burnham's son) and his wife.

the Paris material: Chapters of *A Moveable Feast* (New York: Scribner's, 1964).

the poems: Probably "To Mary in London" and "Second Poem to Mary"; see letter 20.

Baron of Pecas: When AEH went into the bullring in Ciudad Real, the posters read "SOBRESALIENTE: EL PECAS [the freckled one]" (*PH,* 223–25).

{116} EH to AEH
6 Sept. 59 (AcardS, 1 p., ViU)
[Alicante *pmk*] [Spain]

This is the town where you first went into the callejon. Bulls tomorrow at Villena up the road from here. Then Madrid 2—Rhonda. Then north to Salamanca—We miss you at everything always—Love Hemingstein (von und zu).

The front of the postcard shows the beach at Alicante.

callejon: In a bullring, the passageway between the fence surrounding the ring and the first row of seats.

(von und zu): Playing off of AEH's signature "Hotchulin, Baron of Pecas," this phrase indicates an aristocrat's birthright and the location of his family's estate.

We miss you: The card was also signed by Mary, the Davises, and Valerie Danby-Smith.

{117} AEH to EH
Sept, 11, 1959 (TLS, 2 pp., JFKL)
A. E. Hotchner R. F. D. 5 Westport, Conn.

Dear Papa:

There has been so much to do to get our CBS plays in motion, no time to write; also, problems non-TV to solve, much time, emotions, all very rough but since when do we list the very rough as something special? However, the two months there, with you, negro [Bill Davis] and assorted classy characters, all very smooth, so un-used to the rough. Am now used to again.

The Fullmer bout, as on TV, fine to watch. Basilio a shell, legs gone, but still the good moves and lots of guts. However, not nearly enough against Fullmer who was greatly improved over last time I saw him. Very good countering and a wonderfully sharp left. Hope you are here next time he fights.

Have had the Paris chapters [*A Moveable Feast*] copied and am returning all to you under separate cover. Now that I have had good chance to read and re-read them, think they are absolutely wonderful. The funny is deep-down funny and the sad things are unexpected and very moving. The more I spend time thinking about the material as a possible stage venture, the more attractive it becomes. But if it is to be ready by the winter of 1960–61, it must be put into motion quite soon. I have to go to Hollywood next week to do preliminary work on our first two plays, and I plan to see Cole Porter just to see how he is. I will let you know. I will also go to see Mr. Burnham in Palm Springs and buy the book. Since we do not have our capitalization arranged, I'll simply purchase it in my name and then we can re-assign ownership whenever you want.

I know it's silly to say so, but ever since I've been back I have an overwhelming feeling of being displaced from my real life which is as a member of your quadrilla in the best of all possible summers. I am also very sorry that before I left I neglected to give Pepe Burke the alternativa for the paseo. I hope Will Lang will send the Ciudad Real photos as he promised, or else how will I ever convince Mac [MacMullen] or George [Saviers] that I had my moment of half-truth?

I have had the three poems you wanted copied and they are in with the other material. Re-reading your long poem, I think it's a good idea to let the Atlantic publish it now. There's only one thing about it you may want to think about—time has obscured the background of the Cardinal Spellman references. But it is a poem for giants.

What is particularly exasperating about this goddam exile from my true life, is that there ain't no accounts nowhere of what Antonio [Ordóñez] is up to. For all I know his ankle may still be on the bum. But then again, knowing Antonio, I suspect he was back in there on crutches inside of three days.

I have phoned Chas. Scribner but he was moving his family back to town last week and I plan to see him Monday. I have already had conference with lawyer, just to give him facts on Speiser, but to do nothing until you return. His opinion: all of the files are recoverable except copies of material originated by Speiser, and all items bearing your signature or relating to matters worked on by Speiser on your behalf, absolutely subject to being enjoined from auction or any other publication. Very good lawyer—sure you will like. Alfred [Rice] has been pretty well punched out by events, realizes his best action is to clinch and hold if possible. Have mentioned <u>nothing</u> to him, as you suggested. Am sure he expects you to at least make a tax break.

Don't know about your reaction, but I was disappointed in Life spread, considering the rich material they covered. Seemed stereotyped, bloodless.

Do you know your come home plans? If through N.Y. please let me know as much in advance as possible so I can be sure to be here and prepare whatever necessary in way of accommodations, etcetera. I hope Mary is okay again and can travel and have fun.

I'm sorry this is such a shitty meat and potatoes letter. Fact is I miss you and Bill and Mary and Annie [Davis] so much I feel pretty sad when I write to you. Please tell Antonio how much I miss seeing him, as buddy and as artist, and give my love to Valerie [Danby-Smith], Nicole and whatever new prisoners may have hired on.

Best always,
Hotttch

A.E.Hotttchner, Barone di Villombrosa & de Roccapendente—Cavaliere del Sacro Romano Impero—Tel. Regina Coeli 233, Roma.

<u>Inquiries Invited</u>.   AEH

The Fullmer bout: Gene Fullmer defeated Carmen Basilio on August 28, winning the National Boxing Association's world middleweight title. *New York Times,* August 29, 1959, p. 9.

our first two plays: Buick Electra Playhouse was a series of television specials based on Hemingway stories. The series was to open with "The Killers" and "The Fifth Column."

I plan to see Cole Porter just to see how he is: The songwriter had recently had his right leg amputated.

I neglected to give Pepe Burke the alternativa for the paseo: An alternativa is a ceremony in which one graduates from novillero to matador; a paseo is the entrance march of bullfighters into the arena. AEH is joking that he forgot to introduce Life photographer James Burke as a new bullfighter to take the place of El Pecas.

the Cardinal Spellman references: In "Second Poem to Mary." In 1949, Spellman, Archbishop of New York City, accused Eleanor Roosevelt of being anti-Catholic; EH criticized him in a letter that was probably never sent. EH to Cardinal Spellman, July 28, 1949, in Baker, *Selected Letters,* 661–62.

Life spread: Photographic essay titled "Historic Duel of Matadors: Stirring Drama in Spain," *Life,* September 7, 1959, pp. 22–31. Photos by Larry Burrows and James Burke; author of text is not identified.

{118} EH to AEH
14/9/59 (ALS, 4 pp., ViU)
HOTEL SUECIA—MADRID
Apartado 67/Malaga [*hw*] [Spain *pmk*]

Dear Hotch,

We are back in Madrid after another swing around the circuit. You will know the towns from your list of the September fights. They finally put Antonio [Ordóñez] in jail in Alicante for backing up his picadors in the situation that you are familiar with from Bilbao. It had to happen so it is good that it is over with now. He loses ten fights which would make about 5,000,000 ptas. + he + Carmen behave as well about it as they do about everything else. Since he has been out of the can we have been busy breaking training + I think can state that training has been really fractured. There are two more fights [5 *chars. indeciph.*] 20th + Nimes 27th and then he goes to Peru and we will meet in Havana November 1st + drive out West. Maybe you can make that run. See if you can get the Buick station wagon to be ready in Key West care T. O. Bruce 605 Simonton Street, Key West, Florida.

How do all our business deals go? Have had nothing about anything from Alfred [Rice] except the normal tax payment. No news yet on what I must pay on 1957. We took Annie [Davis] on the trip north + through Estremadura + she was wonderful all the time + really had fun. We picked up Mary + Valerie [Danby-Smith] for the coming south to Valencia a little town outside of Alicante. Two fights in Murcia where I got my pocket picked signing autographs + then over to Ronda where Antonio was magnificent and then up to Salamanca where he was cancelled out. The suspension is for a month. There is not any news except that Mary is much better and feels better about everything in general. I have no news as usual. Wonderful pictures of you, Antonio + Miguel [Dominguín] that Bill Lang brought. We were all happy yesterday seeing them. He said he was sending them to you but I will pinch them anyway + have Cano copy them for you. One you ought to have blown up.

Sorry not to write a better letter. We all miss you very much. Antonio asked me to send his best last night when I told him I was writing you this morning. Look for Mary in New York on October 5th. I will be going direct to Havana on the 18th Oct. Having written piece I hope or anyway breaking the balls of it, and finishing on the boat. Write to Morgan Guaranty address as we will go up to Paris to see Mary off. Hope the Lancia will be ok by then. Nimes is the last fight + will think of you there + how Peter [Viertel] would not even get out of the car to see the Maison Carre.

Keep in good shape + write me the gen. We have very fine ops in prospect.

Yours Baronialy

Hemingstein

Von und zu

Atop AEH's letter 117, EH wrote "Answered 17/9/59," which suggests he had not received it before dictating this letter.

This is the first letter that EH dictated to Valerie Danby-Smith. Unlike Juanita Jensen, who seems to have worked from wire recordings in typing EH's letters, Valerie took down his words in longhand as he spoke.

They finally put Antonio in jail . . . for backing up his picadors: Ordóñez's picadors repeatedly violated the taurine code in Bilbao on August 18 and were fined and barred from performing for the remainder of the season. When they continued to perform with Ordóñez, they were jailed in Albacete on September 11. Ordóñez showed his support by not hiring substitutes to replace them. He appeared at the ring alone and the bullfight was cancelled. Miriam Mandel, e-mail message to DeFazio, November 21, 2004.

the Buick station wagon: Provided by the sponsors of *Buick Electra Playhouse* in exchange for an endorsement.

Cano: Spanish photographer and friend who joined the Hemingways for EH's 60th birthday party (*HIW,* 472).

Hope the Lancia will be ok by then: A blown tire caused Bill Davis to mow down several stone slabs along the road. Neither Davis nor his passengers EH and Valerie Danby-Smith were hurt, but the car had to be left in Madrid (*Story,* 549).

{119} AEH to EH
Sept. 15ᵗʰ [1959] (ALS, 2 pp., JFKL)
A. E. Hotchner R. F. D. 5 Westport, Conn.

Dear Papa—

Two items information: Buick station wagon all set, fully insured. It will be in Key West, but Buick would like to know approximately when you will be there. Friend of mine who is automotive engineer, says Buick station wagon is second best to Chrysler, much superior to Pontiac. As the owl said, we shall see.

Other item: spoke to Chas. Scribner—will have another talk next week, but gen is he would like to publish preface plus old stories + new stories as regular trade edition, not for colleges. He thinks preliminary page, as we discussed, fine idea. He wants to have another session about it but I think it's okay now, as you want it. (The suggestion of English publication was exactly right.)

I am working hard on our shows, trying to make them good. I think <u>The Killers</u> will be okay if I can get the right actors—am going to Hollywood end of this week. <u>The Fifth Column</u> will be second show, <u>Kilimanjaro</u> third.

It has suddenly turned Fall + the smell of hunting-to-be is exciting. Wonderful crisp winds + the leaves are turning crisp too. I hope everything turns out as we planned for Ketchum—it is the look-forward-to life, + that's what counts.

Love to all my "family,"

Pecas

preface: EH wrote a preface for a proposed students' edition of his short stories. Scribner and Mary found it inappropriate; when Scribner suggested publishing the stories without the preface, EH withdrew the project from consideration. The preface was published posthumously as "The Art of the Short Story," *Paris Review,* spring 1981, pp. 85–102.

{120} EH to AEH
16/9/59. (ALS, 7 pp., ViU)
Apartado 67,/Malaga [*hw*] [Spain]

Dear Hotch-maru,

Thanks for the two letters with all the gen. everything sounds fine. Will Lang said he would send you or had sent the Ciudad Real pictures. They really came out wonderfully. If you don't get them from him I will have Cano copy them for you, as I pinched the lot to have copies made + then will turn the originals over to Miguel [Dominguín] + Antonio [Ordóñez.] since they are Life property you be careful to see they fall into no one else's hands. Much of the stuff they did not use is better than that in the lay-out, but if we can think of it on a mass production basis rather than on an insider's basis I think they did a really excellent job. It was amazing the stuff Larry [Burrows] got without being a nuisance or ever lousing up the passes or the killing. I watched him closely to flag him down and after instruction + explanation he moved around the callejon as cannily as a good banderillero. Bill Lang was also very good about everything: loyal + fast and understanding within the limits of his intelligence which are considerable.

We ran into disaster when Antonio finally got put into the can on the picador deal. You were familiar with it so we summarize only. They arrested his picks (the two Cerabes brothers) at 2.30 in the afternoon after the apartado. The whole thing was set up + planned well in advance + at 5.30 they arrested Antonio + Miguelin in the patio de Caballos just before the paseo was due, on the charge, technical, that they were intending to go on without picadors which had been announced. The real charge of course, was rebellion, which is serious, + repeated violation of orders that these picadors who had been fined + suspended were used in fights from Bilbao on through Ronda. Actually Chopera, that tall, rather good-looking boy, whose father is the former horse contractor who committed some of the worst abuses which nearly put bullfighting out of business. (It was his promotion in Zaragoza you will remember when we were together + the bulls came out doped so they were like sleepwalkers.) This Chopera boy had in the contracts announced both Antonio's picadors who were barred under other names to get them by the scrutiny of the authorities in small towns. Antonio knew nothing of this. Whether Pepe [Dominguín] did, I do not know. Antonio was very angry about it + with Chopera as otherwise he had an immaculate case of backing up his picadors against an unjust + capricious banning. As it was we all had to shut up + just take it on the chin since any explanation you would give would be countered by the charge of deceit + fraud. At the time it happened no-body stuck with Antonio. Miguelin was arrested by surprise + had no choice to take a stand but Antonio said he behaved very well in the car + acted like a man. They were quite rough with them. Kept them incommunicado sleep on the stone floor without blankets or covering but Miguelillo was allowed in with some food + got a message out to Carmen [Ordóñez] who telephoned us at Salamanca. We knew nothing about it. She had been calling repeatedly, but we had read no papers in the morning at Bayonne where we slept. We talked to her. She was very calm + wonderful in any kind of jam + then went on to Madrid where we met Antonio that night when he arrived after being sprung in Alicante about 5.30 + escorted to the provincial border. He misses ten fights with the suspension, all the September ferias are ruined. Ostos and some other fighters are refusing to substitute for Antonio or rather than be in rebellion are asking a million ptas. to substitute. The facts of the whole thing will come out eventually although reading it under censorship you get no idea of what really happened nor what is behind it all. Antonio's leaving for Lima after he finishes the season at Nimes on the 27th + as of now is meeting us at the finca in Cuba to drive up to Sun Valley on November 1st.

Negro Davis, Valerie [Danby-Smith] + I + probably Annie [Davis] will drive up to Paris from Nimes to see Mary off + have fun for four days. Will search for one for Auteuil. Mary is feeling fine now. Did not get ill at all on the trip + is feeling good in the head + cheerful. We had a very good trip all around although it is always lonesome without you.

What always threw me off about publishing that poem in the Atlantic was the Spellman reference which seemed to be the only thing that dated. I will see what I can do about it.

We had a letter from my brother which gave his address + asked permission to print letters. I wrote him my general attitude about books about people when they are alive + especially one member of a family writing about a family especially one as vulnerable as ours where my mother was a bitch + my father a suicide. It always seemed better to me to skip the whole thing + try for a better record, + I am damned if I will permit the Baron [Leicester] to write about it + drudge up all the trouble I've ever been in as well, just to make money. It might be better to buy the whole thing from him + get a release but as I explained to him no Hemingstein has ever yet paid blackmail + I would rather break him if he thinks he is tough which is one thing that he is not. Am sure it will work out OK once I know what he is up to.

As of now I plan to sail direct to Havana on the Rena del Mar a new ok ship if they have decent accomoddy. Have given or will give you messages. Called your telephone no. at Regina Coelli but they said you were out answering inquiries. Your [indeciph.] is very handsome.

Best love from everybody here.

Papa.

Despite the discrepancy in dates, this is apparently the letter indicated by EH's notation "Answered 17/9/59" on AEH's letter 117.

Thanks for the two letters with all the gen.: Since AEH wrote letter 119 the day before, this must refer to 117 and either 115 or an unlocated letter.

Larry [Burrows]: LIFE photographer.

(the two Cerabes brothers): Their name was actually Salitas.

Pepe [Dominguín]: Pepe and his brother Domingo acted as managers for their brother Luis Miguel Dominguín and for Antonio Ordóñez.

Miguelillo: Sword handler for Ordóñez. Hemingway, *Dangerous Summer,* 70.

{121} EH to AEH
20.9.59 (ALS, 4 pp., ViU)
Apartadp 67, Malaga [*hw*] [Spain]

Dear Boxman,

Thanks for the one of Sept. 15th enclosing the station wagon. Tell them to deliver it to T. O. Bruce 605 Simmonton Street Key West Florida + he can run it up over the Quays a few times + the Unger Buick Agency can get the bugs out of it or get it gone over in Miami. I will have to roll fast in it when we hit Key West to get out to the Valley + you know an un driven new car is a headache. Tell the Buick people I will pick it up the first week in Nov. + will stand for the pictures. End of Buick problem, except that they are so damned low once you take them off the road or on to a dirt-high centered road the kind we use in Idaho, they knock the whole transmission out. Maybe I can get the transmission armoured the way we do with the land rovers in Africa but it should be wonderful for the long passe. I drove one in Ketchum + the pontiac is much the better car for out west but this is free + free is wonderful.

Thanks for talking to Charlie Scribner. Sounds O.K. Let me know any new gen. I just wrote a long letter to Harry Brague that kid you met in the office + asked him to show it to Charlie. Mary is coming in to New York on Pan American's first flight leaving Paris Oct. 4th. She is in fine shape healthy + cheerful.

Good luck on the coast. I will sail from Le Havre on the Liberté Oct. 27th arriving Nov. 2nd + fly down to the finca, check out there + go to Key West. Will plan to drive out but if time schedule too bad may have to fly. Fall has come here too + it is lovely. Annie [Davis] + Valerie [Danby-Smith] + Bill [Davis] + I will drive up to see Antonio [Ordóñez] finish his season at <u>Nimes</u> and shoot some stuff for Life. They want to make a colour picture for whenever the piece comes out + get some more stuff. Larry [Burrows] should be able to shoot some wonderful stuff in the big arena there. Then we will drive to Paris + see Mary off. She went up today to Madrid + will be at the Ritz if you want anything brought over. She will crank George [Scheuer] up on the horses. Will report to you from Paris. Certainly hope we will be able to work together in Ketchum. Am going to build some log cabins for sleeping purposes not motel style but the kind they used to have on the ranch that you can throw up fast. Anyway you know there are lots of good accommodations in Ketchum + if you can get one with sound proof walls you ought to be able to work. Am very anxious to get this bull stuff wrapped up so I will be free to go back + to finish the novel [*The Garden of Eden*] + then let it rest awhile. It is all done but the end + I should have the advantage of coming to that from a long way away.

Will knock this off now as you must be over your head in work. I certainly hope you get the actors that you want. Your family sends love.

Papa—

Harry Brague that kid you met in the office: Editor at Scribner's.
Mary is coming in to New York on . . . Oct. 4th: Mary, who felt like a "ghost wife" in Spain, returned stateside ahead of EH to arrange for her removal from his life. She intended to locate an apartment in New York before returning to the finca (*HIW,* 549).

{122} AEH to EH
Sept. 23, 1959 (TLS, 1 p., JFKL)
Chateau Marmont/8221 Sunset Boulevard/Hollywood 46, California/Oldfield 6-1010

Dear Papa:

Thanks very much for letter with all the news. I had heard nothing about Antonio [Ordóñez]'s jailing, etc., and it's still a mystery to me what happened re the Lancia. From the sound of all, however, I think it can be stated that it has not been a summer full of placid stretches. On second thought, I can't remember a summer that has, but if we enter this summer in the Placid Sweepstakes I think we have a winner. Please tell Antonio that during his suspension, any of the ten fights he wants to honor, I stand ready to come on a moment's notice. Just have my traje de luce (?) pressed.

I'm going back to N.Y. on Monday. I have a place in town, 6 West 77th, Apt. 11A. telephone ENdicott 2-8180, so by all means have Mary phone when she arrives. Actually, if she knows what theatre she wants to see, she might send me an advance note and I can try to have tickets by time she arrives. There is one thing she could bring with her if you are agreeable to doing it. Now that our Buick shows are in the works, the Buick people have made a request which, in light of the dough they're giving us, I don't think is unreasonable, but it just depends on how you feel. They would like you to speak onto one of your Mohawk tapes a sentence or two about THE KILLERS. Anything at all that can be used at the start of the show. It can be something about where it was written, or what motivated it, or whatever. This is strictly a favor, so if you don't feel like doing it they are prepared for that. If you do record something, please give the tape to Mary to bring with her. By the way, the Buick station wagon is all set and will be waiting for you at Bruce's. This will be a 1959; when the new model comes out a little later, it will be sent to Ketchum to replace the 59. [Arrow points to comment in margin:] Just this minute had a call from Buick—they do not want you to have a '59 so there is a special crew in Detroit assembling a 1960 model for you—so you will have the first if not the best.

I have had my pictures developed and there are some wonderful ones of you and Antonio. I'm having prints made and will either send them now or save them for Ketchum. Unfortunately, I won't be able to make the Nov. 1 drive because THE KILLERS goes into rehearsal on that very day, for telecast Nov. 19th, but my plan is to have my game bag packed for departure immediately after the show and to join up Nov. 20. I'm sure the Edelweiss (that was the name, wasn't it?) will be glad to re-welcome its distinguished huntsman, especially since he ascended to his barony. I can't tell you how much I miss my Malaga mob. I'm working on a ditty now: My Old Malaga Mob. One of the tear-provoking choruses ends with, "How I yearn to pinch my Annie's fanny." Gives you an idea of the sentiment involved.

All the best,
Walter B. Hotchler (Dearborn Branch)

Have contract now for Burnham book.

Walter B. Hotchler (Dearborn Branch): Alludes to Walter Percy Chrysler, founder of the Chrysler Corporation.

{123} EH to AEH
[*indeciph.*] Oct .59 [**October 3, 1959**] (ALS, 6 pp., JFKL)
Hotel Ritz/15, Place Vendôme/Paris [France]

Dear Hotch

Thanks for the letter. Will not go into all the gen about Antonio [Ordóñez] etc. since you will be seeing Mary. I cannot do the thing with the [Mohawk tape recorder] box as we got your letter yesterday + the box is in Malaga. If you really need something let me know to Malaga where we should be by the 8th or 9th of this month. Have to work like hell now + really bite on the nail. It may not be smart to give box stuff since they are really not paying us any more than we deserve—+ I hate to do something without you there to advise me and to check on how it goes. You can explain, satisfactorily the difficulties. If the box was here I would just talk into it + send the things over + you could use it or not.

Thank you very much for handling the station wagon deal + I will let [Otto] Bruce know that he should expect it + run it in. Let me know about the box thing by cable to Apartado 67.

This is a busy day as Mary is going out in the morning. George [Scheuer] + I are working seriously on an out-sider in the forth race today at Longchamp. We broke a little better than even yesterday although George was very gentle and told the group we had dropped 6,000 francs. This beast today is strictly not an investment but Georges is reaching. Tomorrow we have the arc de triomphe which is the last classic flat race of the season + which is strictly something to stay away from except as a spectacle. I worked on it last night + since five o'clock this morning on the form + there is one outsider who figures. Will let you know how it comes out. We miss you always very much on all the roads + in all the places. We have had very good luck in everything + especially the weather through province + north through Burgundy. It and things in general were never better and I hope you have some luck too. Love from your family.

Papa.

{124} AEH to EH
14 Oct. 59 (TLS, 2 pp., JFKL)
A. E. Hotchner R. F. D. 5 Westport, Conn.

Dear Papa:

Saw Mary, she looks fine, certainly seems recovered physically. We had dinner and went to see the Merman musical [*Gypsy*] which, unfortunately, neither of us liked very much. She seemed very anxious to get back to Cuba and breathe in a little home grounds.

I had a meeting with Chas. Scribner and Harry [Brague] and we went through the situation which is now clarified—I think best thing is for me to discuss it with you when you get here, rather than trying to get it into this letter. There is, really, only one important point they make and my personal feeling is that it has much validity.

I have purchased the Burnham property and we are now owners. The best way to handle is for you to pay your share into our corp. which will, in turn, buy the contract from me. We can do this when you come in—only take a couple of minutes.

Please don't disturb yourself about the tape. If you want to make a brief statement about The Killers you can do it with me when you're here—I have an evil box too, now. Matter of fact, we can now communicate by simply sending each other tapes. The same tape can be sent back and forth indefin[i]tely.

I have only a couple of the Ciudad photos so if you could get me some copies of the others—through Cano's copying them or whatever—I'd certainly appreciate it—and of course would want to pay Cano for them.

Work is very hard, right now, much to do in a short time. Fall weather splendid but not much time to enjoy it. Really appreciate getting such good news from you, via Valerie [Danby-Smith]. Sounds like Paris was grand and I'm sorry, as always, to miss the races with you.

I will be at the boat to meet you on Nov. 2 which, incidentally, is the start of rehearsals for The Killers. We had a terrible time finding an actor who could play Ole Andreson—someone who would look like a heavyweight and move like a heavyweight and not look like Victor Mature. So rather than settle for second rate, I have got the Swede himself in the part—Ingo J [Ingemar Johansson; see letter 114]. I had him read it, and talked with him, and I think it will perform it okay. I told him you had gone with him in the ring, and he was pleased. "Now I hope he bets on me as an actor," he said. Very nice, bright boy.

Please give brother Bill and sister Annie [Davis] much affection, along with Valerie and whoever else of the inner cuadrilla may be around.

As ever,
Ciudaddy-o-

{125} AEH to EH
27 OCT 1959 (Cable, 1 p., JFKL)
Westport, Connecticut

JUST RECEIVED BILL [Davis]'S CABLE MEETING BOAT DON'T TAKE KITNER DECISION SERIOUSLY YOU'RE IN CONTROL BEST
HOTCH

DON'T TAKE KITNER DECISION SERIOUSLY: Kitner was EH's pet name for Mary. She had written him: "The essence of it is that all evidence, as I see it, shows that you have no further use for me in your life. I am therefore beginning to arrange my removal from it, and hope to establish a new life for myself" (*HIW,* 549).

On November 1, EH returned to New York aboard the Liberté *with Antonio and Carmen Ordóñez and Antonio's friend Ignacio "Natcho" Angulo. EH delivered A* Moveable Feast *to Charles Scribner and then flew to Cuba on November 4 with the Ordóñezes.*

{126} EH to AEH
8/11/59 [November 8, 1959] (ALS, 2 pp., ViU)
FINCA VIGIA, SAN FRANCISCO DE PAULA, CUBA

Dear Hotch:

Good flight. All S: F. de Paula at the airport with banners. Mary very friendly but holds to same program. Very pleased about flat. Consents to go to Ketchum to help me out with Carmen and Antonio [Ordóñez] on these conditions—^Awill not be required to cook—^Bthat I not ever shoot with Mrs. [Nietz] Gray unless she present.

I've kept reasonable and I hope kind and affectionate although have not much way of judging what that is anymore. Not thanked for pin. Was clearly told, as I should have known, she did not want pin. If got pin my own fault. Don't tell her about difficulties. But all kind and impersonal. Took no interest in arranging of Alfred [Rice]'s tax mistakes and assessments. Thought that was all this year's taxes. Vaguely recalled me having mentioned tax assessment in Churriana. Not interested. Not angry now. Not jealous of anyone except hates Nietz who now refers to formally as Mrs. Gray. OK for Valery [Danby-Smith] to come over and help me. Christ knows I need her with 92 letters piled on the table. Weary business. No ink in house. Anyway Mary plans to go to Ketchum and help out with Carmen and Antonio then she plans to go to N.Y. in Jan. to flat where won't have to simply do chores and can do her writing. I move as cheerfully as possible like in a Kafka nightmare.

Antonio and Carmen and Natcho [Angulo] having wonderful time. Really. I act cheerful like always but am not.

I'm bone tired and very beat up emotionally.

Will try to get in very good shape out west. Natcho not going. Returning Spain on family and business.

What want to do most is get back to writing. That's one of the big issues too; that I expect other people to subordinate themselves to <u>my</u> writing and thus make them lead the lives of drudges. Well maybe I can start some sort of working life in Jan. Though it may be a little tough working here with all that goes on—will do it though unless it becomes impossible.

Will tell you very interesting things when I see you. It is a real revolution— Hope to Christ U.S. won't cut the sugar quota. Having been here in the old days you would be amazed at the changes.

Hope show ["The Killers"] goes good. Hold all mail. Enclose the check for corporation[.]

If we are going to get away day after tomorrow I better knock off and start on the endless chores (mine).

Antonio, Mary and Carmen send very best. We had very jolly celebration of my Saint's Day yesterday—

San Ernesto.

All S. F. de Paula at the airport with banners: EH's arrival in Cuba on November 4 marked his first time in the country since Castro had taken control, and a crowd was on hand to cheer his return (*HIW,* 551).

Mrs. [Nietz] Gray: According to AEH, a shooting companion of EH in Ketchum who was innocent of any designs upon him.

pin: A $4,000 platinum and diamond piece (*Final,* 335).

Hope . . . U.S. won't cut the sugar quota: In July 1960, the United States responded to the nationalizing of American-owned oil refineries in Cuba by canceling the sugar quota.

Mary helped EH make their guests comfortable and then flew to Chicago with Lola Richards, their Jamaican maid, to purchase items for their new house in Ketchum. EH, the Ordóñezes, and Roberto Herrera followed by car, arriving on November 19 (Story, 550).

{127} EH to AEH
19/12/59 (ALS, 2 pp., ViU)
Box 955/Ketchum [Idaho *pmk*]

Dear Hotch:

Nothing new. Mary sleeps well and so far as we know bones healing OK. Will have the gen when the cast comes off for pictures the day after christmas. If ok then (good union and all crevasses (mis-spelled) and cracks filled in) George [Saviers] and Dr. Moritz will start manipulation and therapy.

Have been trying to write the comment about the commercials [during "The Killers"]. Hard to do without getting mixed up in the business which have avoided for many reasons one of main ones being to not breathe down your neck etc. I think you should tell Buick that I found the commercials in excellent taste and less up-setting to the continuity of the picture than any I have ever seen. I would like to congratulate them on this not for publicity but personally and sincerely. You can excerpt this from the letter and explain it is not written for advertizing nor for quotation but to tell them personally how pleased I was with the way the advertizing of the cars was handled and how little it interfered with your continuity.

Hope you have a good christmas and that Gerry and the kids are fine.

Very best from everybody out here. Hope we see you soon. Plans still are to hit the Finca by Jan. 16th. Tell Alfred [Rice] to pay you the month's rent on flat 1st of each month. Please let me know what I owe on other things and will send check.

Good luck old Hotch

Papa.

bones healing OK: Mary had fallen on the frozen ground while hunting and shattered her left elbow (*Story,* 551).

Dr. Moritz: John Moritz practiced in Sun Valley and was acquainted with EH since 1939.

the month's rent on flat: AEH had acquired "a modest half-furnished apartment at 1 East Sixty-Second Street," in EH's name, for Mary's use (*HIW,* 559; AEH, phone call with DeFazio, June 14, 2005).

_1960_

{128} EH to AEH
16/1/60 (ALS, 2 pp., ViU)
Ketchum [Idaho _pmk_]

Dear Hotch:

Thanks for tending to the business.

We are getting off tonight. I just signed the papers for banking for the corporation and after signing noticed that the way they are made out Ernest Hemingway is not my banking signature but the one Scribner's have on my books and that I have signed all over the world.

Anybody imitating it could, presumably, draw out funds without Morgan Guaranty questioning it. Think better to send down Ernest M. Hemingway cards and papers to the Finca and will hold these meantime and then destroy.

Am packing and organizing to leave so send this off in a hurry. Good luck with everything.

Best from everybody

Papa

Thanks for fine pictures. Could you have some made up of you and me and the one of me to send to friends in Europe? EH.

We are getting off tonight: EH, Mary, and Lola Richards left Ketchum at 2 a.m. on January 17 (_Final_, 339).

{129} AEH to EH
1/30/60 (ALS, 2 pp., JFKL)
A. E. Hotchner R. F. D. 5 Westport, Conn.

Dear Papa—

I think the play ["The Fifth Column"] came off very well. The response has been wonderful and gratifying for all the hard, hard work. Enclosed are all of the New York reviews. I think you would have been pleased to see how fully the people you created 20 years ago, came to life on the box today—end of flowery statements.

I saw Valerie [Danby-Smith] for lunch Thursday, tried to reach her all day Friday but she was visiting relatives on L. I. [Long Island] + no way to contact her. These two show days very tough but wanted to see her again so please tell her; didn't mean to neglect her but combination of the show + her absence caused it. Hope she got there okay + all well. Gave her dough + briefing on the comels [commercials].

Alfred [Rice] says he made the 25 G deposit + sent you slip.

Please give Lola [Richards] the enclosed color shots. I think she'll be able to get pretty good prints off them. I'll get the prints you wanted (at [Peter] Buckley prices) next week. You know, everytime I think of that cheapness my blood chills.

Reviews of Irwin Shaw's new book [*Two Weeks in Another Town*] broke today—all really terrible—Poore's in the Times, especially.

I'm delighted that you are cleared enough to be back at work. I can hardly wait to read the mano a mano. By the way, I have received several magazine inquiries re The Paris Book (+ so has Scribner's)—what shall I tell them—Sat. Eve. Post, McCall's, etc.? Will they eventually have opportunity to read + submit proposals on price, etc., or is it locked up with Life? Also, when you decide on the Broadway thing let me know, so can or cannot make plans. All love to Mary, + luck on the busted wing +, as always, all good things to you.

<u>Pecas</u>

---

the New York reviews: "The Fifth Column" aired on *Buick Electra Playhouse* on January 29. Reviews were favorable (Ben Gross, "What's On?" *Daily News,* January 30, 1960, p. 24; Sid Bakal, "TV Review: Electra Playhouse," *New York Herald Tribune,* January 30, 1960, p. 9; Atra Baer, "Hemingway's Prose Stronger than Any Stage," *New York Journal American,* January 30, 1960, p. 19) and mixed: "[V]ery substantially rewritten. . . . The main pity was that Mr. Hotchner did not go farther" (Jack Gould, "The Fifth

Column": Ernest Hemingway's Play of Civil War in Spain Presented over Channel
2," *New York Times,* January 30, 1960, p. 43).

everytime I think of that cheapness my blood chills: Buckley wanted to charge EH for prints
of bullfight photos. AEH, phone call with DeFazio, June 14, 2005.

Poore's in the Times: Charles Poore, review of *Two Weeks in Another Town,* by Irwin Shaw,
New York Times, January 30, 1960, p. 19.

the Broadway thing: AEH remembers this as a plan to dramatize the Paris sketches.

{130} AEH to EH
Sunday [January 31, 1960] (ALS, 1 p., JFKL)
A. E. Hotchner R. F. D. 5 Westport, Conn.

Dear Papa—

Will phone you tomorrow but wanted to get these things to you before
departure.

Our corporation is set—please sign the card as president, + the other two
papers under "confirmed by."

Hope the business I have with Shor tomorrow goes okay.

Love to Mary, + all the always best.

Hotcho

wanted to get these things to you: EH signed "Title of Account" and "Corporate Certificate—Cash Account" forms as president and AEH signed as secretary/treasurer. Also
enclosed was a cash-account form (ViU, 6250f). The corporation, H & H Ltd., was
organized under the laws of the state of Delaware.

the business I have with Shor: According to AEH, this concerned winnings from a bet EH
had placed with Toots Shor on the Johansson-Patterson fight (see letter 114). AEH,
fax to DeFazio, November 29, 2004.

{131} EH to AEH
8/2/60 [February 8, 1960] (ALS, 3 pp., ViU)
FINCA VIGIA, SAN FRANCISCO DE PAULA, CUBA

Dear Pecas,

Thanks for the letter and the clippings and for looking after Val [Danby-
Smith]. She arrived in fine shape + work is going good. Came in with no problems. First off the plane + through the customs + immigration. Glad the show

["The Fifth Column"] went well. I had to call Alfred [Rice] yesterday about some business of Bumby [John Hemingway]'s and asked him how it had gone + he was appropriately gloomy. I imagine he only read the Times review. Am waiting for a call now from the Bank and we are getting these letters off as the call would interrupt work + I had finished well over 8.000 words on the second part of the [*Life*] piece yesterday. It goes good + I'll make it go a damn sight better when the weather clears up + we can get out in the boat + get rid of the staleness.

Have to do one thing at a time so am not even thinking about the Paris book. Have no plans for serialization but Life would have first call since George Plimpton mentioned it to them first + they would have been glad to give me an advance + so forth on it if I wanted to. After all they did publish The Old Man but I do not want to go into any aspect of the Paris thing now while I'm busy writing this one.

Mary's arm is coming along very well with massage + therapy. She is feeling good too and is now fairly optimistic about the arm + it makes her feel much better to be able to type even though it is slow + tiring. Weather has been one norther after another with short breaks of decent weather in between. Please thank Mary Dos [Schoonmaker] very much for looking after Val. I'll write her a letter + send her something from town. It was a hell of a thing her having to be out there at the [air]field + we appreciate it very much. Will send the two signature cards for the corporation off to Rice today. He explained satisfactorily about the deposits. Always let me know if anything is not as it should be or as you would like it to be. Am in the early third of this and do not really think about anything else properly. Lots of things going on here that would drive it out of your head if you let them. So I'm in a sort of vacuum of work. It is wonderful + cheerful having Val here + things are getting properly organized.

Good luck with the next show ["The Snows of Kilimanjaro"]. Is it true what Rice said yesterday that they are doing it live on the coast. Don't answer if you are busy. We read everything eventually in the funny papers.

Best always,
Papa.

She arrived in fine shape + work is going good: Valerie Danby-Smith arrived in Cuba on February 8 to continue serving as EH's secretary.

Mary Dos: Mary Schoonmaker (see letter 115) was sometimes called Mary Dos; Mary Hemingway was Mary Uno.

{132} AEH to EH
[**February 10, 1960** *pmk*] (ALS, 2 pp., JFKL)
CBS Television Network/Office Communication [New York *pmk*]

Dear Papa—

Here are a few more reviews which have filtered in. The overall response has been very, very good—probably as good as any of the shows I have ever done. The mail from viewers is heavy + all praiseworthy. But I must tell you that I had a great deal of trouble from the Buick advertising agency + from Flint. They turned into the usual Madison Avenue shits. I held the line against them but it takes so fucking much out of your insides to do it. Aside from their niggling interference, the problem of how to present Dorothy—the mores of TV being what it is—was a bastard, but all in all most everything worked.

I have to go to Hollywood for Kilimanjaro. I leave Monday, 15th + will be at the Chateau Marmont, Sunset Blvd., + at CBS Television City, Buick Play House, Fairfax + Beverly, Hollywood Number there is OLIVE 12345 in case you have need, or at Chateau.

Terrible about Gigi [Viertel], wasn't it? Woman I know wrote Peter a condolence letter + got a reply that beats the cold feet—says he doesn't need condolences because he has no guilt.

Please thank Valerie [Danby-Smith] for her note—I'll write her when I get a little time—if ever. I'm delighted she likes it there so much. She's a lovely girl + I wish I could have seen more of her while she was here.

All love to Mary whose wing, I hope, is mending okay. I hope your work is moving as you indicated + that you're feeling as good as in Ketchum.

All the best

Hotcho

a few more reviews: Don Kirkley, "Look and Listen," *Baltimore Sun,* February 1, 1960, 8;
     Cecil Smith, "The TV Scene: Fifth Column Superb Production," *Los Angeles Times,*
     February 1, 1960, sec. 2, p. 10; "The Fifth Column," *Variety,* February 3, 1960, p. 39.
Dorothy: In "The Fifth Column," the mistress of the protagonist, Philip Rawlings.
Terrible about Gigi: Virginia Viertel died in 1960 as a result of burns suffered when her
     nightgown accidentally caught on fire. Meyers, *Hemingway,* 611n11.

{133} AEH to EH
13 February 60 (TLS, 2 pp., JFKL)
A. E. Hotchner R. F. D. 5 Westport, Conn.

Dear Papa:

That slow-baking project of ours, the readings, is just about set now, as you can tell from this article which appeared, a bit prematurely I'm afraid, in The Times. When it says I will co-produce, actually it will be our corporation, with all financial risk borne by the other producer and us receiving through our corporation, as you and I have discussed. I hope to complete the casting while I'm in Hollywood. I realize you are working, and I don't want to bust in on you in any way, but I just send you this for information. I think it will be a very exciting presentation, especially now that I have been able to work with some of the material on television. I guess Alfred [Rice] will draw contracts and do what legal work necessary, but unless you tell me otherwise, I am going to make it clear to him that this is a corporation project and he will not repeat not be putting the 10 percent squeeze on it.

I meant to ask you whether you saw Eric Hemerroid [Sevareid]'s piece in Esquire on the Mano a Mano. Did you know that he was at lunch that day, and at our table at the hotel, in the guise of an expert for Esquire? Came as a shock to me. Thought it was all social, or else why would you have discussed stuff you might use in his presence?

Took Mary Dos [Schoonmaker] to a very fancy dinner and otherwise feted her for being such a good girl, which she is. Wish I could have taken Val [Danby-Smith] to the theatre. Well, next time.

Sorry Astute Alfred was gloomy about the show. I only wish I could have such gloom visited on me every time out. I do not want to become a clipping addict, so have passed, on getting the wash of out-of-town reviews now coming in, but was told by CBS they are unanimously good, and many hysterical, with not a negative voice other than [New York Times critic] J. Gould's. We beat them about 230–1.

Have sent word to the magazines that inquired about the Paris book, that all is tabled for now and to drop further inquiry. As you know, never intend to press; sorry if it came in at work time and interrupted. Always please disregard that which should be disregarded. One thing I got, as fellow-sufferer, is understanding. End Paris inquiries.

Address of Chateau Marmont is 8221 Sunset Blvd., Hollywood 46; will be there from Feb. 15th to March 25th, if I can survive.

Wonderful about Mary's arm. Give her a kiss and Val a kiss and you can even give Lola [Richards] a kiss, if you want to.

Fidel Hotchtro

this article which appeared . . . in The Times: Sam Zolotow, "Hemingway Work to Become
    Drama: Novels, Short Stories and Play Will Be Adapted by AEH for Stage," *New York*
    Times, February 11, 1960, p. 38. The Times identifies the play as *Of Love and Death;*
    it was ultimately produced in 1967 as *The Hemingway Hero.*
Eric Hemerroid's piece in Esquire: Eric Sevareid, "Mano a Mano: Dominguín vs. Ordoñéz:
    What Really Happened," *Esquire,* November 1959, pp. 40–44.

{134} EH to AEH
18/2/60 (ALS, 2 pp., ViU)
FINCA VIGIA, SAN FRANCISCO DE PAULA, CUBA

Dear Hotch,

Thanks very much for the word on the [stage] project. I hadn't seen the piece in the Times + reading it explains the other poop I had not understood in the papers. Hope it goes good. Let me know when you have more gen. I know how hard you are working + do not want to bother you either but would like to know status of various things when you have time.

Sevareid is the usual character who comes to lunch + then steals you blind, always running as a man of unimpeachable ethics, lucky he did not steal any of Negro [Bill Davis]'s silver. Believe his piece will be forgotten by the time this one comes out but everybody has torn what chunks off it that they could.

Alfred [Rice] sent me some cuttings which only proved he had read nothing but the Times review.

Wrote 1536 words today on piece which is above my usual batting average. Have something over 17,000 done since started working here 25th. Mucho piece. Hope it will turn out. It has to.

Have noted address and will sent this to the Marmount. Mary's arm going good. Will get to work on it now. Be a good boy on the coast + bet on Benny Paret to beat Don Jordan. Will let you know later what to bet for me. How are facilities out there. Suerte, Pecas.

Dr. Hemingstein y Mykoyan

bet on Benny Paret to beat Don Jordan: Paret, a Cuban fighter, did defeat Jordan. *New York*
    Times, May 28, 1960, p. 16.

Dr. Hemingstein y Mykoyan: Soviet deputy premier Anastas Mikoyan had visited Cuba the
week of February 1, 1960, to sign a trade agreement.

{135} AEH to EH
5 March 60 (TLS, 1 p., JFKL)
CBS Television Network/A Division of Columbia Broadcasting Systems, Inc.
Television City, Hollywood, California—Olive 1-2345

Dear Papa:

I've been meaning to write you for days now, but I get so pooped from the
load of work that by the time I stagger back to my pad I'm not fit for a postcard. There is a mighty battle with those ant brains, the censors, and there are
three teams of them—CBS, the McCann-Erickson Advertising Agency, and the
splendid little Buick group at Flint, Mich. The ignorance, prejudice and
hypocrisy are appalling, and no matter how many unbelievable stories you
hear on this subject, the real thing, when you are up against it, is even more
unbelievable. But I am slowly, and without too many loss of troops, winning
most of the major positions, but Christ, I wish we were in Valencia watching
the fireworks. Cast for Kilimanjaro, very good, Robert Ryan to play Harry, and
I think, when the chicken-shit battles are over, we will come out okay.

Our theatre-readings project moves very quickly now, and so far so good.
Beneficent Alfred [Rice] has phoned me several times to discuss his participation. He would like to receive a percentage of our take as his fee. The fact is
that Alfred, as usual, had nothing to do with the formation of this project, and
his work now mostly consists of looking over contracts drawn by other
lawyers. Also, the booking agent will draw the contracts with the actors. If
however, because of the complexities involved, you want to give him one percent participation, that is certainly okay with me. That is considered a very
generous amount. It means that every week this show performs, Alfred will get
one-percent of its take. Never has one man given so little for so much. But let's
give it to him anyway because that's the way we operate. Okay?

Now one more thing. As you know, Coops [Gary Cooper] wanted to get
into something with us, so I have gone ahead with AFTER THE STORM and
developed it and he is very anxious to do it. I told him to look into it with U-I
[Universal-International], for our corp. to do it with his, U-I money to finance
it, and that's what he's doing now. When I get something that looks okay I'll
pass it on to you + we'll discuss it. If it works okay, it should take care of us

very well for a couple of years. The big thing is to avoid the Leland [Hayward] shit-ism + have what we have. I'm delighted your work goes so well. I have a little house at 1129 Horn Ave. (not horn-y) + will be here till Mar. 25ᵗʰ when I go back to N.Y.

Love to Val [Danby-Smith], Mary, et al.

Dr. Frank Hotchton

AFTER THE STORM: AEH recalls completing this adaptation of a Hemingway story, but it was never produced and no copy survives. AEH, fax to DeFazio, November 29, 2004. AEH later adapted the story as a screenplay; the Trimark Productions film debuted on the USA Network in 2001.

Dr. Frank Hotchton: Alludes to Frank Stanton, president of CBS from 1946 to 1971.

{136} EH to AEH
12/3/60 [March 12, 1960] (ALS, 4 pp., ViU)
FINCA VIGIA, SAN FRANCISCO DE PAULA, CUBA

Dear Hotch,

Thanks for the letter + the gen. Alfred [Rice] has not written me anything about his participation. Whatever you decide on that is OK with me but let me know. Coops [Gary Cooper] called me up from N.Y. about 3 days ago and said he would see you when he got to the coast—probably this week. He seemed very enthusiastic about "After the Storm" but spooked in general about pictures due to the strike. I think it would be a good idea to tie him up on "After the Storm" as something for him to have in reserve when strike's + etc. settled—+ for us to take an advance payment on it. In that business + with those people nothing means anything until cash money changes hands for the property as an advance against what we hold. And then it only means something if the sum is very large. You sound as though you had an excellent property in the screen play + I think it would be a good idea to close on it if all the conditions are favorable + if we do not have to put up anything except the property. All of these people plan to go way beyond their budget + then charge practically 100%-150% for the money they spend + you get nothing back. They call it double negative cost plus 50% + they are the auditors, not us.

Coops was very enthusiastic about doing the Burnham series. He sees the possibilities in it + is completely sold on it. I think you ought to tie him up on that as he really wants to go into T.V.

I referred everything that Coops talked about to you so don't believe anything else no matter who tells it or prints it. Sorry you're having trouble with the censorship on the K [Kilimanjaro] film. Don't know how I can help. Wrote it as morally as I could the first time. Did you ever see it as the Snows of Zanuck. That should be an inspiration to you.

Here nothing but work. There are no fish in the Gulf at all so have the Pilar on the ways this weekend cleaning her up for when things start running. We've had some good cock fighting + swim + take walks. Very bucolic. Mary's arm is coming along very well + she'll do much better when it gets warm. She sends her love. Val can add a P.S. to this if she feels like it.* Always remember your triumph in Ciudad Real if times get hard. From your letter it sounds as though times might get pretty good but have no faith repeat NO [faith] in any movie thing unless a large sum of money changes hands. They have no respect for you otherwise + the price + the category goes down. All of those bastards have money instead of blood in their veins + it is best to always consider that the money is counterfeit until you've banked it.

Papa

*P.S. From your ole pal Val.

the strike: The Screen Actors Guild had called a strike over the issue of payment of residuals for movies broadcast on television.
Snows of Zanuck: Darryl F. Zanuck's 1952 production of the story, in which the character of Harry Street was allowed to live (see letter 56).
P.S.: Written on the middle leaf of a three-leaf clover drawn by Valerie Danby-Smith.

{137} AEH to EH
22 March 60 (TLS, 2 pp., JFKL)
CBS Television Network/A Division of Columbia Broadcasting Systems, Inc.
Television City, Hollywood, California—Olive 1-2345

Dear Papa:

Thanks very much for letter giving me all the gen. I'm going to have lunch with Cooper today and see just what he has in mind. I agree thoroughly on Hollywood dough, that what you don't get in your mitt doesn't exist, and I certainly intended that whatever deal is made, a good deal of the green must come our way. However, I think we are much better off making our deal as an independent venture than with a big studio that will pay a lump sum and that's the end of it. Anyway, I'll pass along Coop's proposal and we can go on from there.

With the Mano a Mano [article] grown to such proportion, I suppose you have thought about the possibility of publishing it as a separate book rather than as an appendix to Death in the Afternoon. As one of your Constant Readers (who writes), I would rather see it published as a book unto itself. Now that's the end of this morning's unsolicited advice.

I have done something about the Buick situation which I hope is okay with you. They called to say your new car was ready and that delivery had to be made. Well, since our Buick entente ends shortly, I told them to deliver it to my joint in Conn. where I can store it in the garage for you. I figure it's best to have it available, and I can just bring it into New York when you arrive there and want it. Also, Mary said she'd like a copy of the bust which we use on the show, and I have that for her. Shall I send it out to your Ketchum place, or where? Or would you rather I store it for now? Would prefer to have it shipped because CBS will crate it and do it properly whereas after this series ends I won't have them (CBS) available. There has been talk of another series next year, nothing definite, but I would like to suggest that we skip the 60–61 season. The material that remains that has TV potential is limited and for that reason, and others (the stage project and the possible movie) I think we should let the tube cool out for a year. Please give me your reading on this.

I am putting Gambler, Nun & Radio into production for the fourth show. I hate to ask you, but would it be possible to dictate to Val [Danby-Smith] a little information that would be helpful to me. I would like to know a little background about the story. At that time, was there a migrant flock of Mexicans who went up to Hailey [Idaho] to work the beet fields? Did they just go there, or was it some kind of floating group? Were there gambling places there then? Was the town pretty wide open? Just a bit of information would be helpful.

Kilimanjaro goes before the cameras today for the first time, on air Friday night. The censorship I mentioned is all about little things, words, not the larger concept of the story. Right now a battle royal is raging over the use of the word "dunghill". I have been told that if I use it I will corrupt half of America. That prospect has cheered me considerably. Now if I can only find a way to corrupt the other half.

We sold The Killers to German TV for $2000, less 10%. Is it okay to take payment abroad, and not have it come through New York?

Hope everyone well and happy. I go back to New York Friday night (25th). All best,

Hotchamanjaro

the bust which we use on the show: When AEH brought a 16mm film of the *Buick Electra Playhouse* program to Sun Valley, "Papa seemed to be in a happy mood until the film opening when a rough-sculptured head of Papa rotated with a narrow beam of light playing on it." Tillie Arnold, *The Idaho Hemingway* (Buhl, ID: Beacon, 1999), 220. The bust was by Robert Berks; other busts of EH by Berks are in the Idaho State Park in Ketchum and the University of Texas, Austin.

{138} EH to AEH
31/3/60 (ALS, 4 pp., ViU)
FINCA VIGIA, SAN FRANCISCO DE PAULA, CUBA

Hear Dotch,

Thanks for the letter with the gen and advice. Have delayed writing thinking might have reviews of the show. We got nothing down here except a cable from the Duke [Forrest MacMullen] from Ketchum but since he is in our stable that is discounted. Thanks for taking over the Buick. Hang on to it use it if it is any good to you. Have them ship bust to Ketchum for us care of Chuck Atkinson.

Can't give you a reading on TV situation as am moderately pooped having just written to Life explaining delay on the mano a mano which is now up to 63,562 words. Am offering to return them the advance or renegotiate. Also wrote to Charlie Scribner scratching the Paris book from fall list due to over extension on time put in on mano-a-mano. Took a day off from working this morning + went out on Pilar. Val [Danby-Smith] caught her first sail fish. Came home + swam and now doing the three important letters. I don't see actual folding money in the stage project or the movie yet for 1960 or '61. But you know about that + I don't. Lennie [columnist Leonard Lyons] had some piece about the Paris book being used in the stage (thing) project. I know we had agreed this was not to be done so figure it must be as balled up ¿is balled up or bawled up? as other pieces that have been published recently. Another piece said that [Lauren] Bacall was to be in the stage thing. Let me know if this is true so I can leave her out of the m-a-m—naturally she is not in by name but if she is a client of ours her picture should hang in its proper place on the wall of Alfred [Rice]'s office.

About Gambler, Nun and Radio, from now on referred to as GNR: it took place in a hospital in Billings MONTANA. The beet workers were migrant Mexicans but I do not think immigration restrictions were so strict then + many of them must have stayed there after the crop was harvested. Since I was in hospital there in November [1930; see letter 19] + there was snow on the ground. I would imagine you could use a mexican quartet in the town complete with local character + gambling. I can't tell you much about how it was as came into the hospital after an accident on the road after dark + never left it until taking a train after dark out of town but it was in the old days a town with gambling + very good saloons and one of the best whorehouses in the west also a famous saddle shop, Pat Connally's + very good restaurants. It was a fine cow town + very nice people lived in it but there was the rough life for the hands who came in from the ranches + there was probably a mexican quarter although I do not know it and can't give you the gen. One thing I remember that could or could not be of any use is that when I came into that hospital + they filled out my address form I gave my occupation as writer. The next day the local head of the Rodeo riders came in to see if he could [do] anything for me + when we recognized each other he said "Christ Ernie whoever told you you were a rider." This to give atmosphere to the hospital. You don't have to make it Billings. I was careful not to so you better not use the name since all the characters were actual people but without using the name. Billings was a clean, lively, cowtown, modern building, airfield up on a butte above town the Wolf mountains out side of town snow on them beautiful small mountains like the first ones around Ketchum, not a hick town at all, a little like Elko where we went through on our way to Vegas but much larger + without any big open gambling place. Remember Nevada, take out the gambling + put in saloons + make it a little more prosperous with a certain amount of Mexicans, + you have it. If you want any other gen, write + will answer promptly as have slowed down on the number schedule with the m-a-m piece. George Saviers is coming here in about 4 days. You can call him in New York at 114 E. 62nd.

Glad you sold the Killers to German TV. Is OK to take payment abroad but you have to declare it as income tax. Everybody sends love.

—Papa—

Chuck Atkinson: Friend of the Hemingways in Sun Valley (*Story*, 367).

{139} AEH to EH
20 April 60 (TLS, 2 pp. JFKL)
CBS Television Network/A Division of Columbia Broadcasting Systems, Inc.
485 Madison Avenue, New York 22, New York Plaza 1-2345

Dear Papa:

Way overdue on writing you. Tried to phone you this afternoon, no answer, guess you are out on Pilar. Had dinner with George and Pat [Saviers] last Wednesday, and Teddy Jo [Paulson] was in town, and of course there was Mary Dos [Schoonmaker], so if only you had been at the table it would have been Pamplona reconvened. We had a fine time, good drinks, solid German food, lot of fun talk. George, for whom I have boundless liking, gave very good report on conditions chez toi, and Pat, in her architecture mood, had very little to say, obviously preoccupied with some Gothic problem for the morrow, so it was a fine evening. George said that he had informed you that the Tommy Ram on Kilimanjaro was not Tommy but some other horned beast, which wounded me deeply, since I had gone to vast trouble and expense to get a real honest-to-God certified Tommy for the part. It was the most exhausting show I have done, and I think in some ways the best. Some of the N.Y. reviews were not good, the out-of-town and mail very good, but critics being what they are, all that matters is one's own small voice. I left Hollywood the night of the show, flew in to N.Y., picked up my two kids and took them down to Sarasota so they could get some sun and I could get a look at the teams. I hadn't seen the kids for a long time and it was good to be away with them. The White Sox looked terrible, so did Pittsburgh, the Cards much improved and [Stan] Musial, with whom I had dinner one night, is going to have a great year you can be sure. The Yanks are not nearly so anemic as the sports pages make them out, and if Mickey [Mantle] goes, the Yanks can take it. Of course, I don't know what the Colavito and Score deals will mean—not anything decisive, I'd guess. When I got back to N.Y. I checked in with Honest Alfred [Rice], who said you had asked him to send reviews, as he did on Fifth Col., so felt no sense in my sending since only complicate. I have been sent a lot of out-of-N.Y. reviews but I don't see any sense in flooding you with them—only four knocks out of about fifty.

I have to go back to Hollywood on April 22 to put GNR in the works. Information you sent wonderful help and thank you very much. I think I did not previously make clear what situation is on next year repeat with Buick. They would like to discuss continuation if I will guarantee all shows with a happy ending. Shows they have in mind are Farewell to Arms, Sun Also Rises, Have & Have not, Macomber. So all we have to do is let Catherine have the baby and we're in. And, of course, no reason why Jake couldn't grow a couple of fresh balls. I just don't want you to think I have, or would ever, pass up anything that was feasibly good without referring it to you. But the Buick situation is intolerable. Zane Grey is really their speed.

The thing with Cooper was about worked out, he had financing pretty well set, when he phoned last week to say that he had been given an emergency reading on his prostate, and was being rushed to Mass. Gen. for a prostectomy. It's going to knock him down for a couple of months and maybe more, so he has temporarily bowed out on After the Storm. However, there is other interest, so I'll pursue it. The operation on Coops was successful, I hear, so that's on the good side. Don't know biopsy report on malignancy.

Sorry that honest Lennie Lyons, boy reporter, keeps feeding out these gin-crazed items. Don't know anything about his source other than it ain't me. Any rate, am not now, nor have ever, nor will ever use or attempt to use any material from the Paris sketchbook. Also, about [Lauren] Bacall, had a drink with her one evening and we discussed project, but that's all. Have no idea, this point, who cast will be, and when I have information on any of these things, you can be sure that you will get the true gen, when its formed, before Mr. Lyons.

Please tell Mary I have finally got around to fixing up the apartment well enough so that it can be lived in—good basic bed, dresser, linens, stuff for the kitchen, and what not. I bought only the bare essentials, to make it basically livable—other stuff to be attended to if and when she wants to. Alfred's desk and sofa in living room, so you have the comfort of knowing the spirit of the Great Advocate is about you.

There are several new items that we should discuss re the future, or I should say, the Future, because like God, it can sure kill one dead if not shown the proper obeisance. But no hurry on these—can wait till after GNR. Am enclosing item came out today in TV Guide, which is now, God help us all (note second reference to Almighty, demonstrating my new religious side) the biggest publication in the U.S. Seems that we haven't lost any ground this past year, although my freckles have paled a little.

So I pack bag, clutch typewriter and mush on to Kleigland. I'm at CBS address there, TV City, home address 1129 Horn Ave., phone OLYmpia 7-2317, CBS phone OLive 12345. Love to everybody,

Hotchum

the Colavito and Score deals: The Cleveland Indians traded Rocky Colavito to the Tigers and Herb Score to the White Sox.

let Catherine have the baby and . . . Jake . . . grow a couple of fresh balls: Catherine Barkley delivers a stillborn baby in *A Farewell to Arms;* Jake Barnes, of *The Sun Also Rises,* has been rendered impotent by a war wound.

enclosing item came out today in TV Guide: "The Hemingway Specials," *TV Guide,* April 23–29, 1960, p. 27, commends the *Buick Electra Playhouse* series.

{140} EH to AEH
9/5/60 [May 9, 1960] (ALS, 2 pp., ViU)
FINCA VIGIA, SAN FRANCISCO DE PAULA, CUBA

Dear Hotch,

Sorry we got scragged up on correspondence and that you couldn't get through on the phone. That must have been while George [Saviers] was here. Have only been out on the boat twice since then, both afternoon deals. Fishing pretty good and with any sort of weather should stay that way.

Thanks for sending the TV Guide Reviews. Alfred sent only N.Y. ones, as depressing as possible. Sometimes it looks like he's working for the other people. I wired Coops [Gary Cooper] to the hospital + had a nice note from him a couple of days ago that he was going to Naples on a picture. He didn't say anything about there being any malignancy. Certainly hope not. He said he was seeing you when he wrote the letter. Did he give you any gen on himself? How do the various (things) projects stand now?

Thanks for the gen on Buick. Is there anything I can give you from here that would help any on the GNR show. Wire me or call here if there is. Not much news from here except working. When I knocked off this morning before breakfast the word count was over 92,000. That's much too many but it is a full length book now. Hope to be finished by the 20th of this month if not before but am going out on the boat tomorrow with Mary + Val [Danby-Smith] to get some juice back into the machine. Mary's arm is really showing progress now that the weather warmed up enough so the pool water relaxed it rather than killing it. She can see the progress herself + is working hard on it now. I think it would be alright + perfectly safe for her to take fish like dolphin or bonito with it now. Val has caught 2 good white marlin + is handling a rod very well, also swam 100 round trips of the pool on her birthday.

Will knock this off so that you'll hear from here even though there's no news that it does any good. Don't bother writing when you're working so hard on the show unless there is something that you need. Oh yes, just remembered something, don't write a piece about that day in the ring at Ciudad Real as I have already written it + we don't want to make liars out of each other. Am afraid this piece of mine may be eaten up quite a little already by the various characters. I haven't read Miss Mary's piece ["Holiday for a Wounded Torero"; see p. 258] because I had quite a lot about Carmen [Ordóñez] in this. I'll have to read it eventually + then can cut out anything of mine that has to come out. I know you weren't planning to write on the C.R. but all of a sudden I woke up in the night + remembered I hadn't asked you not to. If you have just let me know + it is OK but mine is pretty good + the dialogue is funny whether true or not. Can remember your voice very well + the event in it within good reason. Don't ever worry about me ever putting any people in the piece that shouldn't be in it nor shouldn't even be in Spain. The piece is cleaner than Buick.

Best from everybody here,
<u>Papa</u>

while George [Saviers] was here: Saviers visited the Hemingways in April (*HIW*, 556).

{141} AEH to EH
20 June 60 (ALS, 3 pp., JFKL)
A. E. Hotchner R. F. D. 5 Westport, Conn.

Dear Papa—

I located the Ford Maddox Ford at Scribner's & they are airmailing it to you right away. Word on Harry B. [Brague]—not heart as feared but pleurisy + will be okay.

I am making up a list of all materials I have and will send it to you this week.

I think I have straightened out Our Legal Leader, Alfred [Rice], on the German situation and all seems to have subsided into peaceful order with all hands satisfied. Payment will be as indicated.

There is one extremely interesting television project, lately reared, which I have been leading through its early stages. The benefactor in this case is General Electric whose solvency need give us no pause, to refresh or otherwise. The meetings so far seem pretty good, but until we get to Stage Concrete, no sense our giving it our Command consideration. If it should fall together, it will happen pretty damn fast, since this is already very late for next season, so if you shove out of your area, or plan to soon, please let me know since communication lines should be open. There are a couple of other projects, not urgent, that we should discuss when we next see each other. Also, the Burnham. But I've held off on all these while you're working.

Editor of TRUE, which is all we have left to believe in now that Bernarr McFadden is dead, wrote me couple of weeks back, asking that I ask you about possibility of using the 600 words about Pamplona in "Death in the Afternoon" in connection with TRUE's 25th Anniversary issue next Feb. They say they will credit the source + run very good photos with the text. Also, they would like to shower you with some coin for this privilege. I would guess around $1000, perhaps $2000 depending on how big an issue this is. Please let me know if you want to grant the reprint privilege.

Ol' Dr. George [Saviers] breezed into town this morning for the fight + I got him a ticket through Toots [Shor]. George is such a grand guy, so cheerful and healthy, always pleasurable to see him. Pat [Saviers] has been here all this time being a lady architect.

I have heard regularly from Negro [Bill Davis], also spoken to him a couple of times, and the London winter seems to have agreed with them very much. Bill + Annie are urging me to come back to Malaga this summer—I would love to—but there is so much to attend to here I haven't been able to figure out time + all that. It's hard to realize that a whole year has already passed since our wonderful times of last summer—the best summer of my life—but then I have had a life not noted for its summers. I don't think I have ever adequately thanked you for putting me in The Spanish mob, or, as they have become known, in Papa's Irregulars. It would be great fun to have a re-union of the Very Irregulars somewhere over Yonder this summer, even if briefly, but I wrote Bill that it doesn't look very promising at the moment. But then this is a rather worthless moment.

All the best to all of you,
Sen. John F. Hotchennedy

---

the German situation: **Having sold "The Killers" to German TV (see letter 138), AEH wanted to receive payment abroad. AEH, fax to DeFazio, November 29, 2004.**

no pause, to refresh or otherwise: **Alludes to the Coca-Cola slogan "The Pause that Refreshes," first used in 1929.**

Bernarr McFadden **(1868–1955): Crusader against prudery who in 1919 started *True Story* magazine, which published "real" tales by its readers.**

Sen. John F. Hotchennedy: On July 14, John F. Kennedy had been nominated as the Democratic presidential candidate.

On June 27, AEH flew to Cuba for nine days to cut the manuscript of the Life *articles (PH, 241–42). He recommended cutting 60,000 words out of a total of somewhat more than 100,000; although EH initially objected to almost every proposed cut, he relented and trimmed the 688-page typescript by about half (see appendix). AEH took the manuscript to* Life's *Ed Thompson in New York. See DeFazio, "HemHotch Letters," Ph.D. diss., University of Virginia, 1992, 97–136, 1579–87.*

{142} EH to AEH
5/7/60. [July 7, 1960] (ALS, 1 p., ViU)
La Vigia [Cuba *pmk*]

Dear Hotch:

Enclose check for $500.<u>00</u> for the apartment expenses + cost of typeing and copying the bull fight mss. Please be sure to let me know what those expenses amount to. You certainly were wonderful down here and very patient. Hope back is fine now and that the trip north was not too bloody. You will have read in the papers what caused the difficulties.

Will be talking to you on the phone probably before you get this.

Still feel bad about the Schoonmaker business.

Best always

<u>Papa.</u>

the difficulties: Castro had shut down Havana Airport, requiring AEH to fly to Key West in a plane piloted by one of EH's friends (*PH*, 24–45).
the Schoonmaker business: Mary Schoonmaker had undergone a medical procedure.

On July 25, EH, Mary, and Valerie Danby-Smith took a ferry to Key West. There, an immigration officer observed that Valerie had not renewed her visitor's visa for the United States. Fearing that the FBI would discover he had brought Valerie into the country illegally, EH began referring to her as "Honor" (a practice that AEH continued in Papa Hemingway*). From Key West, the two women boarded a train for New York; EH flew to New York, arriving August 4. He met with AEH to discuss the stage play AEH was working on, and the next day he flew on to Lisbon and Madrid (*Final, 348; HIW, 559*).*

{143} AEH to EH
[**early August 1960**] (Cable, 1 p., JFKL)
Westport, Connecticut

PUBLICATION'S THIRD INSTALLMENT SEPTEMBER FIFTEENTH ARRANGED YOUR
DEADLINE MIDNIGHT SEPTEMBER SEVENTH THREEHUNDRED WORDS MAXIMUM
HOPE OKAY BEST HOTCH

THIRD INSTALLMENT: LIFE ran the mano a mano article in three installments: "The
Dangerous Summer," September 5, pp. 78–109; "The Dangerous Summer Part II:
The Pride of the Devil," September 12, pp. 61–82; "The Dangerous Summer Part III:
An Appointment with Disaster," September 19, pp. 74–96.

DEADLINE... THREEHUNDRED WORDS MAXIMUM: Probably refers to "One Year Later, a
Cable to 'Life,'" which appears as an addendum to the third installment. Dated
September 6, 1960, the cable complains of horn shaving (altering the points of a
bull's horns to make them less deadly), praises Antonio Ordóñez, and provides a
mixed review of Luis Miguel Dominguín.

{144} AEH to EH
Aug. 7, 1960 (ALS, 2 pp., JFKL)
A. E. Hotchner R. F. D. 5 Westport, Conn.

Dear Papa—

Just quick word let you know have made all changes requested your cable.
Think good libel move if horn-shaving difficult to prove—I mean court prove
if necessary. Checked with Ed Thompson—all moves ok at Life.

Always so God-damned empty when you go. Sorry I was so business-like +
not very cheerful—but this was big responsibility + wanted it to go okay + so
gave it all juice. I was really touched by your wanting me to share some of the
loot—came as a surprise since had no thought this was anything but your project that I enjoyed helping on. I appreciated the dough, of course, but please
remember we are not on a dough basis although we do seem to mutually make
quite a lot of it. But that is only incidental to main business of being friends +
helping each other. I envy your seeing Annie + Bill [Davis] who are also friends
bases + such lovely people.

Love to all
A. E. Pecas

your cable: For what appears to be the text of this cable, see appendix, pages 316–17.

I appreciated the dough: AEH declined EH's offer to pay him for helping edit the *Life* articles, accepting only reimbursement for travel expenses.

{145} EH to AEH
7/8/60 [August 7, 1960] (ALS, 2 pp., ViU)
LA CONSUELA/CHURRIANA/MALAGA [Spain *pmk*]

Dear Hotch:

Am sending enclosed cable so as to protect on libel. Just found out Luis Miguel [Dominguín] going hog wild on suing people here in Spain on anything to do with horns being shaved. The fact everybody knows they are shaved means nothing. Legally you would have to prove it and you cannot prove it unless the govt. took action against the ring, the breeders, or the promoters. The fact you know it is true means nothing. I do not think there would be any libel suit but do not want to expose Life to any possibility. L.M. might do it for publicity. They certainly should be protected on the Spanish edition and on the regular too. He could bring suit in U.S.

Sending this off in a hurry. Drove here from Madrid—got in 10.30. One day's part rest—Today received by finding out L.M. gone law crazy—He's been fighting very badly. See him tomorrow.

Every sort of bad stuff going on. Will be back in Madrid Tuesday to talk to Antonio [Ordóñez]. He is doing wonderfully and everything framed against him and plenty of sordid stuff—whole set up bad.

The sentence referred to in cable should read "But a diet of this type of bull if his defences were altered etc."

It looks as though the horn cutting is going on worse than ever but that they are only cracking down when A. [Antonio]'s bulls involved. But they now have 2 strikes on him on Picadors as well. Breeders who are convicted of cutting horns will be banned on 2nd offense.

Will be at Suecia in Madrid—on Tuesday—Wed.—Saw Bill Lang there Friday and will see him Tuesday—.

Much love from everybody here. Love from me to you all. Tell Mary I haven't written on acct. being dead. Don't feel too good—Had figured on resting today when this came up. Trip across very good—

Best

Papa

enclosed cable: Likely the undated cable on pages 316–17 in the appendix.

the sentence referred to in cable: The sentence is set up by the text that precedes it: "The horns of Luis Miguel's bulls had been cut off at the points, then shaved back to normal shape and I could see the shine of the used crankcase oil that hid the manipulations that had been made and gave the healthy looking polish of normal horns. . . . But a diet of this type of bull with his defenses altered would unfit him, subtly but permanently, for the real bulls when he had to face them." Hemingway, "The Dangerous Summer Part II: Pride of the Devil," *Life,* September 12, 1960, p. 68, col. 1; Hemingway, *Dangerous Summer,* 107.

{146} AEH to EH
8 August 1960 (TLS, 1 p., JFKL)
A. E. Hotchner R. F. D. 5 Westport, Conn.

Dear Papa:

What with the Associated Press World Desk phoning me at 2 am a week ago to tell me they had just received a Stockholm report that you had died in Churriana that afternoon, and Life's monumental double-cross this has been one hell of a week.

I phoned Ed Thompson a week ago, told him I had cable changes to make, he told me to hold them until they had a clean copy. I then told him that I was going to take my kids on a camping-fishing trip to Maine for five days, and he said that was fine because they wouldn't have anything to work on until Saturday (Aug. 6th). I told him I would phone him during the week just to check on situation. I phoned. Was told all okay. When I got back Saturday, I phoned Ralph Graves [*Life* senior editor], was told that in my absence they had sent entire manuscript with a lot of new cuts to you, that you had worked over manuscript, okayed some, etc. Well I'm a sad son of a bitch if that isn't the shittiest trick of the year. I made a firm deal with Thompson that the manuscript as delivered was it, no more changes, etc. Also, I was waiting for a final clean from them in order to check all names, places, technical stuff and the rest against the original ms. I brought back from Cuba, because as we both knew it was hurriedly typed and a lot of errors were in it. So they loaded you with that. I have said nothing to them. I will still double check the manuscript against the original, and they want some help on non-technical captions and other stuff, and I will comply, but it's a shit-eating trick and all I can say is that I'm sorry you got hit with another reading of the manuscript and another assault of cuts. I do not want you to think that I let down on this end—but obviously I knew nothing about the by-pass which was taken in order to re-open the cutting which I had closed.

Mary seems tranquil and happy. Has seen plays with Val [Danby-Smith] and is enjoying the apartment. I think Valerie is ready to shove, probably to Paris and then back to Ireland. She hasn't said when, but that seems to be her intent. Mary may come out for a couple of days.

I am going to be here from now on, so any problem, cable or phone. Thanks very much for your letter. Situation sounds horrible. Must be depress-ing after the wonderful time last summer.

Give all love to all + remember me to Ciudad Real.

Antonio

---

the Associated Press . . . phoning me . . . a week ago: AEH received the false report of EH's death on August 8 and immediately relayed it to Mary; several tense hours passed before EH cabled "REPORTS FALSE" (*HIW*, 560–62). AEH accidentally described this call as taking place "a week ago," at the same time as the call to Ed Thompson in the next paragraph.

Valerie is ready to shove: On August 20, at EH's request, Mary sent Valerie to Europe to help with his work and ease his mind (*Final*, 346).

Antonio: In jest, AEH and Antonio swapped names occasionally.

{147} EH to AEH
8/9/60 [September 8, 1960] (ALS, 1 p., ViU)
La Consula [hw] [Málaga, pmk]

Dear Hotch,

Excuse hurried note to send this check on this Burnham thing. Will write shortly. Been in really lousy shape but feeling better. Please see Alfred [Rice] pays you what he owes as it comes in. Will write good letter soon. Off to Ronda in 1/2 hour. Hope to clean up work for book before too long. Never was so dead in the head in my life but it is starting to pull out of it. The head I mean.

Pedro Ro Papa

Thanks always for everything.

EH.

---

dead in the head: Mary remembered EH feeling "poor-to-terrible" before leaving for New York and Spain on August 4; on August 15 he wrote her: "Only thing I am afraid of, no, not only thing, is complete physical and nervous crack-up from deadly over-work." EH sent similarly desperate messages into September, but, Mary confessed, she "failed totally to evaluate the importance of these successive warning signals" (*HIW,* 564–65).

{148} EH to AEH
17/9/60 (ALS, 4 pp., ViU)
Apartado 67 [*hw*] [Málaga *pmk*]

Dear Hotch:

Got back here for 4 days rest and handle business and correspondence. After Ronda (wonderful[—]Antonio super), Tarifa (blown out by near hurricane), Jerez de la Frontera (very nearly called off by wind but civil Governor said fight or jail). Antonio wonderful in final bull—Then Salamanca 2 days (bulls worthless—Antonio OK and very good. Saw the new boy Camino twice).

In the bank mail Sept. statement showed you never cashed the 5000.^{00} check. This has me worried. Wish you would cable Hotel Suecia—Madrid—check cashed.

Life really crossed us up on pictures of basic passes in 2nd issue. After me working literally weeks for them to get wonderful pictures—fair to both boys—showing things at their best and okayed by Lang after arguments—they used the most inferior ok-ed pictures and one of Miguel that they took last year in Bayonne labeled <u>Pase Ayudado</u> that is the kind photographers use to blackmail bull fighters. After all the hours and days of checking and re-checking—

Can you see that they at least do <u>not</u> use that picture Page 62—Pase Ayudado in their Spanish edition?—

I'm the laughing stock of anyone who knows anything about bull fighting and has seen piece and regarded as the crook and double crosser of all time—After guaranteeing pictures would be accurate and good and show both men at their best—The picture is malicious—when I saw that page of pictures it made me feel worse than any kind of wound or disaster—To be made both a fool (all time) and a double crosser (which can not explain as Antonio and Miguel know how carefully I went over the pictures and the hours put in)—Nobody had a copy to show me at Salamanca though the Life-Time-people had seen it or I could have made some explanation to Antonio and tried to have him make Miguel understand. Never felt so completely sunk—Head was getting in good shape and I thought with the right pictures the fatigue and over-work to point of destruction was justified if we had the results—Does no good to try to explain that promises to me were not kept—Nobody would believe that—Now have to sweat out what there may be in 3rd number—would shoot myself if it would do any good—But have to get things neatened up for any such luxury as that—Had just gotten letter from Mary that 2nd number was fine—so was not worrying and was figureing was starting to have the fatigue beat and that everything would work out fine. Hell—wish you were here to talk to—will try to do some good with a cable to Antonio at Arles—But what the hell good can you do with a cable and he's in France today and tomorrow and probably dressing at some friend's house instead of at the hotel—

It is ok to say that what difference does a page of pictures make—But the work that went into getting these pictures right and straight and my obligation to be straight and see things through makes you sick right through your bones—would rather be smashed up like in Africa any number of times than have the feeling that page of pictures gave me.

So—A—Have to try not to think that am destroyed as an honest guy. B—Try to make the people involved believe it was not done by me in carelessness or malice. C—wait for more awful stuff in 3rd. D—wait for what they do to really put us all out of business in the Spanish edition—What is actual date on that? For what sum would they let me not have it published?

I had intended not to be critical and be cheerful and co-operate all the way—and I did—Then with the wonderful pics we researched and okayed they had to make Miguel look a fool in that Bayonne shot and me a fool (permanent) and a double-crosser.

You can't just say the hell with it because it is the hell with yourself permanently—

Otherwise it is a good day—Please cable about the check. Please let me know amount of any dough I owe. Want to get things really straight in re dough and would rather send check for whole sums than have the Alfred system—Took notes on all the Extremadura Country and we are correcting all book stuff where I slipped up. Been working good and head was getting cheerful when this last thing hit two days ago—Best to you always

Papa

one of Miguel that they took last year: In contrast to Ordóñez's erect posture in the other photographs, Dominguín seems to be awkwardly leaning in this photograph.

The following cables concern AEH's adaptation of several of Hemingway's Nick Adams stories; the resulting motion picture, Hemingway's Adventures of a Young

Man, *was released in August 1962. In a letter or cable that remains unlocated, AEH apparently proposed selling film rights for several stories to producer Jerry Wald; according to AEH, EH believed that if "The Snows of Kilimanjaro" had been worth $100,000, then seven stories should be worth $700,000 (PH, 248).*

{149} EH to AEH
1960 SEP 18 (Cable, 1 p., ViU)
Spain

THAT MANY STORIES IS A BOOK HOTCH WOULD ASK FOR SEVEN NOT 90 UNDER FIVE BEST PAPA=

{150} EH to AEH
SEP 19 60 (Cable, 1 p., ViU)
Spain

CABLE MEANT BELIEVED YOU SHOULD TRY FOR BOOK LENGTH PRICE SAY SEVEN HUNDRED THOUSAND REDUCING AS NECESSARY STOP STUDIO'S VALUE ACCORDING TO PRICE THEY PAY TEN STORIES MINE SHOULD BE EXPENSIVE PACKAGE BEST=PAPA

{151} EH to AEH
SEP 22 60 (Cable, 1 p., ViU)
Spain

=AT 0400 STILL WAITING CALL, CABLE FASTEST WHEN RECEIVE THIS AS HELD HERE UNTIL HEAR FROM YOU

{152} EH to AEH
SEP 24 60 (Cable, 1 p., ViU)
Spain

WILL CALL YOU 0700 YOUR TIME TUESDAY MORNING UNLESS YOU CABLE MAKE MONDAY CALL SAME HOUR ANTONIO GREATESTLONGRONO

Unsure of EH's rationale for insisting on an exorbitant fee and sensing that all was not well with him, AEH flew to Madrid on October 2. His fears were confirmed when he learned that EH believed that Bill Davis was trying to kill him by wrecking the Lancia (PH, 251). EH returned to New York on October 8 and traveled to Ketchum shortly thereafter. The rights to the stories were subsequently sold for $125,000.

{153} EH to AEH
1960 OCT 21 (Cable, 1 p., ViU)
Idaho

HAVE INFORMATION WALD WANTS FILM BADLY STOP INFORM OUR GUEST IF ARRIVED NO FINANCIAL PROBLEMS NO WORRIES WRITING SOONEST TRIED CALL YOU BEST PAPA

OUR GUEST: Valerie Danby-Smith. Mary was nonplussed by Valerie's arrival in Cuba in February 1960 and had reservations about her joining EH in Spain the following August. When EH left Madrid for New York on October 8, Valerie went to visit her home in Dublin. She did not arrive in New York until October 21, after EH had already left for Ketchum. Valerie Hemingway, *Running with the Bulls,* 149–50.

{154} EH to AEH
25/10/60 (ALS, 1 p., ViU)
Ketchum [Idaho *pmk*]

Dear Hotch:

Enclosed is check for 1500.$\underline{^{00}}$ to apply on Val's tuition at the Dramatic Academy and on her living expenses while she is our guest in N.Y. during her studies this semester. I do not want her to arrive in New York and not know that she has something to back her up in her studies and N.Y. is a murderously expensive place to live in—Not only room but to eat properly.

Am getting this off to you in a hurry. Will write more fully later.

Papa.

Val's tuition: Valerie describes this as payment for secretarial services that could not be made directly to her in Cuba because she lacked the proper worker's permit. She claims that EH paid her from his winnings on the Johanssan-Patterson fight (see letter 114; Valerie Hemingway, *Running with the Bulls,* 144). Valerie was not enrolled in school; EH invented this fiction as a means of getting money to her under auspices that Mary could not disapprove of (*Final,* 348).

Enclosed with this letter was a letter to Valerie in which EH expressed concern for her well-being and suggested a means by which she might contact him in Ketchum without Mary's knowledge. According to AEH, EH telephoned him before the letters arrived and instructed him not to deliver the enclosure to Valerie, whom he was afraid would be interrogated by federal authorities about her passport (*PH,* 266–67). His biographer Michael Reynolds writes: "For reasons he was never able to articulate fully, Hemingway was certain that state and federal agencies were pursuing him for unnamed crimes" (*Final,* 349). The letter to Valerie reads:

Dearest Val,

It is impossible to work unless I know that you are all right or that you understand how things are (they are difficult for everybody) so if you want to let me know how you are without annoying anyone you can enclose a sealed letter to EH in a typewritten envelope to Dr. George Saviers Box 181 Sun Valley—Idaho. Put on some name beginning with A. and any return address you like. He has an enormous amount of mail but that way will identify that it is a communication for me. There is no chance of it being returned.

I love you very much and miss your help all of the time. This is a rough fall and the whole purpose of being here to work is destroyed unless I know you are well and doing well. So far it has been like being in Limbo or you being in Limbo or both.

Please have good luck and take care of yourself and know I love you and want everything good for you.

EH

Ketchum
25/10/60.

On November 14, AEH visited the Hemingways in Ketchum. Two weeks later, EH checked into the Mayo Clinic in Rochester, Minnesota, under the name of George Saviers. On January 2, 1961, he granted AEH power of attorney regarding motion picture rights to ten short stories. "Outgoing Correspondence 1961," JFKL.

1961

{155} EH to AEH
1961 JAN 10 (Cable, 1 p., ViU)
Minnesota

HOPE OLD EYES OK NWA ON STRIKE. CAPITOL BEST DIRECT MINNEAPOLIS THEN BRANIFF OR OZARK HERE OR JEFFERSON TRANSPORTATION LIMOUSINE NINETY MINUTES HERE EVERY FOUR HOURS EIGHT BUCKS. WEIGHED ONE SEVENTY THREE AND A QUARTER TODAY: ALL OF IT GLAD TO SEE YOU. LOVE PAPA MARY.

{156} AEH to EH
1961 JAN 16 PM 3 15 (Cable, 1 p., JFKL)
West Los Angeles, California

DEAR PAPA, SO SORRY OUR VISIT WAS SO BRIEF. EVERYTHING FINE HERE. TWEN-TIETH CENTURY FOX TELEPHONE CRESTVIEW 62211, MY ADDRESS SUNSET TOW-ERS WEST 8400 SUNSET BLVD. LOS ANGELES 46 TELEPHONE OLDFIELD 60735. PLEASE INFORM ME WHEN RETURNING KETCHUM. WILL TELEPHONE YOU WEDNESDAY NOON YOUR TIME. LOVE TO MARY AND YOU=
HOTCH==

OUR VISIT: AEH visited the clinic on January 14 and found EH besieged by irrational fears (*PH,* 266). EH was released on January 22.
Atop this message EH wrote: "George Saviers—calling Coopers 9 pm our time Thursday". On verso, he wrote: "Call Alfred Rice Circle G-0200. Ask him to deposit

304

Hotch money. 30 as 20 cash 10 cash what is holding up other deposit 74—deposit. 30,000 not deposited 2,000 in Mary's account—Rice sent her Pay april 15/ Rice paid last estimated payment 1960 have paid 60,000 Hotch a m <u>noon</u> 9–11 L A Alfred 8–<u>9/30</u> Hotch called 1230—money not deposited yet—Jerry Wald promises a percentage [*several chars. indeciph.*]."

{157} EH to AEH
30/1/1961 (ALS, 2 pp., ViU)
Box 555/Ketchum/Idaho [*hw*]

Dear Hotch:

Am enclosing the only thing which came which was not a carbon. The envelope from Jo Mielziner [set designer] office 1 west 72nd street signed Frank Corasro [Corsaro, director] was a 5 page carbon dated December 29. You said not to send it nor Alfred [Rice]'s of Jan. 17 which was a carbon of letter sent to Beverly Hills Hotel. Snowing hard outside.

Working hard as I told you last night. Weight down to 170 which is too low.

Will be hearing from you shortly. Have the Corsaro notes so we will know what we are talking about on the phone since we had no chance to talk at any length about that. Good luck in your deals. Mary sends love. Will listen for you on Friday Feb. 3—6pm our time.

In haste and best always
Papa

Please wire when contracts signed and ask Alfred to wire me when deposits are made.

the Corsaro notes: According to AEH, notes concerning his stage play *A Short Happy Life,* based on a number of Hemingway works. The play, directed by Frank Corsaro, opened in Seattle in October 1961 but closed in Los Angeles before reaching Broadway.

{158} EH to AEH
18 Feb. 61 (ALS, 1 p., ViU)
Box 555/Ketchum [*hw*] [Idaho *pmk*]

Dear Hotch:

Last Monday I had a wire from Alfred [Rice] phoned in which said "Fox Deal Closed For Both You and Hotch. Please Advise in which amount

Deposit." I called him on the phone to tell him I probably thought it should be deposited 70% in tax account and 30% in checking account. He thought that too high a percentage but he had not figured, I thought, of me having a book done in the fall etc. Plus how taxes may rise and then at the end he started talking about your theatrical show [*A Short Happy Life*], that there was a new money man, that you were the producer but had no financial responsibility for the show (which you had told me), that there were subsidiary rights to be settled, what was our arrangement for this, what for that, what was my interest in the show since you were producer, etc. etc. aside from author's equity. I told him I could not take down all these questions nor give him answers—I had not raised the questions and certainly nobody could give subsidiary television rights or any rights that were not owned and for him to put all this in writing—I wanted you to know that he brought all this up—So you would know I was not going behind your back on the matter.

You write me when you have time and explain the play situation. He said, when asked by me, that you had considerable expenses as producer and would have to give up a large share to the new money man. Alfred said he had never seen why he etc. could not put up the money so you would not have to split your share as producer with anyone. I said I did not back plays and did not believe he should either. That you were absolutely definite that as a producer you nor I had any money responsibility. In the T.V. I wished to split 50/50 with you since you did all the work and negotiating and I only furnished the story or stories. I hope everything has been done ok on this by him and on everything else. I have no copies of anything here and if am to get strictly the author's equity, if that was our agreement it is absolutely OK with me. He wanted me to say something about this but I asked him to put it into writing.

Hope everything is OK with you. Please let me hear from you.

Am working hard. If there is anything that I should send you for any expenses since I did not understand Alfred please let me know.

Best always,

Papa

He deducted 5% for the 20th Century Fox and 5% for the other agent. That plus 70% for taxes—(they may not, of course, [*indeciph.*] be needed) left only 20,250$\underline{^{00}}$ for cash acct.

EH.

Fox Deal Closed: **For the movie** *Hemingway's Adventures of a Young Man.*

{159} EH to AEH
March 2, 1961 (TLS, 3 pp., ViU)
[Idaho]

Dear Hotch:

I think you, I and Alfred [Rice] all agree that for the sake of no future mis-understandings, there should be definitely stated the subject matter of the rights you are free to use in connection with the play written by you based upon my properties, originally authorized by me by letter to you dated April 23, 1959 [see note on page 251].

You have indicated to me that for the proper exploitation of the play, those who put up the money properly expect to share in the ultimate sale, if any, of the motion picture, television, and other collateral rights in the play.

You have indicated to me that you have drawn upon the following of my properties in the writing of the play:

Books* entitled: A FAREWELL TO ARMS
FOR WHOM THE BELL TOLLS
ACROSS THE RIVER AND INTO THE TREES
TO HAVE AND HAVE NOT
THE TORRENTS OF SPRING
DEATH IN THE AFTERNOON

and
Short Stories
entitled: HILLS LIKE WHITE ELEPHANTS**
THE UNDEFEATED***
THE LIGHT OF THE WORLD**
THE SNOWS OF KILIMANJARO***

I agree that pursuant to the terms of the minimum basic production con-tract between you, as producer, and you and myself as authors, in addition to the live legitimate stage presentation of the play, you may further acquire, but only of the play as dramatized by you, motion picture, television, radio, sec-ond-class touring performances, stock performances, amateur performances, and foreign language performances, subject, however, to the following limita-tions:

1. It is understood that the right to consent to the exploitation of the play

in the above media shall be arranged only by our mutual agreement, and that no other entity or person has any right to negotiate or sell the exploitation of the play in the media above described.

2. I shall alone at all times be free to negotiate and sell, for any media of exploitation, the individual properties referred to above, and you, as producer of the play, or anyone claiming through you, shall have no right to any of the proceeds obtained by me from the sale of such rights.

3. With respect to the book ACROSS THE RIVER AND INTO THE TREES, such portions used by you in the dramatization, performance rights of which I have heretofore granted you, are confined to the use of this portion in your play for legitimate stage presentation, in English only, in the United States and Canada, and specifically such portion of that work utilized in the play may not be used in any presentation of the play via motion pictures, television, radio, or foreign language performances.

4. Naturally, the exploitation of the play in the media permitted are agreed to be subject to any motion picture or television commitments now outstanding with respect to any of the properties listed in the third paragraph of this letter (page 1).

5. The copyright, if any, to the play shall be in my name, and I shall be the owner of the play as dramatized by you.

With regard to my royalty as author from the use of my basic rights in these properties, it is agreed that I shall receive 5% of gross weekly box office receipts.

Because I know that you had special expenses as producer and negotiating obtaining funds to finance the play, I am willing that the producer's net profit from the exploitation of the play shall be divided 60% to you and 40% to me.

I am sure Alfred will see to it that the restrictions on the use of the various rights to the various properties I have set out above will be incorporated into the production contract since you and I both agree that this should be done.

For the sake of formality, please sign this letter under the word "Accepted".

As ever,
Ernest Hemingway

ACCEPTED:

A E Hotchner

---

[*] Books—only fragments utilized and, in the case of Across the River and into the Trees, use made of only two pages

[**]—entire story utilized

[***]—substantial parts of story utilized

This letter, signed by EH and AEH, was probably written by Rice, based upon his discussions with EH.

{160} EH to AEH
March 4 1961 (ALS, 1 p., ViU)
Box 555/Ketchum/Idaho [*hw*]

Dear Hotch:

This is the agreement Alfred [Rice] sent that you confirmed over the phone.

Sent the copy to him for you to sign that you said would be attached to the equity agreement.

Thanks very much for attending to this and I hope it is all in order.

Best always,
Papa

{161} EH to AEH
March 6 61 (ALS, 1 p., ViU)
[Ketchum, Idaho *pmk*]

Dear Hotch-Maru:

Please remember when you write that letters are scarce around here and that everyone, including myself, picks up my letters, at the post office. Then when they are opened here (by me of course) they are discussed since letters are scarce and of interest so if you ever have any problems of yours you don't want discussed put them on a separate sheet of paper.

I have no plans except working out the present book as I have to go day to day on the health business and the weight is a little low and want to be sure on that end of it before planning further work and movements. Don't want to worry Mary on that nor anything else nor worry myself. I'm learning to be strong at 169 and 170 after eating well but it is too low to fool with. I write this so you have the true Gen. Am following Dr.'s orders exactly and pressure is good. But weight re-action's a little spooky. But [5 *chars. indeciph.*] I'm sure in the end, probably, [5-6 *words indeciph.*] away from you. But right now need to check closely.

Was awfully sorry to hear your daughter had the virus infection and hope she is better. It is a bad thing but am sure you have a good man looking after her and I'm glad your winter is lighter now. It really sounded terrible over the radio and T.V.

Being cabin bound so much there is a tendency for everyone to listen over the phone and while it is perfectly natural this cramps my style.

Hope it was the correct thing to send the other agreement direct to Alfred [Rice]. They could just as well have both gone to you but since he brought it up and was not to sign [*indeciph.*] it being [*indeciph.*] I thought it was only polite.

Best always

Papa.

the present book: Both *The Dangerous Summer* and *A Moveable Feast* were in progress; Michael Reynolds suggests that in March EH was probably working on the introduction to the latter (*Final*, 353).

AEH remembers, "[T]his was the last letter I received from Ernest. The handwriting was now small and cramped and several words were slurred and unintelligible." (See page 249.)

On April 21, Mary discovered EH with a shotgun, and a few days later found him trying to get to the gun and load it (HIW, 573–74).

AEH continues, "After only a few more months back in Ketchum, Ernest again attempted suicide and was flown back to St. Mary's Hospital [in the Mayo Clinic] in a small plane. On re-admittance, Ernest was administered additional electric shocks. I visited him again [in June] and found his mental condition deplorable although he had some lucid exchanges with me. Before I left the hospital, with Spain as my destination, I had a meeting with Mary who promised not to allow Ernest to return to Ketchum in the state he was in, but a few days later the doctors persuaded her otherwise. On July 2, 1961, shortly after Ernest returned to his Ketchum home, he again attempted suicide, this time with a double-barreled Boss shotgun he had taken from a storage room in the basement. He went upstairs to the vestibule inside the front door, loaded two cartridges in the chambers, placed the gun on the floor with his forehead pressed against the barrels and pulled both triggers. He was buried on July 5 in Ketchum Cemetery." AEH to DeFazio, December 2004.

Appendix

Notes on *The Dangerous Summer*

Hotchner's Proposed Cuts, Their Disposition in the Scribner's Edition, and Hemingway's Written Responses

Hotchner's twenty-seven suggested cuts are here divided into eighteen groups. On a sheet of notepad, Hotchner listed the typescript page numbers of his suggested cuts; these appear in column 1. The resulting cuts sometimes started or ended on different pages; column 2 specifies these page and line numbers and the number of words involved. Columns 3 and 4 state the disposition of the suggested cuts in the *Life* articles (see page 295) and the Scribner's edition (New York: Scribner's, 1985). Hemingway's responses are scattered throughout the notepad; those that were written directly on the sheet with Hotchner's list of page numbers are identified as such. The notepad is housed at the Clifton Waller Barrett Library, University of Virginia.

1.

AEH sug. cut	Typescript	Life	Scribner's
20–21	330 wds.	retained	retained

EH: "[(]Takes out humor, mood-setting and people) also Mary's illness—a predominant motif throughout piece." Writing directly on sheet of page numbers: "(Takes out humor and people)."

2.

AEH sug. cut	Typescript	Life	Scribner's
47–50	44.6–60.10	cut	1,170 wds.
58–60	(2,630 wds.)		restored

EH: "Eliminates Mario (important character-(people)". "Eliminates evidence of intimacy with Ordonez (plans for African trip—and explanation of health—<u>referred to later</u>—)." On sheet: "(Leaves no explanation for health business later)."

3.

AEH sug. cut	Typescript	Life	Scribner's
61–64	61.11–65.1	cut	130 wds.
	(550 wds.)		restored

EH: "Eliminates extent of contact between 2 families—(necessary) only saves 161 words by eliminating trip from Ketchum to K[ey] W[est] which makes us seem normal american people with whom reader can identify self)"

4.

AEH sug. cut	Typescript	Life	Scribner's
65–70	66.10–70.14	retained	cut
	(700 wds.)		

EH: "Deprives reader of pleasure of vicarious travel—is well written—Establishes the Southern Coast and the almost fatally bad driver—Has the details that interest traveller who cannot travel. Also wish to be just to extraordinary way Govt. handles tourists. Is a possible cut—but has effect of making things happen no-where)"

5.

AEH sug. cut	Typescript	Life	Scribner's
72	160 wds.	retained	retained

EH: "If put name of ship in on 64 as I did better to leave in—"

6.

AEH sug. cut	Typescript	Life	Scribner's
84–86	80.7–85.11	cut	300 wds.
	(870 wds.)		restored

EH: "This can be cut if you want to eliminate the counter-point between the States and Spain which I have tried for—But it <u>can</u> go."

7.

AEH sug. cut	Typescript	Life	Scribner's
86–98	2,170 wds.	retained	retained

EH: "Cutting this piece of country out that we went through so often and is such a big part of the summer—is like cutting the country part out of The Sun Also Rises—It is a road that is very little driven—country—storks—wine-fields and the conversation in market place and tavern important to me and what am trying to do EH."

8.

AEH sug. cut	Typescript	Life	Scribner's
~~107–109~~ [lined through]			
132–134	107.5–164B.1	90 wds.	3,040 wds.
140–170	(9,570 wds.)	retained	restored

EH seems to have written the following instructions after he had rejected most of Hotchner's proposed cuts: "Where to cut—San Isidro [manuscript page 132] was a miserable feria etc. but Antonio had two interesting bulls: — Must keep in 125–132 136–140—Keep in Cordoba—Sevilla—Aranjuez—Be sure to keep in last paragraph in 162. Put in Cordoba [149]—cut to leaving Sevilla [164A]—cut after the cornada at Aranjuez to the infirmary [191]— then recovery—cut rest at ranch? [219–224] Cut to Ronda [224]—Include the Zaragoza Alicante—Barcelona-Burgos fights. Pamplona—cut birthday/all except the part about death—Cut to Valencia—Put in hospital at Madrid— Cut to mano a mano in Malaga—Bayonne—Ciudad Real—Bilbao (leave other things intact) (Don't try to save sentences at a time) EH." Elsewhere in the notepad, he adds: "Suggest start cut and space at bottom page 140 where have made pencil mark before ¶ and cut to page 146—and continue on to 157—

Then leave space=to 165—where I have marked—Keep on to 170 and continue to 191—cut from 191–194 <u>OK.</u>"

9.

AEH sug. cut	Typescript	Life	Scribner's
191–194	191.16–194.8	cut	cut
	(640 wds.)		

For EH's response, see final sentence of previous response.

10.

AEH sug. cut	Typescript	Life	Scribner's
218–224	218.7–230.13	209 wds.	1,340 wds.
	(2,200 wds.)	retained	restored

EH: "Start cut and space at bottom of page—need those 7 lines to establish Miguelin and Mondeño—LEAVE IN RANCH 219–224 (believe necessary in their relations)"; "Hotch: If absolutely necessary to save piece we could cut from end of 1st ¶ on 219 to beginning of last ¶ on page 224. But this would be grossly unfair to Luis Miguel. To be at <u>all</u> fair to Miguel we would have to, as final concession, cut from end of 1st ¶ on 219 to Beginning of last ¶ on 221—If we have to cut last ¶ on 224—This could be inserted before that ¶ Luis Miguel had been wonderful all though the fight and I had never admired him more. He had the sword back now and all his confidence with it and his great knowledge was never more apparent and his art with [breaks off]"

11.

AEH sug. cut	Typescript	Life	Scribner's
233–236	232.4–236.10	460 wds.	790 wds.
		cut	restored

EH: "agree to cut 233–236"

12.

AEH sug. cut	Typescript	Life	Scribner's
250–253	244.2–284.17	cut	5,220 wds.
258–260	(7,630 wds.)		restored
261–262			
279–282			
~~282–284~~			

EH: "on cut 251–253 Suggest make cut as indicated on 250 to where I have marked on 251"; "282–284 Scrapped—"

13.

AEH sug. cut	Typescript	Life	Scribner's
303–323	302.2–323.11	cut	1,560 wds.
	(3,790 wds.)		restored

EH: "pick up at place marked Space on 280—continue on through 303–323 (These should stay as they show L[uis] M[iguel]'s high point of the season and explain the causes of his disaster. They also show how Antonio consciously learned to fight in the particular high wind of Valencia and how in the bull he dedicated to George he was able to make a perfect faena in a heavy wind. It shows all the movement toward L.M.'s disaster."

14.

AEH sug. cut	Typescript	Life	Scribner's
329–333	329.7–334.10	cut	340 wds.
	(510 wds.)		restored

EH: "Leave in."

15.

AEH sug. cut	Typescript	Life	Scribner's
356–358	356.15–359.5	cut	190 wds.
	(510 wds.)		restored

EH: "Leave in."

16.

AEH sug. cut	Typescript	Life	Scribner's
359–36[indeciph. digit]			
363–370	359.9–372.2	270 wds.	1,050 wds.
	(2,290 wds.)	retained	restored

EH: "Cut from 364 to 370 Leave space—put in date."

17.

AEH sug. cut	Typescript	Life	Scribner's
392–395	391.13–401.2	104 wds.	1,000 wds.
399A–399C	(1,980 wds.)	retained	restored

EH: "392–394—cut—Leave space Date"; "399A—399—C Leave in 399A—B—2nd paragraph 399C—Cut 1st ¶ 399C."

18.

AEH sug. cut	Typescript	Life	Scribner's
488	488.7–490.11	220 wds	cut
	(380 wds.)	retained	
	491.8–492.7	120 wds.	cut
	(170 wds.)	retained	
	493.11–688.15	cut	cut
	(33,320 wds.)		

EH: "Cut second ¶ and 1st ¶ of 489. End Page 493 after 'I've kept the apartment,' he said."

In addition, in an undated (and possibly unmailed) note to AEH on Finca Vigia letterhead, EH wrote: "Severe horn wounds until July 31—56—not counting fractures of skulls, backs, chest, arms and legs, brain damage and severe traumatic shock," signing it "EH" and adding: "Will verify Corde de Tebas—(Believe that correct spelling)" (LOC). This change appears in the *Life* serialization as follows: "That was the way it was that year and there had been more than fifty severe horn wounds until July 31, not counting fractures of skulls, backs, chests, arms and legs, brain damage and severe traumatic shock" ("The Dangerous Summer Part II: The Pride of the Devil," *Life,* September 12, 1960, p. 82).

EH also sent instructions to AEH in an undated cable, apparently from 1960 (LOC):

PLEASE CUT FROM END OF SECOND SENTENCE ON PAGE 216A TO FIRST SENTENCE ON PAGE 217 STOP IN LAST SENTENCE IN FIRST PARAGRAPH PAGE 217 CHANGE TO HORNS APPEARED TO HAVE BEEN TAMPERED WITH STOP IN SECOND PARAGRAPH STOP PAGE 217 CHANGE KNEW TO SAW IN FIRST SENTENCE AND KNOW TO SEE STOP

CUT FIRST FOUR WORDS PAGE 218 AND FIFTH SENTENCE SHOULD READ IF HIS DE-
FENCES WERE ALTERED STOP IF THIS TOO COMPLICATED CUT SOMETHING FROM
FIRST SENTENCE 216A ON THUS GAINING THREE PAGES CUTS STOP REASON POSSI-
BLE LIBEL RETURNING MADRID MONDAY NIGHT WRITING

    PAPA

AEH did not make the first cut, not finding it necessary to cut pages 216A,
216B, and 217 (the "three pages" EH refers to), but he did make all of the
other emendations that EH suggested.

Textual Commentary

These commentaries provide information about the letters and envelopes that is not included in the notes accompanying the letters. For each letter the following information is provided if it is available: the writer or typist's name, if different from the sender; the postmark; the address; the inside address; and any other remarkable features of the envelope. Addresses that appear frequently are provided in full upon their first occurrence and cross-referenced in subsequent appearances. For cables, the address, time, and point of origin are drawn from the dateline.

Alterations, emendations, and remarkable features of the manuscripts are noted. Identifying evidence of multiple hands, damaged manuscripts, and other peculiarities not noted elsewhere are keyed to paragraph and line. So that they may be easily identified, the salutation and closing are counted as paragraphs.

Most often, the alterations in the manuscripts conform to the four general categories described by Fredson Bowers.[1] Following the paragraph and line number, the glossed word is reproduced as it appears in the text. When the gloss concerns a phrase, the first and last words are given and the intervening words are represented by an ellipsis. Editorial comments are italicized; comments that appear amid text from the documents, such as *faint* or *indeciph.,* are enclosed in brackets.

Simple insertions are identified as *interl.* (interlined) when the insertion appears above the line and as *insert.* (inserted) when it appears elsewhere. If the location of a noninterlined insertion seems significant, it is indicated along with other pertinent information, including whether the change was made by the author, a secretary, or the recipient and whether, in a typewritten letter, the

1. Fredson Bowers, "Transcription of Manuscripts: The Record of Variants," *Studies in Bibliography* 29 (1976): 212–64.

alteration appears to have been made immediately in type or upon revision in autograph (*auto.*).

Simple deletions are described relative to words they precede (*prec.*) or follow (*fol.*). For example, if the second word in the sentence "Joe got tired easily" were deleted by hand, the commentary would read: "Joe] *fol. by auto. del.* got."

Sometimes an insertion is accompanied by a deletion. If in the sentence "Joe tired" the word *got* has been cancelled after *Joe* and the word *tired* interlined above *got,* the commentary would read: "tired] *interl. ab. del.* got."

Alterations by superimposition, whether they appear to reflect a bona fide revision or the repair of an inadvertent slip, are also recorded. If in the typewritten word *their* the *i* and *e* were transposed and then corrected, the commentary would read: "their] ei *over* ie." Subscripted carets indicate the points at which missing punctuation was added.

{1}

typed by secretary identified as "cb"

inside address: Mr. Ernest Hemingway/San Francisco de Paula/Cuba/*followed by* AEH:cb

¶8.1–7 The contract . . . 1950."] *on a preprinted form with* Cosmopolitan *printed at head and* Lot 709 50M 3–48 *at foot*

{2}

postmark: Key West Fla Jun 28 1948 6 pm

address: A. E. Hotchner Esq./Associate Editor/Cosmopolitan Magazine/57th Street and 8th Avenue/New York, 19 N.Y./Editorials Department/Estados Unidos

verso of envelope: Hemingway/San Francisco De Paula/Cuba *preprinted in red on white stock*

¶2.3 days'] days∧

¶3.5 free if] i *over* .

¶4.5 straighten] *prec. by* x's *over* starighten up

¶6.6 Francisco.] Francisco∧ *fol. by* x *over* f

¶7.3 (un-inhabited),] *auto. interl. ab. caret*

¶7.6–7 Took . . . photographer.] *auto. insert.*

¶9.1 and . . . again] *auto. insert.*

¶11.1–2 Mary . . . again] *auto. insert.*

¶11.1 wife.] wife∧

¶11.2 again.] again∧

{3}

¶3.5 the eye] theeye

¶4.5 used] *fol. by* x *over* .

¶6.4 shows] *fol. by* 2 *or* 3 *chars. auto. del.*

{4}

From New York, 6 pm

stamped: San Francisco de Paula (Habana) July [*faint*] 1948 *and dateline reads* 6pm *although* 6.30. pm. *appears at conclusion of cable*

{5}

¶4.3 articles] s *auto. insert.*
inside address: *same as {1}, excluding typist's initials*

{6}

¶4.1 N.y.] N∧y∧
¶6.1 always).] always)∧

{7}

top left margin reads Rec Mar. 10 49 Ans. Mar 10 49
¶3.1 elections] *1st* e *over* l

{8}

postmark: *faint*
address: Ed. Hotchner/Editorial Department/COSMOPOLITAN/ 57th and 8th Avenue/New York 19, NY/Estati Uniti D'America/Personal for Mr. Hotchner only.
verso of envelope: E. Hemingway/Villa Aprile/Cortina D'Ampezzo/Italy
¶3.1 years] *fol. by* x's *over* eb
¶3.2 Probably] P *over* p
¶3.2 press] *fol. by* x *over* s
¶5.1 get] *prec. by* x's *over* come
¶5.4–5 (Story . . . you.)] *auto. interl.*
¶5.4 4500] *auto. insert. again to clarify previous.* 4500
¶7.8 with a lot] *prec. by* x's *over* with
¶9.4–5 concession] *prec. by* x's *over* concetion *and* consceion
¶12.1–5 We . . . possible.] *auto. insert.*

{9}

dictated to Juanita Jensen
postmark: *faint*
address: Ed. Hotchner Esq./415 West 21st Street/New York City, NY/Estados Unidos
inside address: Ed. Hotchner, Esquire/COSMOPOLITAN Magazine/ Hearst Magazines, Inc./57th at 8th Avenue/New York 19, NY
envelope: *see {2}*
¶3.2 as it is] *auto. insert. by EH*

{10}

Top right margin EH writes answered July 8
¶5.3 individual] *final* i *over char.*

¶5.4 DiMaggio] M *over* m
¶6.2 cos.] cos∧
¶6.3 mm.] mm∧
¶7.1 I] *over* i
¶7.2 Sept.] Sept∧
¶7.3 book] *2nd* o *over* k
¶7.4 occured] e *over* 4
¶10.1–2 I . . . job.] *auto. insert.*

{11}

postmark: *faint*
address: Personal for Mr. Hotchner Only./Mr. Ed. Hotchner/ Editorial Department/
   COSMOPOLITAN/Fifty Seventh Street at 8th Avenue/New York, 19 N.Y./Estados
   Unidos
envelope: *see {2}*
July 8 1949] *auto.*
¶2.6 1100] *prec. by* x's *over* eleven and
¶2.11 piece] *fol. by auto. del.* sometime
¶2.13 and] a *over* .
¶2.13 and . . . 1840] *auto. interl.*
¶2.13 1840.] 1840∧
¶3.1 (with one eye)] *auto. insert.* (*and*)
¶4.2 Indianapolis] o *over* l
¶4.2 appreciate] *1st* e *over* c
¶5.5 mis-spelled).] mis-spelled)∧
¶6.8 N.Y.] N∧Y∧
¶6.9 that] a *over* t
¶7.2 card] *prec. by* x's *over* crad as
¶7.3 (Joke.)] *auto. insert.*
¶7.4 twice] ic *over* ov
¶9.2 Inf.] Inf∧
¶9.3 war] r *over* y
¶9.4 railway] *auto. insert.* w
¶9.4 impressive).] impressive)∧
¶11.2–3 balance . . . August] *auto. insert. ab. caret*
¶12.4 3/4] *auto.* / *over* ?
¶12.5 far).] far)∧
¶12.6–7 He'll . . . covering.] *auto. insert.*
¶12.10 keep] k∧ep
¶12.10 happy] hoppy
¶12.12 (Pinched . . . Faulkner.)] (Pinched . . . Faulkner∧) *auto. insert.*
¶13.1 So for] *auto* S *over* s
¶13.2 me.] me∧
¶13.3 funny] funnyn
¶13.4 Sort . . . though.] *auto. insert.*

{12}

¶3.4 like] line

¶3.5 In] *fol. by* x's *over* this

¶3.8 band] d *over* b

¶4.3 Collier's] Collier∧s

¶4.6 anything] *prec. by* x's *over* anty

¶6.9 midsections] c *over* t

¶7.13 see] x's *over* sh

¶7.17 because] a *over* z

¶8.1 protestations] a *over* i

¶9.1 mm.] mm∧

{13}

postmark: Habana Cuba Ago 29 1949 3 pm

address: *same as {11} except that EH capitalizes* EDITORIAL DEPARTMENT PER-
SONAL FOR MR. HOTCHNER ONLY.

verso of envelope: *same as {2} except that stock is grey and EH inserts an* E *beneath return address on verso of envelope*

¶3.7 drowned)] *fol. by* x's *over* were

¶3.8 (You . . . settlement.)] *auto. insert.* (*and*)

¶3.10 a] *fol. by* x's *over* harmen

¶3.12 18.25.] 18.25∧

¶3.14 INTELLIGENCE:] *fol. by* X's *over* $$

¶3.16 said] a *over* q

¶4.3 they] e *over* a

¶5.2–3 Appointment] x *over char. prec.* o

¶5.4 half-lace] - *auto. insert.*

¶5.9 writing] *auto. insert.*

¶7.1 "Don't] ""Don't

¶8.5 bro.)] bro∧

¶9.6 out on] *auto.* n *over* f

¶10.1 we] *prec. by auto. del.* We

¶10.2 going] *1st* g *over* i

¶12.5 stories] stroies

¶15.1–16.4 PS. . . . EH.] *auto. insert.*

¶16.2 Don't] Don∧t

{14}

Dateline reads 5pm *although* 5.45. pm. *appears at conclusion of cable*

{15}

postmarks: *on recto* New York Sept 27 1949 1:30 pm *and on verso* Habana Cuba Sept. 28
1949 2 pm *also on verso* San Francisco de Paula Sep 30 1949 [*remainder faint*]

envelope: *recto stamped* VIA AIR MAIL; *atop verso envelope EH writes* answered Sept 30 EH

address: *see {1}*

¶2.1 writing] r *over char.*

¶3.7 landing] a *over char.*

¶3.7–8 citizenship] n *over char.*

¶3.8 without] i *over* h

¶3.9 but you] y *over* I

¶3.10 got] o *over* e

¶3.10 little] *fol. by auto. del.* d

¶3.11 said] *auto.* id *over* y

¶3.14 contain,] , *auto. insert.*

¶3.22 listing] g *over* t

¶3.23 thing] i *over* n

¶4.6 to] t *over char.*

¶4.11 Scribner's] n *over* e

¶4.16–17 anything] a *and* n *merged*

¶4.18 it] i *over* t

¶4.20 about] abo *over* bou

¶4.20 from] r *over* f

¶5.2 and] an *over* nd

¶5.7 be] b *over* e

¶6.5 the] h *over* e

¶6.6 mention] o *over* n

¶7.2 tossed] *1st* s *over* o

¶9.3 word] d *over char.*

¶11.1–2 If . . . E.] *auto. insert.*

{16}

postmarks: *on recto* New York 28 Sept 1949 4 pm *and* New York 29 Sept 1949 [*remainder faint*] *and* San Francisco de Paula Habana 1949 [*remainder faint*]

address: *see {1}*

verso of envelope: *airmail envelope reads* Hearst Magazines Inc./and affiliated companies/ 57th Street at Eighth Avenue/New York 19, N.Y.; *atop envelope EH writes:* answered Oct 3 '49 EH.

recto of envelope: *stamped* Returned for additional postage of 2 cents Foreign Air Mail must be fully prepaid Weight of letter ½ ounce 8 cents for each G.P.O.D.M. Clerk No. 112 *all numbers auto. insert. by unknown hand*

¶2.1 the] e *over* 4

¶2.11 whose] s *over* '

¶4.4 courier] *prec. by* x's *over* cuo

¶4.10 thinking] nki *merged*

¶5.7 grow young] *1st* g *over* f

¶5.9 seasons] g *auto. del. fol.* n

¶5.11 it] it's

¶7.1 us] u *over* t

{17}

Atop letter reads Rec'd Oct 2.48 [8 *altered from* 9]

¶2.1 the] *fol. by* x *over char.*

¶2.6 Scribner] *divided at edge of sheet between* b *and* n

¶2.9 sturdy] *prec. by* x's *over* strud

¶4.1 alarmed] *prec. by* x's *over* la

¶5.4 especially] *final* l *appears at edge of sheet*

{18}

dictated to Juanita Jensen

postmark: *faint*

address: Edward Hotchner/COSMOPOLITAN MAGAZINE/57th at 8th Avenue/New York 19, New York

inside address: Edward Hotchner, Esquire [*then as above*]

verso of envelope: see {2}

¶2.3–4 Hotchner . . . Sigel.] *auto. insert.*

¶3.2 old,] *auto. insert.* ,

¶3.2 lovely,] *auto. insert.* ,

¶3.13 Layed] *auto. over* Laided

¶3.13 (I . . . layed)] *auto. insert.*

¶3.16–17 (she did it)] *auto. insert.*

¶5.7 weeks] *auto. insert.*

¶8.1 this] *insert. ab.* /

¶9.1 proofs] p *over* o

¶12.1 destroyed] *interl. ab.* x's *over* disappointed

¶13.2 Ernest] *auto. insert. by Juanita Jensen*

{19}

postmark: Habana Cuba Oct 3 1949 2 pm

address: *see {13}*

verso of envelope: *see {2}*

Following date EH writes (0645)

¶3.1 accurately,] *auto. insert.* ,

¶3.3–4 Can . . . Charlie.] *auto. interl.*

¶5.3 purpose] puorpuse *auto.* orp *over* rpo

¶6.2–3 We . . . security.] *auto. interl.*

¶8.5 yesterday] yesterday.

¶8.5 Sunday.] *auto. insert.*

¶8.7 Nourish] *auto. insert.* u

¶9.1 Earl] *prec. by* x's *over* ear

¶9.1–2 I . . . birthday.] *auto. interl.*

¶9.2 bucks'] bucks∧

¶10.3 leaves?] *auto. insert.* ?

¶10.4 long] g *over* f

¶10.5 word).] word)∧
¶10.7 Yellowstone] n *over* m
¶10.8 deck] *auto. del. fol.* e
¶12.3 buy] bbuy *2nd* b *over* e
¶13.1 Sat.] Sat∧
¶13.4 Very . . . charge.] *auto. interl.*
¶14.5 Ringlings] *auto. insert. 1st* n
¶15.1 noble] b *over* v
¶15.8 dedicates] *2nd* d *over* s
¶16.1 front] *prec. by* x's *over* feet
¶17.1 wouldn't] t *over* 'y
¶17.4–5 But . . . line.] *auto. interl.*
¶20.1–23.2 Roberto . . . EH] *auto. insert.*
¶20.1 etc.] etc∧
¶21.1 don't] don∧t
¶21.3 isn't] isn∧t
¶21.3 Tolstois] *interl. ab. caret*
¶22.1–2 OK EH] *circled*

{20}
Top margin reads Rec Oct 6.48 *in unknown hand*
¶2.4 dead] *final* d *over* l
¶2.6 recapitulate] lat *over* ale
¶2.6 see] *fol. by* x's *over about 47 chars.*
¶2.12 letters] *prec. by* x's *over* letter
¶3.1 received] rec *merged*
¶3.1 with] *prec. by* x's *over* wit
¶3.9 Scribner's] Scribner∧s
¶3.11 well . . . Cosmo] *auto. insert.*
¶5.1 couple] *prec. by* x's *over* cople
¶5.3 is] s *over* a
¶6.3 read] *prec. by* x's *over* cons
¶6.3 beyond] o *over* n
¶7.1 and there's] andthere's
¶7.3 battle.] battle∧
¶8.4 had] h *over* I
¶9.1 sure] u *over* r

{21}
letterhead: *on a preprinted form with* Cosmopolitan *printed at head and* Lot 709 50M
    4–48 *at foot*
Top margin reads Rec Oct 7.48 *in unknown hand*

{22}

dictated to Juanita Jensen

postmark: Habana Cuba Oct 12 1949 12 [*faint*]m

verso of envelope: *see {2}*

inside address: *see {18}*

¶10.1–2 Mister . . . Nita)] *auto. insert. by Juanita Jensen*

{23}

postmark: New York Oct [*faint*] 1949 1:30 [*faint*]

verso of envelope: Hotchner/405 East 54th/New York City *and recto marked by EH* answered October 20 1949 *and stamped* VIA AIR MAIL

¶2.4 (a . . . achieved)] *auto. insert.* (*and*)

¶2.5 loosen] *prec. by* x *over* p

¶2.5 will] *auto. insert. ab. caret*

¶3.8 the way] theway

¶3.8 fit] *fol. by indeciph. chars. interl.*

¶3.9 sports] r *over* t

¶3.9 Woodling,] Woodling∧ *appears at edge of sheet*

¶3.10 Raschi] *auto. insert.* s

¶4.4 fact] t *over* e

¶4.6 Yankees] a *over* z

¶4.8 artist] *fol. by* x *over* s

¶4.10 prefer] *1st* e *over* f

¶4.12 better] *2nd* e *over* r

¶4.13 work] *fol. by* x's *over* all

¶5.2 checks] *auto.* e *over char.*

¶5.4 very] e *and* r *merged*

¶5.8 Sat. Eve.] Sat∧ Eve∧

¶5.9 holds up] holdsup

¶5.10 $37,000.] *joined by an arrow with* two-installment

¶5.15 that] *fol. by* x's *over* I can't

¶5.19 read] e *over* a

¶5.21 wanted] *fol. by* x's *over* us to publish

¶5.24–25 how you] *fol. by* x's *over* would

¶5.29 and it] andit

¶5.31 Ernest] E *over* e

¶5.31 contract] a *over char.*

¶5.37 Roper),]) *fol. by* x *over* ,

¶5.41 not] t *over char.*

¶5.43 quietly to] *fol. by* x's *over* the

¶8.1–4 Nita . . . time.] *auto. insert.*

{24}

dictated to Juanita Jensen

postmark: Habana Cuba Oct [*faint*] 1949 6 pm

envelope: *same recto as {2}; EH adds E fol. return address*

¶3.1 Dick] d *over char.*

¶7.5 you.] *Up to this point, Jensen uses pica type; page 2 is in elite type. Signature and post-script in EH's hand.*

¶11.1 Love . . . beautiful.] Love . . . beautiful∧ *auto. insert. by EH*

{25}

letterhead: *see {21}*

¶2.2 Scribner] n *over* m

¶2.3 one] o *over* I

¶2.6 trouble] b *over* v

¶2.8 future] t *over* r

¶2.12 it's] *2 or 3 chars. auto. del.*

¶2.13 Scribner] *foll. by* x's *over* was what I wasz

¶3.1 and] *interl. ab. caret*

¶4.1 delay] *interl. ab. del.* dealy

¶4.4 go] g *over* d

¶4.10 cable] *prec. by* x's *over one word*

¶4.12 because] a *over* z

¶4.16 But] *auto. insert. over chars.*

¶4.18 handle] *foll. by* x's *over rest of*

¶5.1 had] d *over* s

{26}

time of cable 10:52 pm

{27}

time of cable 15 10:10 am

{28}

time of cable 9:42 am

¶1.2 605] *auto. interl. ab. caret by unknown hand*

¶1.2 KEY WEST FLORIDA] KEYWESTFLORIDA

¶1.7 NEW YORK] NEWYORK

¶1.12 SO FORTH] SOFORTH

¶1.13 COMMA] COMA

{29}

In this letter dated "Sunday" AEH claims to "have just written" Nita Jensen; his letter to Jensen is dated 30 November 1949 (JFKL), which would suggest that this missive was written on the following Sunday, December 4, 1949.

¶2.1 are having] arehaving
¶2.3 on] o *over* n
¶3.2 on] o *over* i
¶3.3 that] *prec. by* x's *over* hat
¶4.3 are] ar *merged*
¶4.3 as I] *fol. by* x's *over* told
¶5.1 and] *prec. by* ad

{30}
postmark: Venezia Ferrovia Espressi 1 2 50•15
address: *see* {8}
return address on verso of envelope: E. Hemingway/Guaranty Trust Co. of N.Y./4
 Place de la Concorde/Paris France
Taped tear on page 2 obstructs nothing
¶8.2 called] *fol. by* x's *over* to
¶11.12 When] *prec. by* x's *over* If
¶20.1 Will . . . EH.] *auto. insert.*

{31}
postmark: Venezia Corrpacchi Espressio 20 2 50•15
address: Ed. Hotchner Esq./415 West 21st St/New York City/Estati Uniti D'America/
 Personal.
¶2.2 practical] *fol. by* x *over* ?
¶5.1 Oh well.] *prec. by* x's *over* We came down from
¶6.4 N.Y.] N∧Y∧
¶6.4 Savoy] o *over* i
¶9.3 and] *fol. by* x's *over* I had picked something up
¶9.6 Crstalymina] s *over* y
¶10.2 Dr.] *prec. by* x's *over* Think that my face
¶20.1 Tell . . . appendicitis] *insert.*

{32}
postmark: Venezia Ferrovia Expressi 9. 3. 50•17
address: *see* {31}
Beneath date EH writes Venice
¶2.1 March] a *over* r
¶2.3 What . . . Hotchnera?] *auto. insert.*
¶4.1 Padova,] *fol. by* x's *over* Verona
¶5.3 spoke] *prec. by* s *over* a
¶6.1 with . . . wind] *auto. interl. ab. caret*
¶7.1 see] *fol. by auto. del. about 16 chars.*
¶7.4 Ladies'] Ladie's
¶8.4 Been . . . good.] *auto. insert.*
¶10.1 gen.] / *over* G

¶10.3 unregistered] *prec. by* x's *over* unti
¶10.4 N.Y.] N∧y∧
¶10.5 Miami.] *fol. by* x's *over* If ferry running
¶13.1 as] as as
¶14.2 here] pere
¶15.2 N.Y.] N∧Y∧
¶16.1 She . . . worries.] *auto. interl.*
¶17.1 the whole] *auto. insert.* t
¶20.1 Best] *auto.*

{33}

Top margin reads Rec. Apr. 22. 50 *in EH's hand and left margin reads* Hutchner *in unknown hand*
¶1.2 for;] *auto. insert.* ;
¶1.8 finished] is *over* si; *fol. by* x's *over* 8 *chars.*
¶2.12 should] o *fol. by* x *over* o
¶3.5 going] n *over* g
¶3.5 gun] g *over* f
¶3.6 may] m *over* a
¶3.6 stationery] *auto.* e *over* a
¶4.8 also,] *fol. by* x's *over* just he
¶4.10 do] d *over* s

{34}

Top margin reads Rec May 12.50 *in unknown hand*
¶4.2 greatly] e *and* a *merged*
¶4.4 beach] a *over* z
¶4.4 grosses] ro *over* or
¶4.6 alcohol] ho *over* oh
¶4.8 Patrick] rick *over* irkc
¶4.10 sent] t *over* d
¶4.19 three] *prec. by* x's *over* the
¶4.20 so] s *over* z
¶5.5 make] m *over* a
¶5.9 pleasant] s *over* z
¶6.1 am] *fol. by auto. del. about* 8 *chars.*
¶6.2 the World] theWorld
¶7.1 and does] anddoes
¶8.1 look] *1st* o *over* l

{35}

Top margin reads Rec May 22. 50 Ans Jul 4.50 *in unknown hand*
¶2.10 had] d *over* s
¶3.7 as] s *over* z

¶4.4 wasn't] w *over* a
¶5.1 Mary,] y *over* i

{36}

Top margin reads Rec Jun. 7. 50 *in unknown hand; rust mark from paper clip obscures noth-*
ing. On a scrap of paper AEH writes Ernest—A carbon of a letter just sent to Ann
Marie. Hotchner. *The letter to Anne Marie is dated* 30 May 1950. *Atop EH's carbon of*
Anne Marie's letter reads Rec Jun 29. 50 *and verso of letter reads* answered with my
　letter of July 4 1950 EH.
¶2.1 enclosed] *interl. ab.* x's *over* following
¶3.1 Captain,] CAptain *half of* A *strikes page*
¶4.1 poor] *1st* o *over* p
¶4.11 in] *fol. by* X *over* t
¶7.1–2 June . . . know.] *auto. insert.*

{37}

Above date, EH types The Finca
¶2.2 give] *interl. and fol. by* x *over* n
¶2.5 trough)] trough∧
¶2.7 One of] *interl. ab.* The
¶4.7 Kid.] Kid∧
¶6.2 on] o *over* a
¶6.3 all.] all..
¶8.2 N.Y.] N∧Y∧
¶8.2 two] *prec. by* x's *over* too
¶8.6 I should] *fol. by* x's *over* have
¶10.1 2] *prec. by* x's *over* "nd
¶10.2 and The] T *over* t
¶10.2 publish The] T *over* t
¶10.7 though] o *over* e
¶16.1 doing] i *over* o
¶19.3 most] *prec. by* x's *over* al
¶19.5–6 and . . . good] *auto. insert.*
¶19.6 was where the] was the
¶22.1 Best always] *auto.*

{38}

postmark: *on recto* Habana Cuba Oct 13 1950 [*remainder faint*]; *verso bears faint post-*
mark
address: Personal/Ed. Hotchner Esq./RFD # 2/WESTON, Connecticut/Estados Unidos
envelope: *recto preprinted* CORRERO AEREO—AIR MAIL *and verso same as* {2}
¶3.1 Here] H *over* h
¶3.1 it] i *over* t
¶3.2 relayed] *prec. by* x's *over 2 chars.*

¶3.2 Louella] *2nd* l *over* k

¶3.6 millions] milions

¶3.9 on the] n *over* f

¶3.9 on] o *over* .

¶3.10 Gentlemen] tl *merged*

¶5.1 97,000] *prec. by auto. del. of* (7

¶5.2 Sep.] Set.

¶5.4 wrote] ro *over* vi

¶5.8 and hung] nd hung

¶5.9 garage] x *over* g *prec.* r

¶6.1 Gigi's] *auto. interl. ab. auto. del. 7 or 8 chars.*

¶6.1 Salsberg] *auto. insert.* Sals

¶6.3 but] *prec. by* x's *over* Also

¶6.5 amputating] p *over* u

¶6.5 saying] s *over* .

¶7.5–6 <u>wunder-kinde.</u>] <u>wunder-kinde</u>∧

¶7.6 Marie] *fol.* r *auto.* i *over 2 del. chars.*

¶8.1 know] *arched line joins* o *and* w

¶9.1 Collier's] Collier∧s

¶9.1 piece] *prec. by* x's *over* pie

¶9.3 and . . . it.] *auto. insert.*

{39}

postmark: *on recto* New York Nov 7 1950 8pm *and on verso* Habana Cuba Nov 8 1950 9pm

envelope: *on recto AEH writes* <u>AIR MAIL.</u> *On verso EH notes* write <u>Hotch</u> Rec'd 9/11/50 answered 15/11/50

return address on verso of envelope: *as in letterhead of {36}*

¶3.4 Paris] P *over* p

¶3.10 indicating] c *over* v

¶3.10 I] I *over* i

¶4.6 than] a *over* z

¶4.7 else,] *auto. insert.* ,

¶4.7 at] a *over* z

¶5.2 Schulberg] Sch *merged*

{40}

postmark: Habana Cuba Nov 16 1951 1 am

address: E. A. [*sic*] Hotchner Esq./415 West 21st Street/New York 11, N. Y./Estados Unidos/<u>Personal</u>.

envelope: *see {38}*

¶2.1 Collier's] Collier∧s

¶2.3 surreptitious] e *over* r

¶2.4 Anyway] *fol. by* x *over char.*

¶6.1 day] d∧ay d *fol. by faint* a
¶8.4 Gregorio).] Gregorio)∧
¶8.5 i.e.] i∧e.
¶8.5 and] *fol. by* x *over* a
¶8.7 was] a *over char.*

{41}

Top margin reads Rec Dec 6. 50 Ans Dec 7. 50 *in unknown hand.* Dated Monday New
   York *by AEH. The conjectural date of December 4 was arrived at by subtracting the two
   days required for air mail delivery from* Dec 6.
¶2.8 stateside] ate *merged*
¶2.9 equal] *fol. by* x's *over* U.S.
¶3.2 gave] *fol. by* x's *over* me
¶4.4 understand] t *over* a
¶4.6 like to] o *over* p
¶4.11 it's] it
¶5.1 a] a *over* i
¶5.4 thought] *fol. by* x's *over* youd
¶5.6 he'd] d *over* s
¶5.9 due] e *over* o
¶7.3 cashiers] *1st* s *over* h
¶7.4 no] *fol. by* x *over* t
¶11.1 for sale.] *auto. insert.*
¶12.1–3 Good . . . monotony.] *auto. insert.*

{42}

postmark: Habana Cuba 1950 9:30 pm [*remainder faint*]
address: *as in letterhead of* {36}
¶1.1 Ed] *fol. by* x *over* f
¶2.3 still] x *over* o *fol.* t
¶4.7 doing] i *over* j
¶5.3 watch] *prec. by* x's *over* wt
¶5.4 it] to
¶6.6 before] foll *by* x's *over* .But
¶6.8 up)] up,
¶6.9 animals] snimals
¶6.10 write] *prec. by* x's *over* right
¶6.12 specialty] p *over* r
¶8.5 child's] chuld's
¶10.1 he] e *over* t
¶10.1 1st] ist
¶10.4 *one*] ione
¶10.4 five] *prec. by* x's *over* fiv
¶11.1 Sir] *prec. by* x's *over* Si5r

¶13.2 carbon.] *prec. by* x's *over* crabon.

¶15.4 ever] even

¶15.4 has] s *over* d

¶17.1 And] and

¶19.3 Collier's] Collier∧s

¶19.4 never] *prec. by* ne *over* ro

¶19.9 their] r *over* t

¶19.9 mystique] i *over* y

¶20.5 more] x's *over* mor

¶20.6–7 uncorrected] *2nd* r *over* f

¶20.8 bite,] bite.

¶20.8 but] *prec. by* x's *over* Bu

¶23.1 and you] and and you

¶23.3 crowded] r *over* f

¶24.1 said] sqid

¶24.1 on] *fol. by* x's *over* q,

¶26.1–3 You . . . Papa.] *on verso*

{43}

postmark: *on recto* New York NY Dec 19 1959 9:30 am *and on verso* San Francisco de Paula Dec 21 1950 4:30 pm *also verso* Habana Cuba Dec 20 1950 2pm

address: *see* {40}

envelope: *recto marked* Air Mail *by AEH and verso marked by EH* write Hotch/Received 21/12/50 answered Jan 5–52

¶3.2 you] y *over* Y

¶3.6 because] a *over* z

¶3.7 air] *auto. interl. ab. caret*

¶3.8 these] *1st* e *over* a

¶3.14 say] *auto.* y *over* w

¶3.19 toward] w *over* s

¶3.27 continent] x *over char. prec. 2nd* t

¶4.1 (if . . . me)] *auto.* (*and*)

¶4.1 if] f *over* s

¶4.2 When] h *over* e

¶5.3 and] a *over* z

¶5.5 demise] d *over char.*

¶5.5 performed] x's *over 8 chars.*

¶5.12 for] f *over* o

¶5.17 deals] s *over* z

¶5.30 writing] x *over* t *fol.* t

¶6.3 health—and] x *over* y *fol. 2nd* h

¶8.1–2 matters] m *over* t

¶8.5 has] *fol. by* x's *over 4 chars.*

¶8.6 has] s *over* z

¶10.1 Television] T *over* t

¶10.6 basis] si *over* is

¶10.7 future] u *over* t

¶10.10 that] a *over* z

¶10.13 them] m *over* .

¶10.22 I] I *over* i

¶10.29 about] a *over char.*

¶10.34 this] t *over* h

¶10.35 offer and] *fol. by* x's *over 17 chars.*

¶11.1 Next] *prec. by* x's *over 2 chars.*

¶11.2 Ritz] z *over* x

¶11.7 you,] *auto. insert.* ,

¶12.1 Your pal,] *auto. insert.*

{44}

postmarks: *on recto* New York NY Jan 2 [*faint*]pm 1951 *and* Habana Cuba 4pm [*remainder faint*] *and* San Francisco de Paula Habana ENE 1951

address: *see* {1}

envelope: *recto marked by EH* Received 4th Jan 51 answered Ed answered Jan 5 51 *and* AIR MAIL *preprinted on recto*

¶2.1 me] *fol. by auto. del.* but

¶4.13 Of . . . contract.] *auto. insert.*

¶4.14 Over] O *over* o

¶4.14 of a] / *fol.* of

¶7.1 good] g *over char.*

¶7.2 guy.] . *over* l

¶9.3 $14,760] X *over* 9 *fol.* 0

¶10.8 Too . . . $750] *auto. insert.*

¶10.15–16 add . . . $16,840] *auto. insert.*

{45}

postmark: Habana 1951 [*remainder faint*]

address and envelope: *see* {40}

¶2.8 A.] A∧

¶4.1 A.'s] A∧'s

¶4.3 Lloyd's] LLoyd's *1st* L *over* l

¶5.1 Mouse] *prec. by* x's *over* Naturally

¶7.2 defects] e *over char.*

¶10.1 that] that.

¶10.4 piece] *prec. by* x's *over* pice

¶10.7 for] *prec. by* x's *over* from

¶11.2 Brown] B *over char.*

¶17.1 can] *prec. by* x's *over* gan

¶18.2 Bitch)]) *over* (

{46}

postmark: *on recto* New York NY Jan 9 1951 10:30 pm *and* New York NY Jan 11 1951
4:30 pm *and on verso* Habana Cuba ENE 12 2 pm *also verso* San Francisco de Paula
[*remainder faint*]

stamped: Returned for additional postage [*indeciph.*] cents Foreign Air Mail must be
fully prepaid Weight of letter . . . Ounce . . . Cents for each 1/2 [*auto. insert.* 1/2 *by
unknown hand*] G. P. O. D. M.

address: *see {1}*

envelope: *On recto EH writes* answered Hotch 7/2/50 *AEH's return address preprinted as
in letterhead of {36}*

¶2.2 finished] *is over* si

¶3.1 that] *fol. by auto. del.* t *and 2 chars.*

¶3.3 yon] *fol. by auto. del. char.*

¶3.3 loose,] *fol. by auto. del.* that

¶3.7–8 I . . . something] *auto. underlined*

¶3.12–13 The . . . files.] *auto. interl.*

¶5.4 Joe] *prec. by x's over* he

¶5.14 cover] *interl. ab. x's over* pick up

¶6.2 be] *fol. by* x *over char.*

¶6.2 pleasant] l *over* o

¶8.1–3 You . . . Ed] *auto. insert.*

¶8.1 enclose] *fol. by auto. del.* d

{47}

postmark: *faint*

address: *see letterhead of {36}*

envelope: *see {2}*

¶2.2 Jan.] Jan∧

¶2.3 1400] *fol. by* x *over* 0

¶2.4 pooped] popped

¶2.4–5 Have . . . win.] *auto. interl.*

¶3.2 week's] week∧s

¶3.8 and] a *over* .

¶4.2 appearances] ear *merged*

¶5.2 Gulf Coast] GulfCoast

¶5.3 February] *prec. by x's over* Ja

¶5.4 from Feb.] from Feb∧

¶5.4 on Feb.] on Feb∧

¶5.5 Holiday] *prec. by* x *over* Hloiday

¶5.5 wish] *fol. by x's over* he

¶5.7 Adriana] Adrianna *prec. by x's over* She has

¶7.3 Maybe] *prec. by x's over* Could

¶8.3 dime's] dime∧s

¶9.3 same, (i.e.)] same∧ (i∧e∧)

¶9.3–4 (i.e.) . . . me.] *auto. insert.*

¶11.4 if] *fol. by* c *over* y

¶13.2 African] c *over* v

¶13.4 cover] *prec. by* x's *over* cobe

¶13.4 Also] *prec. by* Maybe a

¶13.5 The] T *over* t

¶13.6 Howrwit's] r *over* i

¶13.6 member] b *over* m

¶17.1 you.] you∧

{48}

postmarks: *on recto* New York, NY Feb 21 1951 10:30 pm *and on verso* San Francisco
    de Paula Feb 24 1951 [*remainder faint*]

envelope: *preprinted return address same as* {36} *and recto marked by EH* Received 23 Feb
    1951

¶2.4 five] *interl. ab.* /

¶2.6 immensely] n *over* e

¶2.9 I've] *prec. by* x's *over* I ne

¶2.12 well] first l *over* e

¶2.23 Society] ie *over* ei

¶2.25 enjoys] enj *merged*

¶2.27 in] *prec. by* x's *over* on

¶3.7 Carl] *half of a strikes page*

¶3.7 of N.B.C.] N *over* B

¶3.9 Rosenthal] *1st* e *over* n

¶3.12 named] d *over* e

{49}

postmark: Habana Cuba Mar 26 1951 6:30 pm

address: *same as letterhead of* {36}

envelope: *see* {2}

Dated Easter Sunday 1951

¶3.4 had;] had.;

¶3.4 so sore] e *over* t

¶5.6 novel.)] novel∧)

¶11.1 dough] h *fol. by* x *over* t

¶13.1 Best always] *auto.*

{50}

¶2.1 wire] *prec. by* x's *over* wri

¶2.3 radio] *arched line joins* d *and* o

¶3.4 Maupassant] p *fol. by auto. del. char.; arched line joins* p *and* s; sa *over* as

¶4.7 model] *auto. del. fol.* e; *arched line joins* e *and* l

¶6.2 Looks] k *over* i

¶6.4 one] n *over* h
¶6.5 certainly] n *over* h
¶6.9 shoe] e *over* w
¶6.11 on you] y *over* m
¶6.12 brake] *prec. by x's over* break

{51}

¶2.1 strike] *interl. ab. x's over* sttrike
¶2.2 in stride] d *over char.*
¶2.6–7 figured it] *fol. by auto. del. char.*
¶2.9 of] *prec. by x's over* oc
¶2.17 introduction] d *over* e
¶3.7 use] *prec. by auto. del.* u
¶4.4 enclosing] o *over* l
¶5.4 apologies] pol *merged*

{52}

postmark: Habana Cuba April 1951 9:30 pm [*remainder faint*]
address: *same as letterhead of {36} followed by* Estados Unidos
envelope: *see {38}*
¶2.3 readily] i *over* y
¶2.5 carefree] carfree
¶2.5 (Am] *prec. by x's over* (
¶2.5 fucking] fuckling
¶2.6 pitcher] tc *over* ct
¶2.7 James.] James∧
¶6.1 and 1157] and *auto. insert.*
¶6.3 week.] *fol. by* c *over* a
¶8.3 really] *prec. by* c's *over* goo
¶9.1 876] *auto.* 8 *over char.*
¶9.3 Colonel's] ' *over* s
¶9.7 exclusively] s *fol. by* x *over* e
¶11.4 in this] in in this
¶12.5 OK.] *auto. and circled*
¶12.5 EH] *auto. and circled*
¶12.5 musician] *prec. by* s's *over* mju
¶13.1 avoid] v *fol. by* x *over char.*
¶13.2 Taste] a *fol. by* x *over char.*
¶16.2 while] w *over* .
¶19.1 your] *auto.* y *over* t
¶19.1–2 Please . . . Jerry.] *auto.*

{53}

Top margin reads rec May 12.51 *in unknown hand*
¶2.6 ulcer] lc *over* ov
¶6.1 As ever] *auto.*

{54}

Top margin marked Rec Oct 13.51
¶2.6 all done] alldone
¶5.5 but that] butthat

{55}

Dated Thursday *and top margin marked* Rec Jan 19.52 *[Saturday]*
¶4.6 senior] s *over* d
¶4.9 could.)] *auto.*)
¶7.4 uncomfortable] *hyphen fol.* t *over* a

{56}

postmark: *faint*
address: A. E. Hotchner Esq./R.F.D 2 Old Redding Road/Weston Connecticut/Estados
    Unidos.
envelope: *recto same as {38}*
¶3.4 thicker] ticker
¶5.2 out] *fol. by* x's *over* and
¶5.3 Scribner's] Scribnerᴧs
¶6.6 editing?] editing.?
¶7.1 mean] *insert. and fol. by* x's *over* men
¶15.4 weather] t *over* r

{57}

Top margin marked Rec. Aug 4.52 Ans Aug 4. 52 *in unknown hand.*
¶2.9 entered] t *over* e
¶2.11 boom.] m *over char.*
¶3.3 nonetheless] *2nd* n *over* e
¶3.6 accomplished] i *over* k
¶4.2 Reader's] s *over* z
¶4.2 Digest] D *over char.*
¶4.8 details, and] *fol. by* x *over char.*

{58}

postmark: Habana Cuba Ago 6 1952 *[remainder faint]*
address: *see {56}*
envelope: *verso same as {38}*
¶2.6 development] devellpment
¶3.2 semitic?] ? *over* .
¶4.3 soon] *fol. by* x *over char.*
¶6.1 I've] I *over* .
¶7.3 Primo] i *over* o
¶7.9 raised] s *over* e

{59}

Top margin marked Rec Aug 24.52 *by unknown hand*

¶4.14 champ] a *over char.*
¶4.15 which] *fol. by* X *over char.*
¶4.15 just] *fol. by* x's *over* the
¶4.16 women's] s *over* z
¶6.3 lots of] lotsof
¶6.4 than] n *over* t
¶7.1 the] *interl. ab. / prec. by* x's *over* he

{60}
postmarks: *on recto* New York NY Feb 25 1953 7:30 pm *and verso* 1953 [*remainder faint*] *and* San Francisco de Paula Feb 27 1953 [*remainder faint*]
address: Mr. Ernest Hemingway, Esq./San Francisco de Paula/Havana, Cuba
envelope: *recto stamped twice* AIR MAIL *and marked* answered March 7 1953 *by EH*
verso of envelope: *same as letterhead of {36}*
¶2.7 also] *prec. by* x's *over* also
¶2.14 splendid] *prec. by* x's *over* speln
¶2.31 have] v *over* e
¶5.2–3 cottage] a *over* z
¶5.3 there] *auto. insert.* t
¶5.5 visit?] *prec. by auto. del. of 6 or 7 chars.*

{61}
postmark: *faint*
address: *same as letterhead of {36} with* Please Forward *added by EH*
envelope: *same as {38}; on verso EH adds* E. Hemingway.
¶2.1 Made . . . awful.] *interl.*
¶2.6 couldn't] couldnʌt
¶2.7 wouldn't] wouldnʌt
¶3.3 didn't] didnʌt
¶3.3 1865).] 1865)ʌ
¶4.4 Haven't] havenʌt
¶5.1 won't] wonʌt
¶7.2 isn't] isnʌt

{62}
postmark: New York NY July 13 1953 3pm [*Monday*]
address: Ernest Hemingway/Guaranty Trust Co/Place Vendome/ Paris, France
envelope: *recto marked* AIR MAIL *by AEH*
Letter dated Saturday
¶2.2 seeing] s *over* x
¶2.4 League.] *below 1st* e *is* _ *of another* e
¶4.8 buck] u *over* e

{63}

postmark: Valencia 25 Jul 53 [*remainder faint*]

address: [*by Mary Hemingway*] Edward Hotchner, Esq./ R.F.D.#2–Old Redding Road/<u>Weston, Conn.</u> (Westport)/Estados Unidos; *marked* Por Av [*remainder obscured by stamp*]

¶2.2 fine.] fine∧

¶2.7 mistake] *fol. by arrow pointing to* for you not to be with us.

¶2.7 M.] *circled*

¶2.7–8 (You . . . matadors!)] *insert. atop card by Mary*

{64}

letterhead: *same as* {62} *with autograph* 5 *altered from* 2 *fol.* R. F. D.

Date 12/1/53 *auto. insert. by AEH*

¶2.6 much,] *auto. insert.* ,

¶2.6 you,] *auto. insert.* ,

¶3.3 to stay] tostay

¶3.7 outside] t *fol. by* - *over* o

¶4.7 World] d *over* .

¶4.8 choreography] y *over* e *fol. by* x *over* r

¶4.12 Today] T *over* r

¶4.19 Thought] x *over* t *fol.* h

{65}

Date includes auto. insert. of 53 *by AEH*

¶]4.3 house] s *over* r

¶]4.3 going] *fol. by auto. del.* to

¶]4.9 only] *auto. interl. ab. caret*

¶]4.18 for] *interl. ab. auto. del. of 1 or 2 chars.*

¶]5.2–4 here . . . Love,] *auto. insert.*

{66}

postmark: Kenya [*city faint but initial* N *and concluding* i *suggests Naroibi*] Dec 24 1953 12:15 pm

address: *same as* {56} *with* USA *and* Estas Unis *added by EH*

envelope: *preprinted* By Airmail Par Avion *on recto and on verso* From E. Hemingway/c/oBarclay's Bank/Queensway/ Nairobi/Kenya./<u>B.E.A.</u>

¶2.3 never] *fol. by del. 9 or 10 chars.*

¶2.6 absolute] *interl. ab.* an release

¶4.1 without] *interl. ab. del. chars.*

¶4.9 mm.] mm∧ *fol. by del. char.*

¶4.10 Jaguar),] Jaguar∧,

¶4.11 M.] M∧

¶4.11 photographing] *fol. by del. char.*

¶4.14 It] *prec. by del.* N

¶5.1 (which]∧which

¶5.2 won't] won∧t

¶5.2 acct.] acct∧

¶6.4 Am] *prec. by del.* Have

¶6.8–9 (anywhere] ∧anywhere

¶9.1 and] *fol. del.* can, truly,

¶9.3 Can't] can∧t

¶9.6 shopping] *fol. by del. several words*

¶9.7 neighboring] *prec. by del. several chars.*

¶11.1 on Jan.] on Jan∧

¶11.2 Jan. 26] Jan∧ 26

¶11.2 15.] 15∧

¶12.4 home)"] home)∧

¶12.5 is] *fol. by del. char.*

¶12.7 donkeys.] *fol. by del.* "I k

¶13.2 service] *interl. ab. del. char.*

¶13.2 K.A.R.] K∧A∧R.

¶13.3 (not] ∧not

¶14.1 I'll] I∧ll

¶19.3 "Bwana] *prec. by del.* The

¶24.1 I] *prec. by del.* "

¶25.2 27th] 7 *over* 2

¶25.4 Dunnottar] *prec. by del.* boat

¶26.1 alleged] *interl. ab. caret*

¶26.3 2000.] *prec. by del. char.*

¶27.2 Paris.] Paris∧

¶29.1 both.] both∧

{67}

postmark: New York, NY Grand Central Station Feb 11 1954 5:30 pm

address: Ernest Hemingway/c/o Barclay's Bank/Queensway/ Nairobi, Kenya Colony/ British East Africa

envelope: *on recto by EH* Letter from hotch Re Ballet Personal to File EH.

¶2.7 pusher's] r's *merged*

¶3.7 Roy] y *over* u

¶3.7 as] *auto.* s *over* n *fol. by auto. del.* d

¶3.9 Theatre] x *over* r *fol.* h

¶3.10 that] *prec. by* x's *over* it

¶4.10 worth] w *over* o

¶5.7 opinion,] *1st* o *over* i

¶10.1–3 The . . . me.] *auto. insert.*

{68}

postmarks: *four faint postmarks*

address: A. E. Hotchner Esq./R.F.D. 5/Westport/Connecticut/U.S.A.

envelope: *on recto preprinted* By Air Mail/Par Avion *and verso auto.* From E. Hemingway/
   Gritti Palace Hotel/Venezia/Italia

¶2.5 good)] good∧

¶2.7 now.] *fol. by paragraph sign*

¶4.7 gliders] *fol. by del.* etc

¶4.10 1] *circled*

¶4.10 2] *circled*

¶5.1 doesn't] doesn∧t

¶5.5 up.] up∧

¶6.3 Governor.] Governor∧

¶6.4 part.] part∧

¶6.6 everything] *fol. by 3 del. chars.*

¶6.7 isn't] isn∧t

¶6.8 command] *prec. by 2 del. chars.*

¶7.1 180] *interl.*

¶7.4 One worthless] *prec. by del.* I

¶7.7 course] *prec. by 2 del. chars.*

¶7.8 don't] don∧t

¶7.9 Ernies] *prec. by 3 del. chars.*

¶7.11 Let's] Let∧s

¶7.12 Let's] Let∧s

¶7.12 everybody).] everybody)∧

¶8.6 better] *prec. by del.* b

¶8.9 something.] something∧

¶8.9 won't] won∧t

¶8.12 can't] can∧t

¶9.3 occasions] *prec. by 2 del. chars.*

¶9.6 Mr. Singh's] Mr∧Singh∧s

¶9.7 Mr.] Mr∧

¶9.7 with] *fol. by del. char.*

¶9.10 Mr.] Mr∧

¶12.3 motors."] motors∧"

¶16.2 Masai] *fol. by 2 del. chars.*

¶18.1 another's] another∧s

¶19.1 drivers] *fol. by del.* have

¶19.3 men] *prec. by del.* mens

¶20.3 release] *prec. by del.* shoot

¶27.1 can't] can∧t

¶29.1 each] *interl. ab. caret*

¶29.4 on] *fol. by del.* all

¶29.4 etc.] etc∧

¶32.10 flying] *fol. by del.* the

¶33.1 didn't] didn∧t

¶33.2 doesn't] doesn∧t

¶33.4 into] *fol. by del. char.*
¶33.12 can't] can∧t
¶33.12 I've] I∧ve
¶34.1 were] foll *by. del. chars.*
¶38.4 Couldn't] couldn∧t
¶38.4 acct.] acct∧
¶38.5 (looks . . . toothpicks)] *interl.*
¶38.7 we] *fol. by 3 del. chars.*
¶39.1 old] *prec. by 3 del. chars.*
¶42.2 Today's] Today∧s
¶44.1 shit] *fol. by del. comma and an arrow pointing to list of injuries*
¶44.1 EH.] EH∧ *circled*
¶44.2 writer.] writer∧

{69}
address: the *Francesco Morosini*
¶2.4 mean] m *over* a
¶2.18 rough] *fol. by* x *over* t
¶2.21 strength] e *over* n
¶3.5 her.] *auto. insert.*
¶3.5 have] a *over* q
¶4.6–7 (This . . . mind . . .)] *auto. insert.* (*and*)
¶5.6 Cordoba] ord *merged*

{70}
postmark: Venezuela Jun 28 1954 [*remainder faint*]
address: *see {68}*
¶2.4 Huston's] Huston∧s
¶3.1 N.Y.] N.Y∧
¶3.6 As] as
¶3.6 with you] *fol. by 2 del. chars.*
¶5.3 right] *prec. by del. chars.*
¶6.2 account] *fol. by del.* had be
¶6.3 by Scribner's] by Scribner∧s
¶6.3 for Scribner's] for Scribner∧s
¶6.5 hasn't] hasn∧t
¶6.9 But] *fol. by del.* it
¶7.3 bleeding] 2nd e *over char.*
¶7.6 out] *fol. by del.* the da
¶7.9 cooled out and] *interl.*
¶7.10 didn't] Didn't
¶9.2 through] *prec. by del.* throug
¶9.2 you] *prec. by del.* we
¶10.1 A.] A∧

¶11.1–2 The . . . bad.] *interl.*
¶13.4 this).] this)∧
¶13.4 A.] A∧
¶15.1–2 I . . . good.] *on verso*

{71}
postmark: *faint*
address: A. E. Hotchner Esq./R.F.D. #5/Westport/ Connecticut/Estados Unidos
envelope: *same as {38} and on verso EH adds* E. Hemingway.
¶2.1 wouldn't] wouldn∧t
¶3.5 etc.] etc∧
¶3.5 length] *fol. by del. chars.*
¶4.4 us] *prec. by del.* me
¶4.6 drunk).] drunk)∧
¶6.1 Mme.] Mme∧
¶6.1 Every] *prec. by 2 or 3 del. chars.*
¶7.4 She's . . . people.] *interl.*
¶9.3 won't] won∧t
¶17.1–18.2 How . . . Papa] *on verso*

{72}
postmarks: *on recto* New York, NY Nov 5 1954 2:30 pm *and verso* San Francisco de Paula
  Cuba 2pm [*remainder faint*]
address: Mr. Ernest Hemingway, Esq./Finca Vigia/San Francisco de Paula/Habana Cuba
envelope: *on recto EH writes* answered with later letter on Dec. 10th.54 EH
¶3.9 and he's] andhe's
¶3.17 had] d *over* v *fol. by auto. del.* e
¶6.3 you] u *over char.*
¶6.3 a] *over* I
¶6.5 my] y *over* e
¶6.7 probably] *prec. by* x's *over* maybe
¶6.14 probable] e *over* y

{73}
postmark: *faint*
address and envelope: *see {71}*
¶2.1 Your] *fol. by del. char.*
¶2.1 Am] am
¶3.1 not to] *fol. by del.* bu
¶3.3 (after . . . day)] (after . . . day∧. *insert.*
¶3.7 about,] *fol. by del.* being
¶3.10 maybe] *fol. by del. char.*
¶3.11 V1.)] V1.∧
¶4.1 etc.] etc∧

¶4.1 won't] won∧t

¶4.5 murder] *interl. ab. del.* muder

¶4.14 won't] won∧t

¶4.15 At] at

¶7.1 of photographers,] *interl.*

¶7.2 don't] don∧t

¶8.3 you've] you∧ve

¶8.9 about] *prec. by del.* how

¶10.3 before.] before∧

¶11.1 About] about

¶11.2 to] *fol. by del.* be

¶11.8 lovely] *fol. by del.* fall

¶14.3 writes] *fol. by 2 or 3 del. chars.*

¶14.4 Africa] *fol. by del.* where

¶14.4 sea. Can't] sea Can∧t

¶14.5 Can't go] Can∧t go

¶14.5 Can't stay] Can∧t stay

¶14.6 isn't] isn∧t

¶14.8 that's] that∧s

{74}

¶3.4 had worked] a *over* z

¶3.7 written you] written You

¶5.1 found] d *over* f

¶6.7 recorder] *1st* e *over* 4

¶6.12 bad] *prec. by* x's *over* poor

¶6.12 one.] *fol. by* x's *over* He came down on a late afternoon plane

¶8.17 people.] people..

¶9.1 resume] e *over* 4

¶9.1 Manning] M *over* m

¶9.15 was not] wasnot

¶9.16 book)] book∧

¶10.4 much] *prec. by* x *over* a

¶10.8 sought,)] *fol. by* y's *and* "#" *signs over 8 chars.*

¶11.6 baseball] basedall

¶13.1 regarding] *interl. ab.* x's *over* regaring

¶13.2 foot ball player] *fol. by* m's *over* and a worthless tennis player.

¶13.4 or] *fol. by* x's *over* fish

¶13.10 public] *prec. by* x *over* a

¶13.10 nor in stadiums] *auto. interl.*

¶13.10 so] *foll. by* x *over* ,

¶14.2 professional] proffesional

¶14.3 characters.] *fol. by* x's *over* I wish to disassociate

¶14.3 done] *fol. by* x's *over* everyt

¶15.2 TRUE'S] TRUE∧S

{75}
envelope: *see {71}*
¶3.3 had] *fol. by auto. del.* had
¶6.3 Japs] p *over* t
¶6.3 al.] al∧
¶9.1 he] he he
¶10.2 story] *fol. by x's over* I had
¶12.4 it] *auto. interl.*
¶12.5 stay] *fol. by auto. del. of 4 or 5 chars.*
¶12.7 how] *fol. by auto. del. 7 or 8 chars.*
¶14.1 Year's] Year∧∧
¶14.3 didn't] didn∧t
¶15.2 Year's] Year∧s
¶15.3 yest.] yest∧
¶15.5 rot] t *over* d
¶15.9 anti-biotics'] anti-biotics∧
¶16.1 Year's] Year∧s

{76}
postmarks: *on recto* Ormond Beach Fla Feb 21 1955 2 pm *and on verso* San Francisco de Paula Feb 23 1955 6 am
address: *see {72}*
envelope: *on recto EH writes* Feb 23 1955 write Hotch call [*indeciph.*] about salmon and [*indeciph.*] write Maestro *and* answered Hotch March 13. *On verso AEH writes* Hotchner, RFD 5, Westport, Conn.
letterhead: Orange Court Hotel, Orlando, Florida
¶3.19 although] *interl. ab. caret*
¶3.19 issue] *fol. by del.* but
¶4.6 ball-less] *fol. by del. 5 or 6 chars.*

{77}
postmark: 1955 [*remainder faint*]
address and envelope: *see {71}*
¶1.1 Dear] *arched line joins* e *and* a
¶3.2 Tourists] *fol. by x's over* that
¶3.3 from] *fol. by x's over 4 chars.*
¶4.1 economics] *prec. by x's over* mechanics
¶4.3 but] But
¶4.4 unless] u *over* i
¶5.2 time] *fol. by c's over* and
¶5.6 forth] *prec. by x's over* for them
¶5.8 help her] *prec. by x's over* get
¶5.11 improperly] impr∧perly
¶7.1 helping] *fol. by x's over* it so
¶9.2 kids I] kidsI

¶9.15 he'd] he's
¶9.19 Went] *fol. by* x's *over* to him
¶9.26 weak] *2nd* a *over* e
¶9.32 averaged] averages
¶9.36 boy's] boy∧s
¶13.4 confidential] *prec. by* x's *over* com

{78}
¶2.1 when] w *over* a
¶2.5 doing] *fol. by* x's *over* what
¶2.5 was] *fol. by* x's *over* being
¶2.9 needed:] *auto. insert.* : *fol. by auto. del.* to hear
¶2.24–25 The . . . man!] *auto. insert.*
¶2.26 Musial;] *auto. insert.* ; *fol. by auto. del.* and
¶2.27 in] n *over* a
¶2.36 no] *fol. by* x *over* t
¶3.5 but,] *fol. by* x's *over* more
¶3.10 ones,] *fol. by* x's *over* from my
¶3.11 quite] t *over* e
¶4.2 I] *fol. by* x's *over* have
¶4.4 candidate] candidate.
¶4.6 overwhelmingly] x *over 2nd* e
¶4.7 authoress] or *over* ro
¶4.10 dough] o *over* a
¶4.12 building] *fol. by* x's *over* the
¶5.2 physical] y *over* s *fol. by* x's *over* tear
¶5.11 Sea] x *over* r *fol.* a
¶5.12 he?] *over 2 chars.*
¶6.15–16 and as] s *over* z
¶6.17 and] *fol. by* x's *over* be
¶7.4 stretch] *auto. interl. ab.* x's *over* time
¶7.5 hope] o *over* p
¶7.6 non-billboarded] *2nd* b *over* l
¶8.1 Please] a *over char.*
¶9.1–11.2 Best . . . bet.] *auto.*

{79}
Top margin reads Rec May 28/55 *in unknown hand*
¶2.5 cards] d *over* x
¶3.3 quité] *auto.* ' *as accent*
¶4.2 Christ'ssake] 's *merged*
¶4.15 who] *fol. by* x *over* m
¶7.4 stay] say

{80}

postmark: Habana Cuba Jun 22 1955 [*remainder faint*]

address: A. E. Hotchner. Esq. etc./The Dawdlings/R.F.D. 5/Westport, Connecticut/ Estados Unidos

envelope: *see {38}*

date: EH typed the second digit of 22 over a 0, then retyped 22 in parentheses.

¶2.1 I'd] I∧d

¶2.2 wasn't] wasm't

¶2.3 Again] g *over* f

¶3.1 The] ∧he

¶4.3 children's] chi;dren's

¶4.4 nearly] y *over* t

¶5.1–2 conditions for] o *over* r

¶5.3 here.] here∧ *fol. by* (*over*)

¶5.3 something.] something∧

¶5.3 pm.] *fol. by* x's *over* and gets here

¶5.4 later and] *fol. by* x's *over* the

¶6.4 Durocher] Durcocher

¶8.3 laying] l *over* k

{81}

postmarks: *on recto* New York NY Jun 27 1955 7:30 pm *and on verso* Habana Cuba June 29 1955 3 pm

address: *see {72}*

verso of envelope: *marked* air mail *and preprinted with AEH's address as in {78}*

¶2.19 at] a *over* i

¶3.2 scripts] c *over* t

¶3.8 et al.] et al∧

¶6.1–2 This . . . Sunday.] *auto. insert.*

{82}

¶]3.3 rosé] *accent replaces* '

¶]3.6 Probably] ba *over* ab

¶]5.3 <over>] *auto.*

¶]6.1–3 Marlene's . . . H] *auto. on verso*

¶]7.1–4 Dear . . . H.] *auto. insert.*

{83}

postmarks: *on recto* Westport Conn Aug 31 1955 7 pm *and verso postmark faint*

address: *see {72}*

envelope: *stamped* Air Mail *on recto and verso*

¶2.3 ate] t *over* r

¶2.8 who] o *over* l

¶2.11 hurricanes] e *over* s

¶3.8 which] i *over* k
¶3.10–11 (I . . . stable)] *auto. insert.* (*and*)
¶3.17 wild] *auto. insert.* d
¶3.19 briefing] *arched line joins* b *and* r
¶3.20 sending] *arched line joins* s *and* e
¶4.7 time] m *over* j
¶5.1 told] d *over* x
¶7.1 well] w *over* s

{84}
postmark: Habana Cuba Dec 15 1955 4 pm
address: *see {71}*
envelope: *address and return address by Mary Hemingway*

{85}
postmark: paris, trier distribuaire No 7 14–9 18th 1956
address: Monsieur A. E. Hotchner Esq./La Residenza/Viale Emilia N. 22/Roma Italy
envelope: *envelope and letter are of same sheet and on verso* E.H./c/o Guaranty Trust Co of NY/4 Place de la Concorde Paris
¶2.1 Sept.] Sept∧
¶2.2 Luz] luz
¶2.3 this.)] this.∧
¶2.6 isn't] isn∧t
¶6.1 Am] am

{86}
postmark: *cut from envelope*
address: Mr. Ernest Hemingway, Esq/Care Guaranty Trust Co of N. Y./4 Place de la Concorde/Paris France
envelope: *on recto AEH writes* Please Forward Immediately *and on verso EH writes* answered Hotch 30/9/56
¶2.3 but Venice] V *over* b
¶2.5 first] s *over* l
¶2.8 Schoendienst] o *over* e
¶3.2 magnified] g *over* t
¶4.1 suggesting] *2nd* s *over* x

{87}
postmark: El Escorial Madrid Set 30 56.7t
address: *see {85}*
¶3.1 couldn't] couldn∧t
¶5.2–3 Jamie Ostos] *interl. ab.* friend of ours
¶7.4 pitchers.] pitchers∧
¶7.8 Valentino's] Valentinoes

¶10.1 haven't] haven∧t
¶11.3 worth).] worth)∧
¶18.1 Mary . . . Xmas.] *insert. top margin*

{88}
¶5.5–8.4 Thanks . . . thought.] *auto. insert.*

{89}
Beneath letterhead AEH includes his return address 33 Viale Villa Massimo, Rome
¶2.2 4th] <u>th</u>
¶2.2 3rd] <u>rd</u>
¶2.2 5th] <u>th</u>
¶2.3 6th] <u>th</u>
¶3.7 apotheosis] *circled by Mary and connected by line to bottom margin which reads* glo-rification, exhaltation—antithisis?
¶4.3–4 The...it?] *underlined by Mary*
¶4.10 27th] <u>th</u>
¶4.11 3rd] <u>rd</u>
¶5.9–6.1 Anyway . . . Hotchfoncied] *insert.*

{90}
postmarks: *recto* Roma pm [*remainder faint*] *and on verso* 17 1957 8 am San Francisco de Paula [*remainder faint*]
address: *see {1}*
return address: *see {85}*
envelope: *preprinted* Air Mail
¶2.7 blocks] l *over* o
¶2.10 crystal] r *over* 5
¶2.15 should] uld *merged*
¶3.4 manicured,] *auto. insert.* ,
¶3.9 Raphaels] h *over* a
¶4.6 *been] auto. underlined*
¶4.9 the man] the *fol. by* /
¶4.15 End] *fol. by* x *over* o
¶4.16 paragraphs] 1st p *over* s
¶4.25 write] e *over* 4
¶4.28 selling] *prec. by* x's *over* settl
¶5.4 to have] h *over* a
¶8.1–3 Hotchorama . . . water!)] *auto. insert.*

{91}
time of cable 8:30 pm
stamped: San Francisco de Paula (Habana)

{92}

postmarks: *verso* San Francisco de Paula Hab. Recibido May 27 1957 4 pm *and postmark on recto faint*

address: *see {72}*

envelope: *AEH's return address same as {82}*

¶2.9 70–10] final 0 *over* o

¶2.15 understand] *prec. by* x's *over* ap

¶3.4 letters] et *merged*

¶4.6 the] *fol. by* /

¶4.6 my] *auto. interl. ab. caret*

{93}

postmarks: *on recto* poste A. D. Roma 14–15 1957 *and on verso* Habana Cuba May 28 12–m 1957

address: *see {90}*

¶2.1 60] 6o

¶2.8 Fifty Fifty on] o *over* a *fol. by* x *over* d *fol.* n

¶2.9 average] *fol.* v *auto. del. char.*

¶3.5 I'm] *fol. by* x's *over* wr

¶3.5 right] r *over* w

¶3.10 Nippon] *prec. by* x *over* the Japanes

¶6.2 deserves] r *fol. by* x's *over* 2 *chars.*

¶7.5 anybody] *fol. by* x's *over* and

¶8.1 140] 14o

¶9.1–10.1 Reference . . . Papa] *auto. insert.*

{94}

postmarks: *on recto* Roma 26.6.957 *and* San Francisco de Paula Habana June 30 1957 8 am

address: *see {72}*

envelope: *see {90}*

AEH's return address atop letter same as address in {85}

¶2.21 aforementioned] *prec. by* x's *over* aofr

¶4.12 apparently] *auto.* e *over* a; *auto. del. fol.* t; *arched line joins* t *and* l

¶4.19 Cipriano] pr *over* rp

¶5.4 ice] e *over* r

¶5.10 because] s *over* x

¶5.11 Wilson's.] s *over char.*

¶7.3 With] *prec. by* x's *over* If you

¶7.5 evening,] *auto. insert.* ,

{95}

postmark: Roma [*remainder faint*]

address: *see {72}*

envelope: *see {90}*

{96}

¶2.3 from] o *over* l
¶2.4 came] *auto. insert.*
¶2.6 ALFRED.] AlFRED∧
¶3.2 I] *over* e *prec. by* x *over* h
¶3.2 acct.] acct∧
¶3.4 So] S
¶3.6 N.Y.] N∧Y∧
¶3.6 Sept.] Sept∧
¶3.7 worried] wrorried
¶3.7 he'd] ' *over* l
¶5.1 6th] *interl. ab.* x's *over* fifth
¶5.4 to] o *over* l
¶5.4 normal). normal∧
¶5.5 tests] *fol. by* d *over* s
¶5.7 ticker] *fol. by* x's *over* under
¶7.1 steadily] stadily
¶7.2 Mary] r *over* f
¶7.2–3 mistreated] x *over* r *prec.* r
¶7.4 had] *fol. by* x's *over* $48
¶7.4 G] g
¶7.6 very] *fol. by* x's *over* exp
¶7.9 But] *fol. by* x *over* h
¶8.2 other] *prec. by auto. del.* toeber
¶8.3 cheer] c *over* s
¶8.5 Madrid] Madris
¶8.5 speed] *fol. by* x *over* m
¶8.7 explaining] p *and* in *auto. insert.*
¶8.9 clean.] clean∧
¶9.1 weights] *prec. by* x's *over* wights
¶10.1 up.] up∧
¶11.1 interrupt] x *over indeciph. fol.* n
¶12.2 interest] *2nd* e *over* r
¶13.1 Jerry] *prec. by* x's *over* your

{97}

¶2.8 3rd] r̲d̲
¶3.11 5th] t̲h̲

{98}

¶2.3 Scuttlebutt] *2nd* u *over* b

{99}

¶3.13 classy] *prec. by* x's *over* calss
¶7.1 Thanks . . . love.] *auto.*

{100}

postmarks: *on recto* New York, NY Nov 16 1957 2:30 am *and on verso* San Francisco de Paula Nov 18 [*remainder faint*]

address: *see {72}*

envelope: *AEH's return address label affixed to verso* A. E. Hotchner R. F. D. 5 Westport, Conn. *also on verso EH writes* Answered Dec 7 1957

¶3.7 land] *prec. by* x's *over* alnd

¶3.8 could] *auto.* c *over* w

¶3.12 speed] *1st* e *over* p

¶5.1–7.2 I have . . . stories.] *auto. insert.*

{101}

postmark: *stamp and postmark removed*

address: Monsieur Ed Hotchner/Hotel Roches Noires/Trouville (Calvados) France/Francia

envelope: *see {38}*

¶2.2 clippings).] clippings)∧

¶3.1 to] *fol. by 2 del. chars.*

¶3.3 Mary . . . both] *interl.*

¶4.1 how] *fol. by del. char.*

¶4.2 in for me] *interl.*

¶4.4 tax] *fol. by del. char.*

¶4.6 months'] months∧

¶4.6–7 collections] *fol. by del.* of

¶4.7 accounting system] *interl.*

¶4.11 Don't] Don∧t

¶5.2–3 Told . . . Indian Fakir] *interl.*

¶7.3–4 on . . . him] *insert. ab. caret*

¶7.4 ignorance] *interl. ab. del. chars.*

¶7.4 him.] him∧

¶8.1 for me] *interl. ab. caret*

¶8.3 demand.)] demand∧)

¶9.1–14.2 Have . . . Papa] *verso*

{102}

time of cable 7:27 am

{103}

postmark: Habana Cuba Ago 28 1958 11 pm

address: *see {71}*

¶2.1 Hadn't] Hadn∧t

¶2.1 acct.] acct∧

¶3.1 must] *interl. ab. caret*

¶3.3 and] *fol. by del.* it

¶3.3 didn't] didn∧t
¶4.1 i.e.] i∧e.
¶4.2 not] *fol. by del. 1 or 2 chars.*
¶5.2 latest] *interl.*
¶7.3 He'd] He∧d

{104}
¶2.7 straight] i *over* g
¶2.9 mobsters] t *over* e
¶2.9 Genoa-on-south] *auto. insert.* - *and* -
¶2.11 though the] *fol. by* x *over* y
¶2.15 unrelated] *2nd* e *over* i
¶2.18 Ritz] z *over* x
¶2.18 after the] afterthe
¶3.4 saw] w *over* y
¶3.6 Spahn's] *2nd* s *over* z
¶3.9 probably] a *over* c
¶4.1–5.2 Would . . . Kai-hetchk] *auto. insert.*

{105}
postmark: Ketchum Idaho Nov 6 1958 10 am
address: *same as {71} excluding* Estados Unidos

{106}
postmark: *on recto* Dec 19 1958 1230 pm *and on verso* Ketchum Idaho Dec 22 1958 4
pm
address: Mr. Ernest Hemingway, Esq./General Delivery/ Ketchum, Idaho
envelope: *preprinted* Air Mail *and return address same as letterhead of {76}*

{107}
¶1.1 Dear] a *over* q
¶3.3 celebrated] l *over* e
¶4.9 it.] *fol. by* x's *over* and make
¶4.15 thing,] *auto.* ,
¶4.16 wander] d *over* t
¶4.17 with] w *over* q *and* i *over* t
¶5.2 fits] t *over* c
¶6.1–7.1 Kiss . . . Hotchminguin] *auto. insert.*

{108}
time of cable 4:28 pm
address: Ernest Hemingway, Care Guaranty Trust Company/4 Place de la Concorde,
Paris *and marked* Refrd. to Madrid 26/5/59 *in unknown clerk's hand, followed by indeciph. initials*

¶1.6 WHEN] HEN
¶1.13 BULLS] GULLS
¶1.14 AL.] AL∧

{109}
¶4.2 minute)]) *over* ,
¶4.2 minute),] *fol. by* x's *over* on July lst
¶4.8 on] o *over* a
¶5.1–6.2 Can . . . bring?)] *auto. insert.*
¶5.2 Blvd.] Blvd∧

{110}
address: Chateau Marmont/8221 Sunset Blvd/Hollywood California
¶4.1–2 can't you can't] can∧t you can∧t
¶4.2 Zaragoza.] Zaragoza∧
¶4.3 doesn't] doesn∧t
¶4.6 don't] don∧t
¶5.1 Bill's] Bill∧s
¶6.5 too.] too∧
¶7.3 Juan] *prec. by del.* the rest
¶7.4 crazies] *fol. by del.* are
¶7.5 prospect.] prospect∧
¶8.3–10.1 All . . . good.] *insert.*
¶8.6 ETA] *prec. by del.* arri

{111}
time on cable 10:23 am
postmark: Malaga Spain Jun 19 1959
address: *see {78}*
¶1.3 ANTONIO'S] ANTONIO∧S
¶1.4 ETC.] ETC∧

{112}
time on cable 12:25 pm
address: Hillandale Road/R. F. D. 5/Westport, Conn.

{113}
postmarks: *on recto* Gibralter Ju 19 59 4 pm [*remainder faint*] *and* Los Angeles Calif
    Terminal Annex June 23 1130 am
address: same *as {110} and forwarded to AEH's address in {112}*
¶2.5 won't] won∧t
¶3.1 find] *fol. by del.* what
¶3.2 you've] you∧ve
¶3.2 winter.] winter∧

{114}

address: Sr. Don A. E. Hotchner/E [*indeciph. char.*]S P.M./ <u>Hotel Suecia</u>
envelope: *on recto preprinted* Hotel Suecia Madrid
¶3.1 6 pm] *fol. by del. char.*
¶3.1 Carleton] *prec. by del.* Carll
¶4.1 Alicante] *prec. by del.* Valea
¶4.3 Kilometer] *prec. by del.* mile
¶6.1 that's] that∧s
¶6.1 Terribly] *fol. by del.* y
¶6.1 today's] today∧s
¶6.1 Am] am
¶6.2 shape.] shape∧
¶11.1–2 We . . . EH.] *insert.*
¶11.1 plates.] plates∧

{115}

Top margin marked ans. 14/9/59 *by unknown hand*
¶2.4 Le] e *over* a

{116}

postmark: Alicante Sept 8 1959
address: *see {112}*

{117}

Atop letter EH writes Answered 17/9/59
¶2.3 special?] *auto.* ?
¶2.5 smooth,] *auto.* ,
¶4.9 I will let] i *over* l
¶5.1 ever] *fol. by* x *over* y
¶8.2 last] l *over* t
¶8.4 opinion:] *auto.* :
¶8.9 him] h *over* l
¶13.1 Cavaliere] C *over* c
¶14.1 AEH] *auto.*

{118}

dictated to Valerie Danby-Smith; signed by EH
postmark: Malaga Sept 17 1959
address: To Baron A. E. Hotttchner, Esq *then same as {112}*
envelope: *on recto EH writes* Attention A. E. Hotchner
¶2.12 Florida.] Florida∧
¶4.4 Oct.] Oct∧
¶4.4 hope] *fol. by del. char.*

{119}
Atop letter Danby-Smith writes 20.9.59
¶2.2 like] *prec. by* lil
¶3.5 (The . . . right.)] (The . . . right∧) *insert.*
¶5.2 Wonderful crisp] *fol. by del.* lel

{120}
dictated to Valerie Danby-Smith; signed by EH
postmark: faint
address: *same as {112} with return address same as in {118}*
envelope: *preprinted* Hotel Suecia—Madrid
¶2.8 insider's] insider∧s
¶3.2 summarize] summarise
¶3.12 promotion] permotion
¶3.12 Zaragoza] Zaragosa; Z *over* S
¶3.25 was allowed] *interl. ab. del.* got
¶3.27 no] *fol. by del.* t
¶3.36 Lima] L *over* l
¶4.3 Auteuil.] Auteuil∧
¶5.1 What] h *over* P
¶6.9 explained] p *over char.*

{121}
dictated to Valerie Danby-Smith
postmark: Malaga Sept 22 1959 [*remainder faint*]
address: *see {112}*
¶2.1 Sept.] Sept∧
¶2.2 deliver] *interl. ab. del.* send
¶2.3 Quays] *interl. ab. del.* keys
¶3.4 American's] American∧s
¶3.4 Oct.] Oct∧
¶4.1 Le Havre] *prec. by del.* New York
¶4.1 Oct.] Oct∧
¶4.11 will] *fol. by del. char.*

{122}
letterhead: Chateau Marmont/8221 Sunset Boulevard/Hollywood 46, California/
    Oldfield 6–1010
Rust stain from paper clip in the upper left-hand corner obscures nothing
¶2.3 stated] *arched line joins* s *and* t
¶2.5 Placid] P *over* p
¶3.14–16 This . . . the 59.] *circled, with an attached arrow pointing to left margin*
¶3.16–19 Just . . . best.] *auto. insert. left margin*
¶4.2 Antonio] *prec. by auto.* /
¶6.1 Have . . . book.] *auto. insert. top margin*

{123}

dictated to Valerie Danby-Smith; signed by EH

postmark: Paris 1959 [*remainder faint*]

address: *see {105}*

¶2.2 etc.] etc∧

¶2.7 hate] t *over* d

¶2.8 satisfactorily] *1st* t *over* a

{124}

¶3.1 Chas.] Chas∧

¶3.1 Scribner] n *over* b

¶3.2 best thing] bestthing

¶3.3 trying] y *over* i

¶4.2 turn] *prec. by auto. /*

¶4.3 contract] *2nd* c *over* d

¶8.1 Nov.] N *over* n

¶8.4 for] f *over* v

¶8.5 have] *fol. by* x's *over* taken

{125}

¶1.1 BILL'S] BILL∧S

¶1.1 DON'T] DON∧T

¶1.1–2 DECISION SERIOUSLY] DECISIONSERIOUSLY

¶1.2 YOU'RE] YOU∧RE

{126}

postmark: Habana Cuba Nov 9 1959 3 pm

address: 6 West 77th Street (Apt 11A)/New York City, New York/Estados Unidos

¶2.1 All] all

¶3.1 I've] I∧ve

¶3.2 pin.] *fol. by interl. del. char.*

¶3.4 Don't] Don∧t

¶3.6 year's] year∧s

¶3.6 me] *interl. ab. caret*

¶3.12 won't] won∧t

¶3.12 simply do] *fol. by del.* s

¶5.1 I'm] I∧m

¶5.1 beat] *fol. by del. char.*

¶7.1 That's] That∧s

¶8.2 won't] won∧t

¶8.3 changes.] changes∧

¶10.1 day after] *interl. ab. caret*

¶10.2 mine).] mine)∧

{127}

postmark: Ketchum Idaho Dec 19 1959 5 pm

address: *same as {126} with EH's return address* Box 955/Ketchum Idaho *above letter's date*

¶2.3 in)] in∧

¶2.4 Dr.] Dr∧

{128}

postmark: Idaho Jan 16 1960 [*remainder faint*]

address: *same as {126} and return address on verso same as {127}*

¶3.3 Scribner's] Scribner∧s

¶4.1 imitating it] *interl. ab. caret*

¶5.1 hurry.] hurry∧

¶5.2 everything.] everything∧

{129}

¶7.3 Scribner's] Scribner∧s

¶7.4 Eve.] Eve∧

{130}

postmarks: *on recto* New York Feb 2 1960 2:30 am *and on verso* San Francisco de Paula Feb 5 1960 [*remainder faint*]

address: *same as {72} except spelling of* Havana

envelope: *on recto EH writes* answered Feb [*over deleted* Jan] 9/60 *and on verso AEH writes* Hotchner/6W77 New York City

{131}

dictated to Valerie Danby-Smith; signed by EH

¶2.9 good] *prec. by del.* pretty

¶2.10 sight] site

¶3.2 serialization] serialisation

¶3.4 to.] to∧

¶4.12 I'm] I∧m

¶4.13–14 organized] organised

{132}

postmarks: *on recto* New York, NY Feb 10 1960 *and on verso* San Francisco de Paula Hab. Feb 13 1960 8 am Recibido

address: *see {130}*

envelope: *on verso* CBS Television Network/485 Madison Avenue, New York 22 N.Y.

¶3.1 15th] th

¶6.1–7.2 All love . . . Hotcho] *insert. left margin*

{133}

¶2.4 borne] born

¶2.4 other] *auto. interl. ab. caret*

¶3.3 Esquire?] *auto.* ?

¶7.1 Chateau] *final* a *over* u

¶7.1 Blvd.,] Blvd∧,

¶8.1 Give] G *over* K

{134}

dictated to Valerie Danby-Smith; signed by EH

postmark: Habana Cuba Feb 20 1960 11:30 pm

address: Chateau Marmont/8221 Sunset Blvd./Hollywood, Calif.

envelope: *see {38}*

¶5.2 25th] th̲

¶6.1 Mary's] Mary∧s

¶6.3 Paret] *prec. by del. char.*

{135}

letterhead: Olive 1–2345 *to this AEH adds* x-787 *circling and adding* phone Olympia 72317 x-787

¶2.2 stagger] r *over* d

¶3.3 receive] *fol. by* x *over* a

¶3.6 will] *1st* l *over* t

¶4.3 with U-I] - *over* *

¶4.5 doing] d *over* g

¶4.6–5.2 okay . . . Hotchton] *auto. insert.*

¶4.9 Ave.] Ave∧

{136}

dictated to Valerie Danby-Smith; signed by EH

postmark: Habana Cuba Mar 12 1960 11:30 pm

address: A. E. Hotchner/1129 Horn Ave/Hollywood, California

envelope: *see {38}*

¶4.1 I referred] *prec. by del.* Sorry you are having

¶4.1 don't] don∧t

¶4.3 know] *fol. by del.* wh

¶5.2 ways] waves

{137}

in left margin of page 2 EH writes Please file under Hotch

¶3.1 grown] *prec. by* x *over* gor

¶3.5 advice] v *over* g

¶4.1 hope] *fol. by* x *over* s

¶4.3 Buick] *auto. interl. ab. caret*

¶4.10 (CBS)] *auto. interl. ab. caret*
¶5.5 fields?] e *over* r
¶6.1 goes] g *over* d
¶6.3 use of] o *over* f
¶6.5 considerably] y *over* e

{138}
dictated to Valerie Danby-Smith; signed by EH
¶2.5 ship] h *over* p
¶3.1 Can't] Canʌt
¶3.3 words.] *auto. interl. by EH*
¶3.3 renegotiate] renegociate
¶3.5 mano-a-mano] *auto. interl. by EH ab.* m-a-m
¶3.7 don't] donʌt
¶3.10 (thing)] (and) *insert. by EH; fol. by del.* ie
¶3.15 is balled] ll *over* w
¶3.11–12 ¿ . . . ?] *auto. insert. by EH*
¶4.2 MONTANA] *prec. by del.* mata
¶4.2 beet] beat
¶4.6 ground.] groundʌ
¶4.7 can't] canʌt
¶4.14 can't] canʌt
¶4.18 recognized] regognised
¶4.19 rider.] riderʌ
¶4.19 don't] donʌt
¶4.21 name.] nameʌ
¶4.25 Elko] Elcol
¶4.26 place. Remember] place remember
¶4.31 62nd.] 62ndʌ

{139}
¶2.7 architecture] *fol. 1st* t *del. char.; arched line joins 1st* t *and* e
¶2.12 was the] wasthe
¶2.16 N.Y.] NʌY.
¶2.16 picked up] pickedup
¶2.19 looked terrible] lookedterrible
¶2.24 checked in] checkedin
¶2.26 been] *fol. by* x *over* n
¶3.1 have to] t *over* g
¶3.3 repeat] x *over* r *fol.* p
¶3.5 have in] havein
¶3.7 grow] *prec. by* x's *over* grow
¶3.10 Grey] e *over* a
¶4.2 emergency] *2nd* e *over* m
¶4.4 knock] c *over* w

¶4.5 temporarily] *prec. by auto. insert. /; e and* m *merged*
¶4.5 After] t *over* g
¶4.6 it.] . *over* l
¶4.7 Don't . . . malignancy.] *auto. insert. left margin*
¶5.1 out] *prec. by* x's *over 3 chars.*
¶5.2 Don't] D *over* S
¶5.4 Also,] so *over* os
¶5.7 before] *fol. by* x's *over* the
¶6.6 about] *prec. by* x's *over* not
¶7.3 obeisance] obesance
¶8.3 12345] 1 *over* i

{140}
dictated to Valerie Danby-Smith
postmark: Habana Cuba May 11 1960 1130pm
address: *see {136}*
¶4.4 That's] that∧s
¶5.5 don't] don∧t
¶5.6 eaten] *prec. by del.* esteen
¶5.15–16 nor . . . Buick] *auto. interl. by EH*

{141}
postmark: *on recto* New York NY June 20 3-pm *and on verso* San Francisco de Paula Habana June 24 1960 8 am
address: *see {72}*
envelope: *on verso* Hotchner RFD 5 Westport Conn *below deleted* CBS Television Network/ Television City, Hollywood, California

{142}
postmark: Habana Cuba Jul 6 1960 3pm
address: *same as {68} except* USA *deleted*
envelope: *see {38}*

{143}
address: Hemingway c/o Ordonez Carlton Hotel Bilbao
¶1.1 PUBLICATION'S] PUBLICATION∧S

{144}
no commentary

{145}
postmark: Malaga Ago 7 1960
address: *see {142}*
envelope: *on verso* E. Hemingway/Apartado 67/Malaga, Spain
¶5.1 sentence] *fol. by. del.* in

¶6.2 A.'s] A∧'s
¶7.1 on . . . Wed.–] on . . . Wed∧ *interl.*
¶8.1 Love . . . all.] *interl.*
¶8.2 acct.] acct∧
¶8.2 Don't] Don∧t

{146}
¶3.5 6th).] 6th)∧
¶3.13 ms.] ms∧
¶4.2 Valerie] V *over* C

{147}
postmark: Malaga Sep 10 1960
address: *see {142}*
envelope: *on verso* E. Hemingway/c/o Davis/Apartado 67/ Malaga, Spain
Above date EH writes La Consuela
¶2.2 really] *interl. ab. caret*

{148}
postmark: Malaga Sep 18 1960
address: *see {142}*
envelope: *see {147}*
Atop letter EH writes Apartado 67 But cable and write Suecia Madrid
¶2.1–2 correspondence. After] correspondence∧ after
¶2.2 Antonio super),] Antonio super)∧ *interl. ab.* (wonderful)
¶2.2 hurricane),] hurricane)∧
¶2.4 jail).] jail)∧
¶2.5 and . . . good] *interl. bel.* Antonio OK
¶2.5 good)]) *over—*
¶2.5 twice).] twice)∧
¶3.1 Sept.] Sept∧
¶4.4 ok-ed] *interl.*
¶6.1 I'm] I∧m
¶6.6 can] *fol. by del.* only
¶6.7 in)] in∧
¶6.17 and was] *interl. ab. caret*
¶6.21 friend's] friend∧s
¶6.22 at] *fol. by del.* a
¶7.4 any] *fol. by del.* tha
¶7.5 me.] me∧
¶10.1 can't] can∧t
¶11.2–12.1 straight . . . Papa] *insert.*
¶11.3 sums] *prec. by del.* some

{149}
time on cable 2:47 pm

{150}
time on cable 3:38 pm
¶1.2 STUDIO'S] STUDIO∧S

{151}
time on cable 6:56 am

{152}
time on cable 11:56 am

{153)
time on cable 11:51 pm

{154}
postmark: Ketchum Idaho Oct 25 1960 3 pm
address: A. E. Hotchner/Apt. 4B/1 East 62/New York, NY
envelope: *on recto* Hotch Please keep this letter to you EH *and on verso* EH Box 555
    Ketchum, Idaho
¶2.2 N.Y.] N∧Y∧
¶2.3 this semester] *interl.*
¶2.4 N.Y.] N∧Y∧

{155}
time on cable 12:34 pm

{156}
¶1.3 BLVD.] BLVD∧

{157}
postmark: Ketchum Idaho Jan 31 1961
address: *see {126}*
Above date EH writes Box 555/Ketchum/Idaho
¶2.3 5 page] *interl. ab. caret*
¶4.4 Feb.] Feb∧
¶6.1 wire when] *prec. by del.* cable

{158}
postmark: *on recto* Ketchum Idaho Feb 18 1960 *and* New York NY Feb 20 1961 10:30
    am
address: *see {126}*
envelope: *on recto* If not delivered in 5 days please return to Box 555 Ketchum Idaho
¶2.2 Hotch.] Hotch∧

¶2.5–6 but . . . rise] *insert. ab. caret*

¶2.9 (which . . . me)] *interl.*

¶2.11 etc. etc.] etc∧ etc.

¶2.11 aside . . . equity.] *interl.*

¶2.13–14 television rights] *fol. by del.* to properties

¶2.14 all this] *interl.*

¶3.6–7 That . . . responsibility.] *insert.*

¶3.7 money] *insert.*

¶3.7 T.V.] *prec. by del. chars.*

¶3.8 only] *prec. by del.* f

¶3.10 get] *fol. by del.* only

¶3.11 strictly] *prec. by del.* striclly; k *fol.* c *del.*

¶3.11 author's] author∧s

¶3.11 agreement] *prec. by del.* eg

¶5.2 since . . . Alfred] *interl.*

{159}

¶17.2 A. E. Hotchner] *AEH's signature*

{160}

¶3.1 attached] *fol. by del.* u

{161}

postmark: Ketchum Idaho Mar 6 1961 7 am

address: *see {126}*

envelope: *on verso EH writes* P.O. Box 555/Ketchum, Idaho

¶2.3 (by . . . course)] *interl.*

¶2.3–4 since . . . interest] *interl.*

¶2.4 don't] don∧t

¶2.5 a separate sheet] a a separate sheet

¶3.1 plans] *fol. by del. char.*

¶3.4 nor . . . else] *interl.*

¶3.5 after . . . well] *interl.*

¶3.7 re-action's] re-action∧s

¶4.1 virus] *prec. by indeciph del.*

¶4.3 I'm] I∧m

Word Division List

The following are possible compounds that were hyphenated at the ends of lines in the manuscripts.

{13} ¶5.4 half-lace
{17} ¶2.5 over-length
{37} ¶8.1 Anne-Marie
{38} ¶5.1 Doubleday-Doran
{48} ¶2.20 theatre-going
{58} ¶7.1–2 semi-Christlike
{69} ¶5.2 McCarthy-Army
{89} ¶3.6 great-great-grandson[1]
{95} ¶2.1 Twentieth-Century
{99} ¶2.8 home-run
{100} ¶2.2 wind-up
{104} ¶3.6 right-handers
{117} ¶4.3 deep-down
{135} ¶2.11 chicken-shit
{135} ¶3.10 one-percent

---

1. The initial hyphen in this word appeared at line end.

$Index$

Page numbers in italics refer to illustrations.